T0133679

TRANSNATIONAL SECURITY

TRANSNATIONAL SECURITY

Marie-Helen Maras

CRC Press
Taylor & Francis Group
Boca Raton   London   New York

CRC Press is an imprint of the
Taylor & Francis Group, an **informa** business

CRC Press
Taylor & Francis Group
6000 Broken Sound Parkway NW, Suite 300
Boca Raton, FL 33487-2742

© 2015 by Taylor & Francis Group, LLC
CRC Press is an imprint of Taylor & Francis Group, an Informa business

No claim to original U.S. Government works

Printed on acid-free paper
Version Date: 20140829

International Standard Book Number-13: 978-1-4665-9444-9 (Hardback)

Visit the Taylor & Francis Web site at
http://www.taylorandfrancis.com

and the CRC Press Web site at
http://www.crcpress.com

Δόξα Σοι, ο Θεός ἡμῶν, δόξα Σοι.

This book is dedicated in loving memory to my grandmother (γιαγιά), Marika Filippopoulou, who grew up at a time when women could not attend school. Against all odds, having survived two wars and having been deprived a formal education, she taught herself to read. She was truly an extraordinary woman. I am eternally grateful to her as she nurtured my love for the written word and instilled in me the drive to pursue an education. For my Γιαγιά, who would always tell me:

"Μάθε γράμματα παιδί μου"

Contents

Preface

Security is not exclusively a domestic issue. It is a transnational phenomenon; and accordingly, it should be examined through this lens. The available books on the market focus on specific transnational security threats (e.g., terrorism, organized crime, and weapons of mass destruction). Current books in this area also often provide a single-discipline approach to the field of transnational security. This book seeks to fill the void in available literature by using a multidisciplinary approach to analyze several transnational security issues, including weapons of mass destruction proliferation, terrorism, organized crime, cybercrime, natural disasters, human-made disasters, infectious diseases, conflict societies, food security, water security, and energy security. In addition, it considers applicable international law to transnational security issues and examines key international organizations and institutions dealing with these issues.

The book is intended to serve as a comprehensive text for graduate courses on transnational security (global security, human security, or security studies) and can also be used for advanced undergraduate students. Moreover, it can be used for crisis management and disaster preparedness courses, as well as global governance courses and courses that focus on specific transnational security threats.

The book will seek to appeal to a wide range of different groups. By steering away from exclusively focusing on a single threat, it will be of interest to a much broader audience of writers and researchers working on transnational security. By providing a detailed account of most threats, countermeasures, and their implications for a number of different fields—law, public policy and administration, security, and criminology, it is likely to be an extremely useful resource for academicians, practitioners, and graduate and upper-level undergraduate students in these areas. In addition, it is an extremely useful resource for academicians, practitioners, and graduate and undergraduate students in political science, history, sociology, and psychology. Criminal justice and socio-legal scholars and professionals will also find food for thought in this work.

Given that this book covers global transnational security practices, it will be of interest to security officials, UN employees, nongovernmental organizations (NGOs), and researchers in the field. Specifically, this book is intended for:

- security officials who wish to expand their knowledge of current transnational security threats;
- students and professionals seeking a career in security, global affairs, or crisis management;
- UN employees and NGOs looking to gain more information on transnational security beyond their specialization;
- international relations and global affairs students who would like to learn about transnational security and its economic, political, and social consequences;
- all students, academicians, researchers, and practitioners seeking to understand the nature and extent of transnational security threats and what can be done to effectively combat them.

Probable users of the book also include government agencies. Anyone interested in learning about this field will also benefit from this book.

The Author

Dr. Marie-Helen Maras is an associate professor at the Department of Security, Fire, and Emergency Management at John Jay College of Criminal Justice. She has a DPhil in law and an MPhil in criminology and criminal justice from the University of Oxford. In addition, she holds a graduate degree in industrial and organizational psychology from the University of New Haven and undergraduate degrees in computer and information science and psychology from the University of Maryland University College. She has taught at New York University and SUNY-Farmingdale.

Dr. Maras has published four major works at Jones & Bartlett, which include: *Computer Forensics: Cybercriminals, Laws and Evidence*, First Edition (2011); *Computer Forensics: Cybercriminals, Laws and Evidence*, Second Edition (2014); *Exploring Criminal Justice: The Essentials* (2012); and *Counterterrorism* (2012). She has also published in peer-reviewed academic journal articles on the economic, social, and political consequences of measures seeking surveillance of telecommunications and electronic communications data of all European Union (EU) citizens in the *European Journal of Law and Economics*, *International Journal of Law, Crime and Justice*, and the *Hamburg Review of Social Sciences*. Moreover, she has provided chapters for edited volumes by Benjamin Goold and Daniel Neyland, titled *New Directions in Privacy and Surveillance* (Willan Publishing, 2009), and Justin Sinclair and Daniel Antonius, titled *The Political Psychology of Terrorism Fears*

(Oxford University Press, 2013). She has also published an edited volume titled *CRC Press Terrorism Reader* (2013).

In addition to her teaching and academic work, her background includes approximately 7 years of service in the U.S. Navy with significant experience in security and law enforcement from her posts as a Navy Law Enforcement Specialist and Command Investigator. While in the Navy, she supervised personnel in conducting over 130 counter-surveillance operations throughout Operation Enduring Freedom and Iraqi Freedom. During the early stages of her military career, she worked as an Electronics and Calibration Technician.

Acknowledgments

I am most grateful to Mark Listewnik and Linda Leggio at Taylor & Francis/CRC Press for their direction and guidance during the development and production of this book. I would also like to warmly thank Tina Tsiokris, Michelle Miranda, Christopher Charles, Lauren Shapiro, and Colette Mazzucelli, for graciously taking the time to review and comment on the chapters of this book.

CHAPTER 1

Transnational Security
An Introduction

It is entirely too limiting to view security solely as a domestic issue. By restricting dimensions of security in this manner, effective security solutions and evaluations cannot be achieved. Additionally, looking at security as a domestic issue fails to see the big picture—that the security of one state affects the security of other states. Indeed, globalization has triggered evolving and exponential threats that challenge the security and stability of countries, by transcending traditional borders and having an international impact. As such, a more accurate way of approaching security is to view it as a transnational phenomenon.

Before such an analysis takes place, existing conceptions of security need to be examined. Accordingly, the objectives of this chapter are twofold. First, this chapter explores the notion of security: looking in particular at the concept of security as a state of existence, its relationship to threats, the provision of security, the costs of pursuing security, and its prioritization over other political and social issues. Second, this chapter examines the overall transformation of security studies and the evolution of security into a transnational phenomenon.

THE STATE OF SECURITY

Security is a state of existence.[*] As a state of existence, security can be either objective or subjective. Objective security can encompass being protected from threats (i.e., some type of danger to survival) and being free from security threats (so-called absolute security).[†] With respect to

---

[*] Lucia Zedner, "The Concept of Security: An Agenda for Comparative Analysis," *Legal Studies* 23:1 (2003), 155.

[†] Arnold Wolfers, "National Security as an Ambiguous Symbol," In Arnold Wolfers (Ed.), *In Discord and Collaboration: Essays on International Politics* (Baltimore, MD: Johns Hopkins University Press, 1962), 150; Arnold Wolfers, "'National Security' as an Ambiguous Symbol," *Political Science Quarterly* 67:4 (December 1952), 481–502.

the former, objective security seeks to protect people from harm and property from damage.* The latter, absolute security, is unattainable. However, this does not mean that the pursuit of security should not be attempted. It merely sheds light on important truths about security—that total security (100%) cannot be achieved and that there are no simple solutions to attaining security.

Objective security encompasses the degree to which a person is (actually) secure. Objective security is based on mathematical calculations. It is calculated based on the likelihood of a threat and the efficacy of countermeasures. Nevertheless, not all threats to security are amenable to such calculations.† Objective security is achieved when the dangers posed by threats are prevented, mitigated, and managed. Objective security can be pursued through various means. The means taken will depend on the threat. Material security measures seek to obtain some measure of objective security or at the very least reduce the likelihood and impact of threats. They include all tangible efforts that provide some measure of safety. Examples of material security measures are access control systems (e.g., locks, personal identification systems, and cameras).

On the other hand, subjective security refers to feeling safe or secure, or being free from fear or anxiety.‡ Symbolic security measures provide subjective security. Symbolic security measures are those that seek to allay concerns of fears of perceived threats. An example of this is radio-frequency identification (RFID) bracelets on infants. These bracelets are attached to babies' ankles to deter infant abductions. Hospitals have had "sensors [placed] on the doors ...[of] the maternity ward, ...if a baby passes through, an alarm goes off... RFID bracelets are a low-cost way to ensure that the parents are more relaxed when their baby... [is] out of their sight."§ The measure itself does not prevent infant abductions; it merely seeks to deter perpetrators from abducting babies and potentially aids authorities in the interception of an individual engaging in the abduction. Other child surveillance technologies (e.g., nanny cams) similarly try to assuage paternal fears over the safety of their children.

These symbolic measures have come to be known as "security theater" (Figure 1.1). These are measures that are designed to make the population feel safer, irrespective of whether or not they actually are (i.e., whether objective security measures are actually in place and effective).

---

* Henry Shue, *Basic Rights: Subsistence, Affluence, and U.S. Foreign Policy* (Princeton, NJ: Princeton University Press, 1996).
† Chapter 2 of this volume explores uncertain security threats and responses to them.
‡ Lucia Zedner, "The Concept of Security: An Agenda for Comparative Analysis," *Legal Studies* 23:1 (2003), 155.
§ Bruce Schneier, "In Praise of Security Theater," *Schneier on Security*, January 25, 2007, https://www.schneier.com/blog/archives/2007/01/in_praise_of_se.html.

FIGURE 1.1 "Security theater" measures are designed to make the population feel safer, irrespective of whether or not they are actually effective or not. (Image courtesy of Shutterstock.com.)

Consider U.S. airport security. While there are no existing measurements to test the effectiveness of these measures (e.g., how many attacks have actually been prevented), these measures are generally perceived as protecting the average traveler and deterring the average criminal/terrorist. However, certain airport security measures implemented after the attacks on September 11, 2001, can be considered symbolic. Specifically, in the aftermath of 9/11, passengers were prohibited from carrying sharp objects onboard a plane such as pocket knives and box cutters; after Richard Reid's 2001 attempt to light explosives concealed in his shoes on a flight from Paris to Miami, passengers were, in addition to the previous restrictions, now required to remove their shoes to be scanned before boarding and were prohibited from bringing cigarette lighters onboard aircrafts. In response to the 2006 foiled liquid bomb plot, passengers were prohibited from bringing liquids onboard—at least liquids of a certain quantity. What security is gained by passengers removing their shoes, discarding their liquids before boarding, and being prohibited from carrying sharp objects on their person, when they are still allowed to bring explosive laptop batteries, bottles of alcohol from duty free, and matches (or cigarette lighters; as of August 2007, the ban was lifted) onboard the aircraft?

Another security measure that has been implemented in U.S. airports to combat terrorism is the whole body imaging device. This device uses X-ray technology to provide security personnel with a detailed image of a person's body revealing any weapons, contraband, or explosives that he or she might have hidden in their clothes or on their person. The attempted terrorist attack by Umar Farouk Abdulmutallab in December 2009 led to the widespread use of these measures at U.S. airports. Specifically, Abdulmutallab passed through airport security in Nigeria and Amsterdam with explosives in his underpants and boarded a U.S. passenger jet, Northwest Flight 253 bound for Detroit. He attempted to light the explosives while onboard the flight. In the current state of implementation, the whole body imaging devices, however, are not designed to deal with a terrorist like Abdulmutallab. First, it is important to note that the airport security of the United States did not fail in the case of Abdulmutallab. Even if all of the airports in the United States had the whole body imaging devices in place (which currently they do not), a similar attempted Abdulmutallab-type attack could not be prevented. Actually, the proliferation of this technology distracts security officials from one important truth: airport security in the United States did not fail in the case of Abdulmutallab. Second, the whole body imaging device would not prevent another Abdulmutallab-like terrorist from boarding an airplane bound for the United States because the use of the whole body imaging device in the United States only tries to prevent Abdulmutallab-type terrorists from leaving or traveling within the United States and not from entering it.

The attempted terrorist attack from Abdulmutallab was not the only important terrorist event that occurred in 2009. In August of that year, Abdullah al-Asiri attempted to assassinate the head of Saudi Arabia's counterterrorism operations, Prince Mohammed Bin Nayef, by detonating explosives that he had inserted in his rectum. Currently, the only U.S. airport security measure that could—technically—prevent an Abdullah al-Asiri-type terrorist from boarding a plane is the whole body imaging device. However, this device is not used at every airport in the United States and passengers have the option to choose not to be screened by this device. Accordingly, a terrorist like al-Asiri can just choose to opt out of the screening by this device (if one opts out, the alternative is a rigorous pat down; this would not uncover explosives hidden inside a person) or the terrorist can take a flight out of an airport that does not have this device. The United States has thus spent millions of dollars on an airport security measure that is easily evaded by terrorists.

The main problem with subjective security measures is that they cost money—money that could have been invested in measures seeking to provide a measure of objective security. In addition, if subjective security measures are in place, citizens and governments alike may be lulled into a false sense of objective security—forgetting, at least in the government's case, that these measures were primarily developed to provide subjective security. Nonetheless, there is value to security theater measures. These measures are designed to reassure citizens and make them feel safer.

In the security discipline, there exists a general lack of questioning of the efficacy of security measures in meeting their intended purposes. Questions of efficacy are also largely absent because individuals may not want to know if security measures work; they may be afraid to hear that these measures might not work or that individuals are vulnerable (or more vulnerable) with these measures than without them. The visible measures of security, such as those at the airport, are designed to demonstrate that the government is doing something to protect its citizenry from threats. However, security, as a state of existence, is not a positive concept. When (real) security exists, it is invisible. In fact, security is a negative concept; it is more easily identified in its absence than in its presence.[*] It is primarily a negative concept because one usually only learns about security when it fails. This is commonplace in the news; one hears about perpetrators evading security or an individual being victimized. Because it is largely invisible, attention is paid to security often after it has failed. Indeed, responses to security threats are often reactive—if an incident occurs (e.g., a school shooting), then security measures are implemented, and/or existing security measures are improved. This, however, is neither a sufficient nor an appropriate response. In order to prevent threats and/or mitigate the impact of threats, security measures should be taken in advance of a threat materializing. Here, security is achieved if the threat is eliminated (wherever possible) or at the very least reduced.

SECURITY AND ITS RELATIONSHIP TO THREATS

Security is provided to protect against threats. Threats can be posed by individuals in the form of human-made threats (e.g., fire and nuclear accidents) and natural phenomena (tsunamis, earthquakes, and hurricanes, to name a few). A security threat refers to some type of hazard to survival. The source of the threat can be military, nonmilitary, or both. David Baldwin conceptualized security with respect to what it defends against. Specifically, he argues that security can be used to defend against

---

[*] Lucia Zedner, "The Concept of Security: An Agenda for Comparative Analysis," *Legal Studies* 23:1 (2003), 158–160.

an individual, nation, and/or international system.* For Baldwin, on the individual level, security can seek to protect against the threats posed by one or more people, a group, the majority of the population, or all of the population. He also noted that on the national level, security can be directed to safeguard against one or more states, most states, or all of the states. He further stated that at the international level, security can center on protection from one or more international systems, most of them, or all of them.

Security is threatened by both internal and external threats. Internal threats are often attributed to distinctive groups within the population (e.g., criminals, pedophiles, and domestic terrorists). External threats include nation states seeking to harm other nation states or foreign agents seeking to harm a nation. However, the division between internal and external security threats is blurred, especially with respect to threats such as crime and terrorism. In fact, security threats often extend beyond a nation's borders impacting other societies worldwide. Ultimately, the conception of security depends on who is defining it and what they perceive to be threats to safety. The emphasis placed on providing security will also depend on the country, and the threat that the country is seeking to protect its citizens from; this differs among countries.

THE PURSUIT OF SECURITY: PRIORITIZING SECURITY AND SOCIETAL VALUES

Security governance involves the participation of a multitude of actors in the public sector, private sector, and civil society. It includes all policies and processes related to security in addition to collective decision making made by actors and institutions with respect to security matters. Governments need to allocate their resources to meet their needs. Baldwin proposed three different methods with which to allocate resources. The first, the prime value approach, holds that security "outranks [all] other values for all actors in all situations."† This means that security will always be the primary concern of societies and all resources need to be invested in the pursuit of security. By contrast, the second method, known as the core value approach, claims that "security is one of several important values."‡ As Baldwin contended, the problem

---

* David A. Baldwin, "The Concept of Security," *Review of International Studies* 23:1 (1997), 13.
† Ibid., 18.
‡ Ibid., 19.

with this approach is that it requires the classification of values into core and noncore values.* The allocation of resources to noncore values could not be justified as the category itself signifies that they are of lesser importance than the core values.† To alleviate the issues arising with resource allocation in the first two approaches, the marginal value approach was proposed. This approach holds that

> security is only one of many policy objectives competing for scarce resources and subject to the law of diminishing returns. Thus, the value...will vary from one country to another and from one historical context to another, depending not only on how much security is needed but also how much security the country already has. Rational policymakers will allocate resources to security only as long as the marginal return is greater for security than for other uses of the resources.‡

Here, governments not only decide on the level of resources devoted to security, but also make allocation decisions between different security threats and the means with which to deal with them. Governments have scarce resources that need to be allocated to competing activities. If more funds are invested in one security measure this means that less will be available for other security measures due to the finite number of available resources. For instance, money invested in countering terrorism may divert funds from other threats (e.g., natural disasters and organized crime). When determining where to allocate resources, what needs to be determined (through a cost–benefit analysis) is which security measure represents the most efficient allocation of resources. This analysis should also be broadened to account for nonsecurity related competing activities. Since there are numerous security threats and only a limited number of resources to spend on security, priority should be given to those which provide the greatest benefits at a low cost. The approach to determining acceptable costs depends on whether security is considered "as having a prime value (the most important value), core value (one of the most important values), or marginal value (the diminishing marginal utility of security depends on how much [of it exists in relation to]... other goods and services)."§

---

* Ibid.
† Ibid.
‡ Ibid., 19–20.
§ Ejdus Filip and Savkovic Marko, "Emergent Concept of National Security Policy in Republic of Serbia," Center for European and North Atlantic Affairs (CENNA), 4, http://cenaa.org/analysis/wp-content/uploads/2013/02/Ejdus-Savkovic.pdf.

THE COST OF PURSUING SECURITY:
THE PROBLEM WITH TRADE-OFFS

Security is provided to protect values. Some examples of values include personal autonomy, physical safety, economic well-being, psychological well-being, protection of morals, and the protection of human rights.[*] Security is valued differently between individuals, groups, nations, and international systems. According to Baldwin, "security necessitates the sacrifice of other values"; as such, he argued that it is essential to ask how important security is with respect to the potentially sacrificed values.[†]

The pursuit of security comes at a cost. These security trade-offs are commonplace and a fact of everyday life. Even when individuals are not thinking about threats, dangers, or attacks (e.g., being mugged when walking down an alleyway at night, having their home broken into when at work, or even becoming a victim of the next terrorist attack), they are making assumptions, judgments, and choices about their security.[‡] For example, when someone chooses to buy a paper shredder for their home, they are making a security trade-off: the inconvenience of shredding each document and the costs incurred of buying this machine in exchange for some security against the threat that their paperwork will be subjected to identify theft.[§] Another example is someone choosing to buy home insurance, where the security trade-off is the inconvenience of the costs of home insurance (which as an added burden requires the purchase of a house alarm and the inconvenience of requiring an individual to make sure the alarm is set and the doors are locked when leaving their home) in exchange for some security against loss through burglary.

Nevertheless, when such trade-offs are made concerning greater security issues, what is being traded off is not merely cost or inconvenience but the human rights of citizens. Both security and human rights are important for individuals and collectively for society. Many problems, however, arise when one good—such as rights—is traded off for another good—such as security. In terms of the latter, many believe that in order to increase one good—security—the other must decrease—human rights. This, however, is a highly fallible assumption, the increase

---

[*] David A. Baldwin, "The Concept of Security," *Review of International Studies* 23:1 (1997), 13.

[†] Ibid., 18.

[‡] For further explanations and examples of security trade-offs, see Bruce Schneier, *Beyond Fear: Thinking Sensibly about Security in an Uncertain World* (New York: Springer, 2006), 7–9.

[§] Identify theft occurs when a person assumes the identity of a target (or targets) by unlawfully using their name, social security number (SSN), bank account number, or other identifying information to commit a crime. For more information on identity theft see Chapter 6, Marie-Helen Maras, *Computer Forensics: Cybercriminals, Laws and Evidence* (Second Edition) (Burlington, MA: Jones & Bartlett, 2014).

in one does not necessarily require a decrease in the other. What's more, this assumption fails to understand the relationship between security and human rights; namely, that security and human rights are mutually dependent and not mutually exclusive.

Loader and Walker posit the idea of security as a social good, whereby security, in this sense, is a term only deserved by measures that can increase, for example, trust, social solidarity, civic participation, and the pursuit of other freedoms.* By contrast, if security erodes civic participation and trust and significantly confines individual choices and freedom to pursue their own interests, goals, and plans, it cannot be characterized as a social good. By way of extension, security cannot be considered as a social good if it violates the rule of law and does not respect human rights. Specifically, even if citizens may be safer in the sense of being protected from threats with such measures, their security is degraded as a good by the resulting distributive degradation in the rule of law and their civil liberties.† Yet, this does not imply that some limitations to rights (within the constraints of human rights instruments and Member States constitutional law) are not legitimate. What is being argued, however, is that security is not inimical to the rule of law and human rights but instead, should be seen as a means to achieve this end (i.e., security). The goods of security and human rights are indeed mutually dependent. The existence of one social good (security), thus depends on the other (human rights). Therefore, one cannot say that security is a social good if the security measure implemented unnecessarily limits or even extinguishes the right to the enjoyment of that which security purports to make possible.‡ The freedom that security provides is the freedom from fear, to live one's life with dignity, and to shape one's life free from coercion. If security measures have significant adverse effects on the exercise of human rights, the result is insecurity (and not security) and should be viewed instead as a failure of the state to provide security—a "social bad."§ As Gabe Mythen and Sandra Walklate rightly pointed out, if "the pursuit of security comes at the expense of human

---

* Ian Loader and Neil Walker, *Civilizing Security* (Cambridge: Cambridge University Press, 2007), 154–160.

† See footnote 23 in Jeremy Waldron, "Security and Liberty: The Image of Balance," *The Journal of Political Philosophy* 11:2 (2003), 204.

‡ Ian Loader and Neil Walker, "Necessary Virtues: The Legitimate Place of the State in the Production of Security," In Jennifer Wood and Benoît Dupont (Eds.), *Democracy, Society and the Governance of Security* (Cambridge: Cambridge University Press, 2006), 183–185.

§ Russell Hardin, "Democracy and Collective Bads," In Ian Shapiro and Casiano Hacker-Cordon (Eds.), *Democracy's Edges* (Cambridge: Cambridge University Press, 1999); Ian Loader and Neil Walker, "Policing as a Public Good: Reconstituting the Connections between Policing and the State," *Theoretical Criminology* 5:1 (February 2001), 26.

rights, then not only is the quality of that security compromised, but the very principles of democracy are threatened."[*]

THE PROVISION OF SECURITY

In addition to the view of security as a social good, it can also be considered as a public, common, private, or club good (see Table 1.1). A public good is nonexclusive (i.e., does not exclude someone from obtaining the good; refers to a good that is available to all) and nonrival (i.e., the benefits of the good does not diminish irrespective of the number of users).[†] A lighthouse signal is considered as a pure public good. Security is considered as a public good only if it fits these parameters. A prime example of a security-related public good is national defense.

By contrast, a state's provision of security may not be considered as a public good if it is not equally distributed nor deals with all threats (at least those that are defined by referents). With respect to the latter, security resources are limited. In the past, security was the primary role of the state and its institutions. However, the state and its respective institutions were unable to deal with the growing demand for security, especially in response to the exponential expansion of security threats. Private security arose to meet the demand for security, which far exceeded the capabilities of the public sector; at least in the areas

TABLE 1.1   Security as a Good

	Categories of Goods	
	Exclusive	Nonexclusive
Rival	Private goods	Common goods
Nonrival	Club goods	Public goods

Source: Elke Krahmann, "Security: Collective Good or Commodity?" *European Journal of International Relations* 14:3 (September 2008), 379–404; Hella Engerer, "Security as a Public, Private or Club Good: Some Fundamental Considerations," *Defense and Peace Economics* 22:2 (2011), 135–145.

---

[*] Gabe Mythen and Sandra Walklate, "Terrorism, Risk and International Security: The Perils of Asking 'What If?'" *Security Dialogue* 39 (2008), 236.

[†] Paul A. Samuelson, "The Pure Theory of Public Expenditure," *Review of Economic Statistics* 36 (1954), 387–389; Elke Krahmann, "Security: Collective Good or Commodity?" *European Journal of International Relations* 14:3 (September 2008), 379–404.

that the government could not (from the view of citizens) appropriately provide security.

A common good is nonexclusive and rival. The benefits of the types of goods included in this category can diminish by the number of individuals that use it. Particularly, the types of goods included in this category are considered common pool resources, such as water, fish in international waters, timber, oil, coal, and natural gas. These common goods can be preserved if they are not overexploited. The key to maintaining these common goods is regulation. This regulation should aim at restricting the extraction and use of these goods by individuals.[*]

A private good is exclusive and rival. Indeed, a private good is restricted to a limited number of a defined set of users.[†] Additionally, the consumption of a private good diminishes its benefits according to the number of individuals who use it.[‡] Examples of private goods include food,[§] clothing, and cars.[¶] Security can be considered as "a private good if it is the result of enhancing the abilities of actors to survive an attack or disaster. It is excludable and rival because the defense or protection of an individual or a state typically excludes others, and because others cannot employ the same resources for their own protection."[**]

Like private goods, club goods or toll goods are not available to all. Club goods are exclusive and nonrival. While this type of good is restricted to a limited number of defined users its benefits do not diminish according to consumption.[††] A club good is only available to the members of the club, which either pay for the good or receive the good because of a membership (e.g., living in a gated community, luxury building, or part of a country club). Some examples of this type of good are cinemas, cable television, access to copyrighted works, and computer programs. In both private and club goods, security is also viewed as a commodity[‡‡]; it is something that can be bought and sold. Therefore,

---

[*] Chapters 11 and 12 of this volume cover certain common goods (i.e., water, oil, coal, and natural gas) and the governance of these resources.

[†] Hella Engerera, "Security as a Public, Private, or Club Good: Some Fundamental Considerations," *Defense and Peace Economics, Special Issue: The Economics of Security: A European Perspective* 22:2 (2011), 137; Elke Krahmann, "Security: Collective Good or Commodity?" *European Journal of International Relations* 14:3 (September 2008), 384.

[‡] Elke Krahmann, "Security: Collective Good or Commodity?" *European Journal of International Relations* 14:3 (September 2008), 384.

[§] This private good is considered in Chapter 11 of this volume.

[¶] Hella Engerera, "Security as a Public, Private, or Club Good: Some Fundamental Considerations," *Defense and Peace Economics, Special Issue: The Economics of Security: A European Perspective*, 22:2 (2011), 137.

[**] Ibid., 387.

[††] Ibid., 384.

[‡‡] Ian Loader, "Consumer Culture and the Commodification of Policing and Security," *Sociology* 33 (1999), 373.

not everyone has equal access to it. Gated communities illustrate this point by segregating society in terms of those who can afford additional security and those who cannot afford it. Similarly, physical security measures such as alarms and cameras help protect certain homes, while others who cannot afford these measures cannot enjoy this benefit.

Against certain security threats, the provision of security has shifted away from the state and onto individuals and the private sector. A case in point is child protection. The responsibility for child protection has shifted "onto individuals, families, and private service companies who promise to meet the social and emotional needs of those who can afford them, whereas others must struggle without much assistance from the state or from employers."[*] This reinforces the socio-economic division in society by making the protection of children a commodity which is available only to those who can afford it. Security in cyberspace has also shifted away from the state to the individual; in fact, cybersecurity is a club good. Individuals and companies need to purchase the necessary software (e.g., antivirus and antispyware software) to protect their systems from internal and external threats. This commodification of security, however, is extremely problematic. As Ian Loader argues, "all citizens within a political community should be entitled (simply on account of their membership) to certain basic levels protection (or, to put it another way, to a 'fair' share of scarce security resources) ... the market cannot rule in this sphere"[†]; at the very least, it should not entirely rule in this sphere. Furthermore, this commodification of security is problematic given the increasing interconnectedness of societies and the impact of one nation's insecurity on the security of other nations around the globe. The next and final sections of this chapter explore this notion of interconnectedness by looking at the evolution of security studies and those responsible for security.

THE TRANSFORMATION OF SECURITY

Security is a multidisciplinary and multifaceted concept. Traditionally, security was not thought of in this manner. Instead, security was viewed through a single-discipline lens (political science) and as a one-dimensional concept. Security, here, was viewed "as security of territory

---

[*] Torin Monahan, "The Surveillance Curriculum: Risk Management and Social Control in the Neoliberal School," In Torin Monahan (Ed.), *Surveillance and Security: Technological Politics and Power in Everyday Life* (New York: Routledge, 2006), 120.
[†] Ian Loader, "Private Security and the Demand for Protection in Contemporary Britain," *Policing and Society* 7 (1997), 377–394; Lucia Zedner, "Too Much Security?" *International Journal of the Sociology of Law* 31 (2003), 177.

from external aggression, or as protection of national interests in foreign policy or as global security from the threat of a nuclear holocaust.* The threat was viewed as that posed by an external enemy or a subversive enemy within a country seeking to overthrow the government.† In line with this notion of security, some scholars have maintained a state-centric approach to analyzing security; security from societies, groups, and individuals focuses on intrastate security (e.g., ethnic conflict and civil war). As a result, security studies were viewed as "the study of the threat, use, and control of military force [and included] the conditions that make the use of force more likely, the ways that the use of force affects individuals, states, and societies, and the specific policies that states adopt in order to prepare for, prevent, or engage in war."‡ This conception of security, therefore, refers to maintaining a state's status quo—that is, the state's political independence and territorial integrity against external military threats.§ However, this conception is too narrow, as there are many other threats beyond those posed by a nation state.

Human security was introduced to separate itself from traditional security studies. Human security covers, among other things, environmental and economic threats to the survival of societies' individuals and groups. More specifically, human security encompasses both "safety from chronic threats" (e.g., hunger and disease) and "protection from sudden and hurtful disruptions in the patterns of daily life—whether in homes, in jobs or in communities."¶ The United Nations Development Programme (UNDP) report includes seven elements of human security:**

1. *Economic security* (e.g., freedom from poverty)
2. *Food security* (e.g., freedom from hunger and physical and economic access to food)
3. *Health security* (e.g., protection from diseases)
4. *Environmental security* (e.g., water scarcity and protection from pollution)
5. *Personal security* (e.g., physical safety from crime)

---

* United Nations Development Programme (UNDP), *Human Development Report, 1994* (New York: Oxford University Press, 1994), 22.
† Ronald D. Crelinsten, "Analyzing Terrorism and Counter-Terrorism: A Communication Model," *Terrorism and Political Violence* 14:2 (2002), 103.
‡ Stephen M. Walt, "The Renaissance of Security Studies," *International Studies Quarterly* 35:2 (June 1991), 212.
§ James Busumtwi-Sam, "Development and Human Security: Whose Security, and from What?" *International Journal* 57:2 (2002), 255.
¶ United Nations Development Programme (UNDP), *Human Development Report, 1994* (New York: Oxford University Press, 1994), 23.
** Ibid., 24; Roland Paris, "Human Security: Paradigm Shift or Hot Air?" *International Security* 26:2 (2001), 90; Barry Buzan, "New Patterns of Global Security in the Twenty-First Century," *International Affairs* 67:3 (1991), 439–451.

6. *Community security* (e.g., protecting the survival of traditional cultures)
7. *Political security* (e.g., protection of human rights and freedom from oppression)

Human security was initially developed by UNDP to draw attention to the fact that security affects the individual—a fact that is often overlooked given the traditional view of security as being a state-centric concept. However, the above list of the elements of human security are extremely broad and all-encompassing; as such, it is a conceptual overreach.[*]

Instead of creating a new term for security, several scholars sought to expand the concept of security and the discipline of security studies. First, scholars expanded the concept of security to include various threats and hazards, such as those posed by migration, environmental issues (e.g., natural disasters and climate change),[†] economic issues, and the loss of human rights, to name a few.[‡] Second, other scholars, such as Weaver et al.,[§] extended security studies to include both state security and societal security. Here, state security focused on state sovereignty, which concerns the right and power of a nation to govern itself and regulate its affairs without external interference; whereas, societal security covered national identity and included the "origins, structures, and dynamics of collective identity formation...and the connection between [collective] identities and [national] interests (and threats to them)."[¶] In light of the dual focus of security, both state and societal security, policies were required to ensure "social autonomy as a group, and a degree

---

[*] Mary Martin and Taylor Owen, "The Second Generation of Human Security: Lessons from the UN and EU Experience," *International Affairs* 86:1 (2010), 216.

[†] Climate change refers to "a change of climate which is attributed directly or indirectly to human activity that alters the composition of the global atmosphere and which is in addition to natural climate variability observed over comparable time periods." See Article 1(2) of the 1992 United Nations Framework Convention on Climate Change.

[‡] Richard H. Ullman, "Redefining Security," *International Security* 8:1 (Summer 1983), 129–153; Myron Weiner, "Security, Stability, and International Migration," *International Security* 17:3 (1992/1993), 91–126; Theodore H. Moran, "International Economics and National Security," *Foreign Affairs* 69 (1990/1991), 74–90; Brad Roberts, "Human Rights and International Security," *Washington Quarterly* 13:2 (1990), 65–75.

[§] Ole Weaver, Barry Buzan, Morton Klestrup, and Pierre Lemaitre, *Identity, Migration, and the New Security Agenda in Europe* (London: Pinter, 1993).

[¶] Iver B. Neumann, "Collective Identify Formation: Self and Other in International Relations," *European Journal of International Relations* 2 (1996), 139–174; Alexander Wendt, "Collective Identify Formation and the International State," *American Political Science Review*, 88 (1994), 384–396; cited in Keith Krause and Michael C. Williams, "Broadening the Agenda of Security Studies: Politics and Methods," *Mershon International Studies Review*, 40:2 (1996), 243.

of political status, [and] not merely to [ensure] the physical survival of individuals within national boundaries."*

Transnational security issues encompass military and nonmilitary threats that traverse borders around the globe, threaten the social, political, and legal order of nations, and adversely impact the quality of life of the population of nations. The impact of transnational security threats are felt beyond a single nation's borders and affect the international community as a whole. Examples of transnational security threats include (but are not limited to): the proliferation of weapons of mass destruction, transnational terrorism, transnational organized crime, cybercrime, natural disasters, human-made disasters, infectious diseases, conflict and post-conflict societies, food shortages, water shortages, and the energy dependence and interdependence of countries.†

Today, the distinction between national and international security has become blurred; especially in regard to threats like cybercrime, which know no physical geographic boundaries. Therefore, security should be examined through a transnational lens to illustrate its scope and effect. The next section examines who is responsible for protecting against transnational security threats.

Dealing with Transnational Security

Thomas Hobbes believed that citizens had to defer to the sovereign in order for the sovereign to secure peace. The sovereign is not only responsible for securing peace but also for the protection of citizenry. The sovereign can be the citizens in a democracy, or a king, queen, or prince in a monarchy. For Hobbes, national interests and state sovereignty are primary concerns. This is in line with the conventional realist approach to security studies which focuses on national security—threats to states as a whole.‡ According to Hans Morgenthau, national security seeks to maintain the "integrity of the national territory and its institutions."§

---

* Joseph S. Nye, Jr., "Problems of Security Studies," Paper Presented at the XIV World Congress of the International Political Science Association, Washington, DC, August 1988, 6.
† Each of these will be examined in this volume: Chapter 3 (nonproliferation), Chapter 4 (transnational terrorism), Chapter 5 (transnational organized crime), Chapter 6 (cybercrime), Chapter 7 (natural disasters), Chapter 8 (human-made disasters), Chapter 9 (infectious diseases), Chapter 10 (conflict and post-conflict societies), Chapter 11 (food shortages), Chapter 11 (water shortages), and Chapter 12 (the energy dependence and interdependence of countries).
‡ The realist theory in security studies is discussed in detail in the next chapter, Chapter 2.
§ Hans J. Morgenthau, *Politics among Nations: The Struggle for Power and Peace* (Third Edition) (New York: Alfred A. Knopf, 1960), 562.

By contrast, Immanuel Kant believed that a global order was possible. Specifically, he believed that "nation-states and dominating national interests can be restructured by an enlightened political order—a republican constitution, a federal state system, and global citizenship—to forge a community of mankind."[*] According to the Kantian view, state sovereignty should be subsumed under an international order. Thus, national interests should take a backseat to the interests of global citizenship (at least according to Kant). A third view by Hugo Grotius holds that "all states, in their dealings with one another, are bound by the rules and institutions they form. But, as opposed to the Kantians, what these imperatives enjoin is not the overthrow of the system of states and its replacement by a universal community of mankind, but rather acceptance of the requirements of coexistence and cooperation in a society of states."[†]

For Kant and Grotius, therefore, security is the responsibility of a society of states as opposed to a single nation. Their views accord with global security and international security. Global security, which is considered as a byproduct of the interdependence of nations, assumed that a "community of mankind" can be developed and "political processes controlled by enlightened men."[‡] International security includes the formation of security regimes and the building of international institutions.[§] Contrary to national security, "international security…implies that the security of one state is closely linked to the security of another state."[¶] Consider the suicide bombing in Afghanistan on September 9, 2001, which targeted and killed Ahmad Shah Massoud, the Afghan Northern Alliance leader. The perpetrators of the suicide bombing were carrying stolen Belgian passports.[**] Specifically, prior to this incident, it was reported that approximately 3,500 passports were stolen in Belgium.[††] At the time the passports were stolen, in several European countries, passports were issued by municipal officials that were poorly secured. In fact, there were several other reported incidents in Europe in which passports were stolen from city halls. The suicide bombing on September 9,

---

[*] Helga Haftendorn, "The Security Puzzle: Theory Building and Discipline Building in International Security," *International Studies Quarterly* 35:1 (1991), 6.

[†] Hedley Bull, *The Anarchical Society: A Study of Order in World Politics* (New York: Columbia University Press, 1977), 24–40; Helga Haftendorn, "The Security Puzzle: Theory Building and Discipline Building in International Security," *International Studies Quarterly* 35:1 (1991), 6.

[‡] Helga Haftendorn, "The Security Puzzle: Theory Building and Discipline Building in International Security," *International Studies Quarterly* 35:1 (1991), 6–7.

[§] Ibid., 7.

[¶] Ibid., 9.

[**] Paul Gallis, "European Counterterrorist Efforts: Political Will and Diverse Responses in the First Year after September 11," *U.S. Congressional Research Report*, RL31612, October 17, 2002, 8, http://digital.library.unt.edu/ark:/67531/metacrs7032/m1/.

[††] Ibid.

2001, and the subsequent terrorist attacks on September 11, 2001, added impetus to EU-wide policy changes on the issuance of passports. Currently, Belgium and many other European countries (e.g., Greece) provide greater security over passports by having centralized the control over the issuance of their passports.*

Transnational security is comparable to international security; with one important difference, transnational security emphasizes the interconnectedness and dependency of countries and the ability of threats to transcend borders and impact countries around the world. In both international and transnational security, states are still primarily responsible for the security of their own countries. However, the international community can intervene (as long as they have the legal authority to do so) when security threats are not appropriately dealt with at the national level and when threats extend beyond the borders of a nation. Ultimately, the provision of transnational security is the responsibility of a multitude of actors, such as individuals, businesses, organizations, institutions, governments, and the international community.

CONCLUDING THOUGHTS

Security is a state of existence. As a state of existence, it is a negative concept; it is usually identified based on its absence rather than presence. The measures implemented to attain security have provided objective and subjective security. Objective security refers to the absence of threats to values. It includes measures that are designed to prevent, detect, deter, defend, and/or mitigate threats that materialize. Subjective security provides a feeling of security. Security theater includes purely symbolic measures. These measures are designed to make individuals feel safer when in fact such security is not provided. The measures taken will depend on the nature and extent of the security threat and the emphasis a country places on security. These measures will seek to protect against internal and external threats; although these types of threats are often indistinct.

There are many security threats that are common to individuals and countries around the world, such as crime, poverty, and human rights violations. The emphasis placed on providing security will depend on the threat the country is seeking to protect its citizens from; this prioritization differs between countries. Traditionally, security was viewed as being related to states rather than individuals. In fact, in its original conception, security focused on safeguarding the core values of nations from external military threats. The conception of security has transformed from a state-focused notion to one that also encompasses threats posed

---

* Ibid., 51.

to individuals and the international community as a whole. Security is accurately thought of as a transnational phenomenon due to its scope and effect. The next chapters in this volume are specifically designed to introduce current transnational security threats and the measures implemented to combat them. Preceding this, the next chapter, Chapter 2, explores theories in security studies in order to better understand the lens that is used to view transnational security, the threats to transnational security, and the ways to create more effective and efficient transnational security measures.

Decisions Under Uncertainty
Theories and Practice
in Security Studies

This chapter examines decisions under conditions of uncertainty. More specifically, it explores the risks and uncertainty surrounding security and how this influences security responses. Particular attention is paid to the pursuit of security through the lens of realism and liberalism. The strategic choices of decision makers are investigated through the security spiral model, the security dilemma, and games. This chapter further analyzes the notions of preemption and misplaced certainty in the decision to go to war. Finally, this chapter considers the role of precaution in security studies and its impact on security decision making.

PERPETRATORS AS RATIONAL ACTORS

The success of security largely depends on the understanding of actors and actor's objectives. Discussions on the pursuit of security are predicated on the belief that the actors engaging in the choice of which type of security to pursue are rational actors. According to Gary Becker, an individual will engage in an activity if the expected gain in a particular activity to him or her exceeds the gain he or she would get by using his or her time and resources on other activities.[*] Actors are viewed as rational decision makers in the sense that they: pursue identifiable goals; link possible actions to the pursuit of these goals; and decide whether or not to act by scrutinizing possible actions in terms of benefits and costs, and assessing each action's probability of success. Moreover, the assumption that actors are rational means that they are:

---

[*] Gary S. Becker, "Crime and Punishment: An Economic Approach," *Journal of Political Economy* 76:2 (March–April 1968), 176.

> cognizant of the possible outcomes of a decision situation; can rank
> these outcomes from most to least preferred; are aware of the possible
> courses of action open to them; can estimate the probability of a given
> outcome upon selection of a particular action; and choose the action
> that they believe will give them the highest expected return—that is,
> each action is evaluated in terms of the outcomes that [they] may obtain,
> discounted by the probability that the action leads to each outcome.[*]

There are two forms of rationality: procedural rationality and instrumental rationality.[†] With procedural rationality, an actor "makes a 'clear, coolheaded ends-means calculation' after considering all possible courses of action and carefully weighing the pros and cons of each of them."[‡] The issue at hand, as Frank Zagare rightly points out, is that the "actor must have an accurate perception of the implications of all his options and a well-defined set of preferences concerning them."[§] Here, the actor must not only consider all potential courses of action and carefully weigh the benefits and costs of each of them, but he or she must also consider all of the choices of others and their preferred outcomes.[¶] This is an inherently complex task; rarely does an actor have absolute knowledge of all possible decisions and outcomes; least of all the intentions and preferences of others.

By contrast, with instrumental rationality, an actor makes comparisons between available options and outcomes and chooses the one that is most beneficial to him or her. This conception of rationality does not require the prediction and assessment of all possible choices and outcomes; only the ones that the actor is faced with when making the decision.[**] Irrespective of which view of rationality one subscribes to, it

---

[*] Kenneth J. Arrow, "Alternative Approaches to the Theory of Choice in Risk-Taking Situations," *Econometrica* 19:4 (October 1951), 404–437; Kenneth J. Arrow, *Social Choice and Individual Values* (New York: Wiley, 1963); Karl H. Borch, *The Economics of Uncertainty* (Princeton, NJ: Princeton University Press, 1968); John S. Chipman, "The Foundations of Utility," *Econometrica* 28:2 (April 1960), 123–124; Gerard Debreu, "Stochastic Choice and Cardinal Utility," *Econometrica* 26 (1958), 440–444; Peter C. Fishburn, *Utility Theory for Decision Making* (New York: Wiley, 1970); R. Duncan Luce and Howard Raiffa, *Games and Decisions* (New York: Wiley, 1957); John von Neumann and Oskar Morgenstern, *The Theory of Games and Economic Behavior* (Princeton, NJ: Princeton University Press, 1944) cited in Lee E. Duttera and Ofira Seliktar, "To Martyr or Not to Martyr: Jihad Is the Question, What Policy Is the Answer?" *Studies in Conflict and Terrorism* 30:5 (2007), 432.
[†] Frank C. Zagare, "Rationality and Deterrence," *World Politics* 42:2 (1990), 239–240.
[‡] Sidney Verba, "Assumptions of Rationality and Non-Rationality in Models of the International System," In Klaus Knorr and Sidney Verba (Eds.), *The International System: Theoretical Essays* (Princeton, NJ: Princeton University Press, 1961), 95, cited in Frank C. Zagare, "Rationality and Deterrence," *World Politics* 42:2 (1990), 239.
[§] Frank C. Zagare, "Rationality and Deterrence," *World Politics* 42:2 (1990), 239.
[¶] Ibid.
[**] Duncan R. Luce and Howard Raiffa, *Games and Decisions: Introduction and Critical Survey* (New York: Wiley, 1957), 50; Frank C. Zagare, "Rationality and Deterrence," *World Politics* 42:2 (1990), 240.

is clear that actors are rational beings who take advantage of opportunities that present themselves to further their own ends. Security should thus focus on predicting such opportunities and preventing actors from achieving their objectives.

THE PERILS OF UNCERTAINTY

Security officials often make decisions under uncertainty; that is, they make decisions in the absence of definite knowledge of the benefits, costs, and unanticipated consequences of a decision. Uncertainty can be traced back to the economist, Frank Knight, who differentiated between measurable and unmeasurable uncertainty.[*] The term "risk" was used to refer to measurable certainty.[†] Risk is a part of everyday life. It can be defined as the uncertainty that exists concerning a potential loss. Risk also involves the possibility of suffering a harm or loss. Risk can be classified according to its measurement; namely, objective and subjective risk. Objective risk is observable and measurable. This type of risk is actually present. On the other hand, subjective risk is based on a person's perception of risk. Usually, this type of risk is based on assessments done quickly and intuitively. Risk assessments are accomplished using a variety of subjective and objective measures.

Measurable certainty refers to objective risk. In its most basic conception, risk involves the calculation of the magnitude of harm (its adverse impact) and the likelihood of harm (its probability of occurring).[‡]

$$\text{Risk} = \text{Criticality} \times \text{Probability}$$

Criticality here refers to the magnitude of the impact of the risk should it materialize. Criticality is assessed by identifying all of the important resources that require protection and by identifying worst-case scenarios and how they would affect each asset. An asset is something of importance or value, and can include people, property, information, systems, and equipment.[§]

Criticality includes both direct and indirect losses. Direct losses involve the harm or damage caused by the risk. Imagine that an earthquake

---

[*] Frank H. Knight, *Risk, Uncertainty, and Profit* (Chicago: University of Chicago Press, 1921) cited in Alessandra Arcuri, "Reconstructing Precaution, Deconstructing Misconceptions," *Ethics & International Affairs* 21:3 (2007), 362.

[†] Ibid.

[‡] Harvard Law Review Association, "Responding to Terrorism: Crime, Punishment, and War," *Harvard Law Review* 115:2 (February 2002), 1230.

[§] "Guidance for Developing Sector-Specific Plans," U.S. Department of Homeland Security, 2004, http://cees.tamiu.edu/covertheborder/TOOLS/SSAGuidance.pdf.

occurred in California. An example of a direct loss would be the loss of life and harm to persons that occur as a result of the earthquake. Moreover, direct losses from the earthquake further include those that have occurred from structural damage to buildings and damage to infrastructures. By contrast, indirect losses follow direct losses and constitute the loss or harm caused indirectly from the materialized risk. Consider once again the example of the earthquake. Imagine that the structural damage caused to the buildings occurred primarily in commercial industries. As a result, the employees of the company are unable to go to work and the company is unable to operate. Accordingly, productivity suffers as a consequence and business is lost; in so doing, this loss of company functioning induces losses in sales and company profits. The employees are also indirectly impacted in the form of a loss of income and wages.

Probability is assessed by first identifying threats. The probability assessment depends on the type of risk, its history, capabilities, and other features of the risk which are identified. Some risk assessments also include another factor: vulnerability. Accordingly, with this addition, risk now involves the calculation of the magnitude of harm (criticality), the probability of harm, and the vulnerability of an individual or organization (depending on what is being assessed). Posed another way,

$$\text{Risk} = \text{Criticality} \times \text{Probability} \times \text{Vulnerability}$$

Here, vulnerability is assessed by identifying potential weaknesses for each asset and evaluating the countermeasures for each asset and their efficacy in reducing vulnerabilities. Vulnerability assessments are absent in tools providing objective measures of the risk of a security threat to an entire country. For example, the Terrorism Risk Index was developed by Maplecroft (a global risks advisory firm) to assess the risk of terrorism in countries around the globe.[*] This tool calculates risk based on the intensity, frequency, and history of terrorist activity in each country.

These assessments assert the calculability of future harms and the plausibility of measuring the probability of a security threat. However, not all threats are amenable to such calculations and measurements. Accordingly, risk fails to address these threats. Knight used "unmeasurable uncertainty" to describe and address these incalculable and unmeasurable issues.[†]

---

[*] In 2013, the risk of terrorism to 197 countries was assessed. See Maplecroft, "2013 Terrorism Risk Index," *Maplecroft*, https://maplecroft.com/about/news/terrorism_risk_index_2013.html.

[†] Frank H. Knight, *Risk, Uncertainty, and Profit* (Chicago: University of Chicago Press, 1921) cited in Alessandra Arcuri, "Reconstructing Precaution, Deconstructing Misconceptions," *Ethics & International Affairs* 21:3 (2007), 362.

Uncertainty is a key factor in explaining the "insecurity" of states. Particularly, uncertainty has played a central role in the pursuit of security. There are two general positivist schools of thought when discussing the pursuit of security: security through conquest (i.e., realism), which includes hard power approaches and alliances, and security through democracy (i.e., liberalism) that encompasses soft power approaches, institutions, and interdependence of actors (each of which are explored below).

Realism

For realists, the "international arena...[is] an anarchical, self-help system,"* "'...where states look for opportunities to take advantage of each other.'"† In an anarchic, self-help system, nations concern themselves "with lessening, preserving, or widening the gap in welfare and strength between themselves and others."‡ In such a self-help system, states mistrust others and unremittingly seek power and security to advance national interests. Due to this mistrust, nations need to be concerned that other states will try to take advantage of them; accordingly, agreements between states must be created and any promises and threats made must be credible.§ From a realist's perspective, "the best way for a state to survive in anarchy is to take advantage of other states and gain power at their expense."¶

Different types of realism have emerged: of particular note are neorealism and neoclassical realism. Neorealism includes "theories that seek to explain international outcomes—for example, the likelihood of great power war, the durability of alliances, or the likelihood of international cooperation."** Neoclassical realism includes "theories that seek to explain the external behavior of individual states—for example,

---

* Anarchy is viewed as "the absence of a worldwide government or universal sovereign." Anarchic institutions are viewed as "those premised upon the full sovereignty of all members." David A. Lake, "Beyond Anarchy: The Importance of Security Institutions," *International Security* 26:1 (Summer 2001), 130.

† Stephen Van Evera, "The Hard Realities of International Politics," *Boston Review* 17:6 (November/December 1992), 19, cited in John J. Mearsheimer, "The False Promise of International Institutions," *International Security* 19:3 (Winter 1994/1995), 9.

‡ Kenneth N. Waltz, "Structural Realism after the Cold War," *International Security* 25:1 (2000), 21.

§ Robert Jervis, "Realism, neoliberalism, and cooperation," *International Security* 24:1 (1999), 43–44.

¶ John J. Mearsheimer, *The Tragedy of Great Power Politics* (New York: W.W. Norton and Company Ltd., 2001), 36.

** Jeffrey W. Taliaferro, "Seeking Security under Anarchy: Defensive Realism Revisited," *International Security* 25:3 (Winter, 2000–2001), 135.

military doctrine force posture, alliance preferences, foreign economic policy, or the pursuit of accommodative or belligerent diplomacy."[*]

Uncertainty of intentions has played a central role in conflict between states. Neoclassical realists believe that military reassurance can be used to mitigate uncertainty.[†] Indeed, hard power approaches by states (such as war) are often self-defeating and result in adverse consequences. To avoid this, states should make their intentions known, and reassure potential adversaries as to their motives. One way to do so is through arms control agreements. The core dilemma in reassurance is that actions taken in pursuit of it may lead states to be vulnerable to greedy states (i.e., states that seek to expand for reasons other than security).

Moreover, uncertainty of intentions is at the core of what has come to be known as the security spiral model and the security dilemma. In the security spiral model, if one state increases their own security, other states see this and in turn, increase their own security.[‡] This produces tensions among states. Consider two states A and B: A and B both seek to increase their security. While each state observes the attempts by the other to increase their own security, they are uncertain about each others' motives for doing so (i.e., is it for survival purposes or is it an act of aggression). Accordingly, the states are likely to misinterpret these actions, sparking a spiral of mistrust.

John Herz defines the security dilemma as "[a] structural notion in which the self-help attempts of states to look after their security needs tend, regardless of intention, to lead to rising insecurity for others as each interprets its own measures as defensive and measures of others as potentially threatening."[§] The essence of the security dilemma is as follows: The actions a state takes to enhance their own security will by default result in a decrease for another state (or other states' security). It is a zero sum game—making it extremely difficult to improve one's security situation. Accordingly, states compete for security. The threatened state or states that seek to improve their own security situation cause unease in other countries and threaten their security. The arms race between the United States and the Union of Soviet Socialist

---

[*] Ibid.

[†] Randall L. Schweller, "Neorealism's Status-Quo Bias: What Security Dilemma?" *Security Studies* 5:3 (Spring 1996), 91–121; Andrew Kydd, "Sheep in Sheep's Clothing: Why Security Seekers Do Not Fight Each Other," *Security Studies* 7:1 (Autumn 1997), 114–154.

[‡] Charles L. Glaser, "The Security Dilemma Revisited," *World Politics*, 50:1 (October 1997), 171–201.

[§] John H. Herz, *Political Realism and Political Idealism* (Cambridge, United Kingdom: Cambridge University Press, 1951), 7; For more information on the security dilemma, see Robert Jervis, "Cooperation under the Security Dilemma," *World Politics* 30:2 (January 1978), 167–214; Charles L. Glaser, "Realists as Optimists: Cooperation as Self-Help," *International Security* 19:3 (Winter 1994/1995), 50–90.

FIGURE 2.1   The Cold War is a prime example of the security dilemma. Pictured here, the remains of the Iron Curtain, Cizov, Czech Republic. (Image courtesy of Shutterstock.com.)

Republics (U.S.S.R.) during the Cold War is a prime example of the security dilemma (Figure 2.1). The United States and U.S.S.R. each felt threatened by the weapons that each had and as such, they built up their arms and military strength in an attempt to match each other's capabilities. In fact, each country repeatedly sought to increase its security to match and even surpass the others' capabilities. As Herz explains,

> [g]roups or individuals... must be, and usually are, concerned about their security from being attacked, subjected, dominated, or annihilated by other groups and individuals. Striving to attain security from such attack, they are driven to acquire more and more power in order to escape the impact of the power of others. This, in turn, renders the others more insecure and compels them to prepare for the worst. Since none can ever feel entirely secure in such a world of competing unity, power competition ensues, and the vicious circle of security and power accumulation is on.[*]

This dilemma that states are faced with is described in the work of the Greek philosopher Thucydides. Specifically, in the *History of the Peloponnesian War*, Thucydides claimed that "[w]hat made war inevitable

---

[*] John H. Herz, *Political Realism and Political Idealism* (Cambridge, United Kingdom: Cambridge University Press, 1951), 157.

was the growth of Athenian power and the fear which this caused in Sparta."[*] Indeed, for realists, war is likely to occur because:[†] states are not prevented from using force to resolve conflict; conflict arises over allocation and scarcity of resources; and structural uncertainty is present.[‡] Additionally, war is likely to occur because a self-help system exists, which triggers mutual suspicions due to each state building arms and forming alliances. This system triggers mutual suspicion (e.g., the security spiral model and security dilemma). States self-help systems do not seek to maximize collective gains.

According to John Mearsheimer, the security dilemma implies that "the best way for a state to survive in anarchy is to take advantage of other states and gain power at their expense. The best defense is a good offense."[§] Mearsheimer was an offensive realist. Offensive realists believe that security is a scarce resource. States compete for power by pursuing expansive policies. Offensive realists, like Mearsheimer, believe that states seek to maximize power because they believe it is the means with which they can secure their nation or that this expansion can provide them with other values they seek.[¶] Offensive realism posits that anarchy provides incentives for state expansion.[**] From the view of offensive realists, the primary motivation of states is to improve their relative power position. These expansionist actions are taken if and only when the benefits of their pursuit outweigh their costs.[††] Accordingly, offensive realists hold that states are restrained from expanding when faced with incentives to do so.[‡‡]

By contrast, defensive realism limits the justification for expansion and states that the existence of an international system limits the

---

[*] Thucydides, *History of the Peloponnesian War* (Thuc 1.23).

[†] Jennifer Mitzen and Randall L. Schweller, "Knowing the Unknown Unknowns: Misplaced Certainty and the Onset of War," *Security Studies* 20:1 (2011), 7–8.

[‡] Structural uncertainty refers to states' uncertainty of the present and future intention of other states.

[§] John J. Mearsheimer, *The Tragedy of Great Power Politics* (New York: Norton, 2001), 21 and 35–36.

[¶] John J. Mearsheimer, *The Tragedy of Great Power Politics* (New York: Norton, 2001).

[**] Jack Snyder, *Myths of Empire: Domestic Politics and International Ambition* (Ithaca, NY: Cornell University Press, 1991), 11–12; Sean M. Lynn-Jones and Steven E. Miller, "Preface," In Michael E. Brown, Owen M. Coté, Sean M. Lynn-Jones, and Steven E. Miller (Eds.), *The Perils of Anarchy: Contemporary Realism and International Security* (Cambridge, MA: MIT Press, 1995), ix–xii; Benjamin Frankel, "Restating the Realist Case: An Introduction," *Security Studies* 5:3 (Spring 1996), xiv–xx; and Sean M. Lynn-Jones, "Realism and America's Rise: A Review Essay," *International Security* 23:2 (Fall 1998), 157–182.

[††] Ibid.

[‡‡] Matthew Rendall, "Defensive Realism and the Concert of Europe," *Review of International Studies* 32:3 (July 2006), 540.

conditions for expansion.* Defensive realism suggests the pursuit of moderate strategies. Those subscribing to this view believe that conquest is self-defeating and costly. According to defensive realism, mutual cooperation can be achieved with the involvement or assistance of international institutions.†

Liberalism

Whereas "realism predicts that states will respond as security maximizers to structural incentives; other theories explain cases when they do not."‡ One such theory is liberalism. According to this theory, the international system creates opportunities for both cooperation and conflict. It is up to states and international organizations (e.g., the United Nations) to take advantage of these opportunities or not. This illustrates one important difference between realism and liberalism: namely, unlike liberals that view the state as one of many important actors in the international system, realists believe that the only important actors are states. Kegley and Blanton describe liberalism as "a paradigm predicated on the hope that the application of reason and universal ethics to international relations can lead to a more orderly, just, and cooperative world, and that international anarchy [lack of a hierarchy/world government] and war can be policed by institutional reforms that empower international organizations and laws."§

---

* Robert Jervis, "Cooperation under the Security Dilemma," *World Politics* 30:2 (January 1978), 167–214; Charles L. Glaser, "The Security Dilemma Revisited," *World Politics* 50:1 (October 1997), 171–201; Jack Snyder, *Myths of Empire: Domestic Politics and International Ambition* (Ithaca, NY: Cornell University Press, 1991), 11–12; Sean M. Lynn-Jones and Steven E. Miller, "Preface," In Michael E. Brown, Owen M. Coté, Sean M. Lynn-Jones, and Steven E. Miller (Eds.), *The Perils of Anarchy: Contemporary Realism and International Security* (Cambridge, MA: MIT Press, 1995), ix–xii; Benjamin Frankel, "Restating the Realist Case: An Introduction," *Security Studies* 5:3 (Spring 1996), xiv–xx; Sean M. Lynn-Jones, "Realism and America's Rise: A Review Essay," *International Security* 23:2 (Fall 1998), 157–182.

† Keohane, "defines institutions as 'persistent and connected sets of rules (formal or informal) that prescribe behavioral roles, constrain activity, and shape expectations.'" Robert O. Keohane, "International Institutions: Two Approaches," *International Studies Quarterly* 32:4 (December 1988), 383; Charles L. Glaser, "Realists as Optimists: Cooperation as Self-Help," *International Security* 19:3 (Winter 1994/1995), 50–90; Robert Jervis, "Realism, Neoliberalism, and Cooperation," *International Security* 24:1 (Summer 1999), 42–63; Kenneth N. Waltz, "Structural Realism after the Cold War," *International Security* 25:1 (Summer 2000), 5–41.

‡ Dale C. Copeland, "The Constructivist Challenge to Structural Realism: A Review Essay," Stefano Guzzini and Anna Leander (Eds.), *Constructivism and International Relations: Alexander Wendt and His Critics* (New York: Routledge, 2006), 21.

§ Charles W. Kegley and Shannon Blanton, *World Politics: Trends and Transformations, 2009–2010* (Boston: Cengage, 2009), 32.

Neoliberals believe that changes in preference in strategy can be mutually beneficial. Such changes are the result of more quantity and better quality of information concerning existing situations, actions of each state, reasons for activity, and potential acts of "others" in the future.[*] Interdependence of states can either promote peace or conflict.[†] Liberalism holds that the role of security institutions are critical to confrontation and cooperation within the international system.[‡] Particularly, neoliberalist theories hold that international institutions can reduce uncertainty. Proponents believe that the existence of these institutions increases the likelihood that nations will cooperate with each other.

Realism is "usually contrasted with idealism or liberalism, which tends to emphasize cooperation."[§] Cooperation "requires that the actions of separate (but in their actions interdependent) individuals and organizations—which are not in pre-existent harmony—be brought into conformity with one another through a process of policy coordination."[¶] Incentives for cooperation exist when national interests are not compromised in doing so. Cooperation can occur by reducing the costs of risks for each party through creating and carrying out agreements between them. This reduction of risk helps facilitate cooperation. Cooperation is maintained through diplomacy.

Those subscribing to this view believe that the only way to achieve security is through "mutual threat reduction."[**] The concept of common security was introduced

> based on the notion that security must be sought and maintained not against one's adversaries but with them. This approach is necessary because states, in searching for security, end up making themselves more insecure by enhancing their military power in response: the

---

[*] Robert Jervis, "Realism, Neoliberalism, and Cooperation," *International Security* 24:1 (Summer 1999), 51.

[†] Kenneth N. Waltz, "Structural Realism after the Cold War," *International Security* 25(1) (Summer 2000), 5–41.

[‡] David A. Lake, "Beyond Anarchy: The Importance of Security Institutions," *International Security* 26:1 (Summer 2001), 129–160.

[§] *Stanford Encyclopedia of Philosophy*, s.v. "Political Realism in International Relations," last revised April 2, 2013, http://plato.stanford.edu/entries/realism-intl-relations/.

[¶] Robert O. Keohane, *After Hegemony: Cooperation and Discord in the World Political Economy* (Princeton, NJ: Princeton University Press, 1984), 51, cited in Helga Haftendorn, "The Security Puzzle: Theory Building and Discipline Building in International Security," *International Studies Quarterly* 35:1 (1991), 9.

[**] Elke Krahmann, "Security: Collective Good or Commodity?" *European Journal of International Relations* 14:3 (September 2008), 379–404; Richard Smoke, "A Theory of Mutual Security," In Richard Smoke and Andrei Kortunov (Eds.), *Mutual Security: A New Approach to Soviet–American Relations* (Basingstoke: Macmillan, 1991), 81.

classic security dilemma.[*] Common security seeks to mitigate the security dilemma by organizing policies concerning security coordination with others to maximize mutual as opposed to unilateral security.[†]

An example of an international organization that seeks common security is the United Nations.

Under liberalism, the preferred strategy is thus mutual security. However, states do not trust each other to cooperate to achieve it. Indeed, as Andrew Kydd has argued, mistrust prevents states from mutual cooperation;[‡] and as a consequence seeking mutual security. This mistrust and the lack of mutual cooperation is depicted in games: particularly, the Prisoner's Dilemma and the Stag Hunt.

Games: Understanding Strategic Decisions

Game theory, which was pioneered by John von Neumann, involves the study of strategic decisions and intentions between agents.[§] These agents make decisions according to their preferences or perceived benefits. Game theory seeks to shed light on how individuals make decisions when the outcomes of their choices are dependent on the choices and decisions of others. Games share a common feature of interdependency; that is, the outcomes depend on the choices of each player. Zero sum games are those in which a player's game will always result in another player's loss. This is considered a pure conflict game. Other games were developed that take a more cooperative form. In cooperative games, players should make their choice and should implement their actions jointly.

The Prisoner's Dilemma[¶] draws players into a bad outcome; that is, in this game, each player pursues his or her private interests which do not provide the best outcome. The Prisoner's Dilemma is as follows (see Table 2.1): Two prisoners are placed in separate interrogation rooms and are not allowed to communicate with each other. The prisoners each face the following choice: confess to a crime or deny it. Each prisoner is

---

[*] John Herz, "Idealist Internationalism and the Security Dilemma," *World Politics* 2:2 (1950), 57–180; N. J. Wheeler and K. Booth, "The Security Dilemma," In J. Baylis and N. J. Rengger (Eds.), *Dilemmas of World Politics: International Issues in a Changing World* (Oxford: Clarendon Press, 1992).

[†] Pinar Bilgin, "Individual and Societal Dimensions of Security," *International Studies Review* 5:2 (2003), 204.

[‡] Andrew H. Kydd, *Trust and Mistrust in International Relations* (Princeton, NJ: Princeton University Press, 2005).

[§] John von Neumann and Oskar Morgenstern, *Theory of Games and Economic Behavior* (Princeton, NJ: Princeton University Press, 1944).

[¶] Albert W. Tucker gave the game the name *Prisoner's Dilemma*. Tucker also provided a numeric value for the sentence each prisoner would receive based on his or her own choice. William Poundstone, *Prisoner's Dilemma: John Von Neumann, Game Theory and the Puzzle of the Bomb* (New York: Doubleday, 1992).

TABLE 2.1   Prisoner's Dilemma

	Prisoner B (cooperates; does not confess)	Prisoner B (defects; confesses)
Prisoner A (cooperates; does not confess)	Both Prisoner A and B receive a short sentence	Prisoner A receives long sentence Prisoner B is released
Prisoner A (defects; confesses)	Prisoner A is released Prisoner B receives long sentence	Both Prisoner A and B receive an intermediate sentence

offered a deal: if he or she confesses to the crime and provides evidence that will implicate the other prisoner, then the confessor will be released. Consequently, the other prisoner would receive a long sentence. If both prisoners confess, they will both receive an intermediate sentence. If neither confess, they will both receive a short sentence. The incentive in this game is not to cooperate but to instead defect;* even though it is not in their best interests to do so.

The Stag Hunt was originally discussed in Jean Jacques Rousseau's work, *A Discourse on Inequality*.† An example of a version of the Stag Hunt is depicted in the following game: Two hunters are searching for food in the forest. They can either hunt for a stag or for a rabbit. A stag can provide a larger meal for them than the rabbit, but requires both of them to cooperate. If one of the hunters decides to pursue the rabbit, he or she alone will have a meal. Additionally, the chance of success for hunting a stag alone is minimal. The best outcome in this game is for the two players, the hunters, to cooperate. This, however, requires trust that the other player will work towards hunting the stag instead of pursuing his or her own self-serving interests by hunting the rabbit.

Trust refers to the "belief that the other side prefers mutual cooperation to exploiting one's own cooperation, while mistrust is a belief that the other side prefers exploiting one's cooperation to returning it."‡ Thus, trust depends upon what individuals or states do with the trust invested in them. If the lack of knowledge of an individual or state's capabilities and intentions triggers mistrust, then can certainty of capabilities and intentions encourage trust?

---

* The person defects even though there is a risk that the prisoner may receive the longest sentence in doing so; especially, if the other prisoner confesses to the crime first.
† Jean Jacques Rousseau, *Discourse on Inequality* (Montana: Kessinger Publishing, 2004).
‡ Andrew H. Kydd, *Trust and Mistrust in International Relations* (Princeton, NJ: Princeton University Press, 2005), 6.

CERTAINTY ALSO MATTERS: THE PITFALLS
OF MISPLACED CERTAINTY

Uncertainty breeds mistrust, which at times leads to inappropriate political decisions. However, there have been times where certainty has resulted in adverse consequences. In fact, certainty can cause conflict. For example, Jennifer Mitzen and Randall Schweller have stated that if the intentions of greedy states were known, states would arm themselves and seek alliances with other states in preparation and anticipation of war.[*]

Certainty is determined by objective and subjective assessments. Objective assessments illustrate the likelihood of some event coming to fruition or the veracity of the information. Subjective assessments include how the actors feel about the evidence. As Mitzen and Schweller note, certainty is a "feeling of knowing."[†] Mitzen and Schweller equate certainty to confidence. They further state that confidence depends on two elements: namely, weight and uncertainty salience. Weight refers to the quality of the evidence and its completeness; whereas, uncertainty salience, refers to the emotional salience of fundamental uncertainty (i.e., it refers to an individual's aversion to uncertainty and how individuals seek to eliminate it when it is significant and vivid).[‡]

Misplaced certainty is problematic. According to Mitzen and Schweller, misplaced certainty refers to "cases where decision makers are confident that they know each other's capabilities, intentions, or both; but their confidence is unwarranted yet persists even in the face of disconfirming evidence."[§] Misplaced certainty exists concerning the intentions of others to do harm. The danger lies when individuals or states take actions based on misplaced certainty. Misplaced certainty thus serves as a self-fulfilling prophecy, which refers to "a false definition of the situation evoking a new behavior which makes the originally false conception come true."[¶] Furthermore, "[w]ith misplaced certainty...if the decision maker encounters new information that objectively undermines the initial judgment he or she does not, as a result, become less certain about it. Rather, as time passes, certainty about the initial judgment or

---

[*] Randall L. Schweller, "Neorealism's Status-Quo Bias: What Security Dilemma?" *Security Studies* 5:3 (Spring 1996), 90–121.

[†] Robert A. Burton, *On Being Certain* (New York, NY: St Martin's Press, 2008), 3; Jennifer Mitzen and Randall L. Schweller, "Knowing the Unknown Unknowns: Misplaced Certainty and the Onset of War," *Security Studies* 20:1 (2011), 24.

[‡] Jennifer Mitzen and Randall L. Schweller, "Knowing the Unknown Unknowns: Misplaced Certainty and the Onset of War," *Security Studies* 20:1 (2011), 27–28.

[§] Ibid., 2.

[¶] Robert K. Merton, *Social Theory and Social Structure* (Second Edition) (New York: The Free Press, 1968), 477.

decision hardens, and incoming information, even when contradictory is assimilated to it."[*] The decision maker in such a situation experiences confirmation bias, which refers to the tendency of individuals to favor information that confirms their own hypotheses and beliefs, irrespective of the veracity of that information.[†] Similarly to uncertainty, misplaced certainty has played a critical role in the security spiral mode and the security dilemma.[‡]

As mentioned earlier, realists believe that uncertainty is the harbinger to wars. However, misplaced certainty has also led to war; namely, the Iraq War. There was misplaced certainty that Iraq had in its possession or intended to possess weapons of mass destruction. For example, despite the lack of evidence, the former U.S. Vice President Dick Cheney stated that "there is no doubt that Saddam Hussein now has weapons of mass destruction. ... There is no doubt that he is amassing them to use against our friends, against our allies, and against us."[§]

There was also misplaced certainty with respect to links between al-Qaeda and Saddam Hussein. Specifically, then U.S. Secretary of the State Colin Powell (Figure 2.2) presented the UN Security Council "with evidence [that] the United States maintained irrefutably and undeniably demonstrated Iraqi noncompliance with Resolution 1441; in particular, Secretary Powell alleged that Iraq concealed [weapons of mass destruction (WMDs)] from inspectors and that a large [al-]Qaeda cell was active in Iraq and working together with Baghdad."[¶] Nonetheless, conclusive evidence of WMDs was not provided; evidence that Iraq was plotting to attack the United States with al-Qaeda was also not provided. In fact, Charles Duelfer, who had been chosen by the Bush Administration to conduct a WMD investigation in Iraq, concluded that Saddam Hussein did not have the capability to develop WMDs and that no solid evidence was found concerning a joint Saddam Hussein and al-Qaeda plot to attack the United States.[**] Even without such evidence, it was argued by members of the Bush Administration that just because WMDs were not found in Iraq, this did not mean that they were not there. In particular, Donald

---

[*] Jennifer Mitzen and Randall L. Schweller, "Knowing the Unknown Unknowns: Misplaced Certainty and the Onset of War," *Security Studies* 20:1 (2011), 21–22.

[†] Raymond S. Nickerson, "Confirmation Bias: An Ubiquitous Phenomenon in Many Guises," *Review of General Psychology* 2:2 (1998), 175–220.

[‡] Jennifer Mitzen and Randall L. Schweller, "Knowing the Unknown Unknowns: Misplaced Certainty and the Onset of War," *Security Studies* 20:1 (2011), 4–5.

[§] The White House, President George W. Bush, "Vice President Speaks at VFW 103rd National Convention: Remarks by the Vice President to the Veterans of Foreign Wars 103rd National Convention," Office of the Press Secretary, August 26, 2002, http://georgewbush-whitehouse.archives.gov/news/releases/2002/08/20020826.html.

[¶] Marie-Helen Maras, *Counterterrorism* (Burlington, MA: Jones & Bartlett, 2012), 121.

[**] Ibid., 122.

FIGURE 2.2   Conclusive evidence of WMDs in Iraq was never provided. Pictured here, Colin Powell and Dick Cheney at a Bush/Cheney campaign rally in 2000. (Image courtesy of Shutterstock.com.)

Rumsfeld famously stated that the "absence of evidence is not evidence of absence...Simply because you do not have evidence that something exists does not mean that you have evidence that it [does not] exist."[*]

THE PROBLEMS WITH PREEMPTION

Preemption is a state's legitimate form of self-defense. A state has the right to protect itself from an aggressor by using force. The right of a state for individual self-defense or states for collective self-defense is enshrined in Article 51 of the UN Charter,

> Nothing in the present Charter shall impair the inherent right of individual or collective self-defense if an armed attack occurs against a Member of the United Nations, until the Security Council has taken measures necessary to maintain international peace and security.

---

[*] U.S. Department of Defense, "Secretary Rumsfeld Press Conference at NATO Headquarters," Presenter: Secretary of Defense Donald H. Rumsfeld, Brussels, Belgium, June 6, 2002, http://www.defense.gov/transcripts/transcript.aspx?transcriptid=3490.

> Measures taken by Members in the exercise of this right of self-defense shall be immediately reported to the Security Council and shall not in any way affect the authority and responsibility of the Security Council under the present Charter to take at any time such action as it deems necessary in order to maintain or restore international peace and security.

In order for self-defense to be justified, the threat must be imminent. An imminent threat can be one that has already occurred or is underway. However, the imminence criteria can be met if a state can provide that there is clear and convincing evidence that an enemy or state is planning an attack.[*] The Iraq war did not meet these criteria.

Preemption occurs because it is considered insufficient to wait until the harm or wrongs have been done. This was emphasized in the Bush Doctrine, where former U.S. President George W. Bush stated that as an act of self-defense, "America will act against...emerging threats before they are fully formed" as it "cannot let [its] enemies strike first."[†] By contrast, deterrence is a strategy that is used to discourage an opponent from acting or stopping them from acting. Unlike deterrence, a preemptive strategy relies not on the threat of force, but its actual use against an enemy that has demonstrated the intent and the capabilities to carry out an attack. Against terrorists, for example, there is a strong case to be made for the use of preemptive tactics. The rationale for strategic change from reactive to preventive was driven largely by the scale of September 11 attacks and by the recognition of the potential lethality of future terrorist attacks. This shift is evident in a speech given by President George W. Bush in June 2002 where he stated:

> For much of the last century, America's defense relied on the Cold War doctrines of deterrence and containment. In some cases, those strategies still apply. But new threats also require new thinking. Deterrence—the promise of massive retaliation against nations—means nothing against shadowy terrorist networks with no nation or citizens to defend. Containment is not possible when unbalanced dictators with weapons of mass destruction can deliver those weapons on missiles or secretly provide them to terrorist allies.[‡]

---

[*] *Nicaragua v. United States* [1986] ICJ 14; Marie-Helen Maras, *Counterterrorism* (Burlington, MA: Jones & Bartlett, 2012), 117.

[†] The White House, "U.S. National Security Strategy of the United States of America," September 2002, http://www.state.gov/documents/organization/63562.pdf.

[‡] President George W. Bush, "Complete Text of Bush's West Point Address," The White House, June 1, 2002, http://www.newsmax.com/archives/articles/2002/6/2/81354/shtml.

The terrorist threat was indeed presented as one that was undeterrable—posed by individuals with no territory to defend.[*]

Proponents of preemption argue for its necessity against unde-terrable terrorists and rogue states[†] and the proliferation of WMDs.[‡] While preemption is authorized in limited circumstances according to international law, there are also disadvantages to its use even when it is justified. First, it may damage a country's legitimacy and authority in the world.[§] Legitimacy is accorded to decision makers not on the basis of how decisions were chosen or how they were arrived at and the decisions implemented (procedural legitimacy), but rather on the basis of the quality of decision makers' acts and the decisions themselves.[¶]

---

[*] See Thomas H. Kean and Lee Hamilton, *The 9/11 Commission Report: Final Report of the National Commission on Terrorist Attacks upon the United States* (New York: W.W. Norton, 2004), 375.

[†] Rogue states: brutalize their own citizens; have a leader that uses the country's natural resources for personal gain; threaten the security of their neighbors; disregard interna-tional law and violate international laws and treaties they are signatories of; seek the acquisition, creation, dissemination and/or use of WMDs; sponsor terrorism; and reject the rule of law and human rights. Michael Klare, *Rogue States and Nuclear Outlaws: America's Search for a New Foreign Policy* (New York: Hill and Wang, 1995); Jason Rose, "Defining the Rogue State: A Definitional Comparative Analysis within the Rationalist, Culturalist, and Structural Traditions," *Journal of Political Inquiry* 4 (2001), http://www.jpinyu.com/uploads/2/5/7/5/25757258/defining-the-rogue-state-a-definitional-comparative-analysis-within-the-rationalist-culturalist-and-structural-traditions...jason-rose1.pdf; Petra Minnerop, "Rogue States—State Sponsors of Terrorism?" *German Law Journal* 3 (2002), http://www.germanlawjournal.com/index.php? pageID=11&artID=188; Isobel Roele, "We Have Not Seen the Last of the Rogue State," *German Law Journal* 13 (2012), 560–578, http://www.germanlawjournal.com/index.php?pageID=11&artID=1432.

[‡] John Lewis Gaddis, "A Grand Strategy," *Foreign Policy* 133 (November/December 2002), 50–57; John Lewis Gaddis, *Surprise, Security, and the American Experience* (Cambridge, MA: Harvard University Press, 2004); Krauthammer, Charles, "The Unipolar Era," In Andrew J. Bacevich (Ed.), *The Imperial Tense: Prospects and Problems of American Empire* (Chicago, IL: Ivan R. Dee, 2003); Robert J. Lieber, *The American Era: Power and Strategy for the 21st Century* (New York: Cambridge University Press, 2005); Robert G. Kaufman, *In Defense of the Bush Doctrine* (Lexington, KY: The University Press of Kentucky, 2007); Hakan Tunç, "Preemption in the Bush Doctrine: A Reappraisal," *Foreign Policy Analysis* 5 (2009), 1.

[§] Ivan Eland, "The Empire Strikes Out: The 'New Imperialism' and Its Fatal Flaws," *Policy Analysis* 459 (2002), 1–27, http://www.cato.org/pubs/pas/pa-459es.html; John Ikenberry, "America's Imperial Ambition," *Foreign Affairs* 81 (September/October 2002), 44–60; Robert Jervis, "Understanding the Bush Doctrine," *Political Science Quarterly* 118 (2003), 365–388; Michael Cox, "Empire, Imperialism and the Bush Doctrine," *Review of International Studies* 30 (2004), 585–608; Neta C. Crawford, "The Road to Global Empire: The Logic of U.S. Foreign Policy after 9/11," *Orbis* 48:4 (2004), 685–703; Ivo H. Daalder and James M. Lindsay, *America Unbound: The Bush Revolution in Foreign Policy* (Washington, DC: Brookings Institution, 2003); Hakan Tunç, "Preemption in the Bush Doctrine: A Reappraisal," *Foreign Policy Analysis* 5 (2009), 1.

[¶] D. V. J. Bell, *Power, Influence, and Authority: An Essay of Political Linguistics* (Oxford: Oxford University Press, 1975), 45.

Substantive legitimacy concerns itself with whether the decisions taken are good ones—particularly, whether they respect the rule of law and human rights. Contrary to procedural legitimacy, grievances concerning substantive legitimacy on the part of the subordinate can undermine the legitimacy of the power structure as a whole. Second, the use of preemption may cause mistrust among allies.[*] Third, it may encourage other states to act in a similar manner.[†] One of the reasons why the United States engaged in a preemptive war in Iraq was that Saddam Hussein allegedly had in his possession WMDs and posed a threat to the United States. The issues, however, are that the UN Security Council did not approve the Iraq war and that no credible evidence was presented as to the necessity of the war. Indeed, it did not meet the basic criteria for justifying a preemptive war. This war may thus have set a dangerous precedent for other countries to similarly pursue preemptive war without clear and convincing evidence of an imminent attack and without the UN Security Council's approval.

The preemptive war in Iraq was meant to convey a threat to rogue states that unless they change their behavior (i.e., harboring terrorists, engaging in terrorism or engaging in the proliferation of WMDs) they too will be subjected to similar preemptive action.[‡] The decision of Muammar Qaddafi (former leader of Libya; now deceased) to end his nuclear development program in 2003 during the Iraq war was heralded as a success story for preemptive action. In fact, Qaddafi had stated "that the Iraq war may have influenced him" in his decision.[§] However, the overall effectiveness of using preemptive war to compel rogue states to change their behavior has not been proven effective; cases in point are Iran and North Korea.

Apart from preemptive war, the United States has engaged in preemptive strikes to prevent potential attacks in the future. A prime

---

[*] Ivan Eland, "The Empire Strikes Out: The 'New Imperialism' and Its Fatal Flaws," *Policy Analysis* 459 (2002), 1–27, http://www.cato.org/pubs/pas/pa-459es.html; John Ikenberry, "America's Imperial Ambition," *Foreign Affairs* 81 (September/October 2002), 44–60; Robert Jervis, "Understanding the Bush Doctrine," *Political Science Quarterly* 118 (2003), 365–388; Michael Cox, "Empire, Imperialism and the Bush Doctrine," *Review of International Studies* 30 (2004), 585–608; Neta C. Crawford, "The Road to Global Empire: The Logic of U.S. Foreign Policy after 9/11," *Orbis* 48:4 (2004), 685–703; Ivo H. Daalder and James M. Lindsay, *America Unbound: The Bush Revolution in Foreign Policy* (Washington, DC: Brookings Institution, 2003); Hakan Tunç, "Preemption in the Bush Doctrine: A Reappraisal," *Foreign Policy Analysis* 5 (2009), 1.

[†] Ibid.

[‡] Hakan Tunç, "Preemption in the Bush Doctrine: A Reappraisal," *Foreign Policy Analysis* 5 (2009), 2.

[§] "Gadhafi: Iraq War May Have Influenced WMD Decision," *CNN*, December 22, 2003, http://www.cnn.com/2003/WORLD/africa/12/22/gadhafi.interview/.

example of this were the actions taken in response to the 1998 Kenya and Tanzania Embassy bombings.* Specifically, in response to these bombings, the United States

> launched…a strike within the territory of a state which presumably is not conclusively, actively and directly to blame for the action triggering retaliation…. launched military strikes at multiple terrorist targets within the territory of more than one foreign nation… [and]… attacked a target where the avowed goal was not to attack a single individual terrorist but an organizational infrastructure instead.†

The actual targets of the preemptive strikes were a chemical manufacturing facility in Sudan and al-Qaeda training camps in Afghanistan. Other preemptive strikes have occurred post–9/11, such as targeted killings.

Targeted Killings: Justified Preemptive Strikes?

A targeted killing is the deliberate government decision to order the death of a designated enemy. Countries have authorized targeted killings in the past and continue to do so today. For example, on September 30, 2011, Anwar al-Awlaki and Samir Khan were killed in a drone strike. Al-Awlaki, a U.S. citizen who was affiliated with al-Qaeda in the Arabian Peninsula (AQAP), was considered a prominent spiritual ideologue for English speaking jihadists in the West. Khan was a U.S. citizen and editor-in-chief of the English-language *Inspire* magazine. The targeted killings of both of these operatives were believed to be detrimental to al-Qaeda.

Targeted killings often are conducted in retaliation to a terrorist attack in order to prevent and deter further acts of terrorism. They can be justified as a way to preempt actions that could pose severe security risks to a nation. They are not to be confused with assassinations or extrajudicial killings which are considered illegal. Contrary to popular belief, targeted killings are legal according to international law—as long as they meet the following criteria:‡

---

* In these bombings 213 died and over 5,000 were injured.
† Ted Dagne, "Africa and the War on Terrorism," *CRS Report for Congress*, 1, January 17, 2002, http://fpc.state.gov/documents/organization/7959.pdf; Raphael F. Perl, "Terrorism: U.S. Response to Bombings in Kenya and Tanzania: A New Policy Direction?" *CRS Report for Congress* 98-733 F, September 1, 1998, 3, http://www.policyarchive.org/handle/10207/bitstreams/674.pdf.
‡ Marie-Helen Maras, *Counterterrorism* (Burlington, MA: Jones & Bartlett, 2012), 238–240.

1. Targeted killings can be justified by a state invoking a legitimate right to self-defense.
2. The permission of the host country where the targeted killing will occur must be obtained before executing an attack.
3. The person should only be targeted if he or she presents a serious security risk based on available evidence and/or reliable, corroborated intelligence information that clearly implicates him or her. A targeted killing is unjustified against an individual with only minor involvement in, for example, terrorist activity and whose actions do not endanger public safety.
4. *This tactic should only be used as a last resort.* International law holds that lethal force should only be used as a last resort. Failure to explore other options before deciding to execute a target amounts to extrajudicial killing, which is illegal. Targeted killings are authorized when incapacitation of targets (e.g., terrorists), through arrest is operationally impossible. Targeted killings are also authorized if less invasive options, such as capture, would pose a great risk to the country executing the attack, at least more so than the risk involved in engaging in the targeted killing.

Unless a targeted killing meets all of these criteria, it should not be used. The real issue, however, is not that targeted killings are used but how they are being used; that is, with the manner and oversight of their use. Indeed, on June 5, 2013, *NBC News* reported that since September 2010, 114 drone strikes were conducted in Pakistan and Afghanistan over a 14-month period.[*] In May 2013, during his speech at the National Defense University, President Obama acknowledged that there had been civilian casualties with the use of targeted killings.[†] He also noted that the use of targeted killings raised questions about who the targets were and why they were being targeted. The question that follows is: Are the criteria that legally justify the use of targeted killings being met? To determine this, an oversight committee is needed to review the reasons why such actions were taken. What is required, therefore, is more transparency and accountability in the process of using targeted killings as a preemptive measure.

It is important to remember that preemption involves more than just hard approaches to security. As Lawrence Freedman notes, even the

---

[*] Richard Engel and Robert Windrem, "CIA Didn't Always Know Who It Was Killing in Drone Strikes, Classified Documents Show," *NBC News*, June 5, 2013, http://investigations.nbcnews.com/_news/2013/06/05/18781930-cia-didnt-always-know-who-it-was-killing-in-drone-strikes-classified-documents-show.

[†] Jonathan Masters, "Targeted Killings," Council on Foreign Relations, May 23, 2013, http://www.cfr.org/counterterrorism/targeted-killings/p9627.

U.S. National Security Strategy includes preemptive measures beyond military strikes, such as in the areas of intelligence, diplomacy, economic assistance, technical guidance, and support for the military and police.[*] Beyond these measures taken for self-defense purposes, are measures that are designed to forestall rather than permit a security threat from materializing; more specifically, prospective security measures known as precautionary measures.

USHERING IN THE AGE OF PRECAUTION

A driving principle behind preemption is the precautionary principle. This principle requires that where there is a threat of serious and irreversible harm, "lack of full scientific certainty" should not be used by governments as a reason for inaction.[†] The precautionary principle has three essential elements: a threat of harm; uncertainty as to the impact of the threats; and a precautionary response.[‡] According to Elizabeth Fisher, the principle should be used in "cases where there are threats to human health or the environment; the fact that there is scientific uncertainty over those threats should not be used as the reason for not taking action to prevent harm."[§] The precautionary principle is enshrined in environmental policy in the European Union. For example, according to Article 174(2) of the Treaty establishing the European Community,

> [c]ommunity policy on the environment shall aim at a high level of protection taking into account the diversity of situations in the various regions of the Community. It shall be based on the precautionary principle and on the principles that preventive action should be taken, that environmental damage should as a priority be rectified at [the] source and that the polluter should pay.

There have been several formulations of the precautionary principle in law. For example, it is included in the Bamako Convention on the Ban of the Import into Africa and the Control of Transboundary Movement and Management of Hazardous Wastes within Africa. Specifically, Article 4(3)(f) of this Convention states that

---

[*] Lawrence Freedman, "Prevention, Not Preemption," *The Washington Quarterly* 26:2 (2003), 113.

[†] Sonja Boehmer-Christiansen, "The Precautionary Principle in Germany: Enabling Government," In Timothy O'Riordan and James Cameron (Eds.), *Interpreting the Precautionary Principle* (London: Earthscan, 1994), 31.

[‡] Stephen M. Gardiner, "A Core Precautionary Principle," *The Journal of Political Philosophy* 14:1 (2006), 36.

[§] Elizabeth Fisher, "Is the Precautionary Principle Justiciable?" *Journal of Environmental Law* 13:3 (2001), 316.

> [e]ach Party shall strive to adopt and implement the preventive, pre-cautionary approach to pollution problems which entails, inter alia, preventing the release into the environment of substances which may cause harm to humans or the environment without waiting for scien-tific proof regarding such harm. The Parties shall cooperate with each other in taking the appropriate measures to implement the precaution-ary principle to pollution prevention through the application of clean production methods, rather than the pursuit of permissible emissions approach based on assimilative capacity assumption.

The precautionary principle has also been applied to the marine envi-ronment. In particular, Article 2(2)(a) of the 1992 Convention for the Protection of the Marine Environment of the North-East Atlantic, holds that

> preventive measures are to be taken when there are reasonable grounds for concern that substances or energy introduced, directly or indi-rectly, into the marine environment may bring about hazards to human health, harm living resources and marine ecosystems, damage ameni-ties or interfere with other legitimate uses of the sea, even when there is no conclusive evidence of a causal relationship between the inputs and the effects.

It is also included in the 1992 Helsinki Convention on the Protection and Use of Transboundary Watercourses and International Lakes under Article 2.5(a). Specifically, according to Article 2.5(a), "[t]he precaution-ary principle, by virtue of which action to avoid the potential trans-boundary impact of the release of hazardous substances shall not be postponed on the ground that scientific research has not fully proved a causal link between those substances, on the one hand, and the potential transboundary impact,* on the other hand."

The U.S. government has also referred to the use of the precaution-ary principle (although not by name) for national and international secu-rity (i.e., responses to terrorists and rogue states) when discussing the need to act under uncertainty in cases of substantial and irreparable harm. For example, in a speech given by President George W. Bush in

---

* Under Article 1.2 of the Helsinki Convention on the Protection and Use of Transboundary Watercourses and International Lakes, transboundary impact refers to "any significant adverse effect on the environment resulting from a change in the conditions of trans-boundary waters caused by a human activity, the physical origin of which is situated wholly or in part within an area under the jurisdiction of a Party, within an area under the jurisdiction of another Party. Such effects on the environment include effects on human health and safety, flora, fauna, soil, air, water, climate, landscape and historical monuments or other physical structures or the interaction among these factors; they also include effects on the cultural heritage or socio-economic conditions resulting from alterations to those factors."

June 2002, he stated "[i]f we wait for threats to fully materialize, we will have waited too long."* The 2002 National Security Strategy also called for precautionary responses against potential enemies (e.g., rogue states) with uncertain intentions and capabilities, before an attack was imminent. In particular, the 2002 National Security Strategy noted that "[t]he greater the threat, the greater is the risk of inaction—and the more compelling the case for taking anticipatory action to defend ourselves, even if uncertainty remains as to the time and place of the enemy's attack."†

The precautionary principle was also evident in the "One Percent Doctrine." Former U.S. Vice President Dick Cheney stated that "if there was even a one percent chance of terrorists getting a weapon of mass destruction—and there has been a small probability of such an occurrence for some time—the United States must now act as if it were a certainty."‡ Here, a "one percent of chance of catastrophe" was treated as a certainty; and "firm evidence, of either intent or capability," was considered "too high a threshold."§ This represents an extreme version of the precautionary principle: the ultraconservative precautionary principle. The ultraconservative precautionary principle holds that "any activity that one has any reason whatsoever to suspect might pose any harm whatsoever" should be banned.¶ Another extreme version of the precautionary principle is the ultraminimal precautionary principle. The ultraminimal precautionary principle holds that "the need to act in a precautionary manner [is required] in exactly one case: we should cross our fingers (or just worry) in the situation where there is a probability of 99.9% that the world is going to end immediately due to this experiment."** Not surprisingly, the application of this principle has not been seen in security practices.

Decisions in the face of uncertainty tend to err on the side of caution. Indeed, precautionary logic drives many current security policies. Precaution is viewed as a risk management or uncertainty management tool. Where there are threats or potential threats of irreversible grave harm, lack of full certainty should not be used as a reason for rejecting

---

* President George W. Bush, "Complete Text of Bush's West Point Address," June 1, 2002, http://www.newsmax.com/archives/articles/2002/6/2/81354/shtml.

† The White House, "V. Prevent Our Enemies from Threatening Us, Our Allies, and Our Friends with Weapons of Mass Destruction," 2006, http://georgewbush-whitehouse. archives.gov/nsc/nss/2006/sectionV.html.

‡ Ron Suskind, *The One Percent Doctrine: Deep Inside America's Pursuit of Its Enemies since 9/11* (London: Simon and Schuster, 2006), 62.

§ Ibid., 150.

¶ Stephen M. Gardiner, "A Core Precautionary Principle," *The Journal of Political Philosophy* 14:1 (2006), 37.

** Stephen M. Gardiner, "A Core Precautionary Principle," *The Journal of Political Philosophy* 14:1 (2006), 38.

or postponing the implementation of security measures. Cost–benefit analysis is required in order to ensure that a form of worst-case thinking is not at work when developing and implementing precautionary security measures.

For security policy, cost–benefit analysis is relevant even in cases of uncertainty. Certainly, it figures prominently in Principle 15 of the 1992 Rio Declaration, which defines the precautionary principle as follows: "Where there are threats of serious or irreversible damage, lack of full scientific certainty shall not be used as a reason for postponing cost-effective measures to prevent environmental degradation." The preamble of the 2000 Cartagena Protocol on Biosafety to the Convention on Biological Diversity reaffirmed "the precautionary approach contained in Principle 15 of the Rio Declaration on Environment and Development." Moreover, Article 3.3 of the 1992 UN Framework Convention on Climate Change holds that precautionary measures should be taken

> to anticipate, prevent or minimize the causes of climate change and mitigate its adverse effects. Where there are threats of serious or irreversible damage, lack of full scientific certainty should not be used as a reason for postponing such measures, taking into account that policies and measures to deal with climate change should be cost-effective so as to ensure global benefits at the lowest possible cost.

Even measures that are based on the precautionary principle "should comply with the basic principles for all other legislation, such as proportionality...and should be based on an examination of the potential benefits and costs of action or inaction."[*] The European Court of First Instance in *Pfizer Animal Health SA v. Council of the European Union* (Pfizer) examined the legitimacy of a proposed measure.[†] Specifically, in Pfizer, when examining the legitimacy of a measure the European Court of First Instance evaluated, within the framework of a cost–benefit analysis, whether the disadvantages caused by the contested regulation were disproportionate by comparison with the advantages which would ensue if no action were taken. A proposed measure should only be implemented if its benefits outweigh its costs. This, however, has not always been seen. The application of the ultraconservative precautionary principle (acting as a threat is a certainty, even when this is not the case) brings to light countries' dangerous overreaction to certain threats.

---

[*] European Commission (EC), "Annexes to Impact Assessment Guidelines," June 15, 2005, 26, http://www.legislationline.org/documents/id/15234.

[†] Case T-13/99 *Pfizer Animal Health SA v. Council of the European Union* [2002] ECR II-3305.

Errors in Decision Making in Response to Uncertainty: Lessons from Psychology

Uncertainty manifests itself in several different ways. Precautionary measures in response to uncertainty should only be taken after the following has been determined: that there are possible dangerous effects of a threat; the assessment of the threat does not allow risk to be determined with scientific certainty; and all available scientific data has been objectively evaluated before taking precautionary measures.[*] Despite these requirements, precautionary measures have been implemented that do not meet these criteria.

Jervis believes that bad decision making can be explained and understood by psychology.[†] Often improper risk assessments and fear have adversely impacted decision making under uncertainty. With respect to risk assessments, cognitive heuristics allow individuals to process a large amount of information quickly and intuitively, but often at the cost of sound judgments (i.e., conclusions that individuals would not have drawn given unlimited time).[‡] When considering risks people tend to rely on heuristics. People collectively rely on heuristics to assess risk. These heuristics can explain why individuals overreact to low-probability but highly publicized risks, such as terrorism and bioterrorism attacks. Emotions, such as fear, also play a central role in overestimations of risk and overreacting to uncertainty. Individuals tend to overreact to risks that are involuntary (e.g., murder and terrorism)[§] and uncommon (e.g., bioterrorism attacks, schools shootings, and terrorism).[¶] Feelings of dread can make decision makers susceptible to implementing aggressive policies with little regard to countervailing dangers that may ensue

---

[*] Robert J. Coleman, "The U.S., Europe, and Precaution: A Comparative Case Study Analysis of the Management of Risk in a Complex World," January 11/12, 2002, European Commission, http://ec.europa.eu/dgs/policy_advisers/archives/experts_groups/docs/coleman_speech_en.pdf.

[†] Robert Jervis, "Introduction: Approach and Assumptions," In Robert Jervis, Richard Ned Lebow, and Janice Gross Stein (Eds.), *Psychology and Deterrence* (Baltimore, MD: Johns Hopkins University Press, 1989), 1–12; Jennifer Mitzen and Randall L. Schweller, "Knowing the Unknown Unknowns: Misplaced Certainty and the Onset of War," *Security Studies* 20:1 (2011), 6.

[‡] Marie-Helen Maras, "Risk Perception, Fear and Its Consequences Following the 2004 Madrid and 2005 London Bombings," In Samuel Justin Sinclair and Daniel Antonius (Eds.), *The Political Psychology of Terrorism Fears* (Oxford, United Kingdom: Oxford University Press, 2013), 227.

[§] John Adams, "What Kills You Matters, Not Numbers," *The Social Affairs Unit*, 2005, 4, http://www.socialaffairsunit.org.uk/blog/archives/000512.php.

[¶] Paul Slovic, "Perception of Risk," *Science* 2 (1987), 280–285; Cass R. Sunstein, *Laws of Fear: Beyond the Precautionary Principle* (Cambridge, UK: Cambridge University Press, 2005), 35; Frank Furedi, *Culture of Fear: Risk-Taking and the Morality of Low Expectation* (London: Cassell, 1997), 51.

with their implementation.* Indeed, precautionary responses "driven by overstated risk assessments and fear of dreaded risks will not yield sound policies;"† especially in the field of security.

CONCLUDING THOUGHTS

Security measures are designed with the rational actor in mind.‡ Good security measures focus on predicting perpetrators' responses and preventing perpetrators from achieving their goals. Discussions about security are made under conditions of uncertainty. Two types of uncertainty exist—measurable and unmeasurable uncertainty. Measurable certainty includes objective risks and implies the calculability of a threat. Unmeasurable uncertainty exists when risk calculations cannot address the threat; in these cases, the threat is unmeasurable.

The pursuit of security is examined through the lens of realism and liberalism. Realism posits that nations exist in an anarchic self-help system characterized by mutual distrust. In this system, states seek to increase their relative power position at the expense of other states. By contrast, liberalism holds that the international system creates opportunities for both conflict and cooperation; according to this theory, international institutions help reduce conflict between states. The mistrust and lack of mutual cooperation that exists between states has been depicted in games. These games provide insights into opponents' strategic choices. Uncertainty of actions and even misplaced certainty can lead (and has led to) conflict; misplaced certainty, for example, was a primary driver for the Iraq war. In response to uncertainty and undeterrable threats, states have taken preemptive action. These measures are legally justified only if they meet certain basic criteria. Even though it is considered as a justified measure according to international law (as long as the criteria for its use are met), there are drawbacks to engaging in preemptive action. Greater transparency and accountability in current preemptive practices is required.

Precautionary responses have been taken against security threats. Such actions are based on the precautionary principle. Extreme versions of the precautionary principle have been included in political discourse; the use of them in security practices, however, is indefensible.

---

* Jessica Stern, *The Ultimate Terrorists* (Cambridge, MA: Harvard University Press, 1999).
† Jessica Stern and Jonathan B. Weiner, "Precaution against Terrorism," In Paul Bracken, Ian Bremmer, and David Gordon (Eds.), *Managing Strategic Surprise: Lessons from Risk Management and Risk Assessment* (Cambridge, United Kingdom: Cambridge University Press, 2008), 181.
‡ The exception to this is when the threat is not posed by individuals, groups, or states.

Precautionary measures should only be taken after the dangerous impact of a threat has been identified, it has been determined that the risk cannot be calculated with scientific certainty, and all available data was accessed before using precautionary measures. Notwithstanding these restrictions, precautionary measures have been implemented that do not meet these criteria.

CHAPTER 3

Weapons of Mass Destruction and Nonproliferation

Nuclear arms control refers to the measures that are created and implemented to regulate, control, reduce, prevent, and/or abolish the acquisition, distribution, and use of nuclear weapons according to international law. This chapter considers nuclear arms control in detail. The focus of this chapter is on the threat of weapons of mass destruction (WMDs), existing measures to counter the proliferation of WMDs, and the future of WMD arms control. Iran and North Korea, among other countries, will be used as case studies in the analysis.

NONPROLIFERATION: ARMS CONTROL IN PRACTICE

Nonproliferation seeks to restrict the acquisition, creation, and distribution of weapons of mass destruction (WMDs). WMDs include chemical, biological, radiological, and nuclear (CBRN) weapons. To limit the proliferation of biological and chemical weapons, international legal instruments have been implemented. For instance, the Protocol for the Prohibition of the Use in War of Asphyxiating, Poisonous or other Gases, and of Bacteriological Methods of Warfare of 1928 was created to prohibit use of chemical and biological weapons. This protocol, also known as the Geneva Protocol, did not, however, cover the creation, acquisition, storage, and dissemination of chemical and biological weapons. The issues were addressed in the Biological and Toxin Weapons Convention (BTWC) of 1972 and the Convention on the Prohibition of the Development, Production, Stockpiling and Use of Chemical Weapons and on their Destruction Convention or Chemical Weapons Convention (CWC) of 1992.

For nuclear weapons, the Nonproliferation Treaty of 1970 was implemented. This treaty seeks to:

- Prevent nuclear weapons states from transferring nuclear weapons to nonnuclear weapons states (Article I)*;
- Prevent nonnuclear weapons states from acquiring and creating nuclear weapons (Article II)†;
- Ensure states use nuclear energy for peaceful purposes (Article III)‡;
- Eventually eliminate nuclear arsenals from nuclear weapons states (Article VI).§

With respect to Article VI of the treaty, nuclear weapons states have yet to fulfill the disarmament agreement. The 2000 Review Conference of the Parties to the Treaty on the Nonproliferation of Nuclear Weapons, which took place between April 24 and May 19, 2000, discussed the ways that states can meet their commitments under Article VI. More specifically, states participating in the 2000 Review Conference agreed to 13 steps to advance nuclear disarmament.¶ These steps included, among other things, the entry into force of the Comprehensive Test Ban Treaty.

The Comprehensive Test Ban Treaty, a legally binding document, seeks to ban nuclear explosives tests worldwide. The Comprehensive Test Ban Treaty has not yet entered into force. In order for it to come into

---

* Article I holds that: "Each nuclear-weapon State Party to the Treaty undertakes not to transfer to any recipient whatsoever nuclear weapons or other nuclear explosive devices or control over such weapons or explosive devices directly, or indirectly; and not in any way to assist, encourage, or induce any non-nuclear weapon State to manufacture or otherwise acquire nuclear weapons or other nuclear explosive devices, or control over such weapons or explosive devices."

† According to Article II: "Each non-nuclear-weapon State Party to the Treaty undertakes not to receive the transfer from any transferor whatsoever of nuclear weapons or other nuclear explosive devices or of control over such weapons or explosive devices directly, or indirectly; not to manufacture or otherwise acquire nuclear weapons or other nuclear explosive devices; and not to seek or receive any assistance in the manufacture of nuclear weapons or other nuclear explosive devices."

‡ Under Article III(1): "Each non-nuclear-weapon State Party to the Treaty undertakes to accept safeguards, as set forth in an agreement to be negotiated and concluded with the International Atomic Energy Agency in accordance with the Statute of the International Atomic Energy Agency and the Agency's safeguards system, for the exclusive purpose of verification of the fulfillment of its obligations assumed under this Treaty with a view to preventing diversion of nuclear energy from peaceful uses to nuclear weapons or other nuclear explosive devices..."

§ Pursuant to Article VI: "Each of the Parties to the Treaty undertakes to pursue negotiations in good faith on effective measures relating to cessation of the nuclear arms race at an early date and to nuclear disarmament, and on a Treaty on general and complete disarmament under strict and effective international control."

¶ For information about these 13 steps, see Claire Applegarth, "The 2000 NPT Review Conference and the 13 Practical Steps: A Summary," *Arms Control Today*, January/February 2005, http://www.armscontrol.org/act/2005_01-02/Scheinman.

effect, 44 states with significant nuclear capabilities need to sign and ratify it.* Countries that have not signed and/or ratified the treaty include:†

- United States (signed; not ratified);
- China (signed; not ratified);
- India (neither signed, nor ratified);
- Pakistan (neither signed, nor ratified);
- Israel (signed; not ratified);
- Egypt (signed; not ratified);
- Iran (signed; not ratified); and
- North Korea (neither signed, nor ratified).

It should be noted that the United States has a de facto moratorium on nuclear testing. It also has a program in place, the Stockpile Stewardship program, that enables the United States to maintain its nuclear capabilities without testing. This program engages in scientific inquiry through a combination of complex computational models and the National Nuclear Security Administration's Advanced Simulation and Computing Program in order to evaluate the reliability, safety, security, and efficacy of the nuclear stockpile.‡ To manage nuclear stockpiles, the Life Extension Program was created to provide the necessary repairs and replacements to nuclear weapons to ensure they meet military requirements.§ The availability of such programs has led certain academicians, professionals, policy makers, and government officials to call for the ratification of the Comprehensive Test Ban Treaty.

Another step in the 2000 Conference concerned fissile material.¶ Particularly, according to Step 3 of the 2000 Conference, states agreed on "the necessity of negotiation in the Conference on Disarmament on a non-discriminatory, multilateral and internationally and effectively verifiable treaty banning the production of fissile material for nuclear

---

* Nuclear Threat Initiative (NTI), "Comprehensive Nuclear-Test-Ban Treaty (CTBT)," http://www.nti.org/treaties-and-regimes/comprehensive-nuclear-test-ban-treaty-ctbt/.

† "Status of Signature and Ratification," Comprehensive Nuclear Test Ban Treaty Organization (CTBTO), http://www.ctbto.org/the-treaty/status-of-signature-and-ratification/.

‡ National Nuclear Security Administration (NNSA), "Stockpile Stewardship Program Quarterly Experiments," U.S. Department of Energy, http://nnsa.energy.gov/ourmission/managingthestockpile/sspquarterly.

§ National Nuclear Security Administration (NNSA), "Life Extension Programs," U.S. Department of Energy, http://nnsa.energy.gov/ourmission/managingthestockpile/lifeextensionprograms.

¶ "Fissile materials are composed of atoms that can be split by neutrons in a self-sustaining chain-reaction to release enormous amounts of energy." "Fissile Material Basics," Institute for Energy and Environmental Research, April 2012, http://ieer.org/resource/fissile-materials/fissile-material-basics/.

weapons or other nuclear explosive devices."* The Fissile Material Cut-Off Treaty was enacted to end the production of fissile material for use in weapons (e.g., high enriched uranium and plutonium). The treaty is an important addition to the nonproliferation regime as it seeks to limit the use of and secure existing fissile material throughout the world.

The 2005 Review Conference of the Parties to the Treaty on the Nonproliferation of Nuclear weapons took place from May 2 to May 27, 2005. In the 2005 Review Conference, some states did not reaffirm their commitment to the 13 steps toward nuclear disarmament from the 2000 Conference (among them were the United States and France). Additionally, no final consensus document on states' commitment to nuclear disarmament was created at the end of the conference; this was due, in large part, to the disputes among participants concerning nuclear weapons programs in the Middle East (e.g., the nuclear programs of Iran and Israel). By contrast, the 2010 Review Conference of the Parties to the Treaty on the Nonproliferation of Nuclear Weapons (hereafter 2010 Review Conference) ended with a consensus document with a renewed commitment to nuclear disarmament. The conference covered issues on nuclear proliferation, nuclear disarmament, nuclear energy use for peaceful purposes, and the creation of a zone free from weapons of mass destruction in the Middle East.

In line with the push toward nuclear disarmament, several initiatives exist that seek to reduce the nuclear arsenal of nuclear weapons states. Particularly, certain treaties were signed between states to reduce their nuclear arsenal (these bilateral agreements were also included in the 13 steps of the 2000 Review Conference). For example, the Strategic Offensive Reductions Treaty (SORT) of 2002 required the United States and Russia to dismantle a portion of their nuclear warheads. The New Strategic Arms Reduction Treaty (New START) of 2011 went further requiring both countries to limit their operationally deployed nuclear weapons to 1550. In 2009, to accelerate global efforts in nuclear disarmament, the United Nations (UN) Security Council passed Resolution 1887. That same year, in a speech given in April in Prague of the Czech Republic, President Barack Obama stated that "as a nuclear power, as the only nuclear power to have used a nuclear weapon, the United States has a moral responsibility to act. We cannot succeed in this endeavor alone, but we can lead it, we can start it."† He additionally restated

---

* "Proposed Fissile Material (Cut-off) Treaty (FMCT)," Nuclear Threat Initiative (NTI), http://www.nti.org/treaties-and-regimes/proposed-fissile-material-cut-off-reaty/.
† The White House, "Remarks by President Barack Obama," Office of the Press Secretary, April 5, 2009, http://www.whitehouse.gov/the_press_office/Remarks-By-President-Barack-Obama-In-Prague-As-Delivered.

"America's commitment to seek the peace and security of a world without nuclear weapons."[*]

The Nonproliferation Treaty seeks to limit arms buildup; however, not all countries are signatories. Three major nuclear weapons states, India, Pakistan, and Israel, have not joined the treaty. Currently, there are 189 countries that are parties to the treaty. Nonetheless, some parties of the treaty have violated provisions of it. A case in point is Iran. Iran has continuously refused to comply with its obligation under the Nonproliferation Treaty. The UN Security Council has passed several resolutions in this regard, such as UN Security Resolution 1737 (2006), UN Security Resolution 1747 (2007), and UN Security Resolution 1803 (2008). The most recent of which is UN Security Resolution 1929 of June 9, 2010. This resolution includes sanctions against Iran for refusing to comply with international proliferation security regulations.

The Nonproliferation Treaty includes a clause that allowed states to withdraw.[†] North Korea withdrew from the Treaty in 2003. Even before North Korea withdrew, it was building and working on a nuclear weapons program in violation of the treaty. Following its withdrawal, North Korea continued this endeavor. Consequently, the UN adopted four major resolutions sanctioning North Korea for its continuing development of its nuclear weapons program. The first resolution, UN Security Resolution 1718, was passed in 2006 after North Korea conducted a nuclear test. The second resolution, UN Security Resolution 1874, was passed in 2009 after North Korea conducted a second nuclear test. The third resolution, UN Security Resolution 2087, was passed in 2013 after North Korea launched a satellite on December 12, 2012, when it was prohibited in doing so under previous UN Security Resolutions because this technology can be used for ballistic missile development. The fourth resolution, UN Security Resolution 2094, was passed on February 12, 2013, after North Korea engaged in its third nuclear test. North Korea had also helped Syria create a nuclear facility.[‡] This partially constructed facility was later bombed by Israel.[§]

---

[*] Ibid.

[†] See Article 10(1) of the Treaty that states that: "Each Party shall in exercising its national sovereignty have the right to withdraw from the Treaty if it decides that extraordinary events, related to the subject matter of this Treaty, have jeopardized the supreme interests of its country. It shall give notice of such withdrawal to all other Parties to the Treaty and to the United Nations Security Council three months in advance. Such notice shall include a statement of the extraordinary events it regards as having jeopardized its supreme interests."

[‡] Greg Miller and Paul Richter, "U.S. Opens Dossier on Syrian Facility," *Los Angeles Times*, April 25, 2008, http://articles.latimes.com/2008/apr/25/world/fg-ussyria25.

[§] David E. Sanger and Mark Mazzetti, "Israel Struck Syrian Nuclear Project, Analysts Say," *New York Times*, October 14, 2007, http://www.nytimes.com/2007/10/14/washington/14weapons.html?pagewanted=all&_r=0.

Diplomatic negotiations concerning North Korea's nuclear program during the Six Party Talks (China, Japan, North Korea, Russia, South Korea, and the United States) have not yielded any fundamental results.* Given the unsuccessful negotiations, some have argued that the United States and the international community suspend foreign aid to North Korea and increase economic sanctions against them.† On the other hand, negotiations have proven successful for other countries. For example, the negotiations of Libya with the United States and the United Kingdom ultimately led to the suspension of the country's nuclear weapons program.‡ A more recent example involves Syria; albeit for a different weapon of mass destruction. Pursuant to negotiations between the United States and Russia, an agreement was reached where Syria would remove and destroy its chemical weapons by 2014.§ Syria also acceded to the Chemical Weapons Convention (effective October 14, 2013).¶

In the European Union, the 2003 European Security Strategy and the 2003 EU Strategy against the Proliferation of Weapons of Mass Destruction identified nuclear proliferation as one of the greatest threats to international security.** These strategies, among other objectives, necessitated the pursuit of the worldwide adoption and ratification of nonproliferation multilateral agreements and reinforced the need to honor these agreements.†† In addition to these strategies, agencies have been developed to monitor nonproliferation efforts. A case in point is the International Atomic Energy Agency (IAEA). The IAEA monitors nuclear weapon and nonnuclear weapon states to ensure their compliance with nonproliferation requirements. This agency is also responsible

---

* Emma Chanlett-Avery and Ian E. Rinehart, "North Korea: U.S. Relations, Nuclear Diplomacy, and Internal Situation," *Congressional Research Service*, R41259, September 13, 2013, 9, http://www.fas.org/sgp/crs/nuke/R41259.pdf.

† Mark E. Manyin and Mary Beth Nikitin, "Foreign Assistance to North Korea," *Congressional Research Service (CRS) Report for Congress*, R40095, June 11, 2013, http://www.fas.org/sgp/crs/row/R40095.pdf; Dianne E. Rennack, "North Korea: Economic Sanctions," *Congressional Research Service (CRS) Report for Congress*, RL31696, October 17, 2006, http://www.fas.org/sgp/crs/row/RL31696.pdf.

‡ American Society of International Law, "U.S./UK Negotiations with Libya regarding Nonproliferation Source," *The American Journal of International Law* 98:1 (2004), 195–197.

§ BBC News, "Syria 'Submits Chemical Weapons Data' to Hague Watchdog," September 20, 2013, http://www.bbc.co.uk/news/world-middle-east-24178830.

¶ Michael R. Gordon, "U.S. and Russia Reach Deal to Destroy Syria's Chemical Arms," *New York Times*, September 14, 2013, http://www.nytimes.com/2013/09/15/world/middleeast/syria-talks.html?pagewanted=all&_r=0.

** European Union, "The EU and Nuclear Non-Proliferation: Managing a Global Security Threat," *EU Insight*, 1, January 2011, http://www.euintheus.org/resources-learning/eu-insight/january-2011-the-eu-and-nuclear-non-proliferation-managing-a-global-security-threat/eu-insight-the-eu-and-nuclear-non-proliferation-managing-a-global-security-threat/.

†† Ibid.

for enforcing nuclear security standards worldwide, implementing the Nonproliferation Treaty, and assisting nonnuclear weapon states in developing civilian nuclear technology and energy development.* Despite these responsibilities, to date, a main problem in the detection, prevention, and punishment of Nonproliferation Treaty violations is the IAEA's inadequate enforcement of the treaty due to its lack of enforcement power and resources.†

Another agency created to, among other things, regulate the peaceful uses of nuclear material, equipment, and technology is the European Atomic Energy Community (Euratom). Euratom was established in 1958 to promote the peaceful production and use of nuclear energy. The Euratom Supply Agency, among other duties, is responsible for "authorizing supply contracts for EU import or export of nuclear materials; checking supply contracts to ensure all end-uses are peaceful and that they include a safeguards clause; and authorizing export procedures for nuclear materials produced in the EU."‡ Such safeguards are necessary as violations of the peaceful use of nuclear energy have occurred. A case in point is India. On May 18, 1974, India conducted its first nuclear test (the code name for this was Smiling Buddha). The nuclear test conducted by India heightened international awareness on how even the peaceful export of nuclear technology can lead to nuclear proliferation,§ since India obtained the nuclear technology and materials from Canada, France, and the United States.¶ India argued that it had carried out the explosion for peaceful purposes and as such, in their view, the bilateral agreements were not violated.** This action by India was condemned by members of the Nonproliferation Treaty.††

---

* "Safeguards to Prevent Nuclear Proliferation," World Nuclear Association, September 2013, http://www.world-nuclear.org/info/Safety-and-Security/Non-Proliferation/Safeguards-to-Prevent-Nuclear-Proliferation/.

† Carl E. Behrens, "Nuclear Nonproliferation Issues," *Congressional Research Service (CRS)* Issue Brief from Congress, IB10091, Library of Congress, January 20, 2006, 3–4, http://www.fas.org/sgp/crs/nuke/IB10091.pdf.

‡ European Union, "Euratom: Fostering the Peaceful Development of Nuclear Energy," *EU Insight*, January 2011, 2, http://www.euintheus.org/resources-learning/eu-insight/january-2011-the-eu-and-nuclear-non-proliferation-managing-a-global-security-threat/eu-insight-the-eu-and-nuclear-non-proliferation-managing-a-global-security-threat/.

§ Moeed Yusuf, "Predicting Proliferation: The History of the Future of Nuclear Weapons," *Brookings Institute, Policy Paper 11*, January 2009, http://www.brookings.edu/~/media/research/files/papers/2009/1/nuclear%20proliferation%20yusuf/01_nuclear_proliferation_yusuf.pdf.

¶ History of Commons, "May 18, 1974: India Tests First Nuclear Device," 2003, http://www.historycommons.org/context.jsp?item=a051874indiatest.

** Ibid.

†† Richard Bruneau, "Engaging in a Nuclear India: Punishment, Rewards, and the Politics of Nonproliferation," *Journal of Public and International Affairs* 17 (2006), 28, http://www.princeton.edu/jpia/past-issues-1/2006/2.pdf.

To promote the peaceful use of nuclear energy, numerous bilateral agreements were also created. Pursuant to the U.S.–India civil nuclear agreement, India is required to separate civilian and military nuclear facilities. Its civilian facilities were to be operated according to IAEA standards.[*] Additionally, pursuant to these agreements, nuclear material, equipment, and technology will be transferred to and from nuclear facilities in India in accordance with IAEA safeguards.[†] Other countries, such as Canada, France, the United Kingdom, Argentina, Russia, Kazakhstan, Mongolia, and South Korea, signed nuclear cooperation agreements with India.[‡] India is currently in discussions with other nations to develop nuclear cooperation agreements; for example, Japan and Australia.[§]

Other legally binding nuclear nonproliferation treaties were also implemented throughout the world. These include: the Treaty for the Prohibition of Nuclear Weapons in Latin America (Treaty of Tlatelolco) of 1968; the South Pacific Nuclear-Free-Zone Treaty (Treaty of Rarotonga) of 1986; the Treaty on the Southeast Asia Nuclear-Weapon-Free Zone (Treaty of Bangkok) of 1995; the African Nuclear-Weapon-Free Zone Treaty (Treaty of Pelindaba), which, while opened for signature in 1996, did not enter into force until 2009; and the Central Asian Nuclear-Weapon-Free Zone Treaty (Treaty of Semipalatinsk) of 2009.[¶] Multilateral informal organizations have also been created. One notable example is the Nuclear Suppliers Group (NSG). NSG is made up of 48 nuclear states (see Table 3.1) that seek the nonproliferation of nuclear weapons by implementing guidelines for nuclear exports and nuclear-related exports.[**] Moreover, a legally binding international convention, the Convention on the Physical Protection of Nuclear Material, was created to protect nuclear materials by "establish[ing] measures

---

[*] "India: Nuclear," Nuclear Threat Initiative, June 2013, http://www.nti.org/country-profiles/india/nuclear/.

[†] "Safeguards to Prevent Nuclear Proliferation," World Nuclear Association, April 2012, http://www.world-nuclear.org/info/Safety-and-Security/Non-Proliferation/Safeguards-to-Prevent-Nuclear-Proliferation/#.UkHE1j_Abqw.

[‡] "Nuclear Power in India," World Nuclear Association, August 13, 2013, http://www.world-nuclear.org/info/Country-Profiles/Countries-G-N/India/#.UkHEfD_Abqw.

[§] "Indian-Japanese Cooperation Deal Moves Closer," *World Nuclear News*, May 30, 2013, http://www.world-nuclear-news.org/NP-Indian_Japanese_cooperation_deal_moves_closer-3005135.html; BBC News, "India and Australia to Begin Nuclear Talks," October 18, 2012, http://www.bbc.co.uk/news/world-asia-india-19987048.

[¶] Robert C. Beckman, "South East Asia and International Law," *Singapore Journal of International & Comparative Law* 1 (1997), 414; "Treaty on a Nuclear-Weapon-Free Zone in Central Asia (CANWFZ)," United Nations Office of Disagreement Affairs, http://disarmament.un.org/treaties/t/canwfz.

[**] For more information on the Nuclear Suppliers Group (NSG), see http://www.nuclear-suppliersgroup.org/A_test/01-eng/index.php.

TABLE 3.1   Nuclear States of the Nuclear Suppliers Group (NSG)

Argentina	Germany	Norway
Australia	Greece	Poland
Austria	Hungary	Portugal
Belarus	Iceland	Romania
Belgium	Ireland	Russian Federation
Brazil	Italy	Serbia
Bulgaria	Japan	Slovakia
Canada	Kazakhstan	Slovenia
China	Republic of Korea	South Africa
Croatia	Latvia	Spain
Cyprus	Lithuania	Sweden
Czech Republic	Luxembourg	Switzerland
Denmark	Malta	Turkey
Estonia	Mexico	Ukraine
Finland	Netherlands	United Kingdom
France	New Zealand	United States

related to the prevention, detection and punishment of offenses relating to nuclear material."[*]

In the United States, the Nunn-Lugar Cooperative Threat Reduction Program (i.e., the Cooperative Threat Reduction or CTR program) is an initiative within the Defense Threat Reduction Agency (DTRA). This program aims to secure and disassemble weapons of mass destruction in former Soviet states.[†] It additionally provides expertise and resources to these countries to secure and eliminate their nuclear weapons arsenals. The program has expanded to include other states as well; some of which are in South Asia and Africa.[‡] Even with these programs, initiatives, agreements, and treaties in place, national and international concerns remain that nuclear weapons and materials will be acquired by individuals or states seeking to harm others.

---

[*] IAEA, "International Conventions and Legal Agreements: Convention on Physical Protection of Nuclear Material," International Atomic Energy Agency, http://www.iaea.org/Publications/Documents/Conventions/cppnm.html.

[†] Defense Threat Reduction Agency, "Cooperative Threat Reduction Program," http://www.dtra.mil/Missions/Nunn-Lugar/GlobalCooperationInitiative.aspx.

[‡] Justin Bresolin, Sam Kane, and Kingston Reif, "Fact Sheet: The Nunn–Lugar Cooperative Threat Reduction Program," Center for Arms Control and Non Proliferation, July 2013, http://armscontrolcenter.org/publications/factsheets/fact_sheet_the_cooperative_threat_reduction_program/.

Nuclear Terrorism

Nuclear weapons, or nuclear materials, can be acquired by a non-state actor from a nuclear weapons state (either willingly transferred or through theft) or the black market.* It is important to note that the Nonproliferation Treaty only addresses proliferation by states; nonstate actors are not included in this treaty. To remedy this, the UN adopted Resolution 1540, a legally binding document calling for countries to refrain from providing nonstate actors with WMDs and preventing them from obtaining WMDs. The UN created a committee, the 1540 Committee, to oversee states' implementation of this resolution.

A particular concern among states is nuclear terrorism. Nuclear terrorism refers to either the use of nuclear materials or the attacking of a nuclear facility in furtherance of a political, religious, or ideological goal in order to cause death or serious bodily harm to persons and property.† Out of all of the forms of weapons of mass destruction terrorism (hereafter WMD terrorism), nuclear terrorism is the one considered least likely to occur. Other forms of WMD terrorism, such as bioterrorism and chemical weapons terrorism, have already occurred. For instance, the Bhagwan Shree Rajneesh cult engaged in bioterrorism by spreading salmonella at restaurants in The Dalles, Oregon, in 1984, in order to influence a local election.‡ In addition, Aum Shinrikyo engaged in the well-known 1995 sarin gas attack in the subway of Tokyo, Japan.

Despite the fact that nuclear terrorism has not yet occurred and it is the least likely (with respect to the other forms of WMD terrorism) to occur, in 2009, U.S. President Barack Obama identified "nuclear terrorism [as] one of the greatest threats to international security."§ Moreover, the European Council President similarly stated in 2010 that: "[n]uclear terrorism, with terrorists getting access to nuclear materials or to radioactive sources, represents a…serious threat to international security with potentially devastating consequences to our societies."¶ To combat this threat, the UN implemented the International Convention for the

---

* Marie-Helen Maras, *CRC Press Terrorism Reader* (Boca Raton, FL: CRC Press, 2013), 83–84.
† Marie-Helen Maras, *Counterterrorism* (Burlington, MA: Jones & Bartlett, 2012).
‡ Peter Chalk, "'Hitting America's Soft Underbelly: The Potential Threat of Deliberate Biological Attacks against U.S. Agricultural and Food Industry," RAND National Defense Research Institute, 2004, 29, http: //www.rand.org/pubs/monographs/ MG135.html; Jim Monke, "Agroterrorism: Threat and Preparedness," *CRS Report for Congress*, RL32521, August 13, 2004, 5, http://www.fas.org/irp/crs/RL32521.pdf.
§ "About NSS," Nuclear Security Summit, https://www.nss2014.com/en.
¶ Herman Van Rompuy, "Statement of President of the European Council on Behalf of the European Union at the Nuclear Security Summit in Washington (PCE 68/10)," European Council, April 12, 2010, http://www.consilium.europa.eu/uedocs/cms_Data/ docs/pressdata/en/ec/113709.pdf.

Suppression of Acts of Nuclear Terrorism (or Convention on Nuclear Terrorism); another legally binding convention. The Convention on Nuclear Terrorism criminalizes acts of nuclear terrorism. It was also created to harmonize and promote cooperation in the detection, investigation, and prosecution of nuclear terrorism. A chief criticism against this convention is that it only includes recommendations.

As part of its National Strategy to Combat Weapons of Mass Destruction, the United States participated in several multinational initiatives aimed at protecting against WMD terrorism. One such initiative is the Proliferation Security Initiative (PSI). The PSI promotes international treaties that seek to criminalize weapons of mass destruction trafficking, and cooperation among states in interdicting and preventing trafficking.[*] Furthermore, the Global Threat Reduction Initiative (GTRI) assists the Department of Energy in preventing "the acquisition of nuclear and radiological materials for use in weapons of mass destruction...and other acts of terrorism."[†] A further initiative is the Global Partnership Against the Spread of Weapons and Materials of Mass Destruction.[‡] This partnership "initiate[s] bilateral and multilateral projects and enhance existing ones" on nuclear nonproliferation.[§]

Nuclear safety, or nuclear security, is defined as "the prevention and detection of, and response to, theft, sabotage, unauthorized access, illegal transfer or other malicious acts involving nuclear material, other radioactive substances or their associated facilities."[¶] The international community has sought to assist states in protecting their nuclear materials weapons. Part of the nuclear safety and nonproliferation regime is the need to secure domestic nuclear arsenals and to monitor and verify nuclear stockpiles. Some countries have implemented measures in this regard. For example, the Nuclear Materials Management and Safeguards System (NMMSS) of the United States was created to monitor nuclear materials.[**] Specifically, NMMSS is a centralized government database that is used to account for nuclear material in the United States. This system seeks to

---

[*] "Proliferation Security Initiative (PSI)," Nuclear Threat Initiative, http://www.nti.org/treaties-and-regimes/proliferation-security-initiative-psi/.

[†] "Office of Global Threat Reduction," National Nuclear Security Administration, http://nnsa.energy.gov/aboutus/ourprograms/nonproliferation/programoffices/officeglobalthreatreduction.

[‡] "Global Partnership against the Spread of Weapons and Materials of Mass Destruction ('10 Plus 10 over 10 Program')," Nuclear Threat Initiative, http://www.nti.org/treaties-and-regimes/global-partnership-against-spread-weapons-and-materials-mass-destruction-10-plus-10-over-10-program/.

[§] Ibid.

[¶] Nuclear Security Plan for 2006–2009 (IAEA GOV/2005/50).

[**] U.S. Nuclear Regulatory Commission, "Nuclear Materials Management and Safeguards System (NMMSS)," December 10, 2012, http://www.nrc.gov/reading-rm/basic-ref/glossary/nuclear-material-management-and-safeguards-system-nmmss.html.

prevent unauthorized users from obtaining this material.[*] In the end, due to state sovereignty, each state makes its own decision on how to secure its nuclear materials. The same holds true for a state's decision to engage in nuclear arms control and disarmament. The question that follows is: what factors influence this decision? To answer this question, the classical arms control theory, the democratic peace theory, and the reasons why nuclear proliferation and arms control occur are examined.

KANT AND THE OBJECTIVES OF CLASSICAL ARMS CONTROL THEORY

According to Immanuel Kant, states have the right to defend themselves.[†] However, he further noted that their choice in the manner in which to choose to defend themselves was not unlimited. The actions taken should consider the response of other states and how they might perceive the defensive actions taken by the state. In other words, the actions taken by a state should be proportionate to the threat. This concept can be applied to WMDs. With respect to the use of force, the damage that weapons cause should be limited. In the case of WMDs, there is an implied limitation to the use of these weapons, as they are considered cruel and destructive weapons due to both the short- and long-term effects of their use; the detonating blast (the pressure shock wave), thermal radiation (heat), and the resultant effects of the radiation (both immediate and late onset) of the nuclear explosion can cause a significant number of casualties.[‡]

Historically, nuclear weapons have only been used in war twice (both times by the United States)—in the 1945 atomic bombings of Hiroshima and Nagasaki in Japan during World War II. Given the magnitude of devastation that could be caused with their use, international communities have sought to regulate, inventory, control, and reduce the stockpile of nuclear weapons in the world. The same can be said with biological and chemical weapons. Chemical weapons, for example, have been used multiple times during war and other conflict situations. For example, World War I was known as the chemist's war because of the existence and use of weapons containing chemical agents (chlorine, mustard, and phosgene) during the war.[§] During the Iraq–Iran conflict,

---

[*] Ibid.

[†] Immanuel Kant, *Perpetual Peace: A Philosophical Essay*, Benjamin F. Trueblood (tr) (Washington, DC: The American Peace Society, 1975).

[‡] M. V. Ramana, "Bombing Bombay? Effects of Nuclear Weapons and a Case Study of a Hypothetical Explosion," International Physicians for the Prevention of Nuclear War (IPPNW) Global Health, *Watch Report*, Number 3, 1999, http://www.ippnw.org/pdf/Bombay.pdf.

[§] New York Times, "A Chemist's War," *New York Times*, September 20, 1920, http://query.nytimes.com/mem/archive-free/pdf?res=9504EFDF1F31E433A25753C2A96F9C946195D6CF.

FIGURE 3.1 Syrian President Bashar al-Assad. (Image courtesy of Shutterstock.com.)

Saddam Hussein used mustard gas and nerve agents (sarin, tabun, and VX) against the Kurdish population in northern Iraq.[*] In addition, Syria was recently accused of using chemical weapons against its citizens. Specifically, the UN mission reported that it "collected clear and convincing evidence that surface-to-surface rockets containing the nerve agent sarin were used [on August 21, 2013,] in Ein Tarma, Moadamiyah and Zalmalka in the Ghouta area of Damascus."[†] Syrian President Bashar al-Assad (Figure 3.1) vehemently denied the chemical weapons attacks; arguing instead that these were perpetrated by the opposition forces.[‡]

[*] *BBC News*, "Thousands Die in Halabja Gas Attack," 1988, http://news.bbc.co.uk/onthisday/hi/dates/stories/march/16/newsid_4304000/4304853.stm.

[†] Ban Ki-Moon, "Secretary-General's Remarks to the Security Council on the Report of the United Nations Missions to Investigate Allegations of the Use of Chemical Weapons on the Incident That Occurred on 21 August 2013 in the Ghouta Area of Damascus," UN, September 16, 2013, http://www.un.org/sg/statements/index.asp?nid=7083; *BBC News*, "Syria Chemical Attacks: What We Know," September 24, 2013, http://www.bbc.com/news/world-middle-east-23927399.

[‡] Jeff Black, "Defiant Assad: 'We Didn't Use Any Chemical Weapons,'" *NBC News*, September 18, 2013, http://worldnews.nbcnews.com/_news/2013/09/18/20565969-defiant-assad-we-didnt-use-any-chemical-weapons?lite; *BBC News*, "Syria Chemical Attacks: What We Know," September 16, 2013, http://www.bbc.co.uk/news/world-middle-east-23927399.

DEMOCRACIES AND ARMS CONTROL

The democratic peace theory holds that democracies are more peaceful in their relations with other democracies; that is, they are hesitant to engage in armed conflict with them.[*] The central tenet of democratic peace theory is that democracies are more peaceful than nondemocracies (i.e., democracies are less likely to go to war). This, however, has not always been practiced. What leads democracies to go to war? Kant argues that states are likely to go to war when faced with an "unjust enemy."[†] This unjust enemy can be thought of as a rogue state. A rogue state is defined as one that:[‡]

- Brutalizes its own citizens
- Has a leader that uses the country's natural resources for personal gain
- Threatens the security of its neighbors
- Disregards international law and violates international laws and treaties it is a signatory of
- Seeks the acquisition, creation, dissemination, and/or use of WMDs
- Sponsors terrorism[§]
- Rejects the rule of law and human rights

For rogue states, weapons of mass destruction are viewed as tools of aggression and intimidation.[¶] The transfer of nuclear material and

---

[*] Azar Gat, "The Democratic Peace Theory Reframed: The Impact of Modernity," *World Politics* 58:1 (2005), 73.

[†] Immanuel Kant, *Perpetual Peace: A Philosophical Sketch*, Ted Humphrey (tr.) (Indianapolis, IN: Hackett, 2003), 5.

[‡] Michael Klare, *Rogue States and Nuclear Outlaws: America's Search for a New Foreign Policy* (New York: Hill and Wang, 1995); Jason Rose, "Defining the Rogue State: A Definitional Comparative Analysis within the Rationalist, Culturalist, and Structural Traditions," *Journal of Political Inquiry* 4 (2011), http://jpi-nyu.org/wp-content/uploads/2011/02/Defining-the-Rogue-State-A-Definitional-Comparative-Analysis-Within-the-Rationalist-Culturalist-and-Structural-Traditions...Jason-Rose1.pdf; Petra Minnerop, "Rogue States—State Sponsors of Terrorism?" *German Law Journal* 3 (2002), http://www.germanlawjournal.com/index.php? pageID=11&artID=188; Isobel Roele, "We Have Not Seen the Last of the Rogue State," *German Law Journal* 13:5 (2012), 560–578, http://www.germanlawjournal.com/index.php?pageID=11&artID=1432.

[§] "State-sponsored terrorism involves the use of violence by governments (or factions within governments) against the citizens of the country, factions within the government, or foreign groups or government." Marie-Helen Maras, *Counterterrorism* (Burlington, MA: Jones & Bartlett, 2012).

[¶] George W. Bush, "U.S. National Security Strategy: Prevent Our Enemies from Threatening Us, Our Allies, and Our Friends with Weapons of Mass Destruction," West Point, New York, June 1, 2002, U.S. Department of State, http://2001-2009.state.gov/r/pa/ei/wh/15425.htm.

weapons by rogue states to other states or nonstate actors poses a grave threat to international security.

While democracies favor arms control, their mistrust for the unjust enemy may lead them to use force. Indeed, democracies generally mistrust totalitarian and authoritarian regimes.[*] A case in point is Iran. Iran's nuclear program has caused concern for the international community, where some countries believe that the program is being built for military purposes and not peaceful purposes as Iran asserts. This mistrust has led to many attempts to slow down the development of Iran's nuclear program: the most prominent of which are sanctions (through UN Security Resolutions)[†] and cyberattacks.[‡] The most well-known cyberattack incident involved Stuxnet. Stuxnet was a computer worm that infiltrated the industrial control system of an Iranian nuclear facility.[§] It is believed that Stuxnet delayed, at least in part, Iran's nuclear program; however, this is something that the former Iranian President, Mahmoud Ahmadinejad (Figure 3.2), fervidly denied.[¶] The existence of nuclear programs and nuclear weapons in nondemocracies may thus lead to mistrust; and in so doing, inhibit peaceful negotiations and agreements. As a result, the existence of an unjust enemy may be used as an argument against arms control. Despite this, nuclear arms and disarmament is still the preferred and more appropriate strategic choice in promoting international security.

CHOOSING ARMS CONTROL: WHAT DETERMINES THIS

National insecurity is believed to be a harbinger of nuclear proliferation. Indeed, states acquire nuclear weapons in response to insecurity. The decision of a state to acquire nuclear weapons will depend on the extent of external security threats that it faces. Consider Israel. Israel built its nuclear arsenal to protect itself against its aggressors. However, neighboring countries in conflict with Israel view Israel's arsenal as a

---

[*] Michael W. Doyle, "Kant, Liberal Legacies, and Foreign Affairs," *Philosophy & Public Affairs* 12:3 (1983), 205–35.

[†] See UN Security Resolution 1737 (2006), UN Security Resolution 1747 (2007), UN Security Resolution 1803 (2008), and UN Security Resolution 1929 (2010).

[‡] A cyberattack refers to the damage, disruption, and/or unauthorized access to computer systems and related technologies. For information on the cyberattacks on Iran's energy sector, see Chapter 12.

[§] Daniel Terdiman, "Stuxnet Delivered to Iranian Nuclear Plant on Thumb Drive," *CNET*, April 12, 2012, http://news.cnet.com/8301-13772_3-57413329-52/stuxnet-delivered-to-iranian-nuclear-plant-on-thumb-drive/.

[¶] BBC News, "Stuxnet 'hit' Iran nuclear plans," November 22, 2010, http://www.bbc.co.uk/news/technology-11809827.

FIGURE 3.2 Former Iranian President Mahmoud Ahmadinejad, pictured here, was certainly no friend of the United States during his time as president. (Photo taken by Agência Brasil, published under the Creative Commons Attribution 3.0 Brazil License, http://creativecommons.org/ licenses/by/3.0/br/deed.en. No image modifications made. Retrieved from Wikipedia.com, March 19, 2014.)

threat. These countries in turn seek to match Israel's nuclear arms.* The security dilemma is apparent in the proliferation of nuclear weapons in the Middle East. It is also apparent in the proliferation of nuclear weapons in India and Pakistan. The security dilemma is observed in the India–Pakistan nuclear arms race as follows: After India conducted its first nuclear weapons test, Pakistan initiated a nuclear weapons program. Pakistan's nuclear program has caused international concern. This concern centers on the internal political instability of the country. The fear is that the instability of the country may lead to the state collapsing, leaving the nuclear weapons of the country to possibly fall into

---

* Seymour Hersh, *The Samson Option: Israel's Nuclear Arsenal and American Foreign Policy* (New York: Random House, 1991), 87.

the wrong hands of militants, terrorists, or others who can use them for nefarious purposes.*

The proliferation of nuclear weapons is not always the result of national security concerns.† Robert Malcolmson holds that nuclear weapons are "symbols of power, status and national prestige. They convey vital messages to others, messages that bespeak a special sort of domination and subordination...nuclear weaponry is, in essential respects, the principal currency of power in the modern world."‡ Other than power and prestige,§ some believe that other important factors play a role in nuclear proliferation such as "domestic political dynamics, technological determinism, and the cognitive frameworks and disposition of national leaders."¶

Democracies and nondemocracies' preference for nuclear proliferation and/or arms control can be understood as a product of their role and identity. A state's "[r]ole refers to the function of states in the international environment. Roles consist in part of the actors' self-perception of their place in the world (ego), and in part of expectations of behavior other actors ascribe to them (alter)."** The latter, the "alter," is what Charles Horton Cooley referred to as the *looking glass self*.†† Here, self-perception is influenced and developed from the perceptions of others and how a person believes that others perceive him or her and how others expect him or her to behave. On the other hand, a state's

---

* Bob Graham, Jim Talent, Graham Allison, Robin Cleveland, Steve Rademaker, Tim Roemer, Wendy Sherman, Henry Sokolski, and Rich Verma. *World at Risk: Commission on the Prevention of WMD Proliferation and Terrorism* (New York: Vintage, 2008), 65–75, http://a.abcnews.go.com/images/TheLaw/WMD-report.pdf#http://a.abcnews.go.com/images/TheLaw/WMD-report.pdf.

† Scott D. Sagan, "Why Do States Build Nuclear Weapons? Three Models in Search of a Bomb," *International Security* 21:3 (Winter 1996/1997), 54–86.

‡ Robert W. Malcolmson, *Nuclear Fallacies: How We Have Been Misguided Since Hiroshima* (Montreal: McGill-Queens University Press, 1985), 67.

§ Richard N. Rosecrance, *Problems of Nuclear Proliferation: Technology and Politics* (Berkeley, CA: University of California Press, 1966), 35.

¶ Nick Ritchie, *A Nuclear Weapons-Free World? Britain, Trident and the Challenges Ahead* (New York: Palgrave MacMillan, 2012), 189; see also Peter Lavoy, "Nuclear Myths and the Causes of Nuclear Proliferation," *Security Studies* 2:3 (1993), 196; Scott D. Sagan, "Why Do States Build Nuclear Weapons? Three Models in Search of a Bomb," *International Security* 21:3 (Winter 1996/1997), 54–86; Stephen M. Meyer, *The Dynamics of Nuclear Proliferation* (Chicago, Illinois: University of Chicago Press, 1984); and Jacques E. C. Hymans, *The Psychology of Nuclear Proliferation* (Cambridge: Cambridge University Press, 2006).

** Knut Kirste und Hanns W. Maull, "Zivilmacht und Rollentheorie," *Zeitschrift für Internationale Beziehungen* 3:2 (1996), 283–312, cited in Una Becker, Harald Müller, and Simone Wisotzkic, "Democracy and Nuclear Arms Control—Destiny or Ambiguity?" *Security Studies* 17:4 (2008), 818–819.

†† Charles Horton Cooley, *Social Organization: A Study of the Larger Mind* (New York: Charles Scribner's & Sons, 1909).

identity "refers to images of individuality and distinctiveness that are formed through relations with significant others."[*] According to Una Becker, Harald Müller, and Simone Wisotzki, "state identities and roles establish which interests, preferences, and strategies can be legitimately formulated; they [also] restrict the range of policy options decision makers have at their disposal when formulating their objectives within a logic of appropriateness."[†] More specifically, they argue that a state's role and identity helps "shape the thrust of [its] foreign policy, its enemy perception and evaluation of nuclear weapons, and its ensuing choices of nuclear arms control policies."[‡] National identities and roles are thus crucial to nonproliferation and arms control strategies. They also help explain why countries seek nuclear weapons. They additionally explain what states do with nuclear weapons once developed or acquired.

Identities and Roles in Practice

The roles and identities of states help explain the stance of countries in nuclear arms control and disarmament. The following countries are examined to see how identities and roles play a part in arms control: the United States, the United Kingdom, France, Germany, Canada, Ireland, Russia, Iran, and North Korea. For countries with nuclear weapons, their maintenance is believed to serve as a deterrent for war. One such country is the United States. The United States sees itself as a superpower and responsible for the protection of the world order.[§] For the United States, the presence of an unjust enemy also justifies the maintenance of its nuclear arsenal. The more pronounced an unjust enemy is, the more likely that nuclear weapons will be used to maintain internal order and the less likely that states with such views will be proactive in nuclear weapons arms control and disarmament.

---

[*] Ronald J. Jepperson, Alexander Wendt, and Peter J. Katzenstein, "Norms, Identity, and Culture in International Security," In Peter J. Katzenstein (Ed.), *The Culture of National Security* (New York: Columbia University Press, 1996), 33–75, 59; Alexander Wendt, "Collective Identity Formation and the International State," *American Political Science Review* 88:2 (1994), 384–396, cited in Una Becker, Harald Müller, and Simone Wisotzki, "Democracy and Nuclear Arms Control—Destiny or Ambiguity?" *Security Studies* 17:4 (2008), 819.

[†] James G. March and Johan P. Olsen, *Rediscovering Institutions: The Organizational Basis of Politics* (New York: The Free Press, 1989) and Hopf, T., "The Promise of Constructivism," *International Security* 23(1) (1998), 171–200, cited in Una Becker, Harald Müller, and Simone Wisotzki, "Democracy and Nuclear Arms Control—Destiny or Ambiguity?" *Security Studies* 17:4 (2008), 818.

[‡] Una Becker, Harald Müller, and Simone Wisotzki, "Democracy and Nuclear Arms Control— Destiny or Ambiguity?" *Security Studies* 17:4 (2008), 818.

[§] Ibid., 825.

Similarly to the United States, the United Kingdom views nuclear weapons as essential in providing the necessary "'insurance' against a military intervention getting so ugly that a major confrontation involving the use of weapons of mass destruction" becomes possible.[*] Like the United States, the United Kingdom views arms control as a responsibility for superpowers. The United Kingdom sees itself "as a 'global power of the first order' with responsibilities around the globe."[†] The United Kingdom also considers itself "a pivotal interventionist power" due in part to "its 'special relationship' with the United States."[‡] It further views "itself... as a mediator between moderate non-nuclear weapons states and the more intransigent nuclear weapons states."[§] Like the United States, the United Kingdom justifies the existence of an unjust enemy as a reason for maintaining their nuclear arsenal; the same holds true for France.

France's stance on nuclear weapons is linked to French nationalism and former president Charles de Gaulle's *force de frappe*.[¶] For France, their nuclear weapons are linked to prestige and status. France sees itself as a "grande nation" and points to France's exceptionalism as a reason for retaining nuclear weapons and justifying its maintenance of its nuclear arsenal to protect itself against foreign occupation, to guarantee its independence, and to be on an equal playing field with the United States.[**] The possession of nuclear weapons places France on an equal playing field with the United Kingdom and Russia, as well.[††] With respect to its position on nuclear proliferation, France orients its own policy according to that of the United States; as it does not favor further limiting the nuclear arsenal beyond the set minimum.

---

[*] Nick Richie, "Relinquishing Nuclear Weapons: Identities, Networks and the British Bomb," *International Affairs* 86:2 (2012), 470–471.

[†] Julian Lindley-French, "Paying for the Privilege: Why an Ethical Foreign Policy Needs an Increase in Defence Expenditure," *RUSI Journal* 144:4 (1999), 7; Una Becker, Harald Müller, and Simone Wisotzki, "Democracy and Nuclear Arms Control—Destiny or Ambiguity?" *Security Studies* 17:4 (2008), 833.

[‡] Nick Richie, "Relinquishing Nuclear Weapons: Identities, Networks and the British Bomb," *International Affairs* 86:2 (2012), 471.

[§] Una Becker, Harald Müller, and Simone Wisotzki, "Democracy and Nuclear Arms Control—Destiny or Ambiguity?" *Security Studies* 17:4 (2008), 834.

[¶] Douglas Brinkley and Richard T. Griffiths, *John F. Kennedy and Europe* (Eisenhower Center Studies on War and Peace) (Louisiana: Louisiana State University Press, 1999), 299.

[**] Una Becker, Harald Müller, and Simone Wisotzki, "Democracy and Nuclear Arms Control—Destiny or Ambiguity?" *Security Studies* 17:4 (2008), 828.

[††] Beatrice Heuser, *Nuclear Mentalities? Strategies and Beliefs in Britain, France and the FRG* (Basingstoke: Macmillan Press, 1998) cited in Matthew Moran and Heather W. Williams, "Keeping up Appearances: National Narratives and Nuclear Policy in France and Russia," *Defence Studies* 13:2 (2013), 199.

The need for maintaining nuclear arsenals is less pronounced in countries where an unjust enemy is believed to be absent. Cases in point are Germany, Canada, and Ireland. In particular, Germany is a "proactive force in nonproliferation and has consistently supported nuclear disarmament."[*] This country embraces arms control and views itself as a faithful ally, preferring to cooperate with nondemocracies.[†] Similar to Germany, Canada seeks cooperation with nondemocracies. Contrary to Germany, Canada sees itself as "as a benign middle power and good international citizen," seeking "multilateralism, commitment, and [the] pursuit of a common good."[‡] Canada further sees itself as the peaceful promoter for the use of nuclear energy.[§] Unlike Germany and Canada, Ireland is a nuclear free state: it does not have any nuclear power plants nor ever had a nuclear program. As Becker, Müller, and Wisotzki rightly point out, it "is one of the most proactive states in nonproliferation and disarmament."[¶] They further note that Ireland views itself as "a pacifist, neutral country with the role of a good international citizen and bridge-builder, and a responsibility to promote nuclear disarmament."[**]

While the presence or absence of an unjust enemy plays a role in the stance of countries on nuclear weapons arms control and disarmament, other factors also play a role. For example, some countries maintain nuclear arsenals for existential deterrence purposes. Existential deterrence refers to the notion that states are deterred from using force

---

[*] Harald Müller, "German National Identity and WMD Nonproliferation," *The Nonproliferation Review* 10:2 (2003), 1–20, cited in Una Becker, Harald Müller, and Simone Wisotzki, "Democracy and Nuclear Arms Control—Destiny or Ambiguity?" *Security Studies* 17:4 (2008), 835.

[†] Thomas U. Berger, *Cultures of Antimilitarism: National Security in Germany and Japan* (Baltimore, MD: Johns Hopkins University Press, 1998); Sebastian Harnisch and Hanns W. Maul (Eds.), *Germany as a Civilian Power? The Foreign Policy of the Berlin Republic* (Manchester: Manchester University Press, 2001); Peter J. Katzenstein (Ed.), *Tamed Power: Germany in Europe* (Ithaca, NY: Cornell University Press, 1997); Una Becker, Harald Müller, and Simone Wisotzki, "Democracy and Nuclear Arms Control—Destiny or Ambiguity?" *Security Studies* 17:4 (2008), 838.

[‡] Don Munton and Tom Keating, "Internationalism and the Canadian Public," *Canadian Journal of Political Science* 34:3 (2001), 531; Una Becker, Harald Müller, and Simone Wisotzki, "Democracy and Nuclear Arms Control—Destiny or Ambiguity?" *Security Studies* 17:4 (2008), 843.

[§] Duane Bratt, "Is Business Booming? Canada's Nuclear Reactor Export Policy," *International Journal* 51:3 (1996), 487–505; Una Becker, Harald Müller, and Simone Wisotzki, "Democracy and Nuclear Arms Control—Destiny or Ambiguity?" *Security Studies* 17:4 (2008), 839.

[¶] Una Becker, Harald Müller, and Simone Wisotzki, "Democracy and Nuclear Arms Control—Destiny or Ambiguity?" *Security Studies* 17:4 (2008), 844.

[**] Ibid., 846.

against countries that can respond with the use of nuclear weapons.[*] One such country is Russia. Russia's nuclear arsenal is linked to its national identity. Russia sees itself as "a great and enduring world power."[†] As Christopher Ford argued, "[o]ne of the few things about which Moscow seems able to feel proud [of] is its formidable nuclear arsenal—which has become, for many Russians, the symbolic coinage of their country's continued status and worth as a great power in a world in which both the United States and China utterly outclass Russia in essentially every other meaningful respect."[‡]

As previously noted, countries pursue nuclear weapons because they are viewed as symbols of power. Iran seeks nuclear proliferation as it sees itself as an "emerging great power."[§] Nuclear weapons are also believed to increase a country's internal prestige. Additionally, some countries (e.g., France) pursue nuclear proliferation because they want to be on an equal playing field with superpowers and other countries with nuclear weapons. Indeed, Jacques Hymans argued that certain countries resist the nonproliferation regime as they believe it is discriminatory and places these countries on unequal footing.[¶] North Korea is one such example of a state that seeks nuclear weapons for this reason. Specifically, for North Korea, their nuclear weapons are linked to prestige, status, and national greatness, making them equal players with other nuclear weapon states. North Korea also justifies the existence of its nuclear weapons arsenal on the grounds of self-defense.[**] While power and prestige may be perceived as benefits to possessing nuclear arms, maintenance of a nuclear arsenal is not without its consequences.

---

[*] Nikolai N Sokov, "The Evolving Role of Nuclear Weapons in Russia's Security Policy," In Cristina Hansell and William C. Potter (Eds.), *Engaging China and Russia on Nuclear Disarmament*, Occasional Paper No. 15 (Monterey, CA: James Martin Center for Nonproliferation Studies, Monterey Institute of International Studies, March 2009) 74, http://cns.miis.edu/opapers/op15/op15.pdf.

[†] Matthew Moran and Heather W. Williams, "Keeping up Appearances: National Narratives and Nuclear Policy in France and Russia," *Defence Studies* 13:2 (2013), 202.

[‡] Christopher Ford, "Nuclear Weapons and Their Role in the Security Environment," Hudson Institute, November 14, 2011, http://www.hudson.org/index.cfm?fuseaction=publication_details&id=9044.

[§] Ibid.

[¶] Jacques E. C. Hymans, *The Psychology of Nuclear Proliferation: Identity, Emotions and Foreign Policy* (New York: Cambridge University Press, 2006), 39.

[**] Charles J. Moxley, Jr., "The Sword in the Mirror—The Lawfulness of North Korea's Use and Threat of Use of Nuclear Weapons Based on the United States' Legitimization of Nuclear Weapons," *Fordham International Law Journal* 27:4 (2003), 1379.

NUCLEAR WEAPONS AND THE
DOUBLE-DAMNED DILEMMA

The nuclear arms race is dangerous as it may lead to a phenomenon known as brinkmanship. Brinkmanship is the practice of engaging in continually escalating and dangerous action to the point (or brink) of disaster in order to obtain an optimal outcome. For brinkmanship to be effective, threats to take actions must be credible and must escalate. The game of Chicken is an example of brinkmanship. Consider how the game of Chicken works: two cars are driving along a single lane on a bridge heading in opposite directions. The best outcome of the game is for the player to continue driving straight ahead while the other player swerves (in order to avoid a crash). To obtain the optimal result, therefore, a grave risk must be taken. The worst-case scenario is for neither player to swerve in order to yield the bridge to the other. This would result in a head on collision.

When dealing with countries that engage in nuclear proliferation, inaction by the international community might result in the proliferators increasing their efforts to obtain nuclear weapons and potentially using them in the future; especially if this inaction is viewed by the proliferators as a sign of weakness. Inaction also undermines the international community's capacity to deter such conduct by the proliferator and any future proliferators. Additionally, the opposite action in this instance, the use of force, may also lead to the future use of nuclear weapons by the proliferators. The proliferation of nuclear weapons by states may thus eventually lead to the future use of nuclear weapons.

The problems associated with both action and inaction are known as the double-damned dilemma. The double-damned dilemma is as follows: "If you attack or launch a reprisal, that is exactly what they [e.g., the aggressors] want—you're damned if you do. But if you hold back and do not respond, you still lose—you're damned if you don't."* A practical example of this dilemma can be demonstrated with terrorism. States' responses to terrorism may be a lose–lose situation. If the state does not respond to an attack with force, it can be viewed as a sign of weakness. If the state responds to terrorism with force, then it may play into the hands of the terrorists. In general, terrorists seek to bleed governments' economies by provoking an overreaction to terrorist attacks, which, in turn, leads to social unrest in these countries and ultimately,

---

* Emanuel Adler, "Damned If You Do, Damned If You Don't: Performative Power and the Strategy of Conventional and Nuclear Defusing," *Security Studies* 19:2 (2010), 200.

the defeat of these governments.* This is a tactic that has been observed with those acts linked to al-Qaeda. To be exact, these terrorists seek an extreme overreaction by a state, where governments spend all of their resources to provide security. This strategy, however, is not original and has been used throughout history by both terrorists and urban guerillas.†

Nonetheless, Emanuel Adler proposed a way out of the dilemma— through defusing.‡ Specifically, Adler proposed that diffusion can occur in one of two ways: defusing by denial (that prevents opponents from placing them in a situation where they would be required to use force) and defusing by restructuration (changing the rules of the game; i.e., changing the structural conditions and rules that make the situation possible).§ Defusing by denial and restructuration require changing existing widespread beliefs. In particular, they necessitate building common knowledge and altering common held beliefs and expectations of enemies, government agents, and institutions.¶

The current situation in Iran with their development of a nuclear program is an example of the double-damned dilemma. Countries view this development with mistrust and believe that Iran seeks to create nuclear weapons for military purposes. Iran's public supports the creation of a nuclear program and views attempts of the United States and other countries to stifle its development with suspicion.** Deterrence practices, such as sanctions, have not stopped Iran's development of its nuclear program. Defusing by denial and restructuration are more viable approaches. The United States has started to work toward this. James Dobbins et al. noted that "the United States has begun shifting toward a balanced approach, placing a greater emphasis on Iranian human rights

---

* Abu Bakr Naji, "The Management of Barbarism," 2004, 7–8, cited in William F. McCants (tr.), "The Management of Savagery: The Most Critical Stage Through Which the Umma Must Pass," *Combating Terrorism Center at West Point*, May 23, 2006, 17–19, http://azelin.files.wordpress.com/2010/08/abu-bakr-naji-the-management-of-savagery-the-most-critical-stage-through-which-the-umma-will-pass.pdf.

† Carlos Marighella, "The Mini-Manual of the Urban Guerrilla," *Marighella Internet Archive*, 1969, http://marxists.org/archive/marighella-carlos/1969/06/minimanual-urban-guerrilla/index.htm; Sinn Fein/Irish Republican Army, "Green Book," 1979, Belfast, Ireland, http://cain.ulst.ac.uk/othelem/organ/ira/ira_green_book.htm; Jarrett Brachman and William F. McCants, "Stealing Al-Qa'ida's Playbook Combating Terrorism Center (CTC) Report," February 2006, https://www.ctc.usma.edu/wp-content/uploads/2010/06/Stealing-Al-Qaidas-Playbook.pdf.

‡ Emanuel Adler, "Damned If You Do, Damned If You Don't: Performative Power and the Strategy of Conventional and Nuclear Defusing," *Security Studies* 19:2 (2010), 218.

§ Ibid., 219.

¶ Ibid., 220–228.

** Michael Herzog, "Iranian Public Opinion on the Nuclear Program: A Potential Asset for the International Community, The Washington Institute, Policy Focus #56, June 2006, http://www.washingtoninstitute.org/uploads/Documents/pubs/PolicyFocus56.pdf.

abuses—a shift that can counter negative Iranian public perceptions of U.S. intentions."* The government's beliefs should also be altered. China's role in this may be pivotal as it can use "its existing economic leverage and diplomatic ties" with Iran to influence the regime.† As Gianna Gale Amul rightly points out, both "Iran and China share common interests in internal security, an organized energy market, and, most importantly, equal recognition and fair treatment in the international system."‡ Thus far, China has been able to maintain relationships and a cooperative environment with Iran due to its view of Iran as an equal and strategic partner. In fact, to defuse the existing situation, China is viewed as a key player in convincing Iran to cooperate with IAEA investigators, who want to verify that Iran is meeting its Nonproliferation Treaty (NPT) obligations. As this example shows, defusing by denial and restructuration may well be the best ways forward in the pursuit of nuclear disarmament and arms control.

CONCLUDING THOUGHTS

Multiple measures and initiatives have been implemented to restrict the procurement, development, and supply of weapons of mass destruction; the most prominent of which is the Nonproliferation Treaty. The Nonproliferation Treaty was created to, among other things: restrict nuclear weapons states from providing nonnuclear weapons states with nuclear weapons; prevent nonnuclear weapons states from acquiring nuclear weapons; assist states in developing and using nuclear technology for peaceful purposes; and eventually, achieve widespread nuclear disarmament. Nuclear weapons states have yet to fulfill the disarmament agreement. Apart from the international, multilateral, and bilateral initiatives toward nonproliferation by states, other laws, policies, and programs were implemented to prevent the proliferation of nuclear weapons and materials by nonstate actors; namely, UN Security Resolution 1540.

There are many reasons why states seek to create and/or acquire nuclear weapons. States seek to obtain nuclear weapons because of

---

* James Dobbins, Dalia Dassa Kaye, Alireza Nader, and Frederic Wehrey, "How to Defuse Iran's Nuclear Threat: Bolster Diplomacy, Israeli Security, and the Iranian Citizenry," RAND Corporation, 2012, http://www.rand.org/pubs/periodicals/rand-review/issues/2012/spring/iran.html.

† Elsa Kania, "Defusing Iran," Institute of Politics: Harvard University, http://www.iop.harvard.edu/defusing-iran.

‡ Gianna Gale Amul, "Perceptions of the Other: Iran's National Identity and Nuclear Policy," E-International Relations, June 14, 2012, http://www.e-ir.info/2012/06/14/perceptions-of-the-other-irans-national-identity-and-nuclear-policy/.

insecurity; more specifically, due to the nature and extent of external threats. The presence of nuclear weapons is believed to be a deterrent of war. Countries also pursue the development and acquisition of nuclear weapons because they are viewed as symbols of power and prestige. Some countries pursue them because they want to be on an equal playing field with other countries with nuclear weapons. The roles and national identities of states can explain the view and stance of countries on nuclear arms control and disarmament. Despite the current trend of some states toward nuclear proliferation, the paramount method with which states can promote security is through nuclear disarmament and arms control.

CHAPTER 4

Transnational Terrorism

Terrorism is not a new phenomenon. The attacks on the United States on September 11, 2001, the 2004 Madrid bombings, and the 2005 London bombings, among other terrorist attacks, have illustrated the transformation of terrorism and its global reach. This chapter covers the nature and extent of terrorism worldwide. Specifically, it identifies various terrorist groups and the measures implemented to counter these threats. In particular, it identifies the structure, mindset, goals, tactics, targets, and ideologies of past and contemporary international and domestic terrorist groups. It further evaluates the efficacy of measures to combat them. Special attention is paid to the evolution of counterterrorism measures and whom they are designed to protect against.

WHAT IS TERRORISM?

There is no universally accepted definition of terrorism. There are, however, elements of terrorism that most academicians, practitioners, policy makers, and governments agree upon and they are as follows:[*]

1. Terrorists pursue a religious, ideological, and/or political goal.
2. Terrorists engage in coercive acts in pursuit of their goal or goals.
3. Terrorists seek to cause harm and/or damage.
4. Terrorist acts are designed to elicit a response from the target government and/or its population (e.g., fear and intimidation) to effect change.

Ultimately, who is considered as a terrorist depends on the individual or state providing the label (i.e., terrorist).

Terrorists can operate in a group or individually. Terrorist groups can have a hierarchical organization or can be composed of decentralized networks. Al-Qaeda, for example, is made up of loosely affiliated individuals, cells, and networks throughout the world. An individual who engages in acts of terrorism alone and without assistance from and/or direction

---

[*] Marie-Helen Maras, *Counterterrorism* (Burlington, MA: Jones & Bartlett, 2012), 11.

by a terrorist organization or government (in the case of state-sponsored terrorism) is known as a lone wolf. There are numerous examples of lone wolf attacks. For instance, on March 19, 2012, Mohammed Merah opened fire on the Ozar Hatorah School, a Jewish school in Toulouse, France, killing four and seriously injuring one person. The weapon used in this attack, a .45 caliber handgun, was similar to that used in the attacks that occurred earlier that month (on March 11 and March 15, 2012) killing French paratroopers in Toulouse and Montauban, France.* Claude Guéant, the French interior minister, had identified Merah as a member of Forsane Alizza, or Knights of Glory, an Islamist organization, which was disbanded in January 2012 for inciting racial hatred.† Merah, who was killed after a 30-hour standoff with police, had told negotiators that he was a member of al-Qaeda and that he engaged in the attacks to protest the deployment of French paratroopers in Muslim lands and to avenge the deaths of Palestinian children.‡ French government officials later stated that Merah actually had no ties to al-Qaeda and was a lone wolf.§

Terrorists can operate in a multitude of areas. Terrorists can operate in a country's borders. These terrorists are known as domestic terrorists. Domestic terrorism refers to "the commission of acts intended to threaten or actually cause harm to persons and property, which are conducted primarily within the territorial jurisdiction of the target country."¶ Terrorists may also operate in more than one country. These terrorists are known as international terrorists. Individuals or groups that engage in international terrorism cross borders (one or more) to conduct their operations. An example of such a group is al-Shabaab, a Somali-based Islamic extremist terrorist organization. This group claimed responsibility for a terrorist attack on a Nairobi mall in Kenya in September 2013, which killed an estimated 70 individuals and injured approximately 175.**

---

* Dan Bilefsky, "Toulouse Killer's Path to Radicalism a Bitter Puzzle," *The New York Times*, March 29, 2012, http://www.nytimes.com/2012/03/30/world/europe/toulouse-killers-path-a-bitter-puzzle.html?_r=0.
† Bryony Jones, "French Attacks Could Inspire Next Generation of Terrorists," *CNN*, March 22, 2012, http://www.cnn.com/2012/03/21/world/europe/lone-wolf-future-of-terrrorists/index.html.
‡ Laura Smith-Spark, "Who Was French Gunman Mohammed Merah?" *CNN*, March 23, 2012, http://www.cnn.com/2012/03/21/world/europe/france-shooting-suspect-profile/index.html.
§ "French Official: No Sign Merah Had al-Qaeda Ties," *The Times of Israel*, March 24, 2012, http://www.timesofisrael.com/french-official-no-sign-merah-had-al-qaeda-ties/.
¶ Marie-Helen Maras, *Counterterrorism* (Burlington, MA: Jones & Bartlett, 2012), 6.
** Faith Karimi, Steve Almasy, and Lillian Leposo, "Kenya Mall Attack: Military Says Most Hostages Freed, Death Toll at 68," *CNN*, September 23, 2013, http://www.cnn.com/2013/09/22/world/africa/kenya-mall-attack/index.html; Michael Pearson and Zain Verjee, "Questions Linger after Kenya Mall Attack," *CNN*, September 25, 2013, http://www.cnn.com/2013/09/25/world/africa/kenya-mall-attack-aftermath/.

In addition to domestic and international terrorism, certain terrorists have fallen under the category of transnational terrorism. Transnational terrorism is associated with terrorists that are diverse, adaptable, complex, and continuously evolving. The word transnational highlights the interconnectivity between individuals around the globe and the lessening/removal of boundaries between countries. While transnational terrorism refers to the terrorism that transcends borders and has a global impact, terrorists within this category affect security worldwide.

Typologies of Terrorism

Terrorism involves the deliberate act to cause harm or damage. The act itself is designed to obtain a specific reaction from the government or population. The act of terrorism can involve a variety of criminal activities including (but not limited to): murder, assault, extortion, kidnapping, and arson, among other crimes. The targets of terrorists can include civilian and military personnel; the latter category is included when terrorists seek to intimidate and terrorize their adversaries. In order for it to be labeled as an act of terrorism innocent people must be deliberately targeted. Terrorism, thus, is considered an illegal act, even during times of war, because it deliberately targets civilians.* The purpose of the attack is to meet one or more of the terrorists' objectives. One primary goal, common in all forms of terrorism, is to provoke and instill fear (or terror) in the target government(s) and population(s). Other than this, these objectives are designed to further terrorists' ideologies.

Terrorists have been classified according to the ideologies they pursue. Terrorists have been known to pursue more than one ideology. The typologies of terrorism include: nationalist-separatist, religious, left-wing, right-wing, and special-interest terrorism. The first type, nationalist-separatist terrorism, is conducted by an ethnic or religious group that believes that it is persecuted by the majority. Examples of groups within this category include the Continuity Irish Republican Army (CIRA), Real Irish Republican Army (RIRA), Basque Fatherland and Liberty (ETA), and Lashkar-e-Jhangvi (LeJ). The second type, religious terrorism, is conducted by individuals that believe that they are acting pursuant to divinely commanded purposes. Al-Qaeda and the Abu Sayyaf Group (ASG), which also pursues a nationalist-separatist ideology, fall under this category.

---

* See International Committee of the Red Cross, Convention (IV) Respecting the Laws and Customs of War on Land and Its Annex: Regulations Concerning the Laws and Customs of War on Land of 1907, http://www.icrc.org/applic/ihl/ihl.nsf/385ec082b509e76c412 56739003e636d/1d1726425f6955aec125641e0038bfd6.

The third type of terrorism, left-wing terrorism, is conducted by those who seek to destroy a capitalistic society and replace it with a communist or socialist regime. The Red Brigades (now disbanded), the Red Army Faction (now disbanded), and the Kurdistan Worker's Party (PKK), are all considered left-wing terrorist groups; the latter group, the PKK, is also considered a nationalist-separatist group. The fourth type, right-wing terrorism, is conducted by individuals that seek to attack liberal democratic governments. Those usually associated with right-wing terrorism are white supremacists and other groups that harbor anti-government and antiregulatory beliefs. An example of a right-wing terrorist group is the Sovereign Citizens Movement. The Sovereign Citizens Movement is made up of loosely associated individuals that believe that the federal government is illegitimate; as such, those affiliated with this organization believe that they should not be held accountable to the government.* Others groups that fall under this category include the Ku Klux Klan (the KKK), the World Church of the Creator (WCOTC), and the Aryan Nations.

The fifth and final type is special interest terrorism. This form of terrorism is conducted to draw attention to a specific issue that people believe resulted from government action or inaction and requires immediate attention (e.g., the environment, animal rights, and antiabortion). For example, the Earth Liberation Front, the Animal Liberation Front, and the Army of God (which also pursues a religious ideology). A very well-known example of a terrorist affiliated with the Army of God is Eric Robert Rudolph, who was charged for and convicted of bombing: the Centennial Olympic Park in Atlanta, Georgia, in 1996; the Otherside nightclub in Atlanta, Georgia, in 1997; and the New Woman Clinic in Birmingham, Alabama, in 1998.†

Much of the focus of the international community is on religious terrorism—especially al-Qaeda, its affiliates, and followers. However, there have been numerous incidents recently both abroad and within the United States that have included other forms of terrorism—especially, left-wing and right-wing terrorism. In particular, on December 7, 2011,

---

* "Sovereign Citizens: A Growing Domestic Threat to Law Enforcement," FBI (September 2011), http://www.fbi.gov/stats-services/publications/law-enforcement-bulletin/september-2011/sovereign-citizens.

† "Atlanta Olympic Bombing Suspect Arrested," CNN, May 31, 2003, http://www.cnn.com/2003/US/05/31/rudolph.main/; "Eric RobertRudolph-Fast Facts," CNN, December 6, 2012, http://www.cnn.com/2012/12/06/us/eric-robert-rudolph-fast-facts/index.html; Counterterrorism Threat Assessment and Warning Unit, National Security Division, "Terrorism in the United States 1998," U.S. Department of Justice, Federal Bureau of Investigation, http://www.fbi.gov/stats-services/publications/terror_98.pdf.

a parcel bomb was sent to Deutsche Bank in Frankfurt, Germany.[*] Two days later, on December 9, 2011, a letter bomb attack occurred at a tax collection agency in Equitalia, Italy.[†] Two days later, on December 11, 2011, a package bomb was sent to the Greek embassy in Paris, France.[‡] A bombing campaign had also occurred earlier in the year and in 2010 by both the Federazione Anarchica Informale (FAI—Informal Anarchist Federation), an Italian anarchist terrorist group, and the Conspiracy of Fire Nuclei, a left-wing domestic terrorist group in Greece. Specifically, in 2011, the FAI had claimed responsibility for the letter bombings at the Korydallos prison in Greece (where members of the Conspiracy of Fire Nuclei were held) and the Swiss nuclear group in Switzerland.[§] In 2010, the Conspiracy of Fire Nuclei claimed responsibility for the parcel bombs that were sent to Prime Minister Silvio Berlusconi of Italy, President Nicolas Sarkozy of France, German Chancellor Angela Merkel, the International Criminal Court in the Hague, and the Belgian and Mexican embassies in Athens, Greece.[¶] Given the socio-economic and political turmoil in both Italy and Greece, left-wing and right-wing terrorism are not expected to cease any time soon; by contrast, more terrorist attacks are expected in the future. The groups have claimed that they are engaging in such attacks and civil disturbances as a way to protest the fiscal austerity measures being imposed upon them by the European Union. The case of Anders Behring Breivik also brought home the lesson that attention needed to be paid to right-wing terrorists. On July 22, 2011, Breivik bombed government buildings in Oslo, Norway (8 killed; at least 30 injured).[**] That same day, he opened fire on a youth camp on Utøya Island, killing 69 individuals.[††]

News media reports in 2012 in the United States served as a reminder that the terrorist threat in the United States includes terrorists beyond Islamic extremists. To be precise, two cases in May of 2012

---

[*] Reuters, "Deutsche Bank CEO Target of Suspicious Envelope: Police," December 7, 2011, http://www.nbcnewyork.com/news/local/Banks-Package-Bombs-Warning-NYPD-Ackermann-Deutsche-Bank-Frankfurt-135192593.html.

[†] "Anarchists Claim Bomb at Italy Tax Office," *USA Today*, December 9, 2011, http://usatoday30.usatoday.com/news/world/story/2011-12-09/italy-mail-bomb/51764090/1.

[‡] Reuters, "Parcel Bomb Sent to Greek Embassy in Paris," December 12, 2011, http://www.reuters.com/article/2011/12/12/us-france-explosive-idUSTRE7BB1A120111212.

[§] "Swiss Nuclear Power Industry Office Hit by Letter Bomb, Wounding 2," *Huffington Post*, March 31, 2011, http://www.huffingtonpost.com/2011/03/31/swiss-nuclear-letter-bomb_n_843214.html.

[¶] "Police Pursue 'Anarchists' in Rome Embassy Blasts," *NPR*, December 23, 2010, http://www.npr.org/2010/12/23/132279275/package-explodes-at-swiss-embassy-in-rome.

[**] "Anders Breivik describes Norway island massacre," *BBC News*, April 20, 2012, http://www.bbc.co.uk/news/world-europe-17789206.

[††]Ibid.

drew attention to the rising number of right-wing terrorist incidents. The first case involved the death of Jason Todd (J. T.) Ready, a former Marine, who was a U.S. right-wing homegrown terrorist harboring neo-Nazi and anti-immigration beliefs.[*] He was found dead by authorities on May 2, 2012. Authorities believe that he killed his girlfriend, her granddaughter, daughter, and the daughter's boyfriend, before killing himself.[†] Approximately two weeks later, on May 18, 2012, the news reported on another U.S. right-wing homegrown terrorist. Joseph Benjamin Thomas, a self-proclaimed domestic terrorist, was suspected of ties to white supremacist groups. He was plotting to attack the Mexican consulate in St. Paul, Minnesota, by spilling oil and gas from a truck, which he was planning to steal, and setting the mixture on fire with a road flare. Thomas, along with an accomplice, Samuel James Johnson, were arrested for amassing weapons and ammunition with the intention of targeting the government, minorities, and others.[‡] These incidents illustrate how the threat of terrorism is much larger than the current narrow focus of religious terrorists. Right-wing and special interest terrorism still pose a great threat to U.S. security and to other countries around the globe.

Terrorists' *Modus Operandi*

Terrorists choose their targets. The choice of their target will depend on their ideology. The target chosen will also depend on their goals. For instance, nationalist-separatists often target the majority that they view has persecuted them—this includes government officials and civilians. Left-wing terrorists tend to target businesses and government officials. Right-wing terrorists engage in attacks against their targets of hatred (individuals of a particular race, ethnic group, or sexual orientation) and for those that harbor antiregulatory and antigovernment beliefs, local, state, and federal law enforcement agents and government officials. Special interest terrorists target those that they hold responsible for the current unfavorable situation and/or mistreatment of a person, place, or object they believe that they have a responsibility to protect

---

[*] Rudolf, J., "JT Ready, Arizona Border Vigilante Blamed for Mass Murder, Had State Republican Party Ties," *Huffington Post*, May 3, 2012, http://www.huffingtonpost.com/2012/05/05/us-border-guards-vow-to-continue _n_1483385.html.

[†] Amanda Lee Myers, "U.S. Border Guard Vows to Survive after Jason Todd 'JT' Ready's Death," *Huffington Post*, May 5, 2012, http://www.huffingtonpost.com/2012/05/05/us-border-guards-vow-to-continue_n_1483385.html.

[‡] "FBI: 2 Minn. Men with Supremacist Ties Had Weapons," *CBS News*, April 27, 2012, http://minnesota.cbslocal.com/2012/04/27/fbi-2-minn-men-with-supremacist-ties-had-weapons/.

(e.g., businesses that harm the environment, laboratories that conduct animal testing, and abortion clinics). Religious terrorists tend to target those opposed to their religion and often those that are simply not part of their religious orientation—the latter, however, may lead to an open-ended category of targets (e.g., al-Qaeda, affiliates, and those inspired by al-Qaeda justify their attacks based on such an open-ended category of what they perceive to be legitimate targets).

Most importantly, the chosen target is symbolic and its targeting is designed to obtain significant media attention. This is the primary reason why targets, such as transportation systems, are chosen. There have been several foiled plots targeting transportation systems. Richard Reid (the shoe bomber) and Umar Farouk Abdulmutallab (the underwear bomber), among others, sought to engage in a suicide attack while onboard an airplane. Additionally, in May 2012, al-Qaeda in the Arabian Peninsula (AQAP) claimed responsibility for a foiled plot targeting a U.S. airline near the anniversary of Osama bin Laden's death.[*] Others have targeted commuter trains and subways: Bryant Neil Vinas informed authorities that al-Qaeda was planning to target the Long Island Railroad out of Penn Station, New York City, in a terrorist attack; Najibullah Zazi plotted to simultaneously blow up Manhattan subway trains on lines 1, 2, 3, and 6, days after the 9/11 anniversary; James Elshafay and Shahawar Matin Siraj were planning to bomb a subway station near Madison Square Garden; and Chiheb Esseghaier and Raed Jaser attempted to bomb a VIA Railway train heading from Canada to the United States.[†] Without media attention, the terrorists' message would not be spread to the target population and government, as well as other individuals around the globe. Terrorists consider media coverage vital not only to spread propaganda and the impact of the attacks around the globe, but also to gain new followers and recruits.

In addition to target selection, terrorists plan and prepare for their upcoming operation. During this stage, terrorists choose from a variety of ways to conduct an attack including: bombings, suicide attacks, arson, assassination, aviation attack, maritime, hijacking of vehicles, industrial and infrastructure attack, and physical intimidation or maiming, among others.[‡] In this stage, terrorists also conduct surveillance of their

---

[*] Greg Miller and Karen DeYoung, "Al-Qaeda Airline Bomb Plot Disrupted, U.S. Says," *Washington Post*, May 7, 2012, http://articles.washingtonpost.com/2012-05-07/world/35455296_1_underwear-bomb-aqap-explos ive-device.

[†] Jessica Zuckerman, Steven P. Bucci, and James Jay Carafano, "60 Terrorist Plots Since 9/11: Continued Lessons in Domestic Counterterrorism," The Heritage Foundation, July 22, 2013, http://www.heritage.org/research/reports/2013/07/60-terrorist-plots-since-911-continued-lessons-in-domestic-counterterrorism.

[‡] Marie-Helen Maras, *CRC Press Terrorism Reader* (Boca Raton, FL: CRC Press, 2013), 66.

potential targets and obtain the necessary materials and equipment to execute the attack. For example, the so-called Virginia Jihad Network had obtained surveillance and night vision equipment to use during the planning phase of their attack.[*] The Miami Seven is another example of a group that conducted extensive surveillance of their targets.[†] The plot of the Miami Seven to bomb the Sears Tower in Chicago and various government buildings in Florida was ultimately foiled. Unbeknownst to them, they requested funds ($50,000) and resources such as, "boots, uniforms, machine guns, bulletproof vests, radios and vehicles" from an FBI informant, whom they believed was an al-Qaeda terrorist.[‡]

The preparation stage may also include the recruitment of personnel to assist in the operation. Consider the case of Quazi Mohammad Rezwanul Ahsan Nafis, a Bangladeshi national, who had traveled to the United States with a student visa. While in the United States, Nafis "attempted to recruit individuals to form a terrorist cell inside the United States ... [He] also actively sought out al-Qaeda contacts within the United States to assist him in carrying out an attack. Unbeknownst to Nafis, one of the individuals he attempted to recruit was actually a source for the FBI."[§] On October 17, 2012, Nafis attempted to detonate the explosives he had placed in a van, which he parked next to the New York Federal Reserve Bank in the financial district of New York City.[¶] The explosives given to Nafis were inoperable. Nafis was arrested after he attempted to detonate the inert explosives and was subsequently charged with attempting to use weapons of mass destruction and attempting to provide material support to al-Qaeda.

After planning and preparation, the next step is implementation.[**] Terrorists could be interdicted during the implementation phase. They

---

[*] Jessica Zuckerman, Steven P. Bucci, and James Jay Carafano, "60 Terrorist Plots Since 9/11: Continued Lessons in Domestic Counterterrorism," The Heritage Foundation, July 22, 2013, http://www.heritage.org/research/reports/2013/07/60-terrorist-plots-since-911-continued-lessons-in-domestic-counterterrorism.

[†] For a more detailed analysis of this group and their operations, see Christopher A. D. Charles and Marie-Helen Maras. "Strengthening Counterterrorism from the Information of Successful Terrorist Attack and Failed Missions," (forthcoming).

[‡] Tony Karon, "The Miami Seven: How Serious Was the Threat?" Time Magazine, June 23, 2006, http://www.time.com/time/nation/article/0,8599,1207412,00.html.

[§] U.S. Attorney's Office, Eastern District of New York, "Joint Terrorism Task Force Arrests Man in Lower Manhattan after He Attempted to Bomb New York Federal Reserve Bank," FBI, October 17, 2012, http://www.fbi.gov/newyork/press-releases/2012/joint-terrorism-task-force-arrests-man-in-lower-manhattan-after-he-attempted-to-bomb-new-york-federal-reserve-bank.

[¶] BBC News, "U.S. Federal Reserve 'Bomb Plot' Foiled by FBI," October 17, 2012, http://www.bbc.co.uk/news/world-us-canada-19985987.

[**] Marie-Helen Maras, CRC Press Terrorism Reader (Boca Raton, FL: CRC Press, 2013), 75.

can also be detected during the planning and preparation phase. This has been seen on many occasions. Consider the foiled 2009 Bronx and Newburgh Terrorism Plot. On the day of the attack, David Williams, Onta Williams, and Laguerre Payen acted as lookouts, while Cromitie placed what he believed to be were real explosive devices at the Riverdale Jewish Center and the Riverdale Temple. The perpetrators did not execute their attack as their devices were inoperable and were arrested after they planted the devices. These individuals were charged after they had placed (and attempted to detonate) what they believed were real bombs at the Riverdale Jewish Center and the Riverdale Temple in Bronx, New York. They also conspired to use missiles to shoot down military aircraft at the New York National Guard Base, at Stewart Airport in Newburgh, New York.

For the nonsuicidal attacks, terrorists must plan their escape and evasion tactics.* Capture is possible during this stage. A case in point is the New York City Times Square bomber, Faisal Shahzad. On May 1, 2010, Shahzad left a parked vehicle laden with explosives in Times Square. A vigilant vendor observed that a vehicle that was abandoned in an unauthorized area had smoke billowing out of it and alerted law enforcement in the area.† Authorities subsequently rendered the bomb inoperable. Shahzad attempted to flee the country by boarding an Emirates airplane from the John F. Kennedy International airport in New York City bound for Dubai.‡ He was arrested before the plane left the airport. A more recent example involved the 2013 Boston bombings. Specifically, two bombs detonated near the finish line of the Boston marathon on April 15, 2013.§ This was not the first time bombings have been attempted at a marathon. One example is the attempted bombing of the annual Belfast, Northern Ireland marathon on May 5, 2003, by the Real Irish Republican Army.¶ The bomb, which was left in a

---

* Ibid., 78.

† "Car Bomb Discovered in New York's Times Square," *CNN*, May 2, 2010, http://transcripts.cnn.com/TRANSCRIPTS/1005/02/bn.03.html; Al Baker and William K. Rashbaum, "Police Find Car Bomb in Times Square," *New York Times*, May 1, 2010, http://www.nytimes.com/2010/05/02/nyregion/02timessquare.html?pagewanted=all&_r=0.

‡ Office of Public Affairs, Department of Justice, "Faisal Shahzad Indicted for Attempted Car Bombing in Times Square," U.S. Department of Justice, June 17, 2010, http://www.justice.gov/opa/pr/2010/June/10-ag-713.html.

§ Josh Levs and Monte Plott, "Boy, 8, One of 3 Killed in Bombings at Boston Marathon; Scores Wounded," *CNN*, April 18, 2013, http://www.cnn.com/2013/04/15/us/boston-marathon-explosions/index.html.

¶ "Bombings at the 2013 Boston Marathon," START, National Consortium for the Study of Terrorism and Responses to Terrorism, University of Maryland, April 2013, http://www.start.umd.edu/start/publications/br/STARTBackgroundReport_BostonMarathon2013.pdf.

FIGURE 4.1   The Tsarnaev brothers: Dzhokhar Tsarnaev (left) and Tamerlan Tsarnaev (right). From video footage acquired and released by the FBI. (From the FBI.)

van, was defused by the police before the marathon began. The Boston bombers, however, were successful; in their attack, Tamerlan Tsarnaev and Dzhokhar Tsarnaev, of Chechen origin, killed three and injured at least 264 individuals[*] (Figure 4.1). Unfortunately, interdiction of terrorists at this stage is after the fact.

Given the devastating consequences of a terrorist attack, the main task of counterterrorism officials is to intervene before a terrorist attack has materialized. Terrorists often refine their modus operandi (method of operation or M.O.) after each attack to enable their survival and future successful attacks. Counterterrorism professionals, thus, need to study terrorists' M.O. in order to anticipate future actions of terrorists.

COUNTERTERRORISM

Counterterrorism involves the implementation of policies and practices designed to detect, protect against, prevent, mitigate, investigate, prosecute, and/or otherwise respond to terrorism. Before examining counterterrorism policies, the threat itself should be examined. Indeed, the success of counterterrorism largely depends on the understanding of terrorism and terrorists' objectives.

Knowledge of the classification of terrorism (e.g., nationalist-separatist, left-wing, right-wing, religious, or special interest) is essential in counterterrorism because the appropriateness of the counterterrorism

---

[*] "Boston Marathon Terror Attack Fast Facts," *CNN*, July 11, 2013, http://www.cnn.com/2013/06/03/us/boston-marathon-terror-attack-fast-facts/index.html.

measures chosen will depend on the type of terrorists. Valuable insight into counterterrorism could also be gained by studying successful and failed terrorist attacks. In addition, understanding the underlying factors that make the existence of terrorist attacks possible is paramount to building effective counterterrorism strategies. Robert Pape argues that terrorism depends on three components for its existence—the strategic, the social, and the individual.* The strategic component includes the legitimizing ideology and the goals of terrorists. This provides the justification for terrorism. The social component includes a legitimizing ideology (mentioned previously) and a supportive and enabling community. The role of the community in terrorism is critical as it provides or assists terrorists in finding resources for their group and missions, including funds, weapons, safe havens, recruits, and operatives (i.e., individuals willing to engage in either suicide or nonsuicide terrorist attacks). Without popular support, a terrorist group could not survive and would eventually cease to exist. The final component, the individual, is often ignored. This component is critical because terrorists need to justify their actions and to reassure themselves that they are acting in an honorable way for their cause. Individuals have desisted from terrorism and terrorist groups have disbanded when counterterrorism measures have effectively targeted one or more of these realms. One way to target these realms is by removing the justification for terrorism. Therefore, an effective counterterrorism strategy should not only be tailored toward dealing with specific types of terrorism but should also be designed to deal with the factors that sustain terrorism.

Drivers for Counterterrorism

In addition to examining the terrorist threats themselves, the driving forces behind countermeasures should also be examined. Consider the EU Declaration of Combating Terrorism.† This measure is truly *sui generis*, including measures of mass surveillance and mass registration. More specifically, it contained the following measures: Passenger Name Record (PNR) data (collected and stored for all flights in and out of the European Union); biometric IDs, visas, and passports; and mass data retention (the collection and storage of the telecommunications and

---

* Robert A. Pape, *Dying to Win: The Strategic Logic of Suicide Terrorism* (New York: Random House, 2005), 21; For a detailed analysis of each component also see Chapter 3, Marie-Helen Maras, *Counterterrorism* (Burlington, MA: Jones & Bartlett, 2012).

† European Council, "Declaration on Combating Terrorism," March 25, 2004, http://www.consilium.europa.eu/uedocs/cmsUpload/DECL-25.3.pdf.

electronic communications data of every EU citizen).* These measures were not only extraordinary, but so too was the manner in which they were passed. The manner in which they were passed revealed a sea change in European perspectives on the appropriateness of measures with which to respond to terrorism. In particular, the European Parliament, on March 9, 2004, declared that any form of mass surveillance was unjustified (in that it does not respect the rule of law and human rights) and that only targeted measures were justifiable. Two days later, on March 11, 2004, the Madrid bombings occurred. Approximately two weeks after this event, the European Council, in the Declaration on Combating Terrorism (adopted on the 25th of March 2004), declared the urgency and necessity to adopt measures such as biometric IDs and wide retention of communications data. As a result, the mass surveillance of movement (PNR and biometric IDs) and of communications (Data Retention Directive; Directive 2006/24/EC) were now all said to be justified.

The measures themselves did not change—they still violate the rule of law and human rights. Yet, the perspectives on their appropriateness did. Two driving forces may well explain this shift†: the presentation of the counterterrorism strategy as a war and the presentation of the terrorist threat as an emergency. To be exact, the characterization of the response to terrorists as a "war on terrorism" licensed governmental use of extraordinary powers usually reserved for situations that threaten the life of a nation. Furthermore, the depiction of the threat as an emergency results in the relaxation of legal restraints on counterterrorism measures and the speeding up of the legislative process, which ultimately leaves little room for democratic debate of proposed measures. Indeed, a shared characteristic of many counterterrorism measures that have been implemented is the speed with which they were passed following a terrorist attack. For example, the UK Prevention of Terrorism (Temporary Provisions) Act of 1974 and the Criminal Justice Act (Terrorism and Conspiracy) Act of 1998 were debated and approved

---

* For a more detailed analysis of the EU Data Retention Directive, see Marie-Helen Maras, "From Targeted to Mass Surveillance: Is the EU Data Retention Directive a Necessary Measure or an Unjustified Threat to Privacy?" In Benjamin Goold and Daniel Neyland (Eds.), *New Directions in Privacy and Surveillance* (Devon, United Kingdom: Willan, 2009); Marie-Helen Maras, "While the European Union Was Sleeping, the Data Retention Directive Was Passed: The Political Consequences of Mass Data Retention," *Hamburg Review of Social Sciences* 6:2 (2012), 1–30; Marie-Helen Maras, "The Social Consequences of a Mass Surveillance Measure: What Happens When We become the 'Others'?" *International Journal of Law, Crime and Justice* 40:2 (2012), 65–81; Marie-Helen Maras, "The Economic Costs and Consequences of Mass Communications Data Retention: Is the Data Retention Directive a Proportionate Measure?" *European Journal of Law and Economics* 33:2 (2012), 447–472.

† For more information on these drivers, see Chapters 5 and 6 in Marie-Helen Maras, *Counterterrorism* (Burlington, MA: Jones & Bartlett, 2012).

after only 17 hours and 27 hours, respectively, after terrorist attacks had occurred.* Likewise, the USA Patriot Act, which is considered the broadest anticrime bill in U.S. history, was passed six weeks after 9/11.† These driving forces behind policies may well explain why certain counterterrorism measures are implemented despite their significant adverse legal consequences.

Criminalizing and Combating Terrorism

While international legislation criminalizing terrorism existed before the September 11, 2001, terrorist attacks on the United States, this event added impetus to the harmonization of practices to combat terrorism worldwide. A prime example of this is the UN Security Council Resolution 1373 (2001), which required states to strengthen their prevention, detection, investigation, and prosecution of terrorism. Particularly, this resolution called upon Member States to bolster their legislative and institutional ability to counter terrorism by:‡

- Cooperating with other Member States in the detection, investigation, and prosecution of terrorists;
- Criminalizing the support of, participation in, and financing of terrorism;
- Engaging in intelligence sharing with other Member States;
- Preventing the funding of terrorism;
- Denying terrorists safe havens in countries.

Incitement to commit terrorism was criminalized by UN Security Resolution 1624 (2005). This resolution required Member States to create laws, if they did not already exist, to criminalize incitement to commit terrorism, and to deny safe havens to anyone that engages in such conduct.§

There are 13 main international conventions and related protocols concerning terrorism, and they are as follows:¶

---

* Marie-Helen Maras, *Counterterrorism* (Burlington, MA: Jones & Bartlett, 2012), 135–136.
† Ibid., 136.
‡ Counter-Terrorism Committee, "About the Counter-Terrorism Committee: Our Mandate," UN Security Council, November 11, 2013, http://www.un.org/en/sc/ctc/aboutus.html.
§ Counter-Terrorism Committee, "About the Counter-Terrorism Committee: Our Mandate," UN Security Council, November 11, 2013, http://www.un.org/en/sc/ctc/aboutus.html.
¶ United Nations Department of Public Information, "International Counter-Terrorism Instruments," Counter-Terrorism Committee, Executive Directorate, September 2006, http://www.un.org/en/terrorism/pdfs/bgnote_legal_instruments.pdf.

1. The 1963 Convention on Offences and Certain Other Acts Committed On Board Aircraft (Tokyo Convention) covering aviation safety.
2. The 1970 Convention for the Suppression of Unlawful Seizure of Aircraft (Hague Convention) concerning airplane hijackings.
3. The 1971 Convention for the Suppression of Unlawful Acts against the Safety of Civil Aviation (Montreal Convention) covering acts of airplane sabotage.
4. The 1973 Convention on the Prevention and Punishment of Crimes against Internationally Protected Persons concerning terrorism perpetrated against government officials and diplomats.
5. The 1979 International Convention against the Taking of Hostages (Hostages Convention).
6. The 1980 Convention on the Physical Protection of Nuclear Material (Nuclear Materials Convention) criminalizing the unlawful possession of nuclear material and mandating countries' protection of their nuclear facilities and materials.
7. The 1988 Protocol for the Suppression of Unlawful Acts of Violence at Airports Serving International Civil Aviation, supplementary to the Convention for the Suppression of Unlawful Acts against the Safety of Civil Aviation, extended the Montreal Convention to include acts of terrorism at only those airports that serve international civil aviation.*
8. The 1988 Convention for the Suppression of Unlawful Acts against the Safety of Maritime Navigation covering terrorism on ships and criminalizing such acts. The 1988 Convention for the Suppression of Unlawful Acts against the Safety of Maritime Navigation covering terrorism on ships and criminalizing such acts. Subsequently, in 2005, the Protocol to the Convention for the Suppression of Unlawful Acts against the Safety of Maritime Navigation criminalized the use of a ship to engage in terrorism or otherwise further acts of terrorism.
9. The 1988 Protocol for the Suppression of Unlawful Acts Against the Safety of Fixed Platforms Located on the Continental Shelf criminalizing acts of terrorism on fixed offshore platforms.
10. The 1991 Convention on the Marking of Plastic Explosives for the Purpose of Detection seeking to control and limit the acquisition, creation, use, or transfer of unmarked and undetectable plastic explosives.

---

* Airports without this international element, domestic airports, are regulated by domestic law as they are within the exclusive domain of the country that they are in.

11. The 1997 International Convention for the Suppression of Terrorist Bombings creating a regime of universal jurisdiction* over acts of terrorism.
12. The 1999 International Convention for the Suppression of the Financing of Terrorism seeking the criminalization, prevention, and combating of terrorism financing.
13. The 2005 International Convention for the Suppression of Acts of Nuclear Terrorism criminalizing this form of terrorism and calling for countries' cooperation in its prevention, detection, investigation, and prosecution.†

To combat terrorism, regional treaties and conventions have also been implemented. Examples of these conventions include the following:

- 1971 Organization of American States Convention to prevent and punish the acts of terrorism taking the form of crimes against persons and related extortion that are of international significance;
- 1978 European Convention on the Suppression of Terrorism;
- 1988 South Asian Association for Regional Cooperation (SAARC) Regional Convention on Suppression of Terrorism;‡
- 1998 Arab Convention on the Suppression of Terrorism;
- 1999 Treaty on Cooperation among the States Members of the Commonwealth of Independent States in Combating Terrorism;
- 1999 Organization of African Union Convention on the Prevention and Combating of Terrorism;
- 1999 Organization of the Islamic Conference (OIC) Convention to Combat Terrorism;
- 2002 Organization of American States Inter-American Convention against Terrorism;
- 2004 Convention against Terrorism by the Cooperation Council for the Arab States of the Gulf;
- 2007 Association of Southeast Asian Nations (ASEAN) Convention on Counter Terrorism.§

---

* This form of jurisdiction allows a state or international organizations to claim jurisdiction over a suspect irrespective of where the crime allegedly took place or the alleged perpetrator's nationality, home of residence, or any other link with the country or organization seeking prosecution. See Madeline H. Morris, "Universal Jurisdiction in a Divided World: Conference Remarks," *New England Law Review* 35:2 (2001), 337–361, http://scholarship.law.duke.edu/cgi/viewcontent.cgi?article=1846&context=faculty_scholarship.

† This Convention was also discussed in Chapter 3 of this volume.

‡ Countries part of SAARC are: Afghanistan, Bangladesh, Bhutan, India, Maldives, Nepal, Pakistan, and Sri Lanka.

§ Countries part of ASEAN are: Brunei Darussalam, Cambodia, Indonesia, Lao People's Democratic Republic, Malaysia, Myanmar, Philippines, Singapore, Thailand, and Vietnam.

In addition to these international and regional conventions, there are numerous national and international counterterrorism measures that have been implemented to deal with transnational terrorism. In the next sections, certain hard and soft approaches to combating terrorism are explored.[*] Hard approaches consist of acts designed to prevent, detect, interdict, investigate, and prosecute terrorism. They include actions taken by all three branches of government (legislative, judiciary, and executive) and include tactics such as the surveillance, intelligence gathering, detection, and detention of terrorists. The soft approaches include efforts to quash terrorists' ideology and delegitimizing terrorism. It consists of measures to rehabilitate terrorists, discredit terrorists, and engage in peace talks with terrorists.

Hard Approaches to Terrorism

Various surveillance measures have been implemented post–9/11.[†] Secure Flight, which was implemented in the United States and seeks to identify terrorists by checking the names of passengers to those listed on the terror watch list (or the "no-fly" list), is one such example. Another example is the Personal Identification Secure Comparison and Evaluation System (PISCES), "a computerized watch-listing system," which is part of the Terrorist Interdiction Program (TIP).[‡] The countries that participate in TIP are chosen based on known terrorist activity in or transit through their territories, "need for a watchlisting system, and political will to cooperate with the United States in counterterrorism efforts."[§]

Databases have also been created for surveillance and intelligence purposes. Cases in point are the Visa Information System (VIS), which includes visa application data and the biometrics of third-party country nationals requiring a visa to enter the Schengen area,[¶] and Eurodac, which collects and stores biometric data (e.g., fingerprints) on all asylum seekers and illegal immigrants in the European Union.[**] Moreover, in the European Union, governments have demanded and continue to demand the biometric data (e.g., fingerprints) of its citizens to be stored in passports and IDs. Member States in the European Union, such as the Netherlands,

---

[*] For a more detailed analysis of soft and hard approaches to terrorism, see Chapters 7–13, Marie-Helen Maras, *Counterterrorism* (Burlington, MA: Jones & Bartlett, 2012).

[†] A more detailed analysis of numerous surveillance measures implemented post 9/11 can be found in Chapter 7 in Marie-Helen Maras, *Counterterrorism* (Burlington, MA: Jones & Bartlett, 2012).

[‡] "Terrorist Interdiction Program (TIP)," U.S. Department of State, http://2001-2009. state.gov/s/ct/about/c16663.htm.

[§] Ibid.

[¶] European Union, Visa Information System, http://ec.europa.eu/dgs/home-affairs/ e-library/docs/vis_passport/visa_information_system_passport_en.pdf.

[**] "Eurodac," European Data Protection Supervisor, https://secure.edps.europa.eu/ EDPSWEB/edps/Supervision/Eurodac.

France, and Lithuania, have even required the creation and management of centralized databases for the storage of this information. The United States has also implemented similar measures; namely, the Enhanced Border Security Visa Entry Act 2002 that required all individuals entering the United States to eventually use travel documents (e.g., visas and passports) that included biometric identifiers, and the Real ID Act 2005, which required biometrics for state driver's licenses and ID cards. The information from these measures are to be stored in databases. What do all of these measures have in common? These measures—and others like them—are designed to identify and deal with "known" terrorist threats. They are not designed to deal with the "unknown" threats—individuals currently plotting to commit terrorist activities under the radar of law enforcement and intelligence agencies.

Many of the homegrown terrorists in the United States were law-abiding citizens—up until the point that they conspired to engage in a terrorist attack. One such example was Emerson Winfield Begolly, a Caucasian U.S. citizen with no prior criminal record. Begolly was an active administrator on an Islamic extremist Internet forum known as Ansar al-Mujahideen English Forum (AMEF). In this forum, he praised attacks by other extremists, encouraged similar acts of violence, and solicited other extremists to engage in acts of terrorism.* Another homegrown terrorist is Zachary Adam Chesser, a Caucasian American citizen who was charged with providing material support to terrorists (namely, al-Shabaab), soliciting violence and communicating threats of violence. With respect to the latter, Chesser threatened the creators of *South Park*, Matt Stone and Trey Parker, after an episode which aired that depicted the Prophet Muhammad in a bear costume.† How would a biometric ID or passport have helped catch these homegrown terrorists? Are there any counterterrorism measures designed to deal with this threat?

A hard approach that can combat this threat and detect such homegrown terrorists is the use of undercover agents and informants. Law enforcement agencies have made effective use of undercover agents and informants to uncover terrorist plots and reveal the identities of terrorists operating within their country's borders; especially the identities of individuals and groups that are inspired by a terrorist organization's

---

* Office of Public Affairs, U.S. Department of Justice, "Pennsylvania Man Sentenced for Terrorism Solicitation and Firearms Offense," Federal Bureau of Investigation, July 16, 2013, http://www.fbi.gov/pittsburgh/press-releases/2013/pennsylvania-man-sentenced-for-terrorism-solicitation-and-firearms-offense.

† Majority and Minority Staff Senate Committee on Homeland Security and Governmental Affairs, "Zachary Chesser: A Case Study in Online Islamist Radicalization and Its Meaning for the Threat of Homegrown Terrorism," Senate Committee on Homeland Security and Governmental Affairs, February 2012, 5, http://www.hsgac.senate.gov/imo/media/doc/CHESSER%20FINAL%20REPORT(1).pdf.

cause rather than directed by them (e.g., lone wolves and homegrown terrorists). Examples of successful operations abound. For instance, in December 2010, Antonio Martinez (or Muhammad Hussain), a 21-year-old U.S. citizen, was arrested for attempting to bomb a military recruitment center in Maryland.* Specifically, he was arrested after attempting to detonate the explosives he had received, which had been rendered inoperable by the FBI (unbeknownst to him). Likewise, in January 2012, Sami Osmakac, a 25-year-old naturalized U.S. citizen from Kosovo, attempted to engage in a car bombing attack in Tampa, Florida.† Osmakac was arrested after attempting to use the disabled explosives given to him by an undercover agent of the FBI. In a similar undercover sting operation, federal law enforcement authorities arrested a lone wolf, Amine El-Khalifi, for planning to engage in a suicide bombing and active shooter attack against the U.S. Capitol Building in Washington DC in February 2012.‡ Like other homegrown terrorists before him, he contacted undercover federal agents, who were pretending to be terrorists, for explosives and firearms. He was arrested by federal agents after he received what he believed to be an operable firearm and suicide vest laden with explosives.

Other than Islamic extremist terrorists, other types of terrorists' plots have also been uncovered using undercover agents and informants. For example, a plot to bomb a bridge in Cleveland, Ohio, by a homegrown terrorist group of self-proclaimed anarchists§ (Brandon Baxter, Anthony Hayne, Joshua Stafford, Connor Stevens, and Douglas Wright)

---

* U.S. Attorney's Office, District of Maryland, "Maryland Man Charged in Plot to Attack Armed Forces Recruiting Center: Inert 'Bomb' Provided by Undercover FBI Agent Posed No Danger to Public," FBI, December 8, 2010, http://www.fbi.gov/baltimore/press-releases/2010/ba120810.htm.

† U.S. Attorney's Office, Middle District of Florida, "Florida Resident Charged with Plotting to Bomb Locations in Tampa," FBI Tampa Division, January 9, 2012, http://www.fbi.gov/tampa/press-releases/2012/florida-resident-charged-with-plotting-to-bomb-locations-in-tampa.

‡ U.S. Attorney's Office, Eastern District of Virginia, "Virginia Man Sentenced to 30 Years in Prison for Plot to Carry Out Suicide Bomb Attack on U.S. Capitol," FBI, September 12, 2012, http://www.fbi.gov/washingtondc/press-releases/2012/virginia-man-sentenced-to-30-years-in-prison-for-plot-to-carry-out-suicide-bomb-attack-on-u.s.-capitol.

§ For anarchists, "[i]ndividual autonomy and collective equality are fundamental and necessary for a functional, civilized society. [Anarchism] resists the existing hierarchical structure of society that gives some people authority and control over others. [According to anarchists] authority imbues power, and power always is used in illegitimate and self-serving ways by those who have it." See Randy Borum and Chuck Tilby, "Anarchist Direct Actions: A Challenge for Law Enforcement," *Studies in Conflict and Terrorism* 28:3 (2005), 202, cited in Jerome P. Bjelopera, "The Domestic Terrorist Threat: Background and Issues for Congress," *Congressional Research Service (CRS)* Report for Congress, R42536, January 17, 2013, 13, http://www.fas.org/sgp/crs/terror/R42536.pdf.

was uncovered in 2012.* The perpetrators informed authorities that they were targeting the bridge to "send a message to corporations and the U.S. government."† These perpetrators were unknowingly working with an FBI informant for months, bought fake explosives from the informant, and subsequently, attempted to remotely detonate these explosives; they were arrested shortly thereafter.‡

Human intelligence has proven vital in counterterrorism efforts, both domestic and abroad.§ For example, a spy serving as a double agent successfully infiltrated al-Qaeda in the Arabian Peninsula (AQAP) and discovered a plot to blow up a U.S. airplane.¶ Online surveillance has also led to the detection and capture of terrorists. For instance, the FBI discovered Assem Hammoud's plot to bomb the PATH commuter train tunnel between New York City and New Jersey by conducting surveillance in online chatrooms frequented by Islamic extremists.** Similarly, Maher Husein Smadi was arrested for plotting to bomb a skyscraper in Dallas.†† Likewise, his plan was uncovered through the FBI's monitoring of online chat rooms known to be frequented by Islamic extremists. In this case, FBI agents posing as members of a terrorist group provided Smadi with an explosive device, which they had rendered inoperable. He was arrested after attempting to detonate the fake explosive.

In addition to human intelligence, the proper interrogation of suspects in custody plays an essential role in the effective investigation and prosecution of terrorists.‡‡ The emphasis of interrogations, however, should be on eliciting the truth and not confessions. The FBI's interrogation guidelines emphasizes the use of rapport building during

---

* Michael Muskal, "5 Arrested in Alleged Terrorist Plot to Blow Up Cleveland-Area Bridge, *Los Angeles Times*, May 1, 2012, http://articles.latimes.com/2012/may/01/nation/la-na-nn-cleveland-bomb-plot-20120501.

† Sophia Pearson, Seth Stern, and Mark Niquette, "Five Men Arrested in FBI Sting Over Plot to Bomb Ohio Bridge," *Bloomberg*, May 1, 2012, http://www.bloomberg.com/news/2012-05-01/five-men-arrested-in-fbi-sting-over-plot-to-bomb-bridge-in-ohio.html.

‡ Kantele Franko and Thomas J. Sheeran, "Cleveland Bridge Plot: Anarchists Angry with Corporate America," *The Christian Science Monitor*, May 2, 2012, http://www.csmonitor.com/USA/Latest-News-Wires/2012/0502/Cleveland-bridge-plot-Anarchists-angry-with-corporate-America.

§ For further information on human intelligence in counterterrorism efforts, see Chapter 8, Marie-Helen Maras, *Counterterrorism* (Burlington, MA: Jones & Bartlett, 2012).

¶ William Maclean, "Al Qaeda Bomb Plot: Undercover Agent in Foiled Plot Was Reportedly British Citizen," *Huffington Post*, May 11, 2012, http://www.huffingtonpost.com/2012/05/11/al-qaeda-bomb-plot-undercover-agent-british_n_1508844.html.

** "Terrorist Plots Targeting New York City," NYPD, http://www.nyc.gov/html/nypd/html/pr/plots_targeting_nyc.shtml.

†† "Texas Terror Suspect Pleads Not Guilty," CNN, October 26, 2009, http://edition.cnn.com/2009/CRIME/10/26/texas.terrorism.hearing/.

‡‡ For more information on interrogations, see Chapter 8, Marie-Helen Maras, *Counterterrorism* (Burlington, MA: Jones & Bartlett, 2012).

interrogation and actually forbids the use of torture.* The use of so-called softer interrogation techniques, such as developing rapport with suspects, has been effective in the past. Despite its proven efficacy, after the attacks on September 11, 2001, some government agencies dismissed this tactic as being too time-consuming; arguing that this approach cannot obtain intelligence quickly, which is needed in cases of terrorism. In light of this, other measures were sought, regardless of their limited reliability. One such measure has been torture.† However, no credible evidence exists that information obtained from interrogations using torture is reliable.‡ Countries using torture have seen an increase in terrorist attacks, increase in recruits and supporters for terrorists, and miscarriages of justice. Torture is based on faulty assumptions, that the person being tortured is actually a terrorist and that the person knows the information that the government seeks to obtain. It occurs at earlier points in time in the criminal justice process before guilt is established.

Another practice that had occurred at earlier points in time in the criminal justice process is preventive detention. Preventive detention is a form of incapacitation but differs from imprisonment in the sense that preventive detention occurs precharge and preconviction. Many countries use preventive detention as a counterterrorism measure (the United States, Australia, Israel, Malaysia, Sri Lanka, and Saudi Arabia, to name a few).§ This measure was often implemented in countries in response to an "emergency" situation (i.e., terrorism or more specifically, in the aftermath of a terrorist attack); usually without the official declaration of a state of emergency. When governments officially declare a state of emergency, they are allowed to derogate from certain rights. The right to derogations is prescribed in international human rights instruments (e.g., the European Convention on Human Rights, International Covenant on Civil and Political Rights, and the American Convention on Human Rights). Consider Article 4 of the International Covenant on Civil and Political Rights. Pursuant to Article 4(1),

> [i]n time of public emergency which threatens the life of the nation and the existence of which is officially proclaimed, the States Parties to the present Covenant may take measures derogating from their

---

* Demetri Sevastopulo, "FBI Concerns on Prisoner Abuse 'Ignored.'" *Financial Times*, May 20, 2008, http://www.ft.com/cms/s/0/0cd821a8-26ba-11dd-9c95-000077b07658. html#axzz1X2sYUB12.

† For more information on torture, see Chapter 8 in Marie-Helen Maras, *Counterterrorism* (Burlington, MA: Jones & Bartlett, 2012).

‡ Mark Costanzo, Ellen Gerrity, and M. Brinton Lykes, "Psychologists and the Use of Terror in Interrogations," *Analyses of Social Issues and Public Policy* 7:1 (December 2007), 7–20.

§ See Chapter 9 in Marie-Helen Maras, *Counterterrorism* (Burlington, MA: Jones & Bartlett, 2012), for further information on preventive detention and its use by countries around the world.

obligations under the present Covenant to the extent strictly required by the exigencies of the situation, provided that such measures are not inconsistent with their other obligations under international law and do not involve discrimination solely on the ground of race, colour, sex, language, religion or social origin.

Not all rights, however, can be derogated.* If a state chooses to derogate from this human rights instrument, other parties to the instrument need to be informed of this and the state's reasons for doing so.† But even in the case of the United Kingdom, which declared a state of emergency, the House of Lords found the practice of indefinite (or preventive) detention to be anathema to the rule of law and beyond that which was necessary to achieve the government's stated objectives.‡

In addition to the House of Lords, this practice is considered illegal according to international law. In fact, the prohibition of indefinite or arbitrary detention exists in international human rights instruments. For example, it is explicitly prohibited in Article 9 of the Universal Declaration of Human Rights, Article 7(3) of the American Convention on Human Rights, Article 9(1) of the International Covenant on Civil and Political Rights, and Article 147 of the Geneva Convention. Apart from being illegal, it is also fraught with accountability and transparency issues—those preventively detained cannot challenge why they are there and are often denied other basic due process rights such as access to lawyers, access to the evidence against them, and a speedy trial, among other rights. Fundamentally, preventive detention is unjustified because it occurs at earlier points in time in the criminal justice process, before the requirement of *mens rea* (i.e., guilty mind), and often even before *actus reus* (i.e., guilty act), have been established.

In addition to the use of incapacitation as a form of punishment, certain forms of individual and collective punishment have been implemented as counterterrorism measures around the globe.§ The choice

---

* For example, Article 4(2) of the International Covenant on Civil and Political Rights states: "No derogation from articles 6, 7, 8 (paragraphs 1 and 2), 11, 15, 16, and 18 may be made under this provision."

† For instance, Article 4(3) of the International Covenant on Civil and Political Rights holds that "[a]ny State Party to the present Covenant availing itself of the right of derogation shall immediately inform the other States Parties to the present Covenant, through the intermediary of the Secretary-General of the United Nations, of the provisions from which it has derogate and of the reasons by which it was actuated. A further communication shall be made, through the same intermediary, on the date on which it terminates such derogation."

‡ *A and others v. Secretary of State for the Home Department and X and others v. Secretary of State for the Home Department* [2004] UKHL 56 (opinions delivered on December 16, 2004, House of Lords Session 2004–2005), para. 74, 47. http://www.publications.parliament.uk/pa/ld200405/ldjudgmt/jd041216/a&others.pdf.

§ See Chapter 10, Marie-Helen Maras, *Counterterrorism* (Burlington, MA: Jones & Bartlett, 2012).

of appropriate punishment will ultimately depend on the perpetrator, and domestic and international laws. Concerning individual punishment, targeted killings have been used against terrorists. As mentioned above, AQAP was successfully infiltrated by a spy serving as a double agent. The information the spy provided about the group was used to engage in a successful targeted killing of Fahd al-Quso (a senior terrorist leader).[*] Additionally, capital punishment has been used against terrorists.[†] For instance, Mohd Arif, a member of Lashkar-e-Taiba (a Pakistani-based Islamic terrorist organization with links to al-Qaeda) was given a death sentence for his role in the 2000 Red Fort attack in Delhi, India.[‡] The primary reason that this form of punishment is used is for its purported deterrent effects. However, this assertion has not yet been empirically proven.[§]

Moreover, consider the United States. The United States has also sentenced terrorists to death. A case in point is Timothy McVeigh (Figure 4.2), who bombed the FBI Alfred P. Murray building in Oklahoma City, Oklahoma. Interviews with McVeigh revealed that he wanted to be a martyr;[¶] and he is (was) not alone. Many terrorists seek martyrdom. Indeed, this brings up an often overlooked point—the purpose of punishment is to impose a hardship on the offender to deter him (or her) and others in engaging in similar conduct. If terrorists seek martyrdom, how can that be considered punishment? When faced with the choice of imposing the death penalty or life imprisonment, the choice should be imprisonment—which actually poses a hardship on the individual as it prevents them from achieving martyrdom.

Furthermore, collective punishment has been used in counterterrorism.[**] Collective punishment is implemented against those that have not actually engaged in the offending behavior. Instead, it is implemented

---

[*] For a more detailed analysis of targeted killings, see Chapter 2, this volume.

[†] For a more detailed analysis of capital punishment in counterterrorism, see Chapter 10 in Marie-Helen Maras, *Counterterrorism* (Burlington, MA: Jones & Bartlett, 2012).

[‡] "Supreme Court Upholds Death Penalty for LeT Terrorist in Red Fort Attack," *India: Daily News and Analysis*, August 10, 2011, http://www.dnaindia.com/india/report_supreme-court-upholds-death-penalty-for-let-terrorist-in-red-fort-attack_1574446.

[§] Chapter 8, Roger Hood, *The Death Penalty: A Worldwide Perspective* (Oxford, United Kingdom: Oxford University Press, 2002); Cass R. Sunstein and Adrian Vermeule, "Is Capital Punishment Morally Required? The Relevance of Life-Life Tradeoffs," *Stanford Law Review* 58:3 (December 2005), 703–750; Michael L. Radelet and Ronald L. Akers, "Deterrence and the Death Penalty: The Views of the Experts," *Journal of Criminal Law and Criminology* 87:1 (Fall 1996), 1–16; Isaac Erlich, "The Deterrent Effect of Capital Punishment: A Question of Life and Death," *The American Economic Review* 65:3 (June 1975), 397–417.

[¶] Julian Borger, "Death Row Diaries Reveal McVeigh's Goal of Martyrdom," *The Guardian*, June 8, 2001, http://www.theguardian.com/world/2001/jun/09/mcveigh.usa.

[**] For more information on collective punishment, see Chapter 10, Marie-Helen Maras, *Counterterrorism* (Burlington, MA: Jones & Bartlett, 2012).

FIGURE 4.2   A young Timothy McVeigh during his time in the military.

against those associated with the terrorist in some way—either by familial, professional association, or geographical location. For the most part, collective punishment is prohibited by international law under Article 33 of the Geneva Convention and Article 50 of the Hague Convention, as it applies to those that have not engaged in the behavior that warranted this punishment. There are, however, exceptions to this prohibition.

One such exception is house demolitions. A house demolition is explicitly prohibited according to international law. In particular, it is considered unlawful pursuant to Article 53 of the Geneva Convention and Article 23(g) of the Hague Convention; except when such demolition of property occurs during a time of war and only when absolutely necessary in military operations. There are, however, other forms of collective punishment, closed borders, blockades, and economic sanctions that can be used in limited circumstances; only when they are in accordance with the law and necessary in a democratic society (i.e., they are in line with domestic, international law, and human rights instruments).

Soft Approaches to Terrorism

In addition to the so-called hard approaches to terrorism, soft approaches have been implemented in counterterrorism as well.* One example of this type of measure is the rehabilitation of terrorists. Rehabilitation programs

---

* For more information on soft approaches to terrorism, see Chapters 11, 12, and 13 of Marie-Helen Maras, *Counterterrorism* (Burlington, MA: Jones & Bartlett, 2012).

seek to treat the terrorist to enable him or her to desist from terrorism. Rehabilitation programs have to be oriented toward a certain type of terrorist. A different program will work for a right-wing terrorist than would for a religious terrorist. There are two types of programs: disengagement and deradicalization programs. Disengagement refers to the process of desisting from terrorist activity. It does not seek to alter the individual's beliefs by changing the manner in which the terrorist thinks. Nationalist-separatist and left-wing terrorists would be better suited for disengagement programs. By contrast, deradicalization seeks to alter the terrorist's view about the morality and legitimacy of engaging in violence in pursuit of his/her and/or the group's goals.

Existing rehabilitation programs have primarily focused on deradicalizing religious terrorists. In fact, several countries have implemented programs targeting religious terrorists such as Yemen, Saudi Arabia, Egypt, Singapore, Indonesia, the United Kingdom, and the United States.* These programs are focused on religious reeducation of terrorists. Overall, these programs worked best when accompanied by reintegration programs for terrorists, which often include (but are not limited to): job training, educational opportunities, job placement, and housing. To a lesser extent, rehabilitation programs have focused on right-wing terrorists. For instance, programs exist in Germany where ex-Nazis campaign against Nazism.† The use of these programs serves another purpose: they remove two justifications for terrorism—government indifference and governments' excessive use of force.

Another soft approach that can be used to combat terrorist radicalization involves targeting terrorists' ideology using noncoercive measures such as counterpropaganda.‡ Propaganda seeks to influence the beliefs and actions of the targeted audience. The counterpropaganda should thus aim to oppose propaganda. One way this can be done is by delegitimizing terrorists' actions. Consider al-Qaeda. Despite the claims of al-Qaeda that it defends Muslims, the majority of the deaths that they have caused have been of Muslims. For example, a study revealed that between 2004 and 2008, "85% of al-[Qaedda's] victims hailed from countries with Muslim majorities and only 15% came from Western

---

* For a more in-depth analysis of rehabilitation programs, see Chapter 11 in Marie-Helen Maras, *Counterterrorism* (Burlington, MA: Jones & Bartlett, 2012).
† EXIT-Deutschland BfV (Aussteigerprogram für Rechtsextremisten vom Bundesamt für Vergassungschutz).
‡ For more information on measures to quash terrorists' ideology, see Chapter 12 in Marie-Helen Maras, *Counterterrorism* (Burlington, MA: Jones & Bartlett, 2012).

countries."* The counterpropaganda strategy should, therefore, stress the deaths of Muslims. The latter will be used to counter terrorists' claims that they are serving Muslim interests. Communities and private organizations should be enlisted to assist in the quashing of terrorists' ideologies. Indeed, domestically and internationally, civil society is a critical partner in delegitimizing terrorists' actions. Another noncoercive tactic that can be used is finding ways to subvert terrorists. Here, governments can undermine terrorists' authority by discrediting them, making it more difficult for them to execute attacks, and publicizing the failures of the terrorists or groups to demoralize supporters and operatives.

The structural conditions that give rise to terrorist groups and help sustain support for them should also be addressed. For example, citizens' grievances against countries have historically and presently led to the rise of terrorist groups. Even worse, these groups sometimes fill the void in economic and/or social services; services which should be provided by the government. Cases in point are Hamas and Hezbollah; both groups are known for providing social services to the population.[†] As long as these services are provided by terrorist groups, the population will be dependent on them and most likely will support them in their endeavors. These services should be provided by government agencies. The international community should assist these countries in providing these services as well. Moreover, it is critical for the international community to ensure that any aid it is providing reaches the target population and is not diverted to the regime for its own agenda.

The final soft approach that can be used are peace agreements and negotiations with terrorists.[‡] There have been both successful (e.g., Good Friday Agreement) and unsuccessful peace agreements with terrorists (e.g., peace agreements between Colombia and the Revolutionary Armed Forces of Colombia and certain peace agreements in the Middle East). Furthermore, there are reasons for both engaging and not engaging in negotiations with terrorists. Some of the main reasons brought forward arguing against negotiations with terrorists are as follows: negotiating

---

* Scott Helfstein, Nassir Abdullah, and Muhammad al-Obaidi, *Deadly Vanguards: A Study of al-Qa'ida's Violence against Muslims* (West Point, NY: Combating Terrorism Center, 2009); Scott Helfstein, "A Third Way: A Paradigm for Influence in the Marketplace of Ideas," *CTC Sentinel* 3:6 (June 3, 2010), 16, http://www.ctc.usma.edu/wp-content/uploads/2010/08/CTCSentinel-Vol3Iss6-art5.pdf.

† Jonathan Masters, "Hamas," Council on Foreign Relations, November 27, 2012, http://www.cfr.org/israel/hamas/p8968; Jonathan Masters, "Hezbollah (a.k.a. Hizbollah, Hizbu'llah)," Council on Foreign Relations, July 22, 2013, http://www.cfr.org/lebanon/hezbollah-k-hizbollah-hizbullah/p9155.

‡ For a more in-depth analysis of peace agreements and negotiations with terrorists, see Chapter 13 in Marie-Helen Maras, *Counterterrorism* (Burlington, MA: Jones & Bartlett, 2012).

can legitimize terrorists' cause; it can send the message to other terrorists that terrorism works; and it has been found to increase the incidents
of terrorism.* By contrast, the primary reasons to negotiate with terrorists include: the possibility of gaining valuable intelligence concerning the terrorist group; the likelihood that negotiations may help reduce
recruitment to terrorism; and the possibility that the negotiations may
provide individuals with a "way out" of terrorism.† The choice in using
this tactic will depend on existing national laws and the type of terrorist
a country is dealing with.

The choice of counterterrorism will ultimately depend on the terrorists or terrorist group a government is faced with and the drivers behind
counterterrorism measures. By understanding how terrorists think and
act, the driving forces behind countermeasures targeting these threats,
and the implications of these policies, one can devise better ways with
which to counter these threats. Ultimately, terrorism can be combated
only through universal countermeasures. Without coordination of counterterrorism measures and cooperation between agencies and countries,
terrorists can evade detection and prosecution by authorities. To combat
terrorism, therefore, a unified, international effort is required.

CONCLUDING THOUGHTS

Transnational terrorism is a great transnational security threat. Terrorists
can be distinguished and categorized according to their ideology and
goals. In addition, terrorists can operate individually or in a group.
Currently, there is no universal definition of terrorism. There are, however, common elements in existing definitions of terrorism that most
academicians, practitioners, and policy makers agree upon and they are
as follows: that terrorists use coercive tactics, such as the threat or use
of violence, to promote control, fear, and intimidation within the target
nation or nations in order to effect change for political, religious, or
ideological reasons.

Several international and regional conventions concerning terrorism have been implemented. The core elements of these conventions

---

* Peter R. Neumann, "Negotiating with Terrorists," *Foreign Affairs* 86:1 (2007), 128;
  Harmonie Toros, "We Don't Negotiate with Terrorists!: Legitimacy and Complexity
  in Terrorist Conflicts," *Security Dialogue* 39:4 (2008), 411; Gabriella Blum and Philip
  B. Heymann, *Laws, Outlaws, and Terrorists* (Cambridge, MA: MIT Press, 2010),
  144–145.
† Gabriella Blum and Philip B. Heymann, *Laws, Outlaws, and Terrorists* (Cambridge,
  MA: MIT Press, 2010), 144–145; Harmonie Toros, "We Don't Negotiate with
  Terrorists! Legitimacy and Complexity in Terrorist Conflicts," *Security Dialogue* 39:4
  (2008), 416, 422.

include calls for criminalizing terrorism and ensuring that countries do not serve as safe havens for terrorists. Hard and soft tactics have been implemented in counterterrorism. Hard approaches include surveillance tactics, the use of undercover agents and informants, preventive detention, and different forms of individual and collective punishment. Soft approaches include rehabilitating terrorists, discrediting terrorists, addressing the structural conditions that give rise to terrorism, peace agreements, and (potentially) engaging in negotiations with terrorists. Effective counterterrorism can only be achieved with international cooperation and coordination in the prevention, detection, investigation, and prosecution of terrorists.

CHAPTER 5

Transnational Organized Crime

This chapter considers various organized crime groups and measures aimed at combating transnational and organized crime worldwide. It also explores how globalization has facilitated the emergence of transnational organized crime groups and their engagement in human smuggling and trafficking in persons, drugs, wildlife, arms, cigarettes, precious metals and gemstones, and cultural property (to name a few). This chapter further explores the strategy used by the United States, other countries, regional institutions, and the United Nations to confront organized criminals within and outside their territories and spheres of influence.

TRANSNATIONAL ORGANIZED CRIME

Organized crime refers to a structured group of three or more persons that act in concert with the goal of committing a serious crime or crimes for financial gain. The United Nations, in its Convention against Transnational Organized Crime, defined an organized crime group, under Article 2(a), as "a structured group of three or more persons, existing for a period of time and acting in concert with the aim of committing one or more serious crimes or offences established in accordance with this Convention, in order to obtain, directly or indirectly, a financial or other material benefit." Additionally, the Federal Bureau of Investigation defined organized crime as "[a]ny group having some manner of a formalized structure and whose primary objective is to obtain money through illegal activities. Such groups maintain their position through the use of actual or threatened violence, corrupt public officials, graft, or extortion, and generally have a significant impact on the people in their locales, region, or the country as a whole."[*] Indeed,

---

[*] "Glossary of Terms," FBI, http://www.fbi.gov/about-us/investigate/organizedcrime/glossary.

organized criminals are well known for using violence, intimidation tactics, and bribery to achieve their goals (e.g., Russian and Albanian organized crime groups).* Moreover, § 601(b) of the Omnibus Crime Control and Safe Streets Act of 1968 describes the activities involved in organized crime. Particularly, pursuant to this section, organized crime includes "the unlawful activities of the members of a highly organized, disciplined association engaged in supplying illegal goods and services, including but not limited to gambling, prostitution, loansharking, narcotics, labor racketeering, and other unlawful activities of members of such [an] organization."

To combat organized crime in the United States, the Racketeer Influenced and Corrupt Organizations (RICO) Act of 1970 (18 U.S.C. §§ 1961–1968) is used. This law enables the prosecution and the provision of extended penalties for criminal enterprises† engaged in racketeering activities. Under § 1961(A) of the RICO Act, racketeering includes, among numerous other crimes,‡ "any act or threat involving murder, kidnapping, gambling, arson, robbery, bribery, extortion, dealing in obscene matter, or dealing in a controlled substance or listed chemical (as defined in Section 102 of the Controlled Substances Act), which is chargeable under State law and punishable by imprisonment for more than one year."

Transnational crime and transnational organized crime are not new phenomena; however, the scope and magnitude of their impact worldwide are. Transnational organized crime affects all countries around the globe. Globalization has created new market opportunities for transnational organized criminals to exploit. Transnational organized crime involves the preparation and implementation of illegal business ventures by hierarchical groups or decentralized networks of individuals that conduct their operations in more than one country. There are numerous drivers of transnational organized crime, such as: political situations; technological advances; local, state, and national economies; lack of or ineffective laws; and lack of or ineffective enforcement mechanisms.§ Transnational organized crime is difficult to combat due to the sheer number in operation of networks and their diversity in structure, tactics, targets, and members (different cultures and languages). It is also difficult to combat because, similarly to transnational terrorism, it often

---

* Stephen L. Mallory, *Understanding Organized Crime* (Second Edition) (Burlington, MA: Jones & Bartlett, 2012), 101; "Balkan Criminal Enterprises," FBI, http://www.fbi.gov/about-us/investigate/organizedcrime/balkan.

† A criminal enterprise includes "any individual, partnership, corporation, association, or other legal entity, and any union or group of individuals associated in fact although not a legal entity" (18 U.S.C. § 1961(D)).

‡ See § 1961(B)–(G) of the RICO Act for more information.

§ Mark Galeotti, "Introduction: Global Crime Today," *Global Crime* 6:1 (2004), 4–6.

includes networks that are loose in structure, flexible, and highly adaptable to situations.

To combat transnational organized crime, the UN Convention against Transnational Organized Crime of 2000,* was implemented "to promote [international] cooperation in prevent[ing] and combat[ing] transnational organized crime more effectively."† The United Nations Office on Drugs and Crime (UNODC) is the international agency tasked with working with governments, other international organizations and agencies, and civil society in strengthening efforts to combat transnational organized crime. This agency assists countries in implementing the UN Convention against Transnational Organized Crime by helping them: create legislation to combat transnational organized crime; adopt existing frameworks for mutual assistance; promote cooperation among law enforcement agencies; enhance information between national agencies, international agencies, and private agencies, among others; and provide countries with training and technical assistance. UNODC is also responsible for creating best practices and overseeing the implementation of measures to combat transnational organized crime worldwide.

Historically and presently, transnational organized criminals have engaged in different forms of trafficking, including (but not limited to): human, body parts, drug, flora and fauna, cigarette, arms, timber, oil, and precious stones and metals. These groups have also engaged in human smuggling and cybercrime.‡ The next sections examine different forms and incidents of trafficking and smuggling (human, drugs, wildlife, arms, cigarette, precious metals and gemstones, and cultural property).

HUMAN TRAFFICKING

Slavery is outlawed in domestic and international legislation. In the United States, it is explicitly prohibited in state and federal statutes.§ It is also prohibited in the 13th Amendment to the U.S. Constitution, which holds that "[n]either slavery nor involuntary servitude...shall exist within the United States, or any place subject to their jurisdiction." Concerning international laws prohibiting slavery, in 1927, the Slavery, Servitude, Forced Labor and Similar Institutions and Practices Convention of 1926 (Slavery Convention of 1926) entered into force. The Slavery Convention

---

* The UN Convention against Transnational Organized Crime of 2000 entered into force in 2003.

† Article 1 of the UN Convention against Transnational Organized Crime of 2000.

‡ Cybercrime is explored in the next chapter of this volume, Chapter 6.

§ See, for example, 18 U.S.C. § 1581 and 18 U.S.C. § 1584. Joey Asher, "How the United States Is Violating Its International Agreement to Combat Slavery," *Emory International Law Review* 8:1 (1994), 215–254.

was one of the first international instruments to define slavery and the slave trade, and call for the abolition of slavery.* Under Article 1(1) of the Slavery Convention, slavery is defined as "the status or condition of a person over whom any or all of the powers attaching to the right of ownership are exercised." Moreover, according to Article 1(2) of the Slavery Convention, slave trade refers to "all acts involved in the capture, acquisition or disposal of a person with intent to reduce him to slavery; all acts involved in the acquisition of a slave with a view to selling or exchanging him; all acts of disposal by sale or exchange of a slave acquired with a view to being sold or exchanged, and, in general, every act of trade or transport in slaves."

In 1930, the International Labor Organization (ILO) Convention expanded the definition of slavery in the Slavery Convention of 1926 to include forced or compulsory labor. Specifically, the Forced Labor Convention (No. 29) holds that forced labor refers to: "all work or service which is exacted from any person under the menace of any penalty and for which the said person has not offered himself voluntarily." Forced labor can involve domestic servitude, agricultural work, and other labor-intensive jobs. There are, however, certain exceptions to this rule listed under Article 2(2) of this Convention (e.g., where domestic compulsory military service laws exist). Moreover, the Supplementary Convention on the Abolition of Slavery, the Slave Trade, and Institutions and Practices Similar to Slavery (1956) broadened the Slavery Convention of 1926 to include forced labor and other practices similar to slavery (see Articles 1, 5, and 6). The ILO Convention concerning the Abolition of Forced Labor (No. 105) of 1957 (which entered into force in 1959) held that those that have ratified the Convention will prohibit and not engage in any of the following forms of forced or compulsory labor:

(a) as a means of political coercion or education or as a punishment for holding or expressing political views or views ideologically opposed to the established political, social or economic system; (b) as a method of mobilizing and using labor for purposes of economic development; (c) as a means of labor discipline; (d) as a punishment for having participated in strikes; (e) as a means of racial, social, national or religious discrimination.[†]

Other international conventions and human rights instruments also explicitly prohibit slavery. For instance, Article 4 of the Universal Declaration of Human Rights (1948) states that "[n]o one shall be held

---

* The League of Nations adopted this convention. In 1953, the Protocol amending the Slavery Convention signed at Geneva on 25 September 1926 (1953) entered into force in order to replace the League of Nations with the institutions of the United Nations.
† Article 1 of the ILO Convention concerning the Abolition of Forced Labor (No. 105) of 1957.

in slavery or servitude; slavery and the slave trade shall be prohibited in all their forms." Similarly, Article 4 of the European Convention on Human Rights (ECHR) of 1950 unequivocally forbids slavery and forced or compulsory labor. Notwithstanding, Article 4(3) includes exceptions to the prohibition on forced labor. Likewise, Article 8 of the International Covenant on Civil and Political Rights of 1966 (which entered into force in 1976) prohibits all forms of slavery, servitude, and forced or compulsory labor.[*]

Human trafficking is modern day slavery. The United Nations Protocol to Prevent, Suppress, and Punish Trafficking in Persons, especially Women and Children, Supplementing the United Nations Convention against Transnational Organized Crime (hereafter Trafficking in Persons Protocol), is a legally binding instrument, which defines human trafficking in Article 3(a), as follows:

> the recruitment, transportation, transfer, harboring, or receipt of persons, by means of threat or use of force or other forms of coercion, of abduction or fraud, of deception, of the abuse of power of a position of vulnerability or of the giving or receiving of payment or benefits to achieve the consent of a person having control over other persons, for the purpose of exploitation. Exploitation shall include, at a minimum, the exploitation of the prostitution of others or other forms of sexual exploitation, forced labor or services, slavery or practices similar to slavery, servitude or the removal of organs.

Section 103 of the U.S. Trafficking Victims Protection Act of 2000 (TVPA) defines "severe forms of human trafficking" as

> (A) sex trafficking in which a commercial sex act is induced by force, fraud, or coercion, or in which the person induced to perform such act has not attained 18 years of age; or (B) the recruitment, harboring, transportation, provision, or obtaining of a person for labor or services, through the use of force, fraud, or coercion for the purpose of subjection to involuntary servitude, peonage, debt bondage, or slavery.

Perpetrators of human trafficking include (but are not limited to) transnational criminals and organized crime groups (Japanese Yakuza, Chinese Triads, and Russian organized crime groups, to name a few).[†] Victims of human trafficking include women, children, and men. In 2009, in Houston, Texas, a Salvadoran man escaped a ranch where he was held

---

[*] The exceptions to forced or compulsory labor are included in Article 8(3)(c).

[†] Joseph E. Ritch, "They'll Make You an Offer You Can't Refuse: A Comparative Analysis of International Organized Crime," *Tulsa Journal of Comparative & International Law* 9:2 (2001), 569–606.

against his will, forced to work without pay, beaten, raped, and tortured (e.g., burned with cigarettes) by traffickers.* Moreover, the victims of this form of crime can come from anywhere in the world. Nevertheless, conflict and post-conflict societies are especially vulnerable to human trafficking. Particularly, according to a report by the United Nations Global Initiative to Fight Human Trafficking,

> [i]n conflict and post-conflict countries, social vulnerabilities that may have existed prior to conflict are exacerbated, and new vulnerabilities (particularly affecting women and children) are created from the conflict and post-conflict atmosphere. Social vulnerabilities arising in conflict and post-conflict countries can include: lawlessness and social dysfunction, disrupted families, increased sexual violence and exposure to HIV/AIDS, increased numbers of street children, orphans and children directly involved in armed conflict, and a lack of schools and employment opportunities.[†]

In these, and developing and developed countries, victims can be lured by promises for a better life with employment opportunities. Human trafficking involves the coercion and unwilling participation of an individual. This person has not given their consent and is being exploited in some way. Generally, victims of human trafficking are duped and/or coerced into illicitly entering the country. Traffickers often provide the victims with documents (commonly unbeknownst to the victims, these are false) to transport them to the destination country. A recent example of this occurred on October 7, 2013, where the individuals responsible for a human trafficking operation to the United States that involved the use of false documentation, were arrested in Gujarat, India.[‡]

Once inside the country, victims can be forced into the sex slave trade, slavery, exploitation, or forced labor. Consider the following case in Switzerland:[§] A business manager of hotels and bars in Sweden forced women who came to work for him to be prostitutes. The women who came to his establishment included six individuals from Latvia (four women) and the Czech Republic (two women). The business manager

---

* Susan Carroll, "Traffickers Force More Men into Servitude," *Houston Chronicle*, July 6, 2009, http://www.chron.com/news/houston-texas/article/Traffickers-force-more-men-into-servitude-1730660.php.

† United Nations Global Initiative to Fight Human Trafficking, "Human Trafficking: An Overview," United Nations Office on Drugs and Crime, 2008, http://www.ungift.org/docs/ungift/pdf/knowledge/ebook.pdf.

‡ Somendra Sharma, "2 Held in Gujarat for Human Trafficking to U.S." *DNA India. Daily News and Analysis (DNA)*, October 7, 2013, http://www.dnaindia.com/mumbai/1899677/report-2-held-in-gujarat-for-human-trafficking-to-us.

§ "UNODC Human Trafficking Case Law Database: Switzerland," UNODC, 2008, http://www.unodc.org/cld/search.jspx?f=en%23caseLaw%40country_label_s%3aSwitzerland.

FIGURE 5.1   Victims of human trafficking are exposed to emotionally distressing and inhumane treatments and conditions. (Image courtesy of Shutterstock.com.)

restricted these women's movement by confiscating their passports and controlling their day-to-day activities.

There are two main drivers for human trafficking: economic and political instability in the host country of the victim and the demand for this form of crime. In fact, demand is primarily responsible for the exponential growth in human trafficking. Human trafficking erodes the capacity of the state to function and protect its citizens. The moral concerns regarding human trafficking and its impact on the human rights of victims is apparent. Victims suffer traumatic and inhumane treatments and conditions (Figure 5.1). Those forced into labor, prostitution, or other forms of sexual exploitation suffer from psychological disorders and/or infectious diseases (transmission of STDs; HIV/AIDS).*

To combat trafficking, the United States implemented the TVPA. States have adopted their own laws as well. The TVPA includes provisions calling for the training of law enforcement agencies in the United States. Law enforcement agencies play a critical role in identifying trafficked persons. The TVPA also provides assistance to victims. It additionally requires any undocumented trafficked persons to be considered

---

* "Fact Sheet: Health Consequences of Trafficking in Persons," U.S. Department of State, August 8, 2007, http://2001-2009.state.gov/g/tip/rls/fs/07/91418.htm.

first and foremost a victim (unless the investigation demonstrates otherwise). This was done to emphasize that trafficked persons were considered as victims and not criminals. Furthermore, the TVPA is primarily designed to assist the prosecution. Victim assistance is secondary. If the victim assists in the prosecution of traffickers, they can be granted temporary stay; what is termed to be "continued presence." This allows the victim to stay in the United States for the duration of the prosecution of the offender(s). Victims, if they choose and are eligible, may pursue T Nonimmigrant Status visas (or T-visas) to obtain nonimmigrant status. If a T-visa is issued, victims can apply for permanent residency after 3 years and petition to have their family members brought to the United States. Nonetheless, few T-visas have been granted. Congress has also limited the number of T-visas that are granted to 5,000 per year.* Apart from domestic efforts in the United States and in other nations abroad, international cooperation in the efforts to prosecute traffickers and protect victims is required. Indeed, cooperation is required from the country of origin of the trafficked person, any transit country, and the destination country.

Child Trafficking

The trafficking of children not only adversely affects the child but also society as a whole. Pursuant to Article 3(d) of the Trafficking in Persons Protocol, a child refers to "any person under eighteen years of age." The UN Convention on the Rights of the Child of 1988 (entered into force in 1990) also defines a child as a "human being below the age of eighteen years unless, under the law applicable to the child, majority is attained earlier."† Child slavery is also explicitly prohibited. For instance, the ILO Convention concerning the Prohibition and Immediate Action for the Elimination of the Worst Forms of Child Labor (No. 182) of 1999 defined the "worst forms of child labor" as follows:

> (a) all forms of slavery or practices similar to slavery, such as the sale and trafficking of children, debt bondage and serfdom and forced or compulsory labor, including forced or compulsory recruitment of children for use in armed conflict; (b) the use, procuring or offering of a child for prostitution, for the production of pornography or for

---

* U.S. Citizen and Immigration Services, "Questions and Answers: Victims of Human Trafficking, T Nonimmigrant Status," Department of Homeland Security, http://www.uscis.gov/humanitarian/victims-human-trafficking-other-crimes/victims-human-trafficking-t-nonimmigrant-status/questions-and-answers-victims-human-trafficking-t-nonimmigrant-status-0.
† Article 1, UN Convention on the Rights of the Child of 1988.

pornographic performances; (c) the use, procuring or offering of a child for illicit activities, in particular for the production and trafficking of drugs as defined in the relevant international treaties; (d) work which, by its nature or the circumstances in which it is carried out, is likely to harm the health, safety or morals of children.

The Optional Protocol to the Convention on the Rights of the Child on the Sale of Children, Child Prostitution and Child Pornography of 2000 (entered into force in 2002) called upon states to criminalize: the sexual exploitation of children; transfer of child organs for profit; child forced labor; sale of children; illegal adoption; child prostitution; and child pornography. Countries have domestic laws in place criminalizing child trafficking. For example, Section 236 of the German Criminal Code, the Child Trafficking and Pornography Act of 1998 of Ireland, and Section 98AA of the New Zealand Crimes Act of 1961, No. 43, criminalize and provide penalties for child trafficking.

Numerous incidents of child forced labor have been revealed by international investigations. Among them is an Interpol-led operation known as Operation Tuy. This operation revealed that 387 children were being forced to work in mining under horrific conditions in Burkina Faso; additionally, girls were being subjected to sexual abuse.[*] Other operations in Africa that revealed child forced labor of more than 400 children include: Operations Bia (2009), Cascades and Bana (2010), and Bia II (2011).[†]

Apart from forced labor, children have also been trafficked for the purpose of commercial sexual exploitation. The commercial sexual exploitation of children (CSEC) is defined by the First World Congress against Commercial Sexual Exploitation of Children as "sexual abuse by the adult and remuneration in cash or kind to the child or a third person or persons. The child is treated as a sexual object and as a commercial object. The commercial sexual exploitation of children constitutes a form of coercion and violence against children, amounts to forced labor and a contemporary form of slavery."[‡] CSEC includes the prostitution of children, sex tourism, and any type of transactional sexual activity performed by a child for remuneration and/or the fulfillment of their basic needs.

---

[*] "Nearly 400 Victims of Child Trafficking Rescued across Burkina Faso in INTERPOL-Led Operation," Interpol, November 22, 2012, http://www.interpol.int/News-and-media/News-media-releases/2012/PR096.

[†] Ibid.

[‡] William Adams, Colleen Owens, and Kevonne Small, "Effects of Federal Legislation on the Commercial Sexual Exploitation of Children," U.S. Department of Justice, Office of Justice Programs, July 2010, https://www.ncjrs.gov/pdffiles1/ojjdp/228631.pdf.

According to Eva Klain et al., signs of children who are victims of trafficking include the following:* a lack of access to identification documents; knowledge of the commercial sex industry; inferences to sexual situations that are not age appropriate; truancy; frequent travel to other cities, states, or countries; an increase in expensive possessions; signs of physical abuse; exhibiting fearful and/or withdrawal behaviors; drug addiction or exhibiting behavior of drug use; and a significant older boyfriend or girlfriend. Those engaged in commercial exploitation of children are parents, relatives, family acquaintances, traffickers, pimps, employers, and strangers.† In the United States, child trafficking takes on many different forms. Children are‡: prostituted on streets, in private residences or in private businesses (e.g., spas, massage parlors, hotels, and clubs); sold to homes or businesses for domestic labor; used by others to receive money from begging; and utilized to sell drugs.

Victims of commercial sexual exploitation with no parent, guardian, or relative in the United States are eligible for the Unaccompanied Refugee Minors (URM) program. Children placed in this program "receive the full range of services available to other foster children in the State, as well as special services to help them adapt to life in the United States and recover from their trafficking experience."§ A primary goal of this program is the safe reunification of the child with his or her family. The extent to which child sexual exploitation occurs in the United States is difficult to assess due to the low-visibility nature of this industry. Federal and state laws have been passed to decriminalize prostitution for all youths under the age of 18. In New York, the Safe Harbor for Exploited Children Act of 2007 did just that by relabeling prostitutes under the age of 18 as sexually exploited children (SEC). Other states have similar laws in place, such as Connecticut (Safe Harbor for Exploited Children Act of 2010) and Minnesota (Safe Harbor for Sexually Exploited Youth Act of 2011).

---

* Eva Klain, Amanda Kloer, Diane Eason, Irena Lieberman, Carol Smolenski, and Robin Thompson, "An Introduction for Children's Attorneys and Advocates," American Bar Association, 2009, http://www.americanbar.org/content/dam/aba/migrated/2011_build/domestic_violence/child_trafficking.authcheckdam.pdf.

† Richard J. Estes and Neil Alan Weiner, "The Commercial Sexual Exploitation of Children in the U.S., Canada and Mexico," Center for the Study of Youth Policy, School of Social Work, University of Pennsylvania, September 19, 2001, http://www.sp2.upenn.edu/restes/CSEC_Files/Exec_Sum_020220.pdf.

‡ Janice G. Raymond and Donna M. Hughes, "Sex Trafficking Women in the United States: International and Domestic Trends," Coalition against Trafficking in Women, March 2001, http://www.uri.edu/artsci/wms/hughes/sex_traff_us.pdf.

§ Administration for Children and Families, "Fact Sheet: Child Victims of Human Trafficking," U.S. Department of Health & Human Services, May 23, 2012, http://archive.acf.hhs.gov/trafficking/about/child_victims.htm.

Organ Trafficking

Humans can also be trafficked for the harvesting of their organs (e.g., kidneys, liver, heart, and so on). The cost of organ transplants in hospitals is prohibitive. The cost alone may be too much for the victim to bear. Voluntary organ donation is also insufficient; most countries fall short of meeting the demands for organs and many have died while on the waiting list for organ donation. The waiting lists for organs are very long and the priority given depends on the age and condition of the patient.

The shortage of organs has led to an increase in demand for them in the black market; even though almost all countries prohibit the sale of organs. Some examples of domestic laws criminalizing this activity include: the Human Tissue Act of 1983 (South Africa), the National Organ Transplant Act of 1984 (United States), and the Human Tissue Act of 2004 (UK). Moreover, the Additional Protocol to the Convention on Human Rights and Biomedicine concerning Transplantation of Organs and Tissues of Human Origin of 2002 (which entered into force in 2006) prohibits both organ and tissue trafficking and calls on EU Member States to provide appropriate sanctions for this crime.

Pursuant to the 1984 Temporary Rules Concerning the Utilization of Corpses or Organs from the Corpses of Executed Criminals, China has authorized the procurement of organs from executed criminals.[*] In 2006, China enacted the Provisions on the Administration of Entry and Exit of Cadavers and Treatment of Cadavers, which prohibited organs from being taken from individuals from China to another country without proper government authorization.[†] In contrast to other countries, kidney trade is legal in Iran. Iran has two nongovernmental agencies (the Charity Association for the Support of Kidney Patients and the Charity Foundation for Special Diseases) that oversee the trade of this organ between donors and recipients.[‡] These organizations are responsible for connecting donors and recipients and conducting the tests to ensure compatibility between donors and recipients. Donors are provided with some form of remuneration by recipients. International and regional legal instruments also prohibit organ trafficking.

Organ traffickers exploit the desperation of the seekers and recipients of organs who are trying to prolong their lives. Perpetrators thus take

---

[*] Joan E. Hemphill, "China's Practice of Procuring Organs from Executed Prisoners: Human Rights Groups Must Narrowly Tailor Their Criticism and Endorse the Chinese Constitution to End Abuses," *Pacific Rim Law & Policy Journal* 16:2 (2007), 431.

[†] Ibid.

[‡] Miran Epstein, "A Market in Organs," In Massimiliano Veroux and Pierfrancesco Veroux (Eds.), *Kidney Transplantation: Challenging the Future* (United Arab Emirates: Bentham Books, 2012).

advantage of the situation and the existing demands for organs. Victims, in desperation, seek the organs on the black market. Transnational organized criminals can obtain organs at the lowest price in a poor country and sell them to the highest bidder in a wealthy country. In fact, on April 29, 2013, five individuals who were part of an organ-trafficking network lured poor people to Kosovo "to sell their kidneys and other organs to wealthy transplant recipients from Israel, the United States, Canada and Germany. Organs sold for as much as $130,000 each."[*] Indeed, this is a lucrative business for criminals. In 2012, Levy Izhak Rosenbaum was prosecuted for organ trafficking (the first case to be prosecuted in the United States). Rosenbaum bought organs from vulnerable individuals in Israel for approximately $10,000 and sold them to patients in the United States for more than $100,000.[†] For his crimes, he received a sentence of 2½ years of imprisonment.

Donors of organs are often coerced through force or the threat of force; sometimes they provide their organs for payment, which is often never received. Apart from the illegality of this action, this act exposes donors and the recipients of the organs to health risks. In particular, black market organ trafficking has several health-related repercussions; especially since transmission of organs often occurs outside of a medical facility with unlicensed doctors and potentially under unsanitary conditions (though this is not always the case).

Human Smuggling

Trafficking and smuggling are often used interchangeably. However, when humans are what is being trafficked or smuggled these two terms cannot be used interchangeably. With human smuggling, an individual willingly participates in his or her transport across the border. This person is in no way coerced into the decision to illegally enter into the country and knowingly engages in the illicit act. Accordingly, these individuals are committing a crime. By contrast, those who are trafficked are coerced and are trafficked against their free will; as such, they should be (and are) viewed as victims. Therefore, the responses of authorities to those smuggled should be different from their responses to those trafficked.

---

[*] Dan Bilefsky, "5 Are Convicted in Kosovo Organ Trafficking," *New York Times*, April 29, 2013, http://www.nytimes.com/2013/04/30/world/europe/in-kosovo-5-are-convicted-in-organ-trafficking.html.

[†] Samantha Henry, "Brooklyn Man Sentenced 2 1/2 Years in Fed Organ Trafficking Case," *NBC News*, July 11, 2012, http://www.nbcnewyork.com/news/local/Kidney-Organ-Trafficking-Levy-Izhak-Rosenbaum-Brooklyn-Federal-Conviction-Sentencing-162046565.html.

The UN Protocol against the Smuggling of Migrants by Land, Sea and Air of 2000 (which entered into force in 2004), defines, under Article 3(a), the smuggling of migrants as "the procurement, in order to obtain, directly or indirectly, a financial or other material benefit, of the illegal entry of a person into a State Party of which the person is not a national or a permanent resident." To implement this Protocol, states not only need to criminalize acts of human smuggling, but also need to criminalize attempts to smuggle persons, participation as an accomplice to smuggling, and directing others to engage in smuggling (Article 6(2)). Domestic law is in place in various countries that criminalize these illicit human smuggling activities. For example, in the United States, Section 274(a)(1),(2) of the Immigration and Nationalization Act of 1952, "provides for criminal penalties under" 18 U.S.C. § 1324 "for acts or attempts to bring unauthorized aliens to or into the United States, transport them within the United States, harbor unlawful aliens, encourage entry of illegal aliens, or conspire to commit these violations, knowingly or in reckless disregard of illegal status."* The UK similarly criminalizes this activity with the Immigration Act of 1971.

Whether voluntary or the result of coercion the transport of human beings across the border is a very lucrative business for transnational organized criminals. To evade detection by border authorities, those seeking illegal entry into a country often enlist the help of organized criminals. A notorious human smuggler, dubbed the Mother of Snakeheads,† Cheng Chui Ping, was convicted and sentenced to 35 years imprisonment for facilitating the smuggling of numerous illegal immigrants from China to the United States.‡

With those who take part in human smuggling, the relationship between the victim and smuggler usually ends after the victim enters the host country. Smugglers are paid to help migrants achieve their goal of illegal entry. There are instances where the smuggler threatens the migrants for more fees than originally agreed upon. Indeed, given the fact that such entry is illegal, these individuals often fall victim to the smugglers who may seek to extort them (by threatening to notify authorities) or coercing them into forced labor or the sex slave trade. Such individuals may also be subjected to violent acts, such as robbery, rape, assault, and or eventually murder.

---

* "Fact Sheet: Distinctions between Human Smuggling and Human Trafficking 2006," U.S. Department of State, January 1, 2006, http://www.state.gov/m/ds/hstcenter/90434.htm.

† Snakeheads is a slang term used to describe Chinese gangs that engage in the smuggling of individuals to other countries.

‡ Julia Preston, "Ringleader Gets 35-Year Term in Smuggling of Immigrants," *New York Times*, March 17, 2006, http://www.nytimes.com/2006/03/17/nyregion/17ping.html.

Migrants have been smuggled under inhumane conditions. People have been smuggled in the floorboards of trucks, hidden compartments of vehicles, undercarriages of vehicles, the glove compartment of cars, trunks in vehicles, and even sewn into the seats of vehicles. Some have been crammed into cargo containers and smuggled to countries on board ships.[*] Many individuals that have been smuggled are confined in spaces with poor ventilation and/or exposed to high temperatures leading some to die from suffocation and/or severe dehydration.[†]

DRUG TRAFFICKING

Drug trafficking involves the illicit cultivation, production, distribution, and sale of controlled substances that violate national and international drug prohibition laws. Nationally, controlled substances are divided into schedules under the U.S. Comprehensive Drug Abuse and Control Act of 1970. These schedules classify drugs according to their medical use (if any), potential for abuse, and level of harmfulness. Some types of controlled substances include narcotics, stimulants, depressants, and anabolic steroids.

According to the United Nations Office on Drugs and Crime, "drugs [that are] under international control include amphetamine-type stimulants, coca/cocaine, cannabis, hallucinogens, opiates and sedative hypnotics. Countries have decided to control these drugs because they pose a threat to health."[‡] International laws have been implemented to control the production and distribution of drugs. The UN Single Convention on Narcotics Drugs of 1961 simultaneously recognized the need to maintain the production and use of drugs for medical purposes and the potential for abuse of drugs. Accordingly, this convention sought, among other things to: limit the production of opium for international trade (Article 24); control the uses of poppy straw (Article 25); control the cultivation of coca bush and coca leaves (Article 26); control of cannabis cultivation (Article 28); regulate the manufacture of narcotics (Article 29); and regulate the trade and distribution of narcotics (Article 30). Article 35 of the convention specifies the need for international

---

[*] Barbara Whitaker, "Immigrant Smuggling Draws New Attention," *New York Times*, January 4, 2000, http://www.nytimes.com/2000/01/04/us/immigrant-smuggling-draws-new-attention.html.

[†] Ray Walser, Jena Baker McNeill, and Jessica Zuckerman, "The Human Tragedy of Illegal Immigration: Greater Efforts Needed to Combat Smuggling and Violence," The Heritage Foundation, June 22, 2011, http://www.heritage.org/research/reports/2011/06/the-human-tragedy-of-illegal-immigration-greater-efforts-needed-to-combat-smuggling-and-violence#_ftnref11.

[‡] "Types of Drugs," United Nations Office on Drugs and Crime, http://www.unodc.org/drugs/en/get-the-facts/types-of-drugs.html.

coordination in the prevention and suppression of drug trafficking. The UN Convention on Psychotropic Substances of 1971 was introduced to create an international control system for psychotropic substances, which includes: stimulants (e.g., amphetamine and methamphetamine); hallucinogens (e.g., LSD and mescaline); and sedative hypnotics (e.g., barbiturates). Like the Single Convention on Narcotics Drugs, this convention also recognized these drugs' potential for abuse and their therapeutic value.

Furthermore, the United Nations Convention against Illicit Traffic in Narcotic Drugs and Psychotropic Substances of 1988 included comprehensive measures against drug trafficking. More specifically, this convention called for: the creation of national laws criminalizing and penalizing the illicit drug trade and trafficking (Article 3); the extradition of drug traffickers (Article 5); the enabling of mutual legal assistance in the investigation and prosecution of drug trafficking (Article 7); and the facilitating of international cooperation and assistance in transit states (Article 10).

Drivers of Drug Trafficking

The UN Single Convention on Narcotics Drugs of 1961, the Convention on Psychotropic Substances of 1971, and the Convention against Illicit Traffic in Narcotic Drugs and Psychotropic Substances of 1988 focus on controlling and regulating the supply of drugs. However, the proliferation of illicit drugs is not only the result of the supply of drugs but also the demand for drugs. Indeed, the main drivers of drug trafficking are poverty, unemployment, and the abuse and accessibility of drugs worldwide. Drug trafficking will continue to exist as long as there is demand—and demand for drugs is high. For that reason, the 1972 Protocol amending the Single Convention on Narcotic Drugs was implemented, which highlighted the need to focus on the demand side of the global drug problem by stressing the need for drug users' treatment and rehabilitation. Particularly, Article 14 of the 1972 Protocol amended Article 36 of the Single Convention on Narcotic Drugs to include that drug "abusers...undergo measures of treatment, education, after-care, rehabilitation and social reintegration" when having committed drug offenses, "either as an alternative to conviction or punishment or in addition to conviction or punishment." Similarly, the UN Convention against Illicit Traffic in Narcotic Drugs and Psychotropic Substances called for drug abuse treatment, education, aftercare rehabilitation, and social reintegration of drug users.

To be effective, drug treatment and rehabilitation programs should monitor individuals after completion. Without such monitoring high rates of recidivism exist. In particular, after being released, drug users are vulnerable to reoffending, as they often have little, if any, financial, family, and emotional support. Those that are newly released from drug treatment and rehabilitation programs should distance themselves from their previous environment which may have contributed to their drug use. When family and friends are also drug users, additional problems arise. Especially in such instances, reintegration programs are critical. In order for such measures to be effective, they should be widespread and used together. With respect to the latter, a combination of drug abuse treatment, education, aftercare, rehabilitation, and social reintegration is required.* When one or more of these programs is lacking, there is a greater likelihood of reoffending. Harmonization of practices across and within countries is also required.

Drug Trafficking Hubs

Countries around the globe have served as host, transit, and/or destination countries for drugs, such as cannabis, cocaine, ecstasy, hallucinogens, heroin, and methamphetamines (to name a few). The 2013 World Drug Report revealed that cannabis is the most widely used illicit drug and virtually all countries produce it.† The United States is a major drug consumption zone. The Caribbean is a production zone for marijuana (e.g., Jamaica and Trinidad and Tobago).‡ Indeed, Jamaican organized crime groups are major producers of marijuana (*ganja*). The Caribbean is located between drug production zones (e.g., Colombia and Bolivia) and drug consumption zones (e.g., the United States). Accordingly, it serves as a main transit country for the shipment of South American cocaine to the United States. The 2013 World Drug Report indicated that cocaine seizures were highest in Colombia and the United States; however, there were also increases in cocaine trafficking and cocaine use in areas not previously associated with it, such as Asia, Oceania, Central and South America, and the Caribbean.§

---

* Jeremy Travis, Amy L. Solomon, and Michelle Waul, "From Prison to Home: The Dimensions and Consequences of Prisoner Reentry," June 2001, Urban Institute: Justice Policy Center, http://www.urban.org/pdfs/from_prison_to_home.pdf.
† "World Drug Report 2013," UNODC, 24, http://www.unodc.org/unodc/secured/wdr/wdr2013/World_Drug_Report_2013.pdf.
‡ Ivelaw Lloyd Griffith, "Drugs and the Emerging Security Agenda in the Caribbean," In Joseph S. Tulchin and Ralph H. Espach (Eds.), *Security in the Caribbean Basin: The Challenge of Regional Cooperation Security in the Caribbean Basin: The Challenge of Regional Cooperation* (Boulder, CO: Lynne Rienner, 2000).
§ "World Drug Report 2013," UNODC, 37, http://www.unodc.org/doc/wdr/Chp1_E.pdf.

This 2013 World Drug Report additionally demonstrated that the use of psychoactive substances were on the rise in various countries around the globe. Specifically, the use of ecstasy (i.e., MDMA or methylenedioxymethamphetamine) was found to be prevalent in Oceania, North America, and Europe.[*] Another example is the hallucinogen ketamine, "a human and veterinary anesthetic which acts as a stimulant at low doses and a hallucinogen at high doses."[†] Ketamine was found to be widely used in Asia.[‡] Moreover, the report revealed that Afghanistan remains the top production zone for opiates (opium and heroin).[§] The report also indicated that methamphetamines were the most commonly used amphetamine-type stimulant around the world.[¶] In addition, large seizures of methamphetamines were reported by Mexico, the United States, and countries in East and South-East Asia.[**]

Transnational organized crime groups have engaged in drug trafficking (Figure 5.2). A case in point involved the arrest of members of an Albanian organized crime network that trafficked cocaine and heroin in Europe.[††] The Chinese Triads and Russian organized crime groups, among others, also engage in drug trafficking.[‡‡] In Operation Lionfish, an Interpol-led investigation, approximately "30 tons of cocaine, heroin and marijuana with an estimated value of USD 822 million" were seized.[§§] This operation targeted organized crime groups trafficking drugs through Central America and the Caribbean. Another Interpol-led investigation, code named Icebreaker, led to the seizure of more than "200 kilos of methamphetamine, cocaine and LSD [, with an estimated value of] USD 2 million" from drug producers and traffickers across the Americas; participating countries included "Belize, Colombia, Costa

---

[*] "World Drug Report 2013," UNODC, 2, http://www.unodc.org/unodc/secured/wdr/wdr2013/World_Drug_Report_2013.pdf.

[†] "World Drug Report 2013," UNODC, 49, http://www.unodc.org/unodc/secured/wdr/wdr2013/World_Drug_Report_2013.pdf.

[‡] Ibid.

[§] "World Drug Report 2013: Opiates," UNODC, http://www.unodc.org/wdr/en/opiates.html.

[¶] "World Drug Report 2013: Amphetamine-Type Stimulants," UNODC, http://www.unodc.org/wdr/en/ats.html.

[**] "World Drug Report 2013," UNODC, 49–50, http://www.unodc.org/unodc/secured/wdr/wdr2013/World_Drug_Report_2013.pdf.

[††] Eurojust, "International Operation Targets Albanian Drug Trafficking Network," *Joint Eurojust—Europol Press Release,* July 9, 2012, http://www.eurojust.europa.eu/press/PressReleases/Pages/2012/2012-07-09.aspx.

[‡‡] Joseph E. Ritch, "They'll Make You an Offer You Can't Refuse: A Comparative Analysis of International Organized Crime," *Tulsa Journal of Comparative & International Law* 9:2 (2001), 569–606.

[§§] "Drugs Worth Nearly One Billion Dollars Seized in INTERPOL-Led Operation across Central America and the Caribbean," Interpol, July 2, 2013, http://www.interpol.int/News-and-media/News-media-releases/2013/PR079.

FIGURE 5.2   Drug trafficking is an illicit multibillion dollar enterprise globally. (Image courtesy of Shutterstock.com.)

Rica, Ecuador, El Salvador, Guatemala, Honduras, Jamaica, Mexico, Nicaragua and Panama."[*]

Drug trafficking operations have flourished online, especially in Darknet. Drugs can be bought and sold in Darknet on websites such as Silk Road 2.0, Atlantis, and BlackMarket Reloaded. These websites enable individuals to buy drugs anonymously anywhere in the world. The currency used for sites like these are Bitcoins.[†] The use of this currency and the anonymity afforded to users of Darknet has made the targeting of organized criminals online particularly challenging for authorities. Besides the Internet, common methods used to distribute drugs are vehicles, package delivery services, drug couriers on commercial aircrafts, and maritime cargo shipments. Drugs have also been trafficked through tunnels. For instance, the U.S. Immigration and Customs Enforcement

---

[*] "INTERPOL-Led Operation Targets Methamphetamine Production and Trafficking across Americas," Interpol, February 5, 2013, http://www.interpol.int/%C3%91%C3%A2%C3%A2en/layout/set/print/News-and-media/News-media-releases/2013/PR008.

[†] Bitcoins are a form of digital cryptocurrency; a peer-to-peer commodity. This means that no third-party involvement exists in money exchange; the money simply is moved between players' accounts. Marie-Helen Maras, *CRC Press Terrorism Reader* (Boca Raton, FL: CRC Press, 2013), 115.

Agency has found numerous tunnels used in the trafficking of drugs.* Traffickers have additionally used a variety of techniques to conceal drugs during transport, such as false compartments in vehicles or cargo containers. A case in point involved a Canadian, Robert Fox, who had concealed Ecstasy pills worth an estimated $7 million in a hidden compartment in the bed of his vehicle.† Marijuana has also been found in the United States concealed in a tractor-trailer that was carrying squash.‡

Countries' drug control strategies have included the destruction of drug manufacturing laboratories, aerial fumigations of drug crops, and alternative crop development. Consider, once again, operation Icebreaker. Clandestine laboratories manufacturing methamphetamines were destroyed during this operation. Aerial fumigations have also been proposed as a way to eradicate illicit crops. A case in point is Plan Colombia, which proposed aerial fumigations to eradicate coca cultivation. This practice has not been found to effectively limit coca cultivation. In Colombia, Bolivia, Peru, and other Andean countries in South America the coca shrub grows naturally. In the Andes, "coca is widely used…as a mild stimulant and herbal medicine."§ Accordingly, its use cannot be eradicated completely. In addition, fumigations tend to displace the coca cultivation to a different location. Moreover, aerial fumigations have been found to result in significant adverse economic, social and health consequences by damaging licit crops, exacerbating poverty, and harming the environment and the health of the affected population.¶ Finally, alternative

---

* Department of Homeland Security, "Written testimony of U.S. Immigration and Customs Enforcement Homeland Security Investigations Executive Associate Director James Dinkins for a House Committee on Homeland Security Subcommittee on Border and Maritime Security hearing titled 'Border Security Threats to the Homeland: DHS' Response to Innovative Tactics and Techniques,'" June 15, 2012, Homeland Security, https://www.dhs.gov/news/2012/06/15/written-testimony-us-immigration-customs-enforcement-house-homeland-security; Dianne Feinstein, "Border Tunnels: Working to Stop the Construction of Tunnels Used to Transport Drugs across the U.S.–Mexico Border," February 2012, http://www.feinstein.senate.gov/public/index.cfm/files/serve?File_id=0d0c6ec0-dc34-4ab6-b5f1-89f4742418e2.

† "ICE Probe Leads to Multi-Million Dollar Ecstasy Seizure: Agents Find Stash of Tablets and Cash Hidden in Bed of Tow Truck," U.S. Immigration and Customs Enforcement, May 21, 2009, http://www.ice.gov/news/releases/0905/090521sacramento.htm.

‡ "ICE Agents Thwart Nogales 1.75-Ton Marijuana Smuggling Attempt," U.S. Immigration and Customs Enforcement, February 10, 2010, http://www.ice.gov/news/releases/1002/100210nogales.htm.

§ Marilia Brocchetto, "Bolivia's Morales to UN: Legalize Coca-Leaf Chewing," CNN, March 13, 2012. http://www.cnn.com/2012/03/13/world/americas/bolivia-morales-coca/index.html.

¶ Morgane Landel, "Are Aerial Fumigations in the Context of the War in Colombia a Violation of the Rules of International Humanitarian Law?" Transnational Law and Contemporary Problems 19:2 (2010), 491–513; Connie Veillette and Jose E. Arvelo-Velez, "Colombia and Aerial Eradication of Drug Crops: U.S. Policy and Issues," Congressional Research Service, RL32052, August 28, 2003, http://www.hsdl.org/?view&did=451623.

crop development has been proposed and implemented to eliminate opium poppy and coca cultivation for illicit purposes. Alternative crop development seeks a legal sustainable socioeconomic alternative for those that harvested opium poppy and coca as their only source of income. Thailand's alternative crop (over the opium poppy) development program has been successful and those growing the alternative crops have increased as opposed to decreased their profits.[*]

WILDLIFE TRAFFICKING

Flora[†] and fauna[‡] trafficking (otherwise known as wildlife trafficking) refers to "the illegal trade, smuggling, poaching, capture or collection of endangered species, protected wildlife (including animals or plants that are subject to harvest quotas and regulated by permits), derivatives or products thereof."[§] According to TRAFFIC, a wildlife trade monitoring network, "[t]his can involve live animals and plants or a diverse range of products needed or prized by humans—including skins, medicinal ingredients, tourist curios, timber, fish and other food products."[¶] Live chimpanzees, turtles, tortoises, crocodiles, parrots, snow leopards, falcons, macaques, chameleons, and pangolions, among other species, have been trafficked (Figure 5.3). Additionally, "illegal elephant ivory, rhino horns, hippopotamus teeth, skins of leopards/zebras/cheetahs/pythons, turtle shells ... and other wild animal products are" traded in the black market.[**] For example, in 2012, an Interpol-led investigation, Operation Cage, seized "more than 8,700 birds and animals, including reptiles, mammals and insects."[††] Even though this "operation focused on the

---

[*] United States of America, General Accounting Office, "Drug Control: U.S. Supported Efforts in Burma, Pakistan and Thailand," *Report to the United States Congress* (Washington, DC: United States Government Printing Office, 1988); David Mansfield, "Alternative Development: The Modern Thrust of Supply Side Policy," UNODC, 1999, http://www.unodc.org/pdf/Alternative%20Development/AD_BulletinNarcotics.pdf; Coletta Youngers, "UN International Guiding Principles on Alternative Development," Transnational Institute, November 9, 2012, http://tnidrogas.org/en/weblog/item/4119-un-international-guiding-principles-on-alternative-development.

[†] Flora refers to plant species in a particular region.

[‡] Fauna refers to animal species in a particular region.

[§] Tanya Wyatt, "Exploring the Organization of Russia Far East's Illegal Wildlife Trade: Two Case Studies of the Illegal Fur and Illegal Falcon Trades," *Global Crime* 10:1 (2009), 145.

[¶] "Wildlife Trade: What Is It?" TRAFFIC, http://www.traffic.org/trade/.

[**] Eric Edroma, "Keynote Address: 9th Governing Council Meeting of the Parties to the Lusaka Agreement," Lusaka Agreement Task Force, October 8, 2008.

[††] "Thousands Arrested in INTERPOL Operation Targeting Illegal Trade in Birds," Interpol, July 25, 2012, http://www.interpol.int/%E2%80%8B@en/layout/set/print/News-and-media/News-media-releases/2012/PR059.

FIGURE 5.3   Wildlife smuggling—and trafficking in animals and animal parts—is an often underpublicized, but widespread problem. (Image
courtesy of Shutterstock.com.)

illegal trade of birds, a number of other fauna and flora were found,
including elephant ivory, turtles, fish and other live wildlife."[*]

Wildlife is trafficked for various reasons: food, fodder (i.e., feed for
livestock), fashion (e.g., leather and fur clothing), collections (e.g., individual private collections and museums), sport (e.g., falconry and trophy
hunting), healthcare (e.g., medicinal purposes), religion (e.g., animals
and plants and derivatives of them are used in religious rituals), fuel

---

[*] Ibid.

(e.g., wood for cooking), and building materials (e.g., timber to create furniture).* This form of trafficking has deleterious effects around the globe. Specifically, wildlife trafficking can lead to the destruction of eco-systems and increase the risk of human exposure to diseases associated with wildlife and plants being introduced into a new environment.

Drivers for Wildlife Trafficking

Unfortunately, while it is one of the top forms of trafficking, it is not accorded the attention it deserves and requires from law enforcement and criminal justice agents. Legislation and its enforcement have also been weak in most countries. The penalties for this crime are much less than for other forms of trafficking. Consider the Philippines. In the Philippines, Article 27(3) of the Republic Act of 1947, prohibits wild-life trading. If perpetrators are caught, they can face anywhere from 2 to 4 years of imprisonment. This sentence is significantly less than one would receive for other forms of trafficking, such as drug trafficking. For criminals, therefore, it is considered a low risk and high profit crime.

A main primary driver for wildlife trafficking is the lack of existing substantial punishment of those convicted of the crime. The penalties for this form of trafficking range from minimal to severe. For instance, in Kenya, the penalty for the possession of elephant meat is a small fine. In Tanzania, its possession can result in a maximum imprisonment of 7 years. Moreover, in Australia, the Environment Protection and Biodiversity Conservation Act of 1999, criminalizes the illegal impor-tation and exportation of wildlife and wildlife products and provides a maximum penalty for this crime of AUD 110,000 and/or 10 years imprisonment for individuals; corporations can receive a penalty of a AUD 500,000 fine.†

Like drugs, there is and will continue to be a demand for wildlife products. Wildlife products, such as rhino horns, tiger parts, and ele-phant ivory are sought by dealers, collectors, and the public in general. The more endangered a species is, the more demand exists for it. Also, certain wildlife and plant products are used for religious and medicinal purposes. For instance, tiger products are used in rituals and medicines in China and Africa. Specifically, tiger wine is used for medicinal pur-poses in Chinese medicine. Wildlife and plant products are also used for

---

* "Wildlife Trade: What Is It?" TRAFFIC, http://www.traffic.org/trade/.
† "Australia Takes on Role of Chair of CAWT," Coalition against Wildlife Trafficking, http://www.cawtglobal.org/australia/.

decorative purposes and good luck charms. Accordingly, it is for these reasons that the trafficking in these products is unlikely to subside. To counter the proliferation of products from endangered animals for religious or medical purposes, functionally equivalent alternatives to these products should be promoted. In order to determine the viability and sustainability of this option, further research in this area is required.

Those complicit in the exponential growth of wildlife trafficking include both industries and consumers. Chiru shawls (*shahtoosh*), which are made from endangered local antelopes in Tibet, are a sought after commodity by the wealthy. Indeed, the illicit fur trade is motivated by the wealthy who seek to purchase this type of fur for status. It is also motivated by the poor who either seek the fur for personal use or to obtain funds from its sale.[*] Poverty is thus also a driver for wildlife trafficking.

Another primary driver for the growth of wildlife trafficking is weak government institutions. Developing countries tend to be the greatest suppliers of flora and fauna. Developed countries tend to demand these products. The countries from which wildlife is trafficked have weak enforcement institutions and a general lack of commitment by custom and law enforcement agencies to combat this crime. Sometimes high-level officials cooperate with traffickers giving them unrestricted access to and from a country.

Weak state institutions facilitate corruption. Corruption also enables this form of trafficking; the same holds true for other forms of trafficking such as human, drug, and arms trafficking. For example, the former head of Peru's national intelligence and antinarcotics services was imprisoned for running international drug operations.[†] Furthermore, corrupt customs and border agents and government officials seize trafficked wildlife and derivatives thereof and either keep them for themselves or sell them.[‡] Other corrupt officials ignore trafficked wildlife and allow them to be transported to or through their territory for a fee.[§]

---

[*] Tanya Wyatt, "Exploring the Organization of Russia Far East's Illegal Wildlife Trade: Two Case Studies of the Illegal Fur and Illegal Falcon Trades." *Global Crime* 10:1 (2009).

[†] "Who is Vladimiro Montesinos?" *CNN*, November 22, 2000, http://news.bbc.co.uk/2/hi/americas/992770.stm; John R. Wagley, "Transnational Organized Crime: Principal Threats and U.S. Responses," *Congressional Research Service*, RL33335, March 20, 2006, 2, http://www.fas.org/sgp/crs/natsec/RL33335.pdf.

[‡] Charles W. Schmidt, "Environmental Crimes: Profiting at the Earth's Expense," *Environmental Health Perspectives* 112:2 (February 2004), A96–A103.

[§] Maira Martini, "Wildlife Crime and Corruption," Transparency International, February 15, 2013, http://www.transparency.org/whatwedo/answer/wildlife_crime_and_corruption.

International Laws and Initiatives

International law has been implemented to combat flora and fauna trafficking. Specifically, an international agreement between countries exists to protect endangered species of fauna and flora. This is known as the Convention on International Trade in Endangered Species of Wild Flora and Fauna (CITES) of 1973. CITES regulates the trade of wildlife in such a way that does not threaten its survival. There are 178 countries that are parties to this Convention.*

The United Nations has also promoted the creation of bilateral and multilateral agreements and initiatives in pursuit of the prevention, investigation, and prosecution of flora and fauna traffickers. For example, several UN Resolutions were passed (Resolutions 2001/12, 2002/18, and 2003/27) by the Economic and Social Council concerning the illicit trafficking in protected species of wildlife. Additionally, the UN Economic and Social Council passed Resolution 2008/25 concerning the "international cooperation in preventing and combating illicit international trafficking in forest products, including timber, wildlife and other forest biological resources." Finally, this Council passed Resolution 2011/36 on "crime prevention and criminal justice responses against illicit trafficking in endangered species of wild fauna and flora." The best practices of each country in combating wildlife trafficking should be shared between states.†

Enforcement of wildlife trafficking laws varies between states. This complicates efforts to combat the spread of wildlife trafficking. Police should also be informed and trained to recognize this form of trafficking. Such training has also been advocated by international agencies (e.g., Interpol). Education in wildlife trafficking is critical. Civil society should be educated as to the nature and extent of this form of trafficking and its consequences. They should also be informed of whom to contact in these instances.

Coordinated efforts are required not only for custom and border agents but also for domestic agencies tasked with the protection of wildlife (e.g., in the United States, this agency is the U.S. Fish and Wildlife Service of the Department of the Interior, which is primarily responsible for investigating wildlife trafficking). Even though national laws may exist, enforcement mechanisms may be weak, due, in part, to limited human and financial resources. Customs and border agents need to pay better attention to the documents that permit the transport of flora and

---

* See Convention on International Trade in Endangered Species of Wild Flora and Fauna, http://www.cites.org/eng/disc/parties/alphabet.php.
† Paragraph 14 of the Salvador Declaration.

fauna. Oftentimes, these documents are fraudulent and include incorrect information that is usually unverified. To combat this form of trafficking, therefore, documents for flora and fauna should only be issued by specific agencies and verified by them. Controlling the location and verification mechanisms for these documents can help reduce the number of instances in which flora and fauna are trafficked. To combat wildlife trafficking, antitrafficking laws, robust law enforcement violations, and an awareness campaign are also required.

A number of programs and initiatives have been implemented to combat this form of trafficking. The International Consortium on Combating Wildlife Crime (ICCWC) is one such example. It provides for coordination, support, and assistance in the investigation and prosecution of this form of trafficking. Another example is the Association of Southeast Asian Nations Wildlife Enforcement Network (ASEAN-WEN). ASEAN-WEN seeks to elevate the importance and frequency of the investigation and prosecution of wildlife trafficking to the same level as is occurring for other forms of trafficking such as drugs, arms, and human trafficking.

Specialized initiatives have additionally been implemented for certain endangered species. Consider tigers. Tigers are an endangered species. There are 13 countries in the world that have the few remaining tigers in the wild. These countries, known as the Tiger Range Countries are: Bangladesh, Bhutan, Cambodia, China, India, Indonesia, Lao People's Democratic Republic (Lao PDR), Malaysia, Myanmar, Nepal, Russia, Thailand, and Vietnam. There are certain initiatives that have been implemented dedicated to tigers. One such initiative is the Tiger Alive Initiative. This initiative was created by the World Wide Fund for Nature (previously known as the World Wildlife Fund) and seeks to prevent the further decline of wild tigers and double the number of tigers in the world.[*] Other endangered species have also fueled separate initiatives. A case in point is elephants. According to the United Nations Office on Drugs and Crime (UNODC) report, "[d]emand for ivory in Asia has fueled a rising rate of poaching in Eastern Africa, undermining the sustainability of the local elephant population."[†] In light of this, and other alarming trends concerning the dwindling elephant population, specialized programs such as the Monitoring the Illegal Killing of Elephants (MIKE) and the Elephant Trade Information System (ETIS) have been implemented to protect elephants. Interpol conducted an operation known as Project Web. This project revealed that ivory was the most

---

[*] World Wide Fund for Nature—China, "Tigers Alive," WWF, http://en.wwfchina.org/en/what_we_do/tigers_alive/.

[†] "Transnational Organized Crime in Eastern Africa: A Threat Assessment," UNODC, September 2013, http://www.unodc.org/documents/data-and-analysis/Studies/TOC_East_Africa_2013.pdf.

widely traded wildlife product on the Internet; here, sellers have few obligations to prove the legality of ivory.*

Specialized initiatives were also implemented to combat timber trafficking. In 2010, UNODC launched a program "in Indonesia promoting good governance, law enforcement and anti-corruption measures in areas affected by rampant illegal logging."† Timber trafficking can result in environmental degradation, deforestation, and habitat loss, all of which can result in species extinction and a significant loss of revenue by governments. Timber trafficking also poses particular challenges to authorities. When timber has been illegally harvested, it has to be subsequently processed to be sold. It is usually moved to countries where it is processed and then sold. It is extremely difficult to track this form of trafficking as illegally obtained timber can be mixed with legally obtained timber at logging mills and subsequently sold in the legal market. This is similar to what happens in the illicit fur trade; where illicitly obtained furs are mixed with legally obtained furs. Indeed, illegal and legal wildlife products are often sold side by side. For example, Interpol, in Operation Stocktake, found markets, restaurants, and shops from India, Indonesia, Malaysia, and Thailand, selling and trading in endangered wildlife along with legal products.‡

ARMS TRAFFICKING

The proliferation of arms is a pressing security threat. According to the UNODC, "firearms are high profit commodities."§ Firearms are long-lasting durable goods. In 1998, the United Nations Economic and Social Council passed Resolution 1998/18 concerning "measures to regulate firearms for the purpose of combating illicit trafficking in firearms." In 2001, the UN Protocol against the Illicit Manufacturing of and Trafficking in Firearms, Their Parts and Components and Ammunition, supplementing the United Nations Convention against Transnational Organized Crime (which entered into force in 2005) was implemented to "promote, facilitate and strengthen cooperation among States Parties in

---

* "Online Ivory Trade Worth Millions, INTERPOL Report Reveals," Interpol, March 7, 2013, http://www.interpol.int/News-and-media/News-media-releases/2013/PR029.
† "Wildlife and Forest Crimes," UNODC, https://www.unodc.org/unodc/en/wildlife-and-forest-crime/.
‡ "INTERPOL Leads Crackdown on Illegal Wildlife Markets in Asia," Interpol, December 19, 2011, http://www.interpol.int/News-and-media/News-media-releases/2011/N20111219.
§ "A Global Problem: Illicit Firearms as a Threat to Global Security," UNODC, (n.d.) http://www.unodc.org/unodc/en/firearms-protocol/introduction.html.

order to prevent, combat and eradicate the illicit manufacturing of and trafficking in firearms, their parts and components and ammunition."[*]

Regional measures on firearms have also been implemented. For instance, in 1997, the Inter-American Convention against the Illicit Manufacturing of and Trafficking in Firearms, Ammunition, Explosives, and Other Related Materials was created by the Organization of American States to combat the illegal manufacturing and trafficking of firearms, ammunition, and explosives. Likewise, Europe adopted several laws to combat illegal arms trafficking, including Council Directive 91/477/EEC[†] concerning the control of the acquisition and possession of weapons and its amendment by Directive 2008/51/EC.[‡]

The United Nations Programme of Action to Prevent, Combat and Eradicate the Illicit Trade in Small Arms and Light Weapons in All Its Aspects of 2001 (hereafter UN Programme) was implemented to supplement international legislation on firearms and specifically address small arms and light weapons. Small arms and light weapons (SALW) refer to "any man-portable lethal weapon that expels or launches, is designed to expel or launch, or may be readily converted to expel or launch a shot, bullet or projectile by the action of an explosive, excluding antique small arms and light weapons or their replicas."[§] The main difference between small arms and light weapons is that the former is intended for use by an individual (e.g., assault rifles), whereas the latter is designed for use by two or more persons (e.g., mortars and grenade launchers).[¶] In 2013, an Interpol-led operation, code named Usalama, revealed human, drugs, wildlife, and arms operations in Eastern and Southern Africa; among the weapons seized included AK-47s.[**]

The Council of the European Union implemented 2011/428/CFSP in support of the 2001 UN Programme. The 2001 UN Programme included recommendations for national legislation and control of small arms and light weapons, and regional and international cooperation and

---

[*] Article 2, UN Protocol against the Illicit Manufacturing of and Trafficking in Firearms, Their Parts and Components and Ammunition.

[†] Council Directive 91/477/EEC of 18 June 1991 on control of the acquisition and possession of weapons. OJ L 256.

[‡] Council Directive 2008/51/EC of the European Parliament and of the Council of 21 May 2008 amending Council Directive 91/477/EEC on control of the acquisition and possession of weapons OJ L 179.

[§] "The UN General Assembly Adopted the International Instrument to Enable States to Identify and Trace, in a Timely and Reliable Manner, Illicit Small Arms and Light Weapons of 2005," http://www.unodc.org/documents/organized-crime/Firearms/ITI.pdf.

[¶] "Small Arms and Light Weapons and Mine Action," NATO, http://www.nato.int/cps/ar/natolive/topics_52142.htm.

[**] "Human, Drugs and Arms Traffickers Targeted in Operations across Eastern and Southern Africa," Interpol, August 8, 2013, http://www.interpol.int/News-and-media/News-media-releases/2013/PR092.

assistance. In 2005, the UN General Assembly adopted the International Instrument to Enable States to Identify and Trace, in a Timely and Reliable Manner, Illicit Small Arms and Light Weapons to "promote and facilitate international cooperation and assistance in marking and tracing and to enhance the effectiveness of, and complement, existing bilateral, regional and international agreements to prevent, combat and eradicate the illicit trade in small arms and light weapons in all its aspects."[*]

The proliferation of small arms and light weapons contributes to the insecurity of a region. Social, economic, and political drivers (e.g., demand, high profit, and corruption) are responsible for the demand and spread of arms in a region. There is a large demand of arms in conflict regions. The illicit trafficking of small arms often contributes to conflicts in societies; these weapons are used by guerrillas, militants, insurgents, warlords, pirates, terrorists, gangs, and organized criminals. Even with arms embargoes in various countries imposed by the UN Security Council, arms are still reaching the above-mentioned individuals. The current situation of the global arms trade enables the free flow of arms around the world. To deal with the supply side of the arms trade, on April 2, 2013, the UN General Assembly adopted the Arms Trade Treaty. This multilateral treaty regulates the international trade of arms and seeks to prevent arms from being supplied to regions in conflict.[†] The Arms Trade Treaty promotes the creation of common international standards to regulate the international arms trade and the prevention of illicit arms trade (Article 1). As of June 2014, there are 118 signatories to the Treaty.[‡]

CIGARETTE TRAFFICKING

National and transnational criminals engage in cross-border trafficking of common goods such as cigarettes and oil to avoid taxation. Cigarette traffickers make cigarettes available at a low cost; thereby increasing consumption. The cigarettes sold on the black market are usually legal products. However, there have been instances where counterfeit cigarettes were trafficked.[§] For example, counterfeit cigarettes from China

---

[*] See the following for the full text of this: http://www.unodc.org/documents/organized-crime/Firearms/ITI.pdf.

[†] "The Arms Trade Treaty," United Nations Office of Disarmament Affairs, http://www.un.org/disarmament/ATT/.

[‡] "The Arms Trade Treaty," United Nations Office of Disarmament Affairs, http://www.un.org/disarmament/ATT/.

[§] European Anti-Fraud Office, "Cigarette Smuggling," European Commission, http://ec.europa.eu/anti_fraud/investigations/eu-revenue/cigarette_smuggling_en.htm.

were found in Germany. Germany was a transit country for the cigarette trafficking operation; these cigarettes were actually destined for
the United Kingdom, which imposes a higher tax rate on cigarettes than
other EU Member States.* Extremely high cigarette tax rates provide a
fertile ground for cigarette trafficking to grow.

Criminals gain great profits from this form of trafficking. A common tactic is to buy cigarettes in states (or countries) with low tobacco
taxes and sell them in states (or countries) with higher taxes. Cigarette
trafficking also occurs in the United States. The tobacco tax varies
between states. Virginia has the second lowest tobacco tax in the United
States. The Virginia State Crime Commission has reported that organized criminals can gain greater profits with cigarettes than with other
forms of trafficking, such as arms or drug trafficking.† Moreover, the
penalties for cigarette trafficking are significantly less than one would
receive for drug trafficking. For example, pursuant to 18 U.S.C. § 2344,
a 5-year maximum sentence is given to those who engage in cigarette
trafficking; whereas those who engage in heroin trafficking receive
life imprisonment.

Cigarette traffickers have been known to hijack cigarettes during
transport and steal cigarettes at warehouses or other facilities that store
them. Another way to engage in cigarette trafficking is through mail
and/or the Internet; however, national laws have been implemented to
combat cigarette trafficking through these forums.‡ Whatever means
that cigarette traffickers use, one thing remains certain: the illicit trade
of cigarettes has significant consequences for a region.

The drivers of this form of trafficking are the demand for cigarettes,
the high costs and taxes on cigarettes in certain countries, and corruption. With respect to the latter, this form of illicit trade helps establish
an environment of corruption that becomes endemic in societies, businesses, and governments. Indeed, businesses and government officials
have been found to be complicit in cigarette trafficking.§ For instance,
in Greece, corrupt public officials, such as police officers and customs

---

* Klaus von Lampe, "The Trafficking in Untaxed Cigarettes in Germany: A Case Study
  of the Social Embeddedness of Illegal Markets," In Petrus C. van Duyne, Klaus von
  Lampe, Nikos Passas, *Upperworld and Underworld in Cross-Border Crime* (Nijmegen:
  Wolf Legal Publishers, 2002), 142.
† "Cigarette Smuggling: The Urge to Smurf," *The Economist*, November 24, 2012,
  http://www.economist.com/news/united-states/21567111-when-government-gets-
  greedy-some-people-turn-crime-urge-smurf.
‡ See, for example, the U.S. Prevent All Cigarette Trafficking (PACT) Act of 2010.
§ Wolfram Lacher, "Organized Crime and Conflict in the Sahel-Sahara Region," Carnegie
  Endowment for International Peace, September 13, 2012, http://carnegieendowment.
  org/2012/09/13/organized-crime-and-conflict-in-sahel-sahara-region/dtjm; Georgios
  A. Antonopoulos, "Interviewing Retired Cigarette Smugglers," *Trends in Organized
  Crime* 11:1 (2008), 70–81.

agents, allow the importation of such illicit goods for a fee or exploit their position demanding fees to allow the goods into their country. Corruption also plays a significant role in oil trafficking. Similarly to cigarette smuggling, inexpensive oil is purchased from one country and sold in another for large profit.[*]

TRAFFICKING IN PRECIOUS METALS AND GEMSTONES

Precious metals (e.g., gold and silver) are trafficked and have been used to fund other transnational criminal activities, such as arms trafficking. Among existing precious metals, gold is the most valuable and sought after commodity. Indeed, a main driver for gold trafficking is the value of gold. The second is the ease with which illegally obtained gold can be introduced into the legitimate market.[†] To combat the trafficking of precious metals, an educational awareness campaign is required. Additionally, vulnerabilities to this form of trafficking should be identified and assessed.

Like precious metals, gemstones have also been sold to fund other trafficking activities. Gemstones (e.g., diamonds, sapphires, emeralds, etc.) are lightweight, portable, and easy to transport (Figure 5.4). Diamonds and colored gemstones are both primarily mined in developing countries and regions that are politically unstable. Like other forms of trafficking, drivers include political instability and corruption. For instance, Zimbabwe's army was accused of trafficking diamonds from Zimbabwe to Mozambique.[‡]

Colored gemstones do not compete with diamonds in terms of cost. Indeed, diamonds are much more valuable. Illicitly obtained diamonds are introduced into the legal trade; this occurs because the origin of diamonds cannot be determined. One way in which such diamonds enter into the legal market is through cutting and polishing centers. Diamonds are virtually untraceable. Any pre-existing identifiable marks can be easily erased once diamonds are cut and polished. To combat the trade of illicit diamonds in legitimate international commerce, systems to identify the origins of diamonds have been implemented.[§]

---

[*] "Energy Subsidy Reform: Lessons and Implications," International Monetary Fund, January 28, 2013, http://www.imf.org/external/np/pp/eng/2013/012813.pdf; Oil trafficking is explored further in Chapter 12 of this volume.

[†] R. T. Naylor, "The Underworld of Gold," *Crime, Law and Social Change* 25:3 (1996), 191.

[‡] Celia W. Dugger, "Africa's Diamond Trade under Scrutiny," *New York Times*, November 3, 2009, http://www.nytimes.com/2009/11/04/world/africa/04zimbabwe.html.

[§] Nicolas Cook, "Diamonds and Conflict: Background, Policy, and Legislation," *Congressional Research Service*, RL30751, July 16, 2003, 14, http://royce.house.gov/uploadedfiles/rl30751.pdf.

FIGURE 5.4   Gemstones are trafficked because they are easily moved and transported. (Image courtesy of Shutterstock.com.)

Conflict (or blood) diamonds is a term used to describe diamonds that are mined in areas that are in armed conflict (e.g., war). These diamonds are used to finance the conflict in the area. Diamonds have been used to fund brutal wars (e.g., Angola, Democratic Republic of Congo, Liberia, and Sierra Leone).[*] To combat the spread of conflict diamonds, the Kimberley Process Certification Scheme (KPCS) of 2003, a joint government, industry, and civil society initiative, was implemented.[†] The KPCS is a form of self-policing for the international diamond trade community. KPC establishes standards to certify the origin of diamonds. In addition to international efforts, domestically, the United States passed the Clean Diamond Trade Act of 2003 to stop the trade of conflict diamonds.

CULTURAL PROPERTY TRAFFICKING

The United Nations Educational, Scientific and Cultural Organization (UNESCO) Convention on the Means of Prohibiting and Preventing the

[*] Nicolas Cook, "Diamonds and Conflict: Background, Policy, and Legislation," *Congressional Research Service*, RL30751, July 16, 2003, 2, http://royce.house.gov/uploadedfiles/rl30751.pdf.
[†] The Kimberley Process, http://www.kimberleyprocess.com/.

Illicit Import, Export and Transfer of Ownership of Cultural Property of 1970 (which entered into force in 1972) defined cultural property as "property which, on religious or secular grounds, is specifically designated by each State as being of importance for archaeology, prehistory, history, literature, art or science" (Article 1). Cultural property has also been trafficked through the Internet. The authenticity of cultural property sold online cannot be established with certainty; forgeries are also sold.*

Apart from the protection of cultural property, the UNESCO Convention on the Protection of the Underwater Cultural Heritage of 2001 was implemented to protect underwater cultural heritage, which refers to "all traces of human existence having a cultural, historical or archaeological character which have been partially or totally under water, periodically or continuously, for at least 100 years."† Subsequently, the UNESCO Convention for the Safeguarding of the Intangible Cultural Heritage of 2003 was adopted to protect another form of cultural heritage, intangible cultural heritage. Intangible cultural heritage refers to

> the practices, representations, expressions, knowledge, skills—as well as the instruments, objects, artefacts and cultural spaces associated therewith—that communities, groups and, in some cases, individuals recognize as part of their cultural heritage. This intangible cultural heritage, transmitted from generation to generation, is constantly recreated by communities and groups in response to their environment, their interaction with nature and their history, and provides them with a sense of identity and continuity, thus promoting respect for cultural diversity and human creativity.

Moreover, UNESCO adopted the Convention on the Protection and Promotion of the Diversity of Cultural Expressions of 2005 to protect and promote the development, distribution, access to, and enjoyment of expressions of "creativity of individuals, groups and societies...that have a cultural content."

Countries prohibit the removal of cultural property from their territories. Consequently, cultural property that has been removed from countries enters the legitimate market through illegal means.‡ False documents, corrupt officials, and complicit art dealers, museums, and

---

* "Basic Actions Concerning Cultural Objects Being Offered for Sale over the Internet," UNESCO, http://www.unesco.org/new/fileadmin/MULTIMEDIA/HQ/CLT/pdf/basic-actions-cultural-objects-for-sale_en.pdf.
† Article 1(1), UNESCO Convention on the Protection of the Underwater Cultural Heritage of 2001.
‡ Kenneth Polk, "Whither Criminology in the Study of the Traffic in Illicit Antiquities?" In Simon Mackenzie and Penny Green (Eds.), *Criminology and Archaeology: Studies in Looted Antiquities* (Oxford: Hart Publishing, 2009).

auction houses enable the trafficking of cultural property.* For example, U.S. authorities discovered that antiquity dealers and collectors from the United States and the United Arab Emirates were involved in the trafficking of cultural property that was stolen from Egypt.† Drivers for this form of trafficking are political instability and high demand for cultural property and cultural heritage. Indeed, wealthy collectors drive up demand for these products. Items are sold for extremely high prices and thus those who purchase these items are from the most prominent socio-economic status.‡ Unlike other forms of trafficking, what is being trafficked here is fragile and scarce.§

CONCLUDING THOUGHTS

Transnational organized crime flourishes in countries where citizens have limited economic alternatives and governments are unable to effectively provide for their citizens through economic and social services.¶ Transnational organized crime also flourishes in countries where government institutions are weak and ineffective because corruption runs rampant in these countries and in the institutions of these countries. Given that corruption plays a major role in the proliferation of transnational organized crime, good governance should be promoted, and legitimate political and legal conduct should be advocated. Cooperative mechanisms should additionally be put in place to prevent, counter, control, and diminish corruption.

Countries ought to adopt legislation and measures (if they are not already in place) to seize illicit proceeds from traffickers. These seizures should be widely publicized to send the message to traffickers that they will be punished for their crimes. Significant penalties need to be given

---

* Neil Brodie, Jenny Doole, and Peter Watson, *Stealing History: The Illicit Trade in Cultural Material* (Cambridge: The McDonald Institute for Archaeological Research, 2000), http://www.stanford.edu/group/chr/stealinghistory.pdf.

† ICE, "ICE Makes Arrests and Seizes Cultural Artifacts Stolen from Egypt: Set of Sarcophagi More Than 2,000 Years Old," U.S. Immigration and Customs Enforcement, July 14, 2011, http://www.ice.gov/news/releases/1107/110714newyork.htm.

‡ Christine Alder and Kenneth Polk, "Stopping This Awful Business: The Illicit Traffic in Antiquities Examined as a Criminal Market," *Art, Antiquity, & Law* 7:1 (2002), 35–53; Blythe A. Bowman, "Transnational Crimes against Culture: Looting at Archaeological Sites and the 'Grey' Market in Antiquities," *Journal of Contemporary Criminal Justice* 24:3 (2008), 226.

§ An exception to this are certain wildlife and wildlife products that are also scarce. David C. Lane, David G. Bromley, Robert D. Hicks, and John S. Mahoney, "Time Crime: The Transnational Organization of Art and Antiquities Theft," *Journal of Contemporary Criminal Justice* 24:3 (2008), 254.

¶ It is important to note that countries that do not have limited economic alternatives and weak/ineffective institutions also suffer from transnational organized crime.

to those who engage in trafficking; irrespective of the type of trafficking committed. To combat all forms of trafficking: the drivers of these crimes should be identified; the nature and extent of these crimes should be known; existing measures should be strengthened; and recommendations on bolstering existing measures to prevent it should be promoted. States alone cannot combat transnational organized crime. A coordinated international response is required. More specifically, inter- or multi-jurisdiction cooperation is required between governments, international agencies, national and international law enforcement agencies, national and international regulatory agencies, private sector companies, and nongovernmental organizations, in the investigation and prosecution of transnational organized criminals.

National data on instances of transnational organized crime should be maintained. This can assist authorities in understanding patterns of these threats and perpetrators; thereby enabling early detection and more effective prevention of these threats. The existence of such data would further enable more complete information sharing at the national and international level. Information sharing is critical to improving intelligence on transnational organized criminals, the structure of their groups or networks, important individuals within the groups or networks, their methods of operation, and the routes they use.

Predominantly, the emphasis of legislation and enforcement mechanisms are on the supply side of trafficking. Demand is responsible for the exponential expansion and growth of all forms of trafficking. Without demand for the items, products, animals, or persons trafficked, transnational organized crime would not survive. Education is thus critical. Governments, businesses, and civil society should be educated as to the nature and extent of different types of trafficking and their devastating consequences. To accomplish this, powerful domestic and international awareness campaigns are required.

CHAPTER 6

Cybersecurity

Technology and the Internet provide cybercriminals with access to individuals, organizations, and companies around the world. The reach of cybercrime challenges conventional notions of jurisdiction, making the targeting of cybercriminals particularly challenging for authorities. This chapter seeks to enter into the complex world of cybercrime by exploring its evolution and critically evaluating the cybersecurity measures needed to combat it. To do so, it first examines cybercrime. It then explores existing cybersecurity efforts and those required to effectively counter this threat. Finally, recommendations are provided on ways to deal with cybercrime more effectively.

COMMITTING CYBERCRIME

For a cybercrime to be committed, the Internet, computers, and/or related technology must be used in the commission of the illicit activity. Cybercrime is not limited by traditional physical and geographical boundaries. Cybercriminals can engage in illegal activities on a far broader scale, reaching targets all over the world. The exponential expansion of the Internet, computers, and related technologies yielded a variety of new crimes and provided cybercriminals with new and more efficient means with which to conduct traditional illicit activities.

New crimes are specifically designed to target computers, smartphones, and similar devices, and would not have been possible without the advent of the Internet, computers, and related technologies (Figure 6.1). With these cybercrimes, a perpetrator attempts to steal information from, cause damage to, and/or gain unauthorized access into a computer system or related device. When individuals gain unauthorized access to a computer or related system this is known as hacking. A perpetrator may also attempt to bombard a system with phony authentication requests to prevent legitimate users from accessing a site (this process is known as a denial of service attack). A perpetrator may further attempt to write and/or distribute malicious code (or malware).

FIGURE 6.1 With the advent of the Internet, computers, and related technologies, new crimes are specifically designed to target computers, smartphones, and similar devices. (Image courtesy of Shutterstock.com.)

Examples of malware include (but are not limited to): computer viruses,[*] worms,[†] and Trojan horses.[‡] Moreover, a perpetrator can engage in computer hijacking. This occurs when a perpetrator gains control over a user's computer (or users' computers) with malicious code (i.e., bot code). In addition to new crimes committed, cybercriminals have found a new forum to commit traditional crimes. Here, computers and related technology could be used in the commission of a crime. These crimes include traditional crimes, such as extortion, harassment, and fraud.

---

[*] A computer virus is "a software program that is designed to spread, through user activity, to other computers and to damage or disrupt a computer, by attaching itself (or piggybacking) on files or programs." Marie-Helen Maras, *Computer Forensics: Cybercriminals, Laws and Evidence* (Second Edition) (Burlington, MA: Jones & Bartlett, 2014), 8.

[†] A computer worm is "a type of malware that does not need to piggyback on a file or program to replicate itself or require user activity to make copies of itself and spread." Marie-Helen Maras, *Computer Forensics: Cybercriminals, Laws and Evidence* (Second Edition) (Burlington, MA: Jones & Bartlett, 2014), 9.

[‡] A Trojan Horse is "a type of malware that tricks the computer user into thinking that it is legitimate software, but actually contains hidden functions. When the computer user downloads and installs the program, these hidden functions are executed along with the software." Marie-Helen Maras, *Computer Forensics: Cybercriminals, Laws and Evidence* (Second Edition) (Burlington, MA: Jones & Bartlett, 2014), 9.

Irrespective of whether it is an old or new illicit activity, cybercrime is currently considered the greatest economic and national security threat facing the United States.* Other countries around the world also consider cybercrime as a top security concern.†

DESPERATELY SEEKING CYBERSECURITY

The International Telecommunication Union (ITU) defines cybersecurity as the "[c]ollection of tools, policies, security concepts, security safeguards, guidelines, risk management approaches, actions, training, best practices, assurance and technologies that can be used to protect the cyber environment and organization and user's assets."‡ Cybersecurity seeks to detect, deter, protect, and defend against threats. Cybercriminals exploit vulnerabilities in computer systems and related technologies. These vulnerabilities are made possible due to the interconnectedness of systems. When systems are interconnected, the security of one system is directly impacted by the security of another system. Connections between stronger and weaker systems, therefore, expose the stronger systems to vulnerabilities. Moreover, the more information is available online and the more interconnected systems are, the greater the likelihood that cybercriminals will exploit these vulnerabilities. Finding ways to deal with these vulnerabilities is at the forefront of national security policy.

U.S. President Barack Obama's Cyberspace Policy Review built upon President George W. Bush's Comprehensive National Cybersecurity Initiative enshrined in National Security Presidential Directive 54/ Homeland Security Presidential Directive 23 (NSPD-54/HSPD-23). The recommendations of the Cyberspace Policy Review included: creating an organized and unified response to cybersecurity threats; improving public–private partnerships; engaging in cybersecurity capacity building; and promoting cybersecurity public awareness and education.§ Each

---

* The White House, President Barack Obama, "The Comprehensive National Cybersecurity Initiative," The White House, http://www.whitehouse.gov/issues/foreign-policy/cybersecurity/national-initiative; Ken Dilanian, "Cyber-Crime Tops Threats to U.S., Intelligence Chief Says," *Los Angeles Times*, March 12, 2013, http://articles.latimes.com/2013/mar/12/news/la-pn-cybercrime-threat-20130312; Elise Ackerman, "Secretary of Homeland Security: Cybercrime as Big a Threat as Al Qaeda," *Forbes*, June 3, 2012, http://www.forbes.com/sites/eliseackerman/2012/06/03/secretary-of-homeland-security-cybercrime-as-big-a-threat-as-al-qaeda/.

† For example, for the UK, see *BBC News*, "Cyber-Attacks and Terrorism Head Threats Facing UK," October 18, 2010, http://www.bbc.co.uk/news/uk-11562969.

‡ "Definition of Cybersecurity," International Telecommunication Union (ITU), http://www.itu.int/en/ITU-T/studygroups/com17/Pages/cybersecurity.aspx.

§ The White House, President Barack Obama, "The Comprehensive National Cybersecurity Initiative," The White House, http://www.whitehouse.gov/issues/foreign-policy/cybersecurity/national-initiative.

of these recommendations are explored individually to determine what, if any, measures have been taken to achieve these objectives, and to critically evaluate the efficacy of these measures in achieving their objectives.

United and Structured Cybersecurity Response

Governance consists of "the coordinated management and regulation of issues by multiple and separate authorities, the interventions of both public and private actors (depending upon the issue), formal and informal arrangements, in turn structured by discourse and norms, and purposefully directed toward particular policy outcomes."[*] To achieve effective governance, centralized coordination of cybersecurity initiatives is required. Currently, cybersecurity standards vary by agency. They are designed to fit an agency's requirements and mission. This fails to consider overarching national needs and leads to an overlap of resource usage.

Cybersecurity requires effective governance both at the national and international level. Nationally, there are numerous agencies that are responsible for some facet of cybersecurity. Specifically, under the U.S. Computer Security Act of 1987, the National Bureau of Standards (NBS), now known as the National Institute of Standards and Technology (NIST), is responsible for establishing federal computer security standards; with the exception of those used for intelligence and defense.

The National Security Agency (NSA) is the primary agency for cybersecurity in the national security sector and the U.S. Cyber Command is the primary agency for cybersecurity in the defense sector. With respect to the latter, cyberspace was added to the military domain, joining land, sea, air, and space. The mission of the United States Cyber Command (USCYBERCOM) is to "prepare to, and when directed, conduct full spectrum military cyberspace operations in order to enable actions in all domains, ensure US/Allied freedom of action in cyberspace and deny the same to our adversaries."[†] USCYBERCOM is responsible for "designing the cyber force structure, training requirements and certification standards that will enable the Services to build the cyber force required to execute our assigned missions."[‡] The Armed Services components of USCYBERCOM are: Air Forces Cyber (AFCYBER); Army Cyber Command (ARCYBER); Fleet Cyber Command (FLTCYBERCOM), and Marine Forces Cyber Command (MARFORCYBER).[§]

---

[*] Mark Webber, Stuart Croft, Jolyon Howorth, Terry Terriff, and Elke Krahmann, "The Governance of European Security," *Review of International Studies* 30:1 (2004), 4.

[†] U.S. Cyber Command," U.S. Strategic Command, August 2013, http://www.stratcom.mil/factsheets/Cyber_Command/.

[‡] Ibid.

[§] Ibid.

In 2002, NIST responsibilities were strengthened with the Federal Information Security Management Act. That same year, the Cyber Security Research and Development Act of 2002 authorized appropriations to the NIST and the National Science Foundation for cybersecurity research. Additionally, Executive Order 13636, passed on February 12, 2013, called on the NIST to develop a cybersecurity framework and a set of best practices for protecting critical infrastructure.

Moreover, the Homeland Security Act of 2002 provided some cybersecurity responsibilities to the Department of Homeland Security (DHS). For example, the Immigration and Customs Enforcement (ICE) Homeland Security Investigations (HSI) investigates cybercrime, among other illicit activities.[*] The Cyber Crimes Center (C3) of HSI, which is made up of three units (the Cyber Crimes Unit, the Computer Forensics Unit, and the Child Exploitation Investigations Unit), provides support, training, and other services to domestic and international law enforcement agencies.[†] Furthermore, the Computer Crime and Intellectual Property Section (CCIPS) of the Department of Justice (DOJ) "is responsible for implementing the Department's national strategies in combating computer and intellectual property crimes worldwide. CCIPS prevents, investigates, and prosecutes computer crimes by working with other government agencies, the private sector, academic institutions, and foreign counterparts."[‡]

One of the greatest challenges that exists is the coordination of efforts between the DOJ, DHS, and the Department of Defense (DOD). To deal with this issue, the 2008 Comprehensive National Cybersecurity Initiative (CNCI) called for the National Cyber Investigative Joint Task Force (NCIJTF), a Federal Bureau of Investigation (FBI)-led, multi-agency task force, to serve as a national focal point for government agencies to share intelligence and coordinate cybersecurity investigations.[§] Effective governance and coordination can be achieved with a single coordination center for cybersecurity. A similar focal point was developed in the European Union. In particular, the European Commission established the European Cybercrime Centre (EC3) in January 2013 at Europol. Like the NCIJTF, EC3 serves as the main focal point in the region to share intelligence, cooperate among agencies, and coordinate

---

[*] "Homeland Security Investigations," U.S. Immigration and Customs Enforcement (ICE), http://www.ice.gov/about/offices/homeland-security-investigations/.

[†] "Investigations: Cyber Crimes Center," U.S. Immigration and Customs Enforcement (ICE), http://www.ice.gov/cyber-crimes/.

[‡] "Computer Crime and Intellectual Property Section (CCIPS)," U.S. Department of Justice (DOJ), http://www.justice.gov/criminal/cybercrime/about/.

[§] See National Security Presidential Directive 54/Homeland Security Presidential Directive 23 (NSPD-54/HSPD-23; "National Cyber Investigative Joint Task Force," Federal Bureau of Investigation (FBI), (n.d.), http://www.fbi.gov/about-us/investigate/cyber/ncijtf.

investigations.* Such cooperation and coordination also depends on the existence of an adequate legal system that can adapt to evolving cyber-crime threats.

International Governance of Cyberspace

The development, use, and protection of the Internet is a multifaceted, complex process. A question often asked is: can a single body be responsible for international Internet governance and universal information policies be implemented? One main barrier to creating universal Internet governance is the requirement of all countries to accept one set of global information policies that cover cultural, social, economic, and legal issues.† However, countries differ significantly in these areas. Accordingly, for different cultures to share the same information policies is impractical. Consider the United States and Brazil. The United States provides a domain that violates cultural norms in Brazil; that is, the .xxx domain, which houses pornographic websites.‡ Countries also tend to disagree on social issues such as freedom of speech, freedom of the press, and privacy. A case in point is China. China is a collectivist society and places the welfare of the state above the rights of the people.§ Additionally, censorship is a common practice in China; here, individuals are unable to speak unfavorably about their government for fear of repercussions for doing so. Accordingly, it is extremely difficult for countries to attain global consensus on social issues.

In addition to cultural and social barriers, economic barriers also exist. Specifically, countries may not be financially capable of implementing universal information policies. Lastly, legal barriers inhibit the development of a single international Internet governance body and universal information policies. Take, for instance, countries that follow religious laws. These countries would not be willing to accept information policies of Western countries that conflict with their religious laws.¶

---

* "EC3, 2013," Europol, https://www.europol.europa.eu/ec3.

† Andrew Whitmore, Namjoo Choi, and Anna Arzrumtsyan, "One Size Fits All? On the Feasibility of International Internet Governance," *Journal of Information Technology & Politics* 6:1 (2009), 7–8.

‡ Declan McCullagh, "Will the U.N. Run the Internet?" *CNET*, last modified July 11, 2005, http://news.cnet.com/Will-the-U.N.-run-the-Internet/2010-1071_3-5780157.html; Andrew Whitmore, Namjoo Choi, and Anna Arzrumtsyan, "One Size Fits All? On the Feasibility of International Internet Governance," *Journal of Information Technology & Politics* 6:1 (2009), 8.

§ Andrew Whitmore, Namjoo Choi, and Anna Arzrumtsyan, "One Size Fits All? On the Feasibility of International Internet Governance," *Journal of Information Technology & Politics* 6:1 (2009), 9.

¶ Patrick, H. Glenn, *Legal Traditions of the World: Sustainable Diversity of Law* (New York: Oxford University Press, 2000); Andrew Whitmore, Namjoo Choi, and Anna Arzrumtsyan, "One Size Fits All? On the Feasibility of International Internet Governance," *Journal of Information Technology & Politics* 6:1 (2009), 9.

Therefore, differing legal traditions play a major role in the current lack of a single, universal Internet governance body. Despite all of these obstacles, a unified and structured response to cybercrime is possible and could be achieved through the harmonization of cybercrime laws between countries and the effective enforcement of these laws.

Cyberspace: The Current Legal Landscape

A legal framework is required for international cooperation in pursuing and prosecuting cybercrimes that transcend international borders. Because of its universal reach, countries cannot effectively deal with cybercrime unless all countries have adequate cybercrime laws. The "I LOVE YOU" computer virus brought home this lesson.[*] This computer virus spread across Asia, Europe, and the United States, causing billions of dollars in damages.[†] Specifically, the creator of the computer virus, Onel de Guzman, a resident of the Philippines, was not prosecuted because his country did not have a cybercrime law criminalizing his behaviors. While Guzman's actions were considered illegal in other countries, he could not be prosecuted in the Philippines nor extradited to another country for prosecution because he had not committed a crime in his own country (given the absence of legislation).

A unified and structured response to cybercrime requires the existence of harmonized cybercrime laws on the national and international level; that is, national cybercrime law should be harmonized with international laws, conventions, and treaties. The harmonization of laws makes the prosecution of cybercriminals possible and eliminates cybercrime safe havens. It is also needed for the extradition of cyber-criminals and the enforcement of countries' mutual legal assistance treaties in cybercrime cases. Indeed, several extradition treaties between countries exist (e.g., U.S./UK Extradition Treaty of 2003). These treaties apply to activities that are considered crimes in the countries that agree to arrest and/or extradite individuals to each other. Mutual legal assistance treaties apply to an agreed upon list of crimes between the respective countries that require each country to assist the other with,

---

[*] How did the I LOVE YOU computer virus work? "The virus hid itself within an e-mail message titled 'I LOVE YOU.' When an individual opened the email, the virus would spread by sending itself to every name in the individual's address book if the computer ran Microsoft Outlook's computer program. For those who opened the e-mail, the computer virus destroyed stored music and picture files on the user's computer and replaced each with a copy of the virus and rerouted users seeking to access websites via Internet Explorer to predetermined sites that contained a program that would scan the individual's computer for usernames and passwords." Marie-Helen Maras, *Computer Forensics: Cybercriminals, Laws and Evidence* (Second Edition) (Burlington, MA: Jones & Bartlett, 2014), 10.

[†] Marie-Helen Maras, *Computer Forensics: Cybercriminals, Laws and Evidence* (Second Edition) (Burlington, MA: Jones & Bartlett, 2014), 10.

for instance, the provision of information on and evidence of the listed crimes. Dual criminality, which necessitates that an illicit activity be considered a crime in both countries, serves as the basis for mutual legal assistance and extradition treaties, and is an essential requirement for countries to cooperate in cybercrime investigations.

Several international and regional agreements were also created to establish principles for international cooperation. Examples of such agreements include: the 2013 African Union Draft Convention on the Confidence and Security in Cyberspace; the 2010 League of Arab States, the Arab Convention on Combating Information Technology Offences; the 2001 Commonwealth of Independent States Agreement on Cooperation in Combating Offences related to Computer Information (Commonwealth of Independent States Agreement); and the 2001 Council of Europe's Convention on Cybercrime (hereafter Budapest Convention). The latter, the Budapest Convention, was introduced on November 23, 2001, and entered into force in 2004. The Budapest Convention broke down cybercrime offenses into four main categories: fraud and forgery; child pornography; copyright infringement (i.e., intellectual property theft); and system interferences. It also adopted a set of tools and powers to enable the effective investigation of cybercrimes and establish strong mechanisms that foster international cooperation. The main objective of this Convention was to eliminate procedural and jurisdictional obstacles that serve as a barrier to conducting efficient and effective international cybercrime investigations. While it has taken steps in this regard, there are still certain barriers to effective cooperation in and coordination of cybercrime investigations; especially given the fact that not all countries are signatories to this Convention (see Tables 6.1 and 6.2). For instance, China and Russia, are not signatories. China and Russia, however, are signatories to other agreements, such as the 2009 Shanghai Cooperation Organization Agreement on Cooperation in the Field of Information Security.*

International cooperation in cybercrime investigations are further complicated due to the divergence in countries' membership in bilateral and multilateral agreements. Some countries have the necessary powers and procedures to cooperate between countries; other countries, however, do not. When such membership does not exist, mutual legal assistance channels are unavailable; as such, these countries are unable (or unwilling) to respond to cooperation requests. By contrast, countries that have these agreements cooperate in cybercrime investigations;

---

* The Shanghai Cooperation Organization is composed of China, Russia, Kazakhstan, Kyrgyzstan, Tajikistan, and Uzbekistan. Alica Kizekova, "The Shanghai Cooperation Organisation: Challenges in Cyberspace," S. Rajaratnam School of International Studies, Nanyang Technological University, No. 033/2012, last modified February 22, 2012, http://www.rsis.edu.sg/publications/Perspective/RSIS0332012.pdf.

TABLE 6.1   Signatories That Are Member States of the Council
of Europe

Albania	Belgium	Czech Republic
Georgia	Ireland	Luxembourg
Netherlands	Serbia	Switzerland
Andorra	Bosnia and Herzegovina	Denmark
Germany	Italy	Malta
Norway	Slovakia	The Former Yugoslav Republic of Macedonia
Armenia	Bulgaria	Estonia
Greece	Latvia	Moldova
Poland	Slovenia	Turkey
Austria	Croatia	Finland
Hungary	Liechtenstein	Monaco
Portugal	Spain	Ukraine
Azerbaijan	Cyprus	France
Iceland	Lithuania	Montenegro
Romania	Sweden	United Kingdom

Source: Council of Europe, 2001 Convention on Cybercrime, CETS No. 185,
Council of Europe, Entry into Force: 2004, http://conventions.coe.int/
Treaty/Commun/print/ChercheSig.asp?NT=185&CL=ENG.

TABLE 6.2   Nonmembers of the Council of Europe

Signatories to Budapest Convention	**Acceded Budapest Convention**
Canada	Australia
Japan	Dominican Republic
South Africa	Mauritius
United States of America	

Source: Council of Europe, 2001 Convention on Cybercrime, CETS No. 185,
Council of Europe, Entry into Force: 2004, http://conventions.coe.int/
Treaty/Commun/print/ChercheSig.asp?NT=185&CL=ENG.

yet this cooperation is not without problems. For instance, there is no
time requirement when cooperative requests are made; namely, countries are not required to respond to requests nor are such requests time
sensitive. Nonetheless, given the nature of cybercrime investigations,
in general, and electronic evidence, in particular, time is of critical
importance. Particularly, due to the volatile nature of electronic evidence, international cooperation requires timely responses to requests

for information. Currently, response times for information sharing often take months, and not minutes; this unnecessarily impedes cybercrime investigations and the prosecution of cybercriminals. Notwithstanding, urgent channels for mutual legal assistance requests exist in certain countries. The impact of using these channels on the response times, however, remains unclear.[*]

Another issue that adversely impacts response times in cybercrime investigations is cybercrime's relative importance with respect to other crimes (e.g., murder); this varies by country. Moreover, even between different types of cybercrime, priority is assigned. Certain economic cybercrimes are usually not considered of great importance (e.g., fraud; unless it is committed on a large scale). These cybercrimes are traditionally given lower priority than other cybercrimes (e.g., child exploitation online) when calls requesting assistance in cybercrime investigations are made. Furthermore, investigators often have to contact law enforcement and other agencies in different parts of the world at inconvenient times. Accordingly, it is very difficult to arrange times when all parties involved could come together. What's more, documents that have been obtained in different countries may have to be translated. This can cause not only significant delays in response times but also cost the requesting country a substantial amount of money. This is particularly problematic for developing countries that lack the necessary funds.

Presently, formal and informal information sharing mechanisms are used to facilitate cooperation. Nonetheless, these information sharing mechanisms do not exist in every country. Consider formal information sharing mechanisms. If they do exist, they are the result of multilateral agreements, bilateral agreements, and mutual legal assistance treaties (discussed earlier). When these do not exist, the Budapest Convention acts as a mutual legal assistance treaty (see Article 25 of the Budapest Convention); however, this only occurs for signatories of the Convention.

Informal sharing mechanisms involve police to police cooperation. The main advantage of using informal cooperative mechanisms is that information is exchanged quickly. There are, however, disadvantages to using informal channels. Specifically, certain countries have legal restrictions preventing or limiting authorities from providing assistance through informal channels. Additionally, it is often difficult to locate investigators that can and will provide assistance. Moreover, the evidence obtained using this mechanism is often inadmissible in court. Actually, because rules of evidence differ between jurisdictions (even in countries that have similar legal traditions), evidence obtained through

---

[*] "Comprehensive Study on Cybercrime," UNODC, 197, February 2013, http://www.unodc.org/documents/organized-crime/UNODC_CCPCJ_EG.4_2013/CYBERCRIME_STUDY_210213.pdf.

informal—and at times, even formal—channels may be rendered inadmissible in the courts of the country requesting the information. In fact, not every country has special evidentiary laws that govern electronic evidence. As a result, electronic evidence obtained from another country may not be accepted in another national court.

The absence of harmonized laws, the divergence of countries' memberships in multilateral and bilateral agreements, the priority assigned to traditional crimes over cybercrimes, and the existence of ineffective formal and informal information sharing mechanisms, all serve as obstacles to successful international cooperation. International cooperation is also affected by barriers to the enforcement of existing cybercrime laws (explored in the next section).

Cybercrime Enforcement

Enforcement occurs when a country compels compliance or punishes noncompliance with its laws. Compliance can be achieved by strengthening the monitoring and enforcement of standards. There are certain factors that influence cybercrime enforcement: most notably, the jurisdiction of the incident and the capacity of countries to conduct investigations.

Jurisdiction   One key task in cybercrime is prioritizing conflicting claims asserting jurisdiction over transnational cybercrimes. Consider the following: The perpetrator of a cybercrime may be physically located in the United States, while her victims are located in the United Kingdom, Japan, Australia, and South Africa. The crime itself, therefore, was not committed in one single, sovereign territory. In such situations, which are commonplace with cybercrime, how is jurisdiction decided?

To determine jurisdiction and resolve competing jurisdiction claims, multiple factors are considered, including (but not limited to): the place of the commission of the crime; custody of the perpetrator; victim nationality; perpetrator nationality; interests of the state seeking prosecution; harm caused; strength of the case against the perpetrator; punishment for cybercrime; and fairness in the criminal justice process.* One factor that is believed to influence cybercrime enforcement is the jurisdiction of the incident. International law recognizes different forms of jurisdiction. Traditionally, jurisdiction has been linked to geographic territory. This is known as the principle of territoriality, where each state can prosecute activity on its territory even when the offender is a foreign citizen. However, this is not used to determine the jurisdiction of a cybercrime case because no geographic boundaries exist in cyberspace. Instead, other guiding principles are often used to determine jurisdiction over a cybercrime: the

---

* For further analysis of these factors, see Susan W. Brenner, "Cybercrime Jurisdiction," *Crime, Law and Social Change* 46: 4–5 (2006), 198–206.

active personality (or nationality) principle (jurisdiction is established by the nationality of the offender); the passive personality principle (jurisdiction is established based on the nationality of the victim irrespective of where the crime is committed); and the protective principle (jurisdiction is not established based on the nationality of the victim or offender; instead, it is established on the basis that the security or the interests of the State is affected by an act committed outside of its territory).[*]

In addition to these principles, the harm caused by the cybercrime is also considered. The harm component, often given priority over other factors, involves both the number of victims and the monetary and non-monetary losses suffered by the country or countries as a result of the cybercrime. Another factor that may help resolve conflict over jurisdiction is the strength of the evidence against the cybercriminal (including the admissibility of the evidence in a court of law).[†] The severity of punishment also plays a critical role in asserting jurisdiction. Consider, for example, the United States. A country that does not provide the death penalty for murder will not extradite a murder suspect to the United States unless the U.S. agrees not to seek capital punishment. Finally, assertions of jurisdiction also take into account the anticipated fairness and impartiality of the criminal justice system and its participants in the country seeking to prosecute the case. All of these factors, along with the interests of the state seeking prosecution and the nationality of the perpetrator and victim(s), are considered when determining which country will prosecute the cybercrime in question.

Cybersecurity Capacity Building A unilateral approach to conducting cybercrime investigations does not exist. Therefore, countries vary in terms of their capability to conduct cybercrime investigations. The capacity of countries to conduct investigations influences cybercrime enforcement. Indeed, capacity building is a critical component in cooperation and coordination of investigative efforts. As such, progressive capacity building programs for national law enforcement agencies and those abroad should be established. It is important to strengthen the capacity of law enforcement because they serve as the first responders in cybercrime cases.

To date, some countries still lack the capacity to conduct computer forensic investigations. Here, capacity is determined by the number of professionals that can conduct investigations and prosecutions, and provide assistance in cybercrime investigations to requesting countries.

---

[*] Cedric Ryngaert, *Jurisdiction in International Law* (Oxford, UK: Oxford University Press, 2008), 85–133.
[†] Susan W. Brenner, "Cybercrime Jurisdiction," *Crime, Law and Social Change* 46: 4–5 (2006), 204.

Specifically, countries do not have the necessary computer forensics professionals or at the very least they do not have enough computer forensic professionals to analyze overwhelming quantities of electronic data. In fact, certain countries have a critical shortage of investigators, prosecutors, and judges who are able to handle cybercrime cases (e.g., Africa).* Additionally, many countries do not have the capacity to handle the number of incoming requests for outside assistance in cybercrime investigations. A 2013 United Nations Office on Drugs and Crime (UNODC) report highlighted that this lack of capacity is the direct result of the challenges that many countries face in recruiting personnel with the sufficient computer forensics skills.† This report also indicated that several countries lacked the necessary resources (e.g., computer forensics tools and equipment) to conduct cybercrime investigations.‡ This prevents law enforcement from being able to collect and analyze electronic evidence during the investigation and assist other nations in their cybercrime investigations. Countries may also lack the financial capabilities to investigate cybercrime and provide outside assistance. The cost of conducting these investigations has increased;§ as such, often only large-scale cybercrime activities are investigated.

Regarding capacity building, the nature and extent of training between countries also varies. Indeed, this was highlighted in the 2013 UNODC Comprehensive Study on Cybercrime report. Specifically, this report pointed out that law enforcement agents either: participated in annual training programs or monthly training by internal and external experts; completed e-learning modules on cybercrime and computer forensics; or attended conferences.¶ Moreover, the report revealed that in numerous countries, nonspecialized law enforcement officers lacked basic cybercrime knowledge and computer forensics skills. However,

---

* "Comprehensive Study on Cybercrime," UNODC, 1172, 177–178 and 229, February 2013, http://www.unodc.org/documents/organized-crime/UNODC_CCPCJ_EG.4_2013/CYBERCRIME_STUDY_210213.pdf.

† "Comprehensive Study on Cybercrime," UNODC, 163, February 2013, http://www.unodc.org/documents/organized-crime/UNODC_CCPCJ_EG.4_2013/CYBERCRIME_STUDY_210213.pdf.

‡ "Comprehensive Study on Cybercrime," UNODC, 152–154, February 2013, http://www.unodc.org/documents/organized-crime/UNODC_CCPCJ_EG.4_2013/CYBERCRIME_STUDY_210213.pdf.

§ "The Growing Global Threat of Economic and Cyber Crime," Study Conducted by the National Fraud Center in Conjunction with the Economic Crime Investigation Institute, Utica College, December 2000, http://www.utica.edu/academic/institutes/ecii/publications/media/global_threat_crime.pdf; "2012 Cost of Cyber Crime Study: United States," Ponemon Institute, October 2012, http://www.ponemon.org/local/upload/file/2012_US_Cost_of_Cyber_Crime_Study_FINAL6%20.pdf.

¶ "Comprehensive Study on Cybercrime," UNODC, 176, February 2013, http://www.unodc.org/documents/organized-crime/UNODC_CCPCJ_EG.4_2013/CYBERCRIME_STUDY_210213.pdf.

training in such areas is crucial because very few crimes have been left untouched by computers and related technology. Therefore, it is reasonable to assume that nonspecialized law enforcement officers will be required to conduct basic computer-related investigations. Initiatives should thus be created to improve cybercrime-related training for nonspecialized law enforcement officers. One such initiative could involve incorporating cybercrime and computer forensics training into the curriculum of police academies.

When countries lack the capacity to deal with cybercrime themselves, technical assistance has been provided by other nations. For instance, UNODC is responsible for providing technical assistance to requesting countries. Interpol also plays a central role in enhancing cooperation and coordination in international cybercrime investigations by providing training and assistance wherever required.[*] Nevertheless, given the global nature of cybercrime, it is imperative that all nations build capacities to independently detect, investigate, and respond to online illicit activities. With respect to dealing with cybercrime, developing countries are particularly disadvantaged. They often lack strong enforcement mechanisms to successfully pursue cybercriminals; their agencies lack the knowledge and skills to conduct cybercrime investigations; and they lack the necessary resources to investigate and prosecute cybercriminals.[†] In these countries, cybercriminals are confident that they will not be prosecuted for committing a cybercrime to such an extent that they do not take precautionary measures to hide their online illicit activities. It is important that steps are taken worldwide to deter perpetrators from engaging in cybercrime.

Deterring Cybercriminals

Responses to cybercriminals have been inconsistent. This inconsistency serves as a barrier to minimizing incidents of cybercrime; instead, it has resulted in its proliferation. Currently, strategies need to be developed to deter cybercriminals. The question that follows is: How can cybercriminals be deterred?

Deterrence occurs when an individual wants to commit cybercrime, realizes that his or her actions may involve punishment, and as a result, changes his or her mind and decides instead to adhere to the law. There are two types of deterrence: specific and general. Specific deterrence holds that punishment should be severe enough to ensure that cybercriminals

---

[*] "Cybercrime," Interpol, January 6, 2014, http://www.interpol.int/Crime-areas/Cybercrime/Cybercrime.
[†] Nir Kshetri, "Diffusion and Effects of Cyber-Crime in Developing Economies." *Third World Quarterly* 31:7 (2010), 1063–1067.

do not repeat their illicit actions; whereas, general deterrence holds that individuals will engage in unlawful activity if they do not fear that they will be punished or apprehended.

Deterring cybercriminals, therefore, requires severity and certainty in punishment. The first element, severity, requires that the penalty for committing cybercrime be sufficient to dissuade someone from committing that activity. Consider the United States that has substantial penalties for cybercrime. More specifically, significant penalties were created in the United States for those who target a protected computer. In particular, the Computer Fraud and Abuse Act (CFAA), which was a 1986 amendment to the Counterfeit Access Device and Computer Fraud and Abuse Act of 1984 (18 USC §1030), criminalizes, among other things, access to a protected computer without authorization and access to a computer that exceeds authorization.* Pursuant to Section 814 of the USA Patriot Act of 2001, the penalty for intentionally damaging a protected computer is 10 years imprisonment. In addition, if an individual has been convicted of cybercrime in the past and/or is charged with two or more cybercrimes, this person can receive 20 years imprisonment for intentionally or recklessly damaging a protected computer.

Another law that enhanced penalties for cybercrimes is Section 255 of the Homeland Security Act of 2002 (also known as the Cyber Security Enhancement Act of 2002). This act increased the penalty for "knowingly or recklessly caus[ing] or attempt[ing] to cause serious bodily injury" to 20 years. It additionally increased the penalty for knowingly or recklessly causing or attempting to cause death to life in prison. Other countries also provide life imprisonment for certain cybercrimes. A case in point is Pakistan. In Pakistan, the Prevention of Electronic Crimes Act of 2007 provides the death penalty or life imprisonment for acts of cyberterrorism.†

The second element, certainty, requires that cybercriminals be punished each time they commit an online illicit activity. This way, cybercriminals know that if they commit a cybercrime they will inevitably be punished. This, however, is not currently the case. Incidents of

---

* A protected computer is used in interstate or foreign commerce or communications. Communications networks and the Internet are channels of interstate commerce and have long been subjected to federal regulation under the Commerce Clause. Because every computer connected to the Internet is used in interstate commerce or communication, one could argue that any computer connected to the Internet is a protected computer under 18 USC §1030.

† Cyberterrorism refers to "the politically, religiously, or ideologically motivated use of computers (or related technology) by an individual(s), group, or state targeting critical infrastructure with the intention of harming persons and/or damaging property in order to influence the population (or segment of the population) or cause a government to change its policies." Marie-Helen Maras, *Computer Forensics: Cybercriminals, Laws and Evidence* (Second Edition) (Burlington, MA: Jones & Bartlett, 2014), 183.

cybercrime have drastically increased over the years,* due in part to the fact that many cybercriminals around the world are not punished for their crimes. Therefore, while there exists severity in punishment, certainty of punishment does not exist. As a result, cybercriminals cannot be effectively deterred in such situations. To do so, more prosecutions of cybercriminals are required.

Additionally, for deterrence to work, attribution is needed. Attribution refers to determining with certainty the individual(s) responsible for a cybercrime. Usually, evidence obtained during a cybercrime investigation cannot determine with certainty who was actually using the computer to commit the crime. For instance, a trace can lead back to the computer used, but not, with certainty, to the perpetrator who was using the computer. The individual behind the computer could be anyone. Indeed, the greatest challenge in cybercrime investigations is attribution.

In international law, the person who engages in the attack must be ascertained. State responsibility is well-established in international law. The state responsibility doctrine holds that every country has an affirmative legal obligation to prevent its territory from being used to plan, plot, coordinate, and execute attacks against other countries. If a country refuses to prevent such incidents it can be held responsible for the attacks on another nation. However, the assessment of the country's responsibility is inherently complex due to the attribution problem in cybercrime: especially with political cybercrimes such as hacktivism,† cyberwarfare,‡ cyberterrorism,§ and

---

* Gordon M. Snow, "Statement before the Senate Judiciary Committee, Subcommittee on Crime and Terrorism," Federal Bureau of Investigation, April 12, 2011, http://www.fbi.gov/news/testimony/cybersecurity-responding-to-the-threat-of-cyber-crime-and-terrorism; "Cybersecurity Overview," U.S. Department of Homeland Security, January 7, 2014, https://www.dhs.gov/cybersecurity-overview.

† Hacktivists use tools and techniques of hackers to promote their political agendas. They "intentionally access a computer system and/or website, without authorization or exceeding authorized access, as a means of achieving political goals." Marie-Helen Maras, *Computer Forensics: Cybercriminals, Laws and Evidence* (Second Edition) (Burlington, MA: Jones & Bartlett, 2014), 181.

‡ Cyberwarfare is a state-sponsored cyberattack against another country's computers or information networks in pursuit of a political goal. Marie-Helen Maras, *Computer Forensics: Cybercriminals, Laws and Evidence* (Second Edition) (Burlington, MA: Jones & Bartlett, 2014), 181.

§ Cyberterrorism is included in the category of political cybercrime because most terrorists, even suicide bombers and religious terrorists, have cited political reasons for engaging in terrorism. Marie-Helen Maras, *Counterterrorism* (Burlington, MA: Jones & Bartlett, 2012); Marie-Helen Maras, *CRC Press Terrorism Reader* (Boca Raton, FL: CRC Press, 2013).

cyberespionage.* It is extremely difficult to determine who the perpetrator is in cyberspace.

Consider cyberespionage. The Office of the National Counterintelligence Executive (NCIX) warned that foreign countries (including allies) are engaging in cyberespionage against the United States. Specifically, NCIX submitted a report to the U.S. Congress, which noted that during 2009 to 2011, academic and research institutions, individual citizens, and intelligence agents in foreign countries have clandestinely obtained information (e.g., trade secrets and patent software and technologies) from private organizations.† China and Russia were identified in the report as the countries from which these crimes have been primarily perpetrated. The specific perpetrators of these crimes, however, have largely remained unidentified. A recent incident involved GhostNet, which involved the theft of documents from government and private offices around the world. Canadians had traced the signal back to systems located in Hainan, China.‡ However, they could not trace them back to the actual perpetrator, who today, still remains unknown. Another cyberespionage incident was Shadows in the Cloud.§ The Shadow network systematically broke into computers of government offices in India.¶ The perpetrators obtained automatic control of the computers they infected. The Shadow network obtained a wide range of classified material, which they stole from the Indian government. This incident was more sophisticated and difficult to detect than GhostNet. The attacks were traced back to Chendu, Tibet.

Some believe that effective cyberdefensive (e.g., protecting against attackers by minimizing vulnerabilities) and cyberoffensive measures

---

* Cyberespionage involves the "theft of trade secret for the benefit of a foreign government, foreign instrumentality, or foreign agent." Marie-Helen Maras, *Computer Forensics: Cybercriminals, Laws and Evidence* (Second Edition) (Burlington, MA: Jones & Bartlett, 2014), 127. Cyberespionage can also be considered as an economic cybercrime depending on the motive and intent of the perpetrator.

† "Foreign Spies Stealing U.S. Economic Secrets in Cyberspace: Report to Congress on Foreign Economic Collection and Industrial Espionage, 2009–2011," Office of the National Counterintelligence Executive, October 2011, http://www.ncix.gov/publications/reports/fecie_all/Foreign_Economic_Collection_2011.pdf.

‡ Paul Rosenzweig, "10 Conservative Principles for Cybersecurity Policy," The Heritage Foundation, January 31, 2011, http://www.heritage.org/research/reports/2011/01/10-conservative-principles-for-cybersecurity-policy.

§ Information Warfare Monito and Shadowserver Foundation, "Shadows in the Cloud: Investigating Cyber Espionage 2.0. Joint Report," JR03-2010, April 6, 2010, http://www.nartv.org/mirror/shadows-in-the-cloud.pdf.

¶ John Markoff and David Barboza, "Researchers Trace Data Theft to Intruders in China," *New York Times*, April 5, 2010, http://www.nytimes.com/2010/04/06/science/06cyber.html?pagewanted=all.

could deter cybercriminals (e.g., proactively penetrating and damaging enemy systems).* Accordingly, many nations are seeking to advance their cybercapabilites. To do so, several countries have in place (or started to build) cyber defensive and offensive capabilities; the same holds true for international, multilateral, bilateral, and regional organizations. For instance, in 2011, the North Atlantic Treaty Organization (NATO) developed a new cyberdefense policy. This policy calls for a coordinated response to cyberattacks and creating the capability to deter, prevent, and respond to attacks against NATO's networks.† NATO, and other organizations, along with governments around the globe, cannot achieve effective cybersecurity on their own. To achieve cybersecurity governance, effective cooperation between public and private sectors should also be promoted. Nowhere is this need more pronounced than in critical infrastructure industries.

Public–Private Partnerships

Critical infrastructure needs to be protected by both physical security and cybersecurity because it includes systems and services that are essential to society. Specifically, in the United States, critical infrastructure is defined as the "systems and assets, whether physical or virtual, so vital to the United States that the incapacity or destruction of such systems and assets would have a debilitating impact on security, national economic security, national public health or safety, or any combination of those matters."‡ In the United Kingdom, critical national infrastructure "comprises those assets, services and systems that support the economic, political and social life of the UK whose importance is such that loss could: (1) cause large-scale loss of life; (2) have a serious impact on the national economy; (3) have other grave social consequences for the community; or (4) be of immediate concern to the national government."§ For Canada, "critical infrastructure consists of those physical and information technology facilities, networks, services and assets which,

---

* Christopher Haley, "A Theory of Cyber Deterrence," *Georgetown Journal of International Affairs*, February 6, 2013, http://journal.georgetown.edu/2013/02/06/a-theory-of-cyber-deterrence-christopher-haley/; Eric Talbot Jensen, "Cyber Deterrence," *Emory International Law Review* 26:2 (2012), 773–824, http://www.law.emory.edu/fileadmin/journals/eilr/26/26.2/Jensen.pdf.

† "Defending against Cyber Attacks," NATO, 2013, http://www.nato.int/cps/en/natolive/75747.htm.

‡ See Section 2 of the Homeland Security Act of 2002; See also Section 1016(e) of the USA Patriot Act of 2001 [42 USC 5195c(e)] and 6 C.F.R. § 29.2.

§ "Protection of 'Critical Infrastructure' and the Role of Investment Policies Relating to National Security," Organization for Economic Co-operation and Development (OECD), 2008, 4, http://www.oecd.org/dataoecd/2/41/40700392.pdf.

if disrupted or destroyed, would have a serious impact on the health, safety, security or economic well-being of Canadians or the effective functioning of governments in Canada."*

Some critical infrastructure is owned by local and state governments; the majority of critical infrastructure, however, is owned by the private sector. Accordingly, to adequately protect critical infrastructure systems it is imperative that common cybersecurity standards are established. For that reason, effective public–private partnerships are required. Public–private partnerships are guided by the National Infrastructure Protection Plan (NIPP). NIPP was created to "provide a unifying framework that integrates a range of efforts designed to enhance the safety of our nation's critical infrastructure. The overarching goal of the NIPP is to build a safer, more secure, and more resilient America by preventing, deterring, neutralizing, or mitigating the effects of a terrorist attack or natural disaster, and to strengthen national preparedness, response, and recovery in the event of an emergency."† The NIPP assigned sector-specific agencies (SSAs) to 18 critical infrastructure sectors (see Table 6.3). The 18 different critical infrastructure sectors in the United States include: food and agriculture; banking and finance; chemical; commercial facilities; communications; critical manufacturing; dams; defense and industrial bases; emergency services; energy; government facilities; healthcare and public health; information technology; national monuments and icons; nuclear reactors, materials, and waste; postal and shipping; transportation systems; and water.

Sector-specific agencies (SSAs) have the requisite knowledge and expertise for the critical infrastructure they are responsible for. In particular, Presidential Policy Directive 21 (PPD-21) defines a sector-specific agency as "the Federal department or agency designated under this directive to be responsible for providing institutional knowledge and specialized expertise as well as leading, facilitating, or supporting the security and resilience programs and associated activities of its designated critical infrastructure sector in the all-hazards environment."‡ PPD-21 designates SSAs for each critical infrastructure. SSAs have the requisite knowledge and expertise for the critical infrastructure they are responsible for. Homeland Security Presidential Directive 7 (or HSPD-7) notes that the SSA designations could change as threats and hazards to the

---

* Ibid.
† "National Infrastructure Protection Plan," Homeland Security, para. 1, 2009, https:// www.dhs.gov/national-infrastructure-protection-plan.
‡ The White House, "Presidential Policy Directive—Critical Infrastructure Security and Resilience (PPD-21)," Office of the Press Secretary, February 12, 2013, http://www. whitehouse.gov/the-press-office/2013/02/12/presidential-policy-directive-critical-infrastructure-security-and-resil.

TABLE 6.3   The Sector-Specific Agencies (SSAs) for Critical Infrastructure Sectors Are as Follows

---

1. *Chemical*. The sector-specific agency for this CI is the Department of Homeland Security. The SSA was specified by Homeland Security Presidential Directive 7 (or HSPD-7).

2. *Commercial Facilities*. This includes facilities in the following areas: public assembly, sports leagues, resorts, lodging, outdoor events, entertainment and media, real estate, and retail. The sector-specific agency for this CI is the Department of Homeland Security.

3. *Communications*. The sector-specific agency for this CI is the Department of Homeland Security.

4. *Critical Manufacturing*. The sector-specific agency for this CI is the Department of Homeland Security.

5. *Dams*. The sector-specific agency for this CI is the Department of Homeland Security.

6. *Defense Industrial Base*. The sector-specific agency for this CI is the Department of Defense.

7. *Emergency Services*. The sector-specific agency for this CI is the Department of Homeland Security.

8. *Energy*. The sector-specific agency for this CI is the Department of Energy.

9. *Financial Services*. The sector-specific agency for this CI is the Department of the Treasury.

10. *Food and Agriculture*. The co–sector-specific agencies for this CI are the U.S. Department of Agriculture and Department of Health and Human Services. The SSAs were specified by HSPD-7.

11. *Government Facilities*. The co–sector-specific agencies for this CI are the Department of Homeland Security and General Services Administration.

12. *Healthcare and Public Health*. The sector-specific agency for this CI is the Department of Health and Human Services.

13. *Information Technology*. The sector-specific agency for this CI is the Department of Homeland Security.

14. *National Monuments and Icons Sector* (NMIS). This sector is designated as a critical infrastructure as it includes federally owned physical structures which represent America's heritage, traditions, or values. The sector-specific agency for national monuments and icons is the Department of the Interior.

15. *Nuclear Reactors, Materials, and Waste*. The sector-specific agency for this CI is the Department of Homeland Security.

16. *Postal and Shipping*. The sector-specific agency for postal and shipping is the Transportation Security Administration.

17. *Transportation Systems*. The co–sector-specific agencies for this CI are the Department of Homeland Security and Department of Transportation.

TABLE 6.3 (continued)   The Sector-Specific Agencies (SSAs) for Critical
Infrastructure Sectors Are as Follows

---

18. *Water and Wastewater Systems.* The sector-specific agency for this CI is
    the Environmental Protection Agency. The SSA was specified by HSPD-7.
    HSPD-8 facilitates a national policy, among other things, to protect water,
    food, and agriculture.

Source: The White House, "Presidential Policy Directive—Critical Infrastructure
Security and Resilience (PPD-21)," Office of the Press Secretary,
February 12, 2013, http://www.whitehouse.gov/the-press-office/2013/
02/12/presidential-policy-directive-critical-infrastructure-security-and-resil.

United States are continuously evaluated.[*] Each critical infrastructure
is deemed to be equally vital and as such, no critical infrastructure is
deemed to be of greater importance than the other. PPD-21 states that
critical infrastructure security and resilience is a shared responsibility of
both public and private entities.

To assist public and private entities, the Industrial Control System—
Computer Emergency Readiness Team (ICS-CERT) of the Department
of Homeland Security works to reduce cyber risks by:[†]

- Partnering with and assisting public agencies and private sector
  partners, upon request;
- Responding to and analyzing control system incidents;
- Providing support for cyberincident response and forensic analysis; and
- Harmonizing efforts and sharing information between local,
  state, federal, and tribal governments and the private sector.

To enhance existing and build new public–private partnerships,
the Cybersecurity Act of 2012 was created. When the Cybersecurity
Act was introduced in 2011 and again in 2012 it was widely criticized.
Among other things, it suffered from overly broad language in the sections that cover monitoring and countermeasures. The final version of
the Cybersecurity Act of 2012 also included provisions that enabled private companies to volunteer to receive assistance by the Department of
Homeland Security on how to develop better cybersecurity performance
standards. Ultimately, the act was not passed.

---

[*] "Homeland Security Presidential Directive 7: Critical Infrastructure Identification,
Prioritization, and Protection (HSPD-7)," Homeland Security, December 17, 2003,
https://www.dhs.gov/homeland-security-presidential-directive-7.

[†] Industrial Control System—Computer Emergency Readiness Team (ICS-CERT), "About
the Industrial Control Systems Cyber Emergency Response Team," ICS-CERT, https://ics-
cert.us-cert.gov/About-Industrial-Control-Systems-Cyber-Emergency-Response-Team.

The following year, Executive Order 13636 (on improving critical infrastructure cybersecurity) was passed on February 12, 2013. This order sought to enhance cybersecurity in both the public and private sector. It also called for information sharing between the public and private sector. However, the information sharing between these sectors was not mandated: it was optional. Yet, what happens if privately owned critical infrastructures with weak cybersecurity (or at the very least weaker cybersecurity than other critical infrastructure industries) do not volunteer? How can enhanced cybersecurity be achieved without mandating that each critical infrastructure have the necessary security measures in place? To enhance the cybersecurity of private companies that own critical infrastructure, a common mandatory framework should be created. Nonetheless, there are barriers to the implementation of any mandatory scheme. Companies may hesitate to participate because they may fear customer backlash, bad publicity, negative attention, and may be reluctant to devote time and resources to implement the standards. The creation of incentives for the private sector to implement cybersecurity standards is a particularly challenging task. However, cost sharing and tax breaks for participating private sectors are steps in the right direction. The key to a successful public–private partnership is to enable information sharing without placing an unnecessary burden on the private industry.

Nevertheless, the protection of critical infrastructure is not solely a domestic task. For example, the European Union (EU) faced a similar dilemma. Pursuant to the proposed 2013 Directive on Network and Information Security (NIS Directive), a mandatory approach to cybersecurity was promoted; due in large part to the fact that the current voluntary approach provided insufficient protection. This voluntary approach resulted in very different levels of capabilities, protection, and preparedness among Member States; in so doing, weakening the cybersecurity of the entire system due to high levels of interconnectedness.[*] Inadequate international coordination and cooperation unnecessarily exposes critical infrastructure to cybersecurity risks.

Nationally and internationally, countries have taken steps to enhance cybersecurity cooperation and coordination and build partnerships between public and private sectors.[†] Indeed, such public–private partnerships exist in the United States. A case in point is the

---

[*] "Network and Information Security Directive," Department for Business, Innovation and Skills (BIS), September 20, 2013, 5, https://www.gov.uk/government/uploads/system/uploads/attachment_data/file/244978/bis-13-1206-network-and-information-security-directive-impact-assessment.pdf.

[†] "G8 Principles for Protecting Critical Information Infrastructures," G8 Justice and Interior Ministers, May 2003, http://www.coe.int/t/dghl/cooperation/economiccrime/cybercrime/documents/points%20of%20contact/24%208%20G8_CIIP_Principles_en.pdf.

National Cyber-Forensic & Training Alliance (NCFTA), which is an alliance between the private sector, academia, and government agencies (e.g., the Federal Bureau of Investigation). These partnerships also exist abroad. For instance, in the EU, the European Union Agency for Network and Information Security (ENISA) created a detailed guide promoting public–private partnerships; namely, the European Public Private Partnership for Resilience (EP3R). The main task of EP3R is to "build upon national…[public-private partnerships] and engage both the public and private sectors in addressing the pan-European dimension of the resilience of critical EU-wide infrastructure."[*] Europol has also built alliances with the private sectors to enable cooperation between them through the International Cyber Security Protection Alliance (ICSPA).[†]

Alliances should also be built among like-minded nations. This has occurred, for example, between the United States and the European Union. These alliances help develop and disseminate best practices for protecting critical infrastructure and minimizing vulnerability. These alliances also promote the sharing of information and best practices in cybersecurity incident response and preparedness. To prepare for cyberattacks, countries can conduct cyberincident exercises. Indeed, a key element in preparedness for cyberattacks involves conducting exercises. In 2002, the U.S. Naval War College hosted a war game titled *Digital Pearl Harbor*, which involved a mock attack on critical infrastructure in the United States by computer security experts. This exercise revealed U.S. critical infrastructure vulnerabilities. Other exercises abound (e.g., Cyber Storm I, II, and III).[‡] A more recent exercise was conducted in 2011 by both the EU and the United States. The exercise, titled *Cyber Atlantic*, involved simulated cyberattacks against critical infrastructure. The purpose of these exercises were to see how the EU and the United States would cooperate in such situations.[§]

---

[*] "European Public Private Partnership for Resilience (EP3R)," European Union Agency for Network and Information Security, 2013, http://www.enisa.europa.eu/activities/ Resilience-and-CIIP/public-private-partnership/european-public-private-partnership-for-resilience-ep3r.

[†] "The International Cyber Security Protection Alliance (ICSPA)—Executing Its Mission Globally," International Cyber Security Protection Alliance (ICSPA), 2013, https:// www.icspa.org/about-us/; "Europol to Lead International Cyber Security Protection Alliance Consultation into the Future of Cybercrime," Europol, https://www.europol. europa.eu/content/press/europol-lead-international-cyber-security-protection-alliance-consultation-future-cybe.

[‡] "Cyber Storm: Securing Cyber Space," Department of Homeland Security, 2013, http:// www.dhs.gov/cyber-storm-securing-cyber-space.

[§] "First Joint EU–U.S. Cyber Security Exercise Conducted Today, 3rd Nov. 2011," European Union Agency for Network and Information Security, November 3, 2011, http://www.enisa. europa.eu/media/press-releases/first-joint-eu-us-cyber-security-exercise-conducted-today-3rd-nov.-2011.

Furthermore, information sharing and analysis centers are instrumental in mitigating cyberincidents. Awareness of system vulnerabilities should be communicated and shared with relevant public and private entities to facilitate efficient responses. In addition, if possible, vulnerability advisories and threat warnings should be disseminated as well. Effective mechanisms should be in place to disseminate information on cybersecurity incidents. If they do not exist, effective cybersecurity incident reporting mechanisms should be developed. An example of an information sharing and analysis center is the Computer Emergency Response Team (CERT). CERT was created to provide information and support against cyberattacks. Other countries have created their own version of CERT, such as Argentina, Canada, Denmark, Greece, Japan, Pakistan, the Philippines, Singapore, Slovenia, and the United Kingdom (to name a few). In the United States, the Federal Computer Incident Response Center (FedCirc) became part of the Department of Homeland Security Directorate of Information Analysis and Infrastructure Protection (IAIP). IAIP is responsible for providing federal civilian agencies with cybersecurity incident information and assisting them with incident prevention and response.

Information sharing is also an essential element of cooperation in cybercrime investigations. However, current reporting and recording practices of cybercrime are insufficient. Existing crime measurement tools, such as the Uniform Crime Report (UCR) and the National Incident Based Reporting System (NIBRS), focus on traditional crimes. These measurements do not include existing cybercrimes. In fact, to date, there are no official crime measurement tools that record cybercrime. Existing police databases record cybercrime in one of two ways. When an offense is registered as a cybercrime, police have two options: if a computer has been used in the crime, a box is checked that says that the computer was either the target of the crime or the computer was used in the commission of the crime. Nonetheless, this is not a helpful measurement of cybercrime as it does not accurately depict what type of cybercrime was committed; only the role of the computer in the crime (i.e., a computer was the target of the crime or was used in the commission of a crime).

Incidents of cybercrime are primarily recorded because of victim self-reporting. However, cybercrime is significantly underreported. The underreporting of cybercrime occurs because of the public's lack of awareness of cybercrime and existing reporting mechanisms; individuals' shame and embarrassment for falling victim to cybercrimes; and the fear that reporting will adversely affect the reputation of the company. To increase reporting: online and hotline cybercrime reporting should be made available and communicated to the public (if this does not already exist); private sector liaisons should be designated to report cybercrimes to public agencies; and public awareness campaigns should be created.

It is essential that a cybersecurity culture be developed, promoted, and maintained on national and international levels. Indeed, efforts should focus on promoting cybersecurity awareness, education, and training both domestically and abroad. Academia can and should play a role in educating the workforce. To do so, it should create and implement cybersecurity programs that cover laws, criminal justice, computer forensics, and computer security (if they do not exist). If such programs are in place, they should be kept up-to-date and offer workshops and training to public and private sectors. Cybersecurity awareness and education programs should be standardized and efforts in this regard should be coordinated. Minimum uniform requirements and qualifications for cybersecurity professionals should also be identified.

CONCLUDING THOUGHTS

The anonymity afforded by the Internet provides perpetrators with an environment to operate with a low risk of detection and a low risk of personal injury. Indeed, technologies today make it easy for individuals to hide their identities. In the online environment, someone can misrepresent himself/herself or make use of somebody else's identity. Accordingly, it is very difficult to know with certainty who is committing a cybercrime. This poses particular challenges for the deterrence of cybercrime and its investigation.

Existing laws and their enforcement play an essential role in the coordination of efforts and cooperation between countries. There are certain factors that influence cybercrime enforcement including: jurisdiction of the incident and the capacity of countries to conduct investigations. In respect of jurisdiction, several factors play a role in the determination of jurisdiction for a cybercrime case, such as the: place of commission of the crime; custody of the perpetrator; harm; victim nationality; perpetrator nationality; strength of case against the perpetrator; punishment; and fairness. Enforcement also depends on the capacity of a country to respond to requests for information and their ability to conduct investigations. Countries have pointed out the difficulty of recruiting personnel with the sufficient skills to conduct investigations and process electronic evidence. Countries have additionally reported a lack of human and economic resources to conduct investigations. Assistance can be provided to such countries. However, this serves only as a short-term solution to an ongoing problem. To effectively deal with cybercrime in the long term, national capacity to conduct investigations independently should be developed. Here, education and training in computer forensics is critical. Training should be provided to criminal justice professionals (law enforcement and prosecutors). Additionally, capacity is essential to respond to requests for evidence and information from other countries.

To facilitate such requests, formal and informal sharing mechanisms have been established. These mechanisms may or may not exist between countries. For formal mechanisms, established agreements, conventions, and treaties make cooperation and information sharing possible. The cooperation provisions in multilateral and bilateral instruments differ in the following: response time obligation; multiple informal law enforcement networks; and variance in cooperation standards. These divergent provisions serve as barriers to international cooperation in cybercrime investigations. For informal sharing mechanisms, the domestic laws and rules of evidence will dictate the nature and extent of the use of the informal channels for cooperation and information sharing. Problems arise with the use of informal mechanisms; especially with respect to potential privacy violations of the individuals' information shared through these channels and the inadmissibility of evidence retrieved through these mechanisms in court.

There are certain cultural, social, economic, and legal challenges to achieving universal Internet governance. Single national bodies should be identified to consolidate cybersecurity initiatives, including awareness campaigns. This would also assist in coordinating efforts among public and private agencies. Ultimately, effective governance requires cooperation and coordination between public and private sectors.

CHAPTER 7

Natural Disasters
A Forgotten Security Risk?

Threats can be posed by individuals in the form of human-made threats (such as fire and nuclear accidents) and by natural phenomena (earthquakes, tsunamis, and hurricanes, to name a few). Hazards constitute a risk or danger. Hazards can be thought of as a condition or possible situation that has the potential to cause or create a disaster. A disaster is "an event in a definite area that has occurred as a result of an accident, hazardous natural phenomena, catastrophe, natural or human-made, which may or have caused significant physical, social, economic and cultural damage to human lives or [the] environment."[*] A disaster has also been referred to as "a serious disruption of the functioning of society, posing a significant, widespread threat to human life, health, property or the environment, whether caused by accident, nature or human activity, and whether developing suddenly or as the result of complex, long-term processes."[†] While not all hazards cause a disaster, all disasters are the result of some form of hazard. Hazards include naturally occurring phenomena, incidents caused by human activity, and incidents caused by conflict situations (e.g., war, genocide, terrorism, etc.). Threats or hazards, depending on their severity, can constitute emergencies.

This chapter explores the catastrophic harm that often results from a natural disaster. A natural disaster is a materialized threat that emanates from a natural cause (for examples of natural disasters, see Table 7.1). In addition to looking at the impact of various types of natural disasters, this chapter: covers the risk of natural disasters; considers the agencies created to deal with these emergencies; and evaluates these agencies' ability to efficiently mitigate, respond to, prepare for, and/or recover from disasters.

---

[*] The Agreement among the Governments of the Participating States of the Black Sea Economic Cooperation (BSEC) on Collaboration in Emergency Assistance and Emergency Response to Natural and Man-Made Disasters of 1998.

[†] Under Article 1(6) of the Tampere Convention on the Provision of Telecommunication Resources for Disaster Mitigation and Relief Operations (or Tampere Convention) of 1998.

TABLE 7.1   Natural Disasters

Floods	Volcanic eruptions
Earthquakes	Severe winter storms
Hurricanes	Droughts
Storm surges	Extreme heat
Tornadoes	Coastal erosion
Wildfires	Thunderstorm/lightning
Landslides	Hailstorms
Tsunamis	Sinkholes, land subsidence, and expansive soils
Avalanches	

NATURAL DISASTERS: COSTS AND CONSEQUENCES

The costs and consequences of natural disasters are significant. Natural disasters cause deaths, injuries, destruction of land and property, and economic damage to the affected area (or areas). Additionally, environmental damage can be caused. For example, in 2002, major wildfires in the United States decimated an estimated 6 million acres of forestland.[*] Individuals have also lost their homes and livelihoods due to natural disasters. Consider the 1906 San Francisco earthquake. This earthquake left up to 250,000 of the city's residents homeless.[†] As devastating as this earthquake was, it is not considered one of the largest earthquakes in American history. The greatest earthquake occurred in 1964 in Prince William Sound, Alaska. This earthquake, which measured 9.2 on the Richter scale, caused a tsunami,[‡] which resulted in 128 deaths (113 lives lost from the tsunami and 15 from the earthquake).[§] This earthquake caused more than 300 million dollars in damages. The largest earthquake in the world occurred in Chile in 1960. It measured 9.5 on the Richter scale and caused landslides, a flood, volcanic eruptions, and tsunamis.[¶] It left 2,000,000 residents homeless and caused approximately 1,886 deaths, 3,000 injuries, and 675,500,000 U.S. dollars' worth of damage in the affected areas of Chile, Japan, the Philippines, Hawaii, and other areas of the United States.

---

[*] George D. Haddow, Jane A. Bullock, and Damon P. Coppola, *Introduction to Emergency Management* (Third Edition) (Boston: Butterworth-Heinemann, 2008), 40.

[†] Richard Worth, *The San Francisco Earthquake* (New York: Facts on File, 2005), 15.

[‡] Tsunamis consist of a series of waves of various large sizes. Tsunamis can be caused by earthquakes, meteor impacts, volcanic eruptions, and landslides.

[§] United States Geological Survey, "Historic Earthquakes: Prince William Sound, Alaska," USGS Earthquake Hazards Program, November 1, 2012, http://earthquake.usgs.gov/earthquakes/states/events/1964_03_28.php.

[¶] United States Geological Survey, "Historic Earthquakes: Chile," USGS Earthquake Hazards Program, November 1, 2012, http://earthquake.usgs.gov/earthquakes/world/events/1960_05_22.php.

Numerous earthquakes have occurred worldwide; some with minimal and others with devastating consequences. For example, in 2001, in India, a 7.7 magnitude earthquake resulted in roughly 20,005 deaths and 166,836 injuries.[*] Also, the 2004 Indian Ocean tsunami, the result of a 9.1 magnitude earthquake, caused the loss of numerous lives and significant destruction. Particularly, 227,898 individuals were killed or missing (but presumed dead), millions were displaced, and thousands were injured by "the earthquake and the subsequent tsunami in 14 countries in South Asia and East Africa."[†] Severe damage was sustained by critical infrastructure (e.g., energy and communications), homes, industries, businesses, and personal property. In addition, in 2005, in Pakistan, a 7.6 magnitude earthquake killed approximately 86,000 and injured at least 69,000 people.[‡] Moreover, in 2008, a 7.9 magnitude earthquake in China killed "[a]t least 69,195 people..., [and injured] 374,177"; additionally, approximately "18,392 [individuals went] missing and [were] presumed dead."[§] Furthermore, in 2010, a 7.0 magnitude earthquake hit Haiti, killing 227,000 and injuring 300,000 individuals.[¶] Millions of Haitians were left homeless, displaced, and or separated from their families.

Certain individuals in the population are disproportionately affected by disasters. Particularly, the World Health Organization (WHO) has recognized that women and children have, historically and presently, been disproportionately affected by natural disasters (in relation to men).[**] One study revealed that "more women than men die in disasters where women's economic and social rights are not ensured."[††] Indeed,

---

[*] United States Geological Survey, "Earthquake Information for 2001," USGS, 2001, http://earthquake.usgs.gov/earthquakes/eqarchives/year/2001/.

[†] United States Geological Survey, "Magnitude 9.1—Off the West Coast of Northern Sumatra," USGS Earthquake Hazards Program, July 8, 2013, http://earthquake.usgs. gov/earthquakes/eqinthenews/2004/us2004slav/#summary.

[‡] United States Geological Survey, "Magnitude 7.6—Pakistan," USGS Earthquake Hazards Program, 2008, http://earthquake.usgs.gov/earthquakes/eqinthenews/2005/ usdyae/#summary.

[§] United States Geological Survey, "Magnitude 7.9—Eastern Sichuan, China," USGS Earthquake Hazards Program, 2008, http://earthquake.usgs.gov/earthquakes/ eqinthenews/2008/us2008ryan/#summary.

[¶] Heidi Koontz and Clarice Nassif Ransom, "Haiti Dominates Earthquake Fatalities in 2010," United States Geological Survey, January 11, 2011, http://www.usgs.gov/ newsroom/article.asp?ID=2679.

[**] World Health Organization, "Gender and Women's Health: Gender and Disaster," WHO Regional Office for South-East Asia, January 19, 2005; "Gender and Women's Health: Gender and Disaster," The Global Fund for Women, December 2005, 1, http:// www.globalfundforwomen.org/storage/images/stories/downloads/disaster-report.pdf.

[††] Eric Neumayer and Thomas Plümper, "The Gendered Nature of Natural Disasters: The Impact of Catastrophic Events on the Gender Gap in Life Expectancy, 1981–2002," *Annals of the Association of American Geographers* 97:3 (2007), 551–566; Nicole Detraz, *International Security and Gender* (Cambridge, UK: Polity, 2012), 190.

men were found to have greater and easier access to relief aid.* What's more, following natural disasters, women have experienced sexual violence (e.g., rape) and domestic violence. This occurs, in part, due to the lack of appropriate security provided to the population after these events. Consider Haiti. Law enforcement agencies were unable to provide adequate security in the wake of the earthquake. As a result of the earthquake, the headquarters of the Haitian National Police (HNP) sustained significant structural damage. Moreover, approximately 500 police officers were killed or missing; this figure reportedly represented 20% of the Port-au-Prince police officers.† Prisons were also damaged as a result of the earthquake leading to thousands of prisoners escaping.‡ The insecurity in Haiti following the earthquake was found to "contribute…to an upsurge in both rapes and domestic violence following the earthquake."§

In the aftermath of natural disasters, children are vulnerable to separation from their families; they are also at risk of being exploited or trafficked. There have been instances where orphans have been abducted, and children have been trafficked, forcibly removed from their parents, or have been taken away from their parents on the false promise that the children will have a better life and that parents can visit them. Often, in these situations, parents find that children have been taken to other countries. These children may also be exploited in the countries they are sent to. A case in point was the attempted kidnapping of 33 children in the immediate aftermath of the 2010 Haiti earthquake.¶ Specifically, those involved attempted to take the children to the Dominican Republic but they did not have the appropriate paperwork to do so. The individuals responsible were charged and taken into custody in Haiti. Subsequently, they were released to the United States; where these individuals were not prosecuted for their crimes. Children have also been sold to agencies that are responsible for intercountry adoption. In such situations, decisions that are made to place the child with other families or with an adoption agency may not serve the best interests of the child. Given the prevalence of this occurrence, countries have placed temporary suspensions on intercountry adoption in areas that either have experienced a severe natural

---

* Nicole Detraz, *International Security and Gender* (Cambridge, UK: Polity, 2012), 176.
† Isabelle Fortin, "Security Sector Reform in Haiti One Year after the Earthquake," The Centre for International Governance Innovation (CIGI), SSR Issue Papers 1, March 2011, 5.
‡ Ibid., 3–4.
§ Lynn Horton, "After the Earthquake: Gender Inequality and Transformation in Post-Disaster Haiti," *Gender & Development* 20:2 (2012), 301.
¶ Edward Cody, "Eight of 10 Missionaries Arrive in U.S. after Release from Haiti Jail," *The Washington Post*, February 19, 2010, http://articles.washingtonpost.com/2010-02-18/world/36873035_1_jorge-puello-laura-silsby-charisa-coulter.

(or human-made) disaster or are experiencing conflict.* Clearly, natural disasters can cause significant adverse consequences should they materialize. The question that follows is: what is the risk of this threat?

THE RISK OF NATURAL DISASTERS

Risk calculations for this phenomenon are based on its probability of occurring and the impact of the natural disaster (i.e., its costs and consequences) should it materialize. A tool that was developed to objectively assess this security risk is the Natural Disaster Risk Index (created by Maplecroft, a global risks advisory firm). Specifically, the Natural Disaster Risk Index (NDRI), used data between 1980 and 2010 to assess the risk of natural disasters in 229 countries.† The calculations of the NDRI are based on frequency (i.e., the incidence of attacks within a country over a specific period of time) and human impact (i.e., deaths per year and number of deaths in proportion to the population).‡ The NDRI ranked 15 of 229 countries as being at "extreme risk" of natural disasters (see Table 7.2).§ High-risk countries for natural disasters included the United States, Italy, and France; whereas medium risk countries were Canada, Germany, and Russia.¶ The United States was ranked as a high risk of a natural disaster due to its susceptibility toward

TABLE 7.2   Countries at Extreme Risk of Natural Disasters

Bangladesh	Sudan	India
Indonesia	Mozambique	China
Iran	Haiti	Sri Lanka
Pakistan	Philippines	Myanmar
Ethiopia	Colombia	Afghanistan

---

* See, for example, Canada. Government of Canada, "Adoption Post–Disaster Situations," Citizenship and Immigration in Canada, http://www.cic.gc.ca/english/immigrate/adoption/disaster.asp.

† "GLOBAL: Asia Most at Risk from Natural Disasters," The Integrated Regional Information Network (IRIN), May 30, 2010, http://www.irinnews.org/report/89305.

‡ Maplecroft, "Disasters Risk Index 2010," May 2010, Prevention Web, http://www.preventionweb.net/english/professional/maps/v.php?id=14169.

§ These countries are listed starting with the top ranked country at extreme risk of a natural disaster. Maplecroft. "Natural Disasters Risk Index 2010: Map," Prevention Web, May 2010, http://www.preventionweb.net/files/14169_NaturalDisasters2010.pdf.

¶ Maplecroft, "Bangladesh, Indonesia and Iran Top Natural Disaster Ranking—France, Italy, USA at 'High Risk,'" Relief Web, May 26, 2010, http://reliefweb.int/report/bangladesh/bangladesh-indonesia-and-iran-top-natural-disaster-ranking-france-italy-usa-high.

hurricanes and severe storms (e.g., tornadoes). Actually, for the last decade, the United States, along with China, India, Indonesia, and the Philippines, have suffered from frequent natural disasters. According to the NDRI, the countries which were found to be least at risk for natural disasters were Bahrain, Qatar, the United Arab Emirates, Andorra, Malta, Gibraltar, Liechtenstein, Monaco, and San Marino.[*]

EMERGENCY MANAGEMENT

Emergency management involves the development of policies and management of principles and concepts such as organization, administration, and planning as applied to emergency situations. Its purpose is to minimize the loss of life by protecting people and properties and aiding affected communities in rebuilding after a natural or human-made disaster. Emergency management has prehistoric roots; humankind during that period experienced some of the security threats that individuals are faced with today: for example, food shortages and infectious diseases. Beyond this era, references to natural disasters and responses to them were made in ancient history and religious texts, such as the Bible (e.g., Noah's Ark and the Flood in the Old Testament). The responses to natural disasters only constitute one phase of emergency management. In fact, emergency management includes four basic phases: mitigation, response, recovery, and preparedness[†] (each of which is explored individually below).

Mitigation

The first step, mitigation, focuses on lessening the effects of emergencies in the event that they occur and reducing vulnerability to potential future disasters. Vulnerability involves an assessment of how well or poorly an area is protected against a natural (or human-made) disaster. The vulnerability to an area or facility is not constant; it can be altered as a result of climate change, land use changes, population patterns, or building codes, among other things. One way to reduce vulnerabilities is through mitigation measures.

Mitigation involves taking measures before a threat or hazard materializes. These measures are, thus, taken in anticipation of a threat or

---

[*] "GLOBAL: Asia Most at Risk from Natural Disasters," The Integrated Regional Information Network (IRIN), May 30, 2010, http://www.irinnews.org/report/89305.

[†] Alvin H. Mushkatel and Louis F. Weschler, "Emergency Management and the Intergovernmental System," *Public Administration Review* 45, Special Issue: Emergency Management: A Challenge for Public Administration (January 1985), 49–56; George D. Haddow, Jane A. Bullock, and Damon P. Coppola, *Introduction to Emergency Management* (Third Edition) (Boston: Butterworth-Heinemann, 2008).

hazard. This step differs from the remaining three because it seeks to implement long-term risk-reducing solutions.* Consider the Midwest flooding of 1993. After the 1993 Midwest flooding, the government initiated one of the largest mitigation strategies, which included voluntary buyouts and relocation programs, in U.S. history in order to move individuals who lived in floodplains out of these areas. Ideally, in areas that are earthquake-prone, populations should settle away from fault lines and coastal areas; however, this is not frequently seen in practice.

Mitigation seeks to lessen the impact of a disaster. This can include regulation, policies, procedures, and warning systems. Early warning systems are one way to reduce vulnerabilities from natural disasters. Early warning systems exist for natural disasters, such as earthquakes, hurricanes, tornadoes, floods, and tsunamis. For example, for tsunamis, the implementation of an early warning system, buoys moored in the ocean, can register the speed and wavelength of tsunamis. The Pacific Ocean has an early warning system; this early warning system was implemented after the 1964 tsunami in Alaska. In 2004, while the earthquake that occurred was registered, there was no early warning system in place in the Indian Ocean to warn countries about the impending tsunami (Figure 7.1). Tsunamis in the Indian Ocean were considered rare. Therefore, an early warning system was not considered a priority given the cost and how it would affect the already weak economies in the region.

FIGURE 7.1   A photo of a tsunami devastated area in Aceh, Indonesia. (Image courtesy of Shutterstock.com.)

---

* George D. Haddow, Jane A. Bullock, and Damon P. Coppola, *Introduction to Emergency Management* (Third Edition) (Boston: Butterworth-Heinemann, 2008), 75.

After the 2004 tsunami, an early warning system was put in place to alert Indian Ocean countries of impending disasters. The UN Office for the Coordination of Humanitarian Affairs (OCHA) reported that this early warning system and the preparedness of several countries were tested after an 8.6 magnitude earthquake occurred in 2012.[*] In response to this earthquake, the early warning system issued alerts and evacuation orders to those that lived in coastal areas at risk of flooding. In 2012, advance warnings of Hurricane Sandy was given to residents and businesses. Nonetheless, Hurricane Sandy devastated certain areas in the Caribbean, United States, and Canada, resulting in 117 deaths in the United States and 69 deaths in Canada and the Caribbean.[†] The economic damage caused by Sandy was 50 billion U.S. dollars; this figure was higher than all of the other natural disasters that occurred in 2012, such as the drought in the United States and the earthquake in Italy.[‡]

The need for effective early warning systems was highlighted in the Hyogo Declaration, a direct outcome of the 2005 World Conference on Disaster Reduction in Kobe, Hyogo, Japan. This declaration represented the commitment of the international community in reducing losses from disasters. The need to create effective early warning systems was additionally emphasized in the Hyogo Framework for Action 2005–2015 on "building the resilience of nations and communities to disasters."[§] Particularly, this framework, under Section III(B)(2)(ii), called on relevant parties to

> [d]evelop early warning systems that are people centered, in particular systems whose warnings are timely and understandable to those at risk, which take into account the demographic, gender, cultural and livelihood characteristics of the target audiences, including guidance on how to act upon warnings, and that support effective operations by disaster managers and other decision makers.

This framework also included other detailed risk-reduction strategies for those involved in the disaster mitigation process.

Given the varying degrees of each natural disaster, mitigation strategies differ for each disaster. For example, wildfires would require some

---

[*] "Indonesia: Early Warning Pays Off after Tsunami Threat," OCHA, May 1, 2012, http://www.unocha.org/top-stories/all-stories/indonesia-early-warning-pays-after-tsunami-threat.

[†] "Hurricane Sandy Fast Facts," *CNN*, July 13, 2013, http://www.cnn.com/2013/07/13/world/americas/hurricane-sandy-fast-facts/index.html.

[‡] Debarati Guha-Sapir, Philippe Hoyois, and Regina Below, "Annual Disaster Statistical Review 2012: The Numbers and Trends," Brussels: Centre for Research on the Epidemiology of Disasters (CRED), August 2013, 17, http://cred.be/sites/default/files/ADSR_2012.pdf.

[§] This framework was also a product of the 2005 World Conference on Disaster Reduction in Kobe, Hyogo, Japan.

form of fire suppression tools; whereas floods would not. For floods, flood insurance can be purchased to mitigate losses after a flood occurs. Additionally, in areas prone to earthquakes, building codes are developed and enforced to ensure that buildings can withstand the impact of earthquakes of specified magnitudes. Indeed, ensuring that buildings are constructed in such a way as to withstand—as best as possible—certain natural disasters is an effective way to reduce vulnerabilities. This measure has been sought when dealing with disasters other than earthquakes, such as floods, hurricanes, and tornadoes (e.g., for storm shelters, hurricane shelters, and safe rooms). There are numerous examples of such mitigation strategies for each natural disaster.

Response

The second step, response, covers actions taken once a hazard or disaster has materialized. This step of emergency management seeks to effectively respond to an emergency in order to save lives, protect property, and meet basic human needs. Multiple agencies can be involved in the response stage of emergency management, such as local, state, volunteer groups, national organizations, federal and/or international agencies. The severity of the threat or hazard will dictate who will be involved in the response stage.

Local Response

First responders include emergency medical service (EMS), fire, law enforcement, and public works personnel. First responders are tasked with providing—first and foremost—medical assistance, setting the boundaries to the disaster or hazard incident, and removing all non-essential personnel from the area. Local emergency managers are responsible for developing, maintaining, and overseeing the implementation of local emergency management plans.

State Response

If the local agencies need assistance in responding to a natural disaster, they can request this assistance from the state. Each state and territory of the United States has a state emergency management office. In regards to disaster response, state emergency managers use the National Guard, which provides "personnel, communications systems, and equipment, air and road transport, heavy construction and earth-moving requirement, mass care, and feeding equipment, and emergency supplies such as beds, blankets, and medical supplies."[*]

---

[*] George D. Haddow, Jane A. Bullock, and Damon P. Coppola, *Introduction to Emergency Management* (Third Edition) (Boston: Butterworth-Heinemann, 2008), 107.

Federal Response

Assistance may be rendered on the federal level, if the local and state resources are overwhelmed or when the interests at stake are federal. The Homeland Security Act of 2002 and the Homeland Security Presidential Directive-5 (HSPD-5) mandated the creation of the National Response Framework. The NRF was created in 2005 and revised after Hurricane Katrina.* The purpose of the National Response Framework (NRF) was "to establish a comprehensive, national, all-hazards approach to domestic incident management across a spectrum of activities including prevention, preparedness, response, and recovery."† Specifically, the NRF

> is a guide to how the Nation responds to all types of disasters and emergencies...This Framework describes specific authorities and best practices for managing incidents that range from the serious but purely local to large-scale terrorist attacks or catastrophic natural disasters. The National Response Framework describes the principles, roles and responsibilities, and coordinating structures for delivering the core capabilities required to respond to an incident and further describes how response efforts integrate with those of the other mission areas.‡

In fact, the NRF provides guidance on how the entire community can work together to respond to threats or hazards. In addition, those whose roles and responsibilities have been outlined in the NSF include: individuals; communities; critical infrastructure; federal agencies; first responders; emergency services; local agencies; nongovernmental organizations (NGOs); private companies; nonprofit entities (e.g., charities); state agencies; tribal agencies; and the nation as a whole.

National Organizations and International Agencies

Many agencies have played a major role in natural (and human-made) disasters. National organizations coordinate the national responses and recovery efforts to natural (or human-made) disasters. Government funded development aid agencies, such as the United States Agency for International Development (USAID), the Swedish International Development Cooperation Agency (SIDA), and the New Zealand Aid Programme (NZAID), provide assistance in the aftermath of disasters. Some volunteer agencies that also assist national, state, and federal agencies include: the American Red Cross, AmeriCares, Feeding America,

---

* "The National Response Framework (NRF)," Environmental Protection Agency (EPA), 2013, http://www.epa.gov/osweroe1/content/nrs/nrp.htm.
† "National Response Plan," Homeland Security, 2004, 2, https://www.hsdl.org/?view= docs/dhs/nps08-010605-07.pdf.
‡ "National Response Framework," FEMA, 2013, http://www.fema.gov/media-library/ assets/documents/32230?id= 7371.

Habitat for Humanity, and Headwaters Relief Organization, to name a few.* Others that can be involved in response efforts are private sectors, nongovernmental organizations (NGOs), and international organizations such as the United Nations.

International intervention in emergency management occurs for a variety of reasons. Factors that play a role in determining whether international assistance is required are the economic resources of the country and the capacity for emergency response. Indeed, international agencies and communities usually intervene when a nation is overwhelmed and cannot respond to or recover from a natural (or human-made) disaster without assistance. The international community cannot intervene unless they have the consent of the state affected by the disaster. This is due to state sovereignty and the prohibition that exists with foreign nations and organizations interfering with domestic matters without the country's permission.

International organizations are governed by international law and their own rules and regulations. One such organization is the United Nations. Article 7 of the UN Charter established six main organs of the United Nations: "a General Assembly, a Security Council, an Economic and Social Council, a Trusteeship Council, an International Court of Justice and a Secretariat." Throughout the years, other agencies and programs were created and became part of the UN. These include (but are not limited to) the: Office for the Coordination of Humanitarian Affairs (OCHA); UN Disaster Relief Co-ordinator (UNDRO); Food and Agricultural Organization (FAO); UN International Children's Emergency Fund (UNICEF); UN Development Programme (UNDP); UN Educational, Scientific and Cultural Organization (UNESCO); UN Environment Program (UNEP); UN Institute for Training and Research (UNITAR); UN High Commissioner for Refugees (UNHCR); International Telecommunications Union (ITU); World Food Programme (WFP); and World Health Organization (WHO). These and other international organizations have legal mandates relating to international disaster response and recovery efforts.

The agency involved will depend on the disaster and the needs of the affected country. For instance, the WFP and FAO provide food during disasters (among other emergency situations). Other examples are the International Organization for Migration (IOM) and the UN Commission for Refugees (UNCHR), which provide assistance to displaced persons. Additionally, among its many responsibilities, the World Health Organization protects displaced persons by natural disasters from disease. Moreover, the United Nations Children's Fund (UNICEF)

---

* See the National Voluntary Organizations Active in Disaster (VOAD) website for more examples of volunteer organizations: http://www.nvoad.org/members.

provides education for children that have been displaced by natural (or human-made disasters).

Rescue Operations and Relief Efforts

History is replete with examples of responses to disasters. Evaluating these responses and their impact on society provides security professionals with greater insight into how to handle such disasters more effectively. Studying disasters and responses to disasters enable better decision making in dealing with them.

The response to a natural disaster can include the mobilization of national and international agencies, the provision of emergency assistance, and the evacuation of those in the affected area. A preliminary assessment of the losses resulting from the natural disaster in order to determine how best to allocate resources is also conducted in the response phase. In the aftermath of a natural disaster, generally, the initial rescue phase lasts approximately 48 hours. However, the rescue phase has lasted longer. Notwithstanding, the resources toward the rescue operations in this phase are generally lessened after 48 hours, owing to the fact that relief efforts need to be subsequently funded. Relief efforts focus on providing the basic necessities to the victims of the natural disaster. These necessities can include "trauma care, food, clean water, sanitation and shelter."[*]

Food and supplies were quickly provided to Haiti in the aftermath of the earthquake. Indeed, "[t]he U.S. Agency for International Development (USAID) sent 90,000 metric tons [of] American crops to Haiti as part of the Food for Progress and its related Food for Peace programs run by USAID and the U.S. Department of Agriculture."[†] When domestic "infrastructure and supply lines were down, foreign food aid helped alleviate the provisional needs of displaced people and disaster victims."[‡] One major concern is whether imported food is helpful during disasters. Emergency food aid can have adverse consequences on local livelihoods. While food was critical in the immediate aftermath of the disaster, the amount of food that was sent actually hampered the local economy by diverting funds from Haitian farmers to U.S. farmers. A better way to respond to food shortages in the aftermath of a natural

---

[*] Andrea Fernandes and Muhammad H. Zaman, "The Role of Biomedical Engineering in Disaster Management in Resource-Limited Settings," *Bulletin of the World Health Organization* 90 (2012), 631, http://www.who.int/bulletin/volumes/90/8/12-104901/en/.

[†] Jacob Kushner, "U.S. Spent $140 Million of Haiti Earthquake Aid on Controversial Food Exports," Pulitzer Center on Crisis Reporting, January 11, 2012, http://pulitzercenter.org/reporting/haiti-earthquake-united-states-usaid-food-aid-exports-program-farmers-clinton-monsanto-rice.

[‡] Oliver Cunningham, "The Humanitarian Aid Regime in the Republic of NGOs: The Fallacy of 'Building Back Better,'" *The Josef Korbel Journal of International Studies* 4 (2012), 110, http://www.du.edu/korbel/jais/journal/volume4/volume4_cunningham.pdf.

disaster was seen in the response of the FAO to the 2004 Indian Ocean tsunami. Specifically, the FAO dispatched resources to help farmers affected by the natural disaster by directly targeting response efforts to the farmers' losses of assets and income; thus enabling "farming and livestock production activities" to quickly resume.[*]

Water was also provided to Haiti after the 2010 earthquake. In fact, to provide the much needed clean drinking water, millions of water bottles were delivered. This provision of water had unintended consequences. Because of the ineffective recycling system in Haiti at the time, the plastic water bottles caused environmental and sanitation problems. Specifically, streets were littered with empty water bottles and sewage canals became blocked with plastic bottles and garbage.[†] In response to this, the government launched an initiative to clean up the streets; in so doing, efficiently removing the plastic bottles and garbage that had littered the streets and sewage canals.[‡]

Recovery

The third step, recovery, involves restoring the disaster-affected area by repairing and replacing damages to pre-incident conditions. This step of the emergency management process focuses on comprehensively assessing the damage that has occurred (directly and indirectly) as a result of the disaster to individuals and property (both public and private). In the aftermath of the 2004 Indian Ocean tsunami UN General Assembly Resolution 63/137 (2009) was passed, which called for the strengthening of disaster relief and recovery. Recital 13 of this resolution recognized the "Tsunami Recovery Impact Assessment and Monitoring System" as "a valuable common analytical framework for assessing and monitoring the impact of tsunami recovery and for informing effective planning and programming."

How long this step of the emergency management process lasts depends on the magnitude of the devastation caused by the disaster. Recovery includes short-term and long-term efforts to return affected areas to their predisaster state (as best as possible). A short-term goal of recovery is to restore infrastructure, clear debris, and rebuild and repair homes, schools, hospitals, and other critical infrastructure. Thus,

---

[*] Wilhelm Kirch (Ed.), *Encyclopedia of Public Health* (Volume 1) (Dresden, Germany: Springer, 2008), 281.

[†] "Rebuilding Haiti: The Long, Hard Haul," *The Economist*, March 17, 2011, http://www.economist.com/node/18390114?story_id=18390114.

[‡] Petra Nemcova, "Each New Day in the New Haiti Brings New Opportunities to Create Happiness," *Huffington Post*, January 16, 2013, http://www.huffingtonpost.com/petra-nemcova/haiti-earthquake-anniversary_b_2482113.html.

one aspect that this step focuses on is recovery from structural damage. Accordingly, major repairs on buildings and structures may be required after a disaster. In this step, financial assistance and other aid should also be provided to individuals, households, and businesses in affected areas. Another aspect of this step is emotional recovery. After the 2004 Indian Ocean tsunami, many citizens and tourists (adults and children) required mental health assistance and counseling as they suffered from anxiety and posttraumatic stress disorder (PTSD).* The emotional distress caused by traumatic events should be factored into the recovery process.

Long-term goals include building a sustainable environment. This may involve "long-term health and livelihood interventions."† To ensure that efforts are sustainable, a partnership between the community and government is required. Community input is critical in order to understand the nature and extent of the impact of a natural disaster on the population. Consider, once again, the 2010 earthquake in Haiti. An unprecedented number of NGOs are in Haiti. In particular, there are approximately 10,000 NGOs in Haiti; many of these organizations provide critical services.‡ Haiti has also been given significant aid. It is important to note that prior to the 2010 earthquake, Haiti relied heavily on foreign aid. The situation was exacerbated in the aftermath of the earthquake. NGOs tend to operate parallel to the government instead of in support of. This leads to a duplication of efforts and inhibits effective coordination. NGOs also inevitably undermine the authority of the Haitian government as they provide services that the government is supposed to be providing. This hinders Haitian economic development and explains why Haiti continues to depend on foreign aid. Indeed, a common and often problematic tendency is for local or national actors to be subordinated by international actors. In this manner, local agencies and authorities are marginalized during the decision-making processes. These types of relationships between local or national and international agencies undermine local capacity, thereby inhibiting effective recovery.

---

* Anto P. Rajkumar, Titus S. Premkumar, and Prathap Tharyan, "Coping with the Asian Tsunami: Perspectives from Tmail Nadu, India on the Determinants of Resilience in the Face of Adversity," *Social Science & Medicine* 67:5 (2008), 844–853; Braj Bhushan and J. Sathya Kumar, "Emotional Distress and Posttraumatic Stress in Children Surviving the 2004 Tsunami," *Journal of Loss and Trauma* 12 (2007), 245–257.
† Andrea Fernandes and Muhammad H. Zaman, "The Role of Biomedical Engineering in Disaster Management in Resource-Limited Settings," *Bulletin of the World Health Organization* 90 (2012), 631, http://www.who.int/bulletin/volumes/90/8/12-104901/en/.
‡ Kevin Edmonds, "Beyond Good Intentions: The Structural Limitations of NGOs in Haiti," *Critical Sociology* 39: (2013), 440.

Preparedness

The fourth and final step, preparedness, requires communities, cities, and nations to get ready for disasters that will or may happen in the future. The National Incident Management System (NIMS) defines preparedness as "a continuous cycle of planning, organizing, training, equipping, exercising, evaluating, and taking corrective action in an effort to ensure effective coordination during incident response."[*] Preparedness helps reduce vulnerability to threats or hazards.

Preparedness for disasters is also the responsibility of individuals, families, businesses, and governments. The preparedness cycle includes: creating a plan; engaging in training and education; conducting exercises; and evaluating and improving the plan based on the exercises. In the past, what has been observed is a general lack of preparedness and planning by certain countries experiencing a natural disaster. For example, Haiti had no adequate preparedness plan in the event of a natural disaster of this magnitude. This, and Haiti's existing economic and political factors, directly contributed to the effects of the earthquake (Figure 7.2).

The training of emergency management personnel and education of the public are critical components of preparedness plans. The public should be informed of ways to prepare for disasters, such as: maintaining emergency food, water, and medical supplies; keeping cash on hand that families can live on for several days; retaining radios; creating indoor safety measures (depending on the type of natural disaster); and setting up family evacuation routes and meeting locations (in the event that such an evacuation is required). Information concerning best practices in emergency management planning should be communicated to the public via the Internet, brochures, and training offered in communities. The education of the public as to the signs of natural disasters is critical as well. For example, the 2004 Indian Ocean tsunami revealed that many individuals believed that receding waters were an indication of safety; which is not the case. Indeed, curious to see the exposed reef area because of the receding waters, several stayed in the coastal areas before the tsunami hit. The public should not only be familiar with warning signs of natural disasters, but also on how to respond to them should they occur.

The final stages of the preparedness cycle consist of conducting exercises and implementing the lessons learned following the completion of these exercises. These stages enable the effective allocation of natural disaster resources. However, this can only occur if the recommendations

---

[*] "Plan & Prepare: Preparedness," FEMA, 2012, http://www.fema.gov/what-mitigation/plan-prepare.

FIGURE 7.2   A Haitian man walks past a sign requesting help and supplies in Port-au-Prince, Haiti, January 19, 2010. Units from all branches
of the U.S. military conducted humanitarian and disaster relief operations as part of Operation Unified Response after a 7.0 magnitude earthquake struck the country January 12, 2010. (From the U.S. Navy, DoD
photo by Mass Communication Specialist 2nd Class Michael C. Barton,
U.S. Navy, Released.)

provided after concluding the exercises are implemented. Consider the
2004 U.S. preparedness exercise known as Hurricane Pam. The scenario
presented in the exercise, a hypothetical Category 3 hurricane, was as
follows: "Hurricane Pam brought sustained winds of 120 mph, up to
20 inches of rain in parts of southeast Louisiana and storm surge that
topped levees in the New Orleans area. More than one million residents
evacuated and Hurricane Pam destroyed 500,000–600,000 buildings."[*]
Emergency management officials from parish, state, federal, and volunteer organizations participated in this exercise. After the exercise,
recommendations were made to improve preparedness for a hurricane
of this magnitude. These recommendations: recognized the need for
approximately 1,000 shelters; determined ways to replenish supplies at
shelters; identified lead and support agencies for search and rescue; created a command and control structure for search and rescue; determined

---

[*] "Hurricane Pam Exercise Concludes," FEMA, July 23, 2004, http://www.fema.gov/
news-release/2004/07/23/hurricane-pam-exercise-concludes.

ways to resupply hospitals; identified alternative locations to provide medical care in the event that hospitals' resources are overwhelmed; and outlined debris removal priorities.* Nonetheless, these recommendations were not implemented before Hurricane Katrina struck. The problem areas identified in the Hurricane Pam exercise were similar to those identified after Hurricane Katrina.

The United States was ill-prepared for Hurricane Katrina. Hurricane Katrina "reached [a] Category 5 at its peak intensity."[†] When it reached Mississippi and Louisiana it was a Category 3 hurricane. What caused massive damage was the storm surge. The storm surge caused the levee system protecting New Orleans from Lake Pontchartrain to fail.[‡] This failure resulted in the severe flooding of New Orleans. To date, Hurricane Katrina is the deadliest, and most destructive and expensive natural disaster in U.S. history. Over 1,800 individuals died as a result of the hurricane. Businesses were ruined and thousands of individuals were displaced as a result of the destruction to their homes. After the terrorist attacks on September 11, 2001, most emergency management resources were diverted to human-made threats—such as terrorism and weapons of mass destruction. When Hurricane Katrina struck New Orleans in 2005, it brought home the lesson that attention needed to be paid to natural disasters as well.

LESSONS LEARNED IN INTERNATIONAL EMERGENCY MANAGEMENT

Numerous international nongovernmental agencies work toward development, recovery, and preparedness for natural (or human-made) disasters. Article 1 of the UN Charter holds that one of the main purposes of the United Nations is to achieve international cooperation in humanitarian issues. Several UN General Assembly resolutions have been implemented in this regard calling for "international cooperation on humanitarian assistance in the field of natural disasters, from relief to development."[§] Other UN General Assembly resolutions promote the

---

* Ibid.
† "About Hurricane Katrina," FEMA, January 28, 2013, http://www.fema.gov/response-recovery/about-hurricane-katrina.
‡ "Summary Report on Building Performance: Hurricane Katrina 2005," FEMA, April 2006, http://www.fema.gov/pdf/rebuild/mat/fema548/548_SumRprt0329fnl.pdf.
§ UN General Assembly Resolution 63/141 of 10 March 2009; UN General Assembly Resolution 64/251 of 30 April 2010; UN General Assembly Resolution 65/264 of 21 June 2011; and UN General Assembly Resolution 66/227 of 15 March 2012.

strengthening and coordination of UN humanitarian assistance during emergencies.* In addition, resolutions have been passed to promote UN cooperation with other relevant international actors, such as NGOs and the International Red Cross and Red Crescent Movement.† Moreover, the United Nations Millennium Declaration of 2000 included a commitment by the international community "[t]o intensify cooperation to reduce the number and effects of natural and manmade disasters." Likewise, the Council of the European Union expressed its commitment to provide humanitarian aid to those countries that are in need.‡ The European Commission Humanitarian Aid Department (ECHO) is responsible for providing this assistance to victims in countries outside of the European Union.§

For the United Nations, the UN Office for the Coordination of Humanitarian Affairs (OCHA) is responsible for overseeing and facilitating humanitarian efforts. Specifically, OCHA "mobilize[s] and coordinate[s] effective and principled humanitarian action in partnership with national and international actors in order to alleviate human suffering in disasters and emergencies."¶ The Inter-Agency Standing Committee (IASC) serves as an interagency coordinator of humanitarian assistance of agencies inside and outside the UN. Additionally, the International Federation of Red Cross and Red Crescent Societies, an international humanitarian organization, oversees and coordinates assistance to victims of natural (and human-made) disasters.**

Cooperation and coordination enable better responses to natural disasters. To enhance coordination and cooperation, regional organizations have also been designated to work with UN organizations. For example, the African Union Commission (AUC) collaborates with OCHA in responses to emergencies. Regionally, organizations have been designated to coordinate responses to natural disasters in their area. For instance, the Caribbean Disaster Emergency Response Agency is responsible for coordinating regional assistance efforts between

---

* UN General Assembly Resolution 63/139 of 5 March 2009; UN General Assembly Resolution 64/76 of 3 February 2010; UN General Assembly Resolution 65/133 of 3 March 2011; UN General Assembly Resolution 66/119 of 7 March 2012; and UN General Assembly Resolution 67/87 of 7 December 2012.

† For example, UN General Assembly Resolutions 60/196 of 2 March 2006 and UN General Assembly Resolution 46/182 of 19 December 1991.

‡ Council Regulation (EC) No. 1257/96 of 20 June 1996 concerning humanitarian aid, OJ L 163.

§ "The EU Explained: Humanitarian Aid," European Commission, February 2013, http://europa.eu/pol/hum/flipbook/en/files/humanitarian-aid_en.pdf.

¶ "Who We Are," OCHA, http://www.unocha.org/about-us/who-we-are.

** "International Federation of Red Cross and Red Crescent Movement: At a Glance," International Federation of Red Cross and Red Crescent Societies, 2007, http://www.ifrc.org/Global/Publications/general/at_a_glance-en.pdf.

governmental and nongovernmental organizations responsible for relief efforts.* Other examples of regional organizations that engage in similar emergency management efforts are the Coordination Centre for the Prevention of Natural Disasters in Central America (CEPREDENAC) and the Southern African Development Community (SADC).

Regional mutual assistance agreements also exist to strengthen cooperation.† Moreover, comprehensive partnership agreements have been developed between regions. A primary example of this is the Cotonou Agreement between developing countries and the European Union. This agreement provides a framework for cooperative relations between the EU and "79 countries in Africa, the Caribbean and the Pacific (ACP)."‡ Furthermore, the North Atlantic Treaty Organization (NATO) has procedures in place coordinating disaster assistance with affected countries and international humanitarian organizations.§ NATO additionally has the Euro-Atlantic Disaster Response Coordination Centre (EADRCC), which manages aid distribution to affected states.

Some countries do not include guidelines on how international cooperation will occur in the event of a disaster. For this reason, international and regional instruments have been implemented to create such guidelines. One notable example is the 2005 ASEAN Agreement on disaster management and emergency response. This agreement sought to: mitigate (and wherever possible prevent) natural (or human-made) disasters; strengthen regional cooperation during disasters; involve civil society and local communities in emergency management plans; provide primary control over emergency management to the affected country; and ensure respect for national sovereignty when responding to natural disasters. In this manner, it sought to remove certain obstacles in order to ensure efficient and effective international disaster management.

International disaster management is a complex process that involves a coordinated effort by local, national, and international agencies. The issue at hand is not the lack of available agencies nor the contributions by these agencies. Instead, the issue is that each agency and government

---

* Wilhelm Kirch (Ed.), *Encyclopedia of Public Health* (Volume 1) (Dresden, Germany: Springer, 2008), 281.
† See, for example, the Memorandum of Understanding between the Government of the United States of America and the Government of Ukraine on cooperation in natural and human-made technological emergency prevention and response of 2000, and the Agreement between the Swiss Federal Council and the Government of the Republic of the Philippines on cooperation in the event of natural disaster or major emergencies of 2001.
‡ "The Cotonou Agreement," European Commission, December 9, 2012, http://ec.europa.eu/europeaid/where/acp/overview/cotonou-agreement/.
§ NATO, "NATO's Role in Disaster Assistance," NATO Civil Emergency Planning, Euro-Atlantic Disaster Response Coordination Centre, 2001, http://www.nato.int/eadrcc/mcda-e.pdf.

has difference priorities and agendas, making the coordination in aid efforts extremely difficult. Indeed, there is no single command and control structure that has been developed in the international disaster response community.

A common complaint in the aftermath of natural disasters is the lack of coordination between international actors during disaster situations. For example, the coordination in relief efforts in the past has left much to be desired. This is especially true regarding relief in the form of donated foodstuffs, clothing, and medical necessities. Concerning foodstuffs, after the flood in Bangladesh in 1974, canned pork was donated and distributed to the victims, ignoring the fact that the majority of them were Muslims, who are prohibited from consuming pork (according to their religion).* Inappropriate clothing has also been sent in response to natural disasters; for example, heavy winter clothing has been sent to tropical climates. This was observed in the donations provided in response to the 2004 Indian Ocean tsunami.† Winter coats were also donated to Hurricane Andrew victims in Florida in 1992.

In addition to errors in foodstuffs and clothing, despite the best of intentions, some drug donations have been more harmful than helpful. There have been instances in the aftermath of a disaster where medication that was provided had expired. There have also been instances where medication provided had inadequate labels or labels in foreign languages. In fact, in response to the earthquakes in Guatemala in 1976 and in Armenia in 1988 many of the medications sent had expired, were not needed, or were inadequately labeled.‡ Moreover, there have been further instances where medication that has been provided is inappropriate to that which is needed by those surviving the disaster. In addition to these errors, oftentimes there have been delays in the receipt of medication due to restrictions on the importation of medications. The Kyoto

---

* Bimal Kanti Paul, "Disaster Relief Efforts: An Update," *Progress in Development Studies* 6:3 (2006), 213.
† Ibid.
‡ David Alexander, *Confronting Catastrophe* (Oxford: Oxford University Press, 2000); Philippe Autier, Marie-Christine Ferir, Araik Hairapetien, Alexandre Alexanian, Veronique Agoudjian, Gerard Schimets, Georges Dallemagne, Marie-Noelle Leva, and Jacques Pinel, "Drug Supply in the Aftermath of the 1988 Armenian Earthquake," *Lancet* 335 (1990), 1388–1390; Robie V. Harrington, "Pharmaceutical in Disasters," In David E. Hogan and Jonathan L. Burstein, *Disaster Medicine* (Philadelphia, PA: Lippincott Williams & Wilkins, 2002), 58; Bimal Kanti Paul, "Disaster Relief Efforts: An Update," *Progress in Development Studies* 6:3 (2006), 213; Philippe Autier, Ramesh Govindaraj, Robin Gray, Rama Lakshminarayanan, Homira G. Nassery, and Gerard Schimets, "Drug Donations in Post-Emergency Situations," *HNP Discussion Paper*, June 2002, http://siteresources.worldbank.org/HEALTHNUTRITIONANDPOPULATION/Resources/281627-1095698140167/Nassery-DrugDonation-whole.pdf; AEDES, PQMD, WHO, and World Bank, "Drug Donations in Post-Emergencies Situation," January 5, 2008, http://www.pqmd.org/assets/drug_donations_in_post-emergency_situations.pdf.

Customs Convention and UN General Assembly Resolutions 46/182 and 57/150 called on states that have been affected by disaster to better facilitate the entry of medications.

Providing timely and reliable information is critical to emergency management planning and the effective mobilization of national and international resources. A determination needs to be made as to which resources are required in the aftermath of a natural disaster. This includes both supplies and services. Resources can be human, material, and financial. Potential sources for these are the private sector, NGOs, governmental bodies, national organizations, and international organizations. Agencies should additionally coordinate the control and monitoring of the sources, uses, and effectiveness of domestic and international donations of resources.

Overall, what is required is a holistic improvement of coordination efforts between local, state, private, national, regional, and international organizations. Coordination is critical as without it resources are wasted, efforts are duplicated, and gaps are left in the coverage of the affected country's needs. Countries should, if they have not already, designate a local, state, or national entity that will be responsible for coordinating responses to natural (or human-made disasters). In this way, if international assistance is needed and provided, there will be a single point of contact in the affected country; thereby reducing the likelihood of the duplication of efforts. This process also works towards ensuring that the resources obtained via outside assistance are those that are needed by the affected country.

CONCLUDING THOUGHTS

Natural disasters are costly; both in terms of their human and economic impact. In addition to resulting deaths, injuries, destruction, and economic damage, natural disasters tend to disproportionately affect particular individuals within the population; this is especially true in developing countries. Specifically, women are at risk of sexual and domestic violence and children are at risk of abduction, exploitation, and/or trafficking.

Natural disasters can be dealt with using emergency management procedures. There are four phases of emergency management: namely, mitigation, response, recovery, and preparedness. Natural disasters cannot be prevented. Mitigation, however, can occur. Mitigation focuses on reducing the impact of a natural disaster should it materialize and reducing the vulnerability of areas to potential future natural disasters. Responses to disasters seek to save lives, protect property, and effectively meet basic human needs. Sometimes responses to disasters fall short of this due to the lack of coordination and cooperation among those involved in the emergency management process. Coordination and cooperation among actors in this, and other stages of the emergency management process, is critical.

Recovery is a vital part of emergency management as it aims to restore a community to its pre-disaster status. Recovery includes short-term (e.g., cleanups and home repairs) and long-term efforts (e.g., livelihood interventions that allow the affected country to obtain economic stability without foreign aid). Finally, to prepare for a natural disaster, emergency management plans should be created (those involved in the process should also be made aware of them). All those involved in the process should obtain training. Exercises should additionally be run as part of existing preparedness plans. The lessons learned from these exercises should be incorporated into the already existing emergency management plans. Hurricane Katrina brought home the lesson that attention needed to be paid to these exercises and that the recommendations from them should be implemented.

CHAPTER 8

Human-Made Disasters

Every community, state, and country, should understand the risks it faces and understand how to manage them. To achieve this, it is necessary to engage in threat, hazard identification, and risk analysis. To identify the threats and hazards to an area, forecasting, historical information about the location, and expertise in past threats and hazards are required. After the threats and hazards are identified, an assessment of how each threat and hazard affects the area is conducted. The all-hazards approach seeks to identify all threats and hazards to an area. According to Presidential Policy Directive 21 (or PPD-21), all hazards is defined as "a threat or an incident, natural or manmade, that warrants action to protect life, property, the environment, and public health or safety, and to minimize disruptions of government, social, or economic activities. It includes natural disasters, cyber incidents, industrial accidents, pandemics, acts of terrorism, sabotage, and destructive criminal activity targeting critical infrastructure."[*] The all-hazards approach has been used in the field emergency management and the protection of critical infrastructure.

Many commonalities exist among threats and hazards that communities are faced with. These commonalities suggest that many of the same strategies can be applied to these threats and hazards. As such, an all-hazards approach seeks an effective and consistent response to threats and hazards, irrespective of their cause.[†] Using the "all-hazards approach," this chapter considers human-made disasters and the agencies that were created to respond to them. It further critically examines national and international responses to well-known human-made disasters. Finally, this chapter recommends ways to more effectively deal with such threats.

---

[*] The White House, President Barack Obama, "Presidential Policy Directive—Critical Infrastructure Security and Resilience," Office of the Press Secretary, February 12, 2013, para. 83, http://www.whitehouse.gov/the-press-office/2013/02/12/presidential-policy-directive-critical-infrastructure-security-and-resil.

[†] It is important to note, however, that other threats and hazards may require a more specific, tailored response.

TYPES OF HUMAN-MADE DISASTERS

A human-made disaster or technological hazard is a materialized threat that can occur either intentionally or unintentionally from human action. Technological hazards or human-made disasters are sometimes referred to as environmental disasters because they are caused by the impact of human action on the natural environment. These types of disasters include: events associated with exposure to hazardous materials, fires, conventional and nuclear power failures, gas line or water main breaks, nuclear accidents, terrorist incidents, and the use of weapons of mass destruction (i.e., nuclear, biological, chemical, or radiological weapons). The following sections examine four human-made disasters: nuclear accidents, chemical accidents, fires, and oil spills.

Nuclear Events: Accidents or Incidents?

Nuclear events are classified as incidents or accidents depending on their severity. The International Nuclear Event Scale (INES), a tool used worldwide to communicate to the public the significance of nuclear and radiological events, makes these classifications.[*] In the INES, nuclear events are classified on a scale of 1 to 7.[†] On this scale, events in Levels 1–3 are classified as incidents and events in Levels 4–7 are classified as accidents.[‡] The next sections focus exclusively on nuclear accidents.

Three-Mile Island Nuclear Power Plant Accident

The Three Mile Island nuclear power plant accident in Harrisburg, Pennsylvania, occurred on March 28, 1979 (Figure 8.1). In this Level 5 accident, a partial nuclear meltdown occurred. Specifically, this event occurred because of a cooling malfunction which caused a partial meltdown of one of the two nuclear reactors. In its report, the U.S. Nuclear Regulatory Commission (NRC) concluded that this accident was the result of equipment malfunctions, flaws in system design, and human error.[§] In particular, according to the NRC report, the event began with

---

[*] "INES: The International Nuclear Event Scale," International Atomic Energy Agency (IAEA), 1, http://www.iaea.org/Publications/Factsheets/English/ines.pdf.
[†] "INES: The International Nuclear and Radiological Event Scale," International Atomic Energy Agency (IAEA), August 16, 2013, http://www-ns.iaea.org/tech-areas/emergency/ines.asp.
[‡] Ibid.
[§] "Backgrounder on the Three Mile Island Accident," U.S. Nuclear Regulatory Commission, 1, February 11, 2013, http://www.nrc.gov/reading-rm/doc-collections/fact-sheets/3mile-isle.pdf.

FIGURE 8.1   President Jimmy Carter leaving Three Mile Island for Middletown, Pennsylvania, April 1, 1979. (From the National Archives and Records Administration.)

> [e]ither a mechanical or electrical failure [that] prevented the main feedwater pumps from sending water to the steam generators that remove heat from the reactor core. This caused the plant's turbine-generator and then the reactor itself to automatically shut down. Immediately, the pressure in the primary system (the nuclear portion of the plant) began to increase. In order to control that pressure, the pilot-operated relief valve (a valve located at the top of the pressurizer) opened. The valve should have closed when the pressure fell to proper levels, but it became stuck open.[*]

The NRC report further noted that the "[i]nstruments in the control room, however, indicated to the plant staff that the valve was closed. As a result, the plant staff … [were] unaware that cooling water was pouring out of the stuck-open valve."[†] In addition, "other instruments available to reactor operators provided inadequate information. [For example,] [t]here was no instrument that showed how much water covered the core."[‡]

Apart from the issues that arose from equipment malfunctions and poor instrumentation design, the operators of the plant also inadequately responded to this event. This inadequate response resulted from the lack of appropriate training that operators had received on emergency procedures. For instance, operators were only required to memorize a few

---

[*] Ibid.
[†] Ibid.
[‡] Ibid.

emergency procedures and were insufficiently "trained to diagnose and cope with unexpected equipment malfunction."[*] In addition, the operators had not been trained to deal with events occurring under conditions of stress. As a result, misunderstandings in communication of the accident and its potential impact led to widespread panic. Contributing to the public's fears was the conflicting information that was being communicated to the public about the event and its potential health effects. Ultimately, only a small amount of radiation was released. This amount of radiation, according to numerous studies, did not pose any significant health concerns for the population.[†]

Despite the findings of these studies, this event had significant consequences for the nuclear energy industry; eventually leading to its sharp decline. Moreover, due to the Three Mile Island nuclear accident, many significant reforms were made in the nuclear energy industry: the upgrading and enhancement of plant design and equipment; improvement of operator training; the enhancement of emergency response and preparedness; stricter adherence to NRC regulations; the requirement of more inspections of facilities to ensure compliance with existing regulations; information sharing on lessons learned both domestically and abroad; and mandating the provision of information to the public about nuclear power plant performance.[‡] The Federal Radiological Emergency Response Plan was also implemented in the aftermath of the Three Mile Island nuclear power plant accident.[§]

At the time the Three Mile Island nuclear accident occurred, it was considered the worst commercial nuclear power plant accident in history. This soon changed following the Chernobyl nuclear accident.

---

[*] Najmedin Meshkati, "Human Factors in Large-Scale Technological Systems' Accidents: Three Mile Island, Bhopal, Chernobyl," *Organization & Environment* 5:2 (1991), 143.

[†] Studies were conducted by academicians, independent groups, the Environmental Protection Agency, the Department of Energy, the Department of Health and Human Services (previously known as the Department of Health, Education and Welfare), the Commonwealth of Pennsylvania, and so on. "Backgrounder on the Three Mile Island Accident," U.S. Nuclear Regulatory Commission, February 11, 2013, 2–3, http://www.nrc.gov/reading-rm/doc-collections/fact-sheets/3mile-isle.pdf.

[‡] "Nuclear Incidents: Three Mile Island Nuclear Plant," Environmental Protection Agency, February 15, 2012, http://www.epa.gov/radiation/rert/tmi.html; "Three Mile Island Accident of 1979 Knowledge Management Digest (NUREG/KM-0001)," U.S. Nuclear Regulatory Commission, December 2012, http://www.nrc.gov/reading-rm/doc-collections/nuregs/knowledge/km0001/.

[§] The Federal Radiological Emergency Response was subsequently replaced by the National Response Framework (the National Response Framework is discussed in Chapter 7 of this volume). "Nuclear Incidents: Three Mile Island Nuclear Plant," Environmental Protection Agency, February 15, 2012, http://www.epa.gov/radiation/rert/tmi.html.

Chernobyl Nuclear Accident

A reactor for the Chernobyl nuclear power plant in the Ukraine malfunctioned on April 26, 1986. Particularly, the nuclear accident, a Level 7 on the INES, was the result of a decision of plant operators to test the safety systems of the reactor. Before the tests were conducted, the security systems of the plant were deactivated. After the test commenced, a series of explosions occurred at the core of the reactor and the cover of the reactor blew off releasing radioactive material. The level of radioactivity in the atmosphere was extremely high.

Unlike the Three Mile Island nuclear accident, ultimately, this event caused radiation deaths and illness. Those working at the site were also exposed to substantial doses of radiation. Some emergency responders were exposed to lethal dosages of radiation. The same was true for plant operators. Within several weeks of the accident, 30 plant workers and emergency personnel had died.[*] Moreover, out of the 600 workers, 134 received high radiation doses and suffered from acute radiation syndrome (ARS).[†] ARS survivors also experienced "skin injuries and radiation-induced cataracts."[‡] Other health consequences were also observed in the aftermath of Chernobyl; the most significant of which was thyroid cancer. In fact, studies showed a link between contaminated food and milk and thyroid cancer. Specifically, "[r]esidents who ate food contaminated with radioactive iodine in the days immediately after the accident received relatively high doses to the thyroid gland. This was especially true of children who drank milk from cows who had eaten contaminated grass. Since iodine concentrates in the thyroid gland, this was a major cause of the high incidence of thyroid cancer in children."[§] Indeed, these studies demonstrated that "a substantial fraction of the more than 6,000 thyroid cancers observed to date [were] among people

---

[*] "The Chernobyl Accident: UNSCEAR's Assessments of the Radiation Effects," United Nations Scientific Committee on the Effects of Atomic Radiation, July 16, 2012, http://www.unscear.org/unscear/en/chernobyl.html.

[†] B. Bennett, M. Repacholi, and Z. Carr, *Health Effects of the Chernobyl Accident and Special Health Care Programmes*, Report of the UN Chernobyl Forum, Expert Group "Health" (Geneva: World Health Organization, 2006), http://www.who.int/ionizing_radiation/chernobyl/WHO%20Report%20on%20Chernobyl%20Health%20Effects%20July%2006.pdf.

[‡] UNSCEAR 2008, Report to the General Assembly with Scientific Annexes, *Sources and Effects of Ionizing Radiation, Annex D in United Nations Scientific Committee on the Effects of Atomic Radiation* (New York: United Nations, 2011), 64, http://www.unscear.org/docs/reports/2008/11-80076_Report_2008_Annex_D.pdf.

[§] "Chernobyl: The True Scale of the Accident: 20 Years Later a UN Report Provides Definitive Answers and Ways to Repair Lives," World Health Organization, 2005, http://www.who.int/mediacentre/news/releases/2005/pr38/en/index1.html.

who were children or adolescents at the time of the accident (by 2005, 15 cases had proved fatal)."[*]

According to NRC, at the time of Chernobyl, the U.S. nuclear energy industry had several measures in place to prevent a Chernobyl-type event from occurring in the United States, including "differences in plant design, broader safe shutdown capabilities and strong structures to hold in radioactive materials."[†] Even though the design of the Chernobyl nuclear power plant was unique to the Soviet Union, the nuclear accident triggered significant changes in the safety procedures of the nuclear energy industries both in the East and West.[‡] Similar to the Three Mile Island nuclear accident, there were flaws in the design of the system. Consequently, in the aftermath of Chernobyl, emphasis was placed on the proper design of nuclear power plant systems and the development and implementation of "backup safety systems to deal with potential accidents."[§] Additionally, like the Three Mile Island nuclear accident, Chernobyl resulted from gross operator error. Accordingly, the reforms post-Chernobyl included "maintaining proper procedures and controls for normal operations and emergencies" and ensuring that "competent and motivated plant management and operating staff" were hired and maintained in nuclear power plants."[¶]

The nature and extent of the damage was not immediately communicated to the media, public, and emergency responders. Even security measures to protect populations close to the plant were not immediately taken. It was not until 30 hours after the explosion that the first security measures were taken. Indeed, buses were sent to Pripyat to evacuate inhabitants, which was located 3 kilometers (km) away from the nuclear power plant, 30 hours after the accident occurred.[**] By that time, inhabitants had already been exposed to high levels of radiation.

Given that a delayed response and insufficient communication of the nuclear accident played a significant role in the outcome, international laws were implemented to prevent unnecessary delays in actions

---

[*] UNSCEAR 2008, Report to the General Assembly with Scientific Annexes, *Sources and Effects of Ionizing Radiation, Annex D in United Nations Scientific Committee on the Effects of Atomic Radiation* (New York: United Nations, 2011), 64–65, http://www.unscear.org/docs/reports/2008/11-80076_Report_2008_Annex_D.pdf.

[†] "Backgrounder on Chernobyl Nuclear Power Plant Accident," U.S. Nuclear Regulatory Commission, June 20, 2013, 2, http://www.nrc.gov/reading-rm/doc-collections/fact-sheets/chernobyl-bg.pdf.

[‡] "Chernobyl Accident 1986," World Nuclear Association, June 2013, http://www.world-nuclear.org/info/Safety-and-Security/Safety-of-Plants/Chernobyl-Accident/.

[§] "Backgrounder on Chernobyl Nuclear Power Plant Accident," U.S. Nuclear Regulatory Commission, June 20, 2013, 2, http://www.nrc.gov/reading-rm/doc-collections/fact-sheets/chernobyl-bg.pdf.

[¶] Ibid.

[**] "Chernobyl Accident 1986," World Nuclear Association, June 2013, http://www.world-nuclear.org/info/Safety-and-Security/Safety-of-Plants/Chernobyl-Accident/.

and communication of nuclear accidents or radiological disasters. The most notable of which were the Convention on Early Notification of a Nuclear Accident and the Convention on Assistance in Case of a Nuclear Accident or Radiological Emergency. The Convention on Early Notification of a Nuclear Accident of 1986 "establishe[d] a notification system for nuclear accidents which have the potential for international transboundary release that could be of radiological safety significance for another State. It require[d] States to report the accident's time, location, radiation releases, and other data essential for assessing the situation."[*] The Convention on Assistance in Case of a Nuclear Accident or Radiological Emergency of 1986 created a framework for international cooperation whereby parties of the Conventions and the International Atomic Energy Agency (IAEA) provide support and assistance to countries that are experiencing or have experienced nuclear accidents or radiological emergencies.[†] Despite these international laws and the safety measures promoted nationally and internationally post-Chernobyl (Figure 8.2), the lack of preparedness, inadequate system design, gross operator errors,

FIGURE 8.2   The exclusion zone at Chernobyl. Pripyat, Ukraine. (Image courtesy of Shutterstock.com.)

---

[*] "International Conventions and Legal Agreements: Convention on Early Notification of a Nuclear Accident," International Atomic Energy Agency, http://www.iaea.org/Publications/Documents/Conventions/cenna.html.

[†] "International Conventions and Legal Agreements: Convention on Assistance in Case of a Nuclear Accident or Radiological Emergency," International Atomic Energy Agency, http://www.iaea.org/Publications/Documents/Conventions/cacnare.html.

and a lack of communication were all present factors in the next significant nuclear accident, the 2010 Fukushima Daiichi nuclear power plant accident.

Fukushima Nuclear Power Plant Accident

On March 11, 2011, an earthquake (9.0 on the Richter scale) occurred in Japan. This earthquake caused a tsunami. These two natural disasters triggered a human-made disaster, the Fukushima Daiichi nuclear power plant accident (a Level 7 accident on the INES). This compound disaster caused critical power failures at the plant. Specifically, emergency generators, located under the facility, were flooded by water. As a result, no power was available for the safety measures, rendering the emergency cooling system inoperable. Consequently, the nuclear reactors overheated causing explosions and critical damage to the facility. Subsequently, radiation leaked from the nuclear facility. This nuclear accident had significant adverse consequences for humans, the environment, and the food supply.

Similar to the nuclear accidents previously mentioned, the design of the plant played a role in the nuclear accident. Specifically, the Daiichi nuclear power plant in Fukushima was not designed to withstand the type of disaster that occurred. Consider the following: nuclear power plants are designed, maintained, and controlled based on the concept of defense in depth. According to the International Nuclear Safety Advisory Group, "defense in depth consists of a hierarchical deployment of different levels of equipment and procedures in order to maintain the effectiveness of physical barriers placed between radioactive material and workers, the public or the environment, during normal operation, anticipated operational occurrences (AOOs) and, for some barriers, accidents at the plant."[*] It "is implemented to provide a graded protection against a wide variety of transients, incidents and accidents, including equipment failures and human errors within nuclear power plants and events initiated outside plants."[†] There are five levels: levels 1 through 5, of defense in depth (see Table 8.1).[‡] In the Fukushima event, Level 3 was

---

[*] "Defence in Depth in Nuclear Safety" (INSAG-10, International Atomic Energy Agency, Vienna), International Nuclear Safety Advisory Group, 1996, cited in IAEA, "Assessment of Defence in Depth for Nuclear Power Plants," *Safety Reports Series No. 46*, 2005, 4, http://www-pub.iaea.org/MTCD/publications/PDF/Pub1218_web.pdf.

[†] IAEA, "Assessment of Defence in Depth for Nuclear Power Plants," *IAEA Safety Reports Series No. 46*, 2005, 1, http://www-pub.iaea.org/MTCD/publications/PDF/Pub1218_web.pdf.

[‡] Information about the levels and what they consist of was obtained from: IAEA, "Assessment of Defence in Depth for Nuclear Power Plants," *IAEA Safety Reports Series No. 46*, 2005, 5, http://www-pub.iaea.org/MTCD/publications/PDF/Pub1218_web.pdf.

TABLE 8.1   Defense in Depth

Defense in Depth Levels	Objectives
Level 1	Prevention of abnormal operation and failures
Level 2	Control of abnormal operation and detection of failures
Level 3	Control of accidents within the design basis
Level 4	Control of severe plant conditions including prevention of accident progression and mitigation of severe accident consequences
Level 5	Mitigation of radiological consequences of significant releases of radioactive materials

Source: Information about the levels and what they consist of was obtained from: IAEA, "Assessment of Defense in Depth for Nuclear Power Plants," Safety Reports Series No. 46, *IAEA*, 2005, 5, http://www-pub.iaea.org/MTCD/publications/PDF/Pub1218_web.pdf.

not obtained as the facility was not designed to withstand the impact of a tsunami of that magnitude.

A combination of other factors also contributed to the nuclear accident, including the plant's physical location. The power plants in Fukushima were built near earthquake faults and areas vulnerable to tsunamis. Countries, other than Japan, have nuclear power plants in such areas; a case in point is the United States. Specifically, there are nuclear power plants in California near earthquake faults. The Fukushima accident illustrated that power plants should not be built near tsunami, earthquake, or other disaster-prone areas.

Generally, emergency management is designed to deal with one incident at a time. What happens when a combination of events occur? There are emergency management plans that consider more than one natural and/or human-made disaster occurring concurrently. Human-made and natural disasters have occurred in tandem. For example, Hurricane Hugo "caused major oil spills at the Hess oil terminal and the Virgin Islands water and power authority on the island of St. Croix."[*] While emergency management plans exist for combined disasters, there is a general tendency to underestimate worst-case scenarios; irrespective of the existence of information that anticipates a worst-case event and its consequences. A case in point is the Fukushima Daiichi nuclear power plant accident. The disaster was predictable. In 2007, an earthquake

---

[*] CDR Charles E. Bills and LT Daniel C. Whiting, "Major Oil Spills, St. Croix, U.S. Virgin Islands," Oil Spills: Management and Legislative Procedures, International Oil Spill Conference (IOSC) Proceedings.

temporarily shut down the Kashiwazaki-Kariwa nuclear power plant.[*] For that reason, in 2010, the Niigata Prefecture sought to conduct a joint earthquake and nuclear disaster drill.[†] However, this plan was not executed as it was believed that it would cause unnecessary public anxiety.[‡]

Two key areas in emergency management failed in the Fukushima Daiichi nuclear power plant accident: preparedness and response. Particularly, the Tokyo Electric Power Company (TEPCO), who owned and operated the Fukushima Daiichi nuclear power plant, had not adequately prepared for tandem disasters and/or worst-case scenarios. To be exact, TEPCO had not anticipated that power would not be available during the response phase to the nuclear accident. Accordingly, procedures to follow in the event that power was unavailable had not been created. Japan's Nuclear Safety Commission (NSC) also did not have provisions in its accident-management policy on the steps to take should an extended loss of power occur. In fact, the NSC did not believe that emergency power systems could be out for long. The belief was that these systems would be repaired quickly. As the Fukushima accident showed, however, this did not occur. The National Diet of Japan's Fukushima Nuclear Accident Independent Investigation Commission (NAIIC) pointed out that TEPCO and the regulatory agencies in Japan were well aware of the risks that a natural disaster, such as a tsunami, posed to the nuclear power plant facility and had several opportunities to take the necessary precautions to prevent or at the very least mitigate the consequences should such an event materialize. TEPCO, while aware of these risks, had not taken any appropriate action to mitigate and prepare for them.

With respect to the responses to the nuclear accident, the public was not adequately informed of the event. Even measures that were created to assist the government in making evacuation decisions were not immediately used nor communicated to the public. A case in point is the System for Prediction of Environmental Emergency Dose Information (SPEEDI). SPEEDI was created to assist governments in deciding when to evacuate residents and from which areas to evacuate them from. The government delayed in releasing the information provided by SPEEDI, thereby unnecessarily exposing nearby residents to radiation.

---

[*] "Impact of the Niigata Chuestu-oki Earthquake on the Tokyo Electric Power Company (TEPCO) Kashiwazaki-Kariwa Nuclear Power Station and Countermeasures," The Tokyo Electric Power Company, Inc., September 2007, http://www.tepco.co.jp/en/news/presen/pdf-1/0709-e.pdf.

[†] Yoichi Funabashi and Kay Kitazawa, "Fukushima in Review: A Complex Disaster, A Disastrous Response," *Bulletin of the Atomic Scientists* 68:2 (March/April 2012), 6.

[‡] Peter Behr, "Nuclear: Fukushima Disaster Compounded by 'Public Myth of Absolute Safety,' Investigators Say," *Energy Wire*, March 2, 2012, http://www.eenews.net/stories/1059960743.

The government tried to downplay the seriousness of the situation. In fact, the level of severity of the event was not accurately communicated (i.e., withheld or misrepresented) to the Japanese public and the international community. Accurate communication and responsible reporting during human-made disasters is critical. Risk communication provides information about the expected outcome from a threat or hazard. Usually, it involves the communication of an adverse consequence (or adverse consequences) and the likelihood of that impact occurring. Care should be taken when communicating information about risk. The language used to communicate the risk may invoke fear or create unease among the population. Uncertainty breeds fear. Therefore, it is important to keep the public informed of the risk and the measures that are being taken to deal with the risk. Information concerning the threat or hazard must be correctly communicated to the public. All affected communities must be promptly informed of the impending risk and the steps that public agencies are taking to deal with it. The public must also be informed during all four phases of emergency management. To be effective, the disaster communications strategy should involve:[*]

- placing the needs of the public first and orientating the informing, management, and response to the emergency accordingly;
- leadership that promotes the open lines of communications between all of those involved in the emergency management process;
- including communications in all aspects of emergency management planning and operations; and
- the development of effective media partnerships.

Common communications plans should be developed and interoperable communications equipment, processes, and standards should be used by both public and private agencies to ensure the accurate and timely flow of information during the emergency and all four phases of the emergency management process.

The government has a responsibility to the public to provide truthful and accurate information. Its failure to do so resulted in significant backlash by the public and the international community. In the aftermath of the aforementioned nuclear accident, Japan implemented new guidelines for emergency management. Prior to the event, Japan had voluntary safety measures in place. After the event, Japan implemented legal mandates on safety measures and accident management procedures. In addition, better coordination and cooperation in the implementation of

---

[*] George Haddow, Jane Bullock, and Damon P. Coppola, *Introduction to Emergency Management* (Third Edition) (Boston: Elsevier, 2008).

such plans was promoted; so too was the need to include evacuation plans (and the practice of evacuation plans) as part of the emergency management process. Citizens should also be made aware of these plans.

Chemical Accidents

There have been a series of public health crises that involved toxic chemicals, such as: the Seveso disaster in Italy in 1976; the Love Canal disaster in the United States in 1978; and the Bhopal disaster in India in 1984. Each of these are explored below.

Seveso Disaster

In 1976, the ICMESA Chemical Company plant, which manufactured trichlorophenol in Seveso, Italy, malfunctioned releasing toxic chemicals into the environment.[*] Nobody was killed in the accident but significant ecological damage occurred; land and vegetation in surrounding areas were contaminated. Inhabitants close to the facility needed to be evacuated and numerous individuals were treated for dioxin poisoning. An investigation into the incident revealed that: industrial safety measures at the plant were inadequate; local authorities were not provided with the necessary information to respond to the incident in a timely manner; local authorities did not have the capability to mitigate the consequences of the disaster; and local residents were not informed of the risks posed by the plant and did not have the resources or information needed to appropriately react to the event.[†] In the aftermath of the Seveso disaster, the Seveso Directive (Council Directive 82/501/EEC) was implemented. It was subsequently amended in 1987 and 1998 by Directives 87/216/EEC and 88/610/EEC, respectively. The Seveso Directive and its amendments govern risk management practices in chemical industries.[‡] In 1996, the Seveso Directive was replaced by the Seveso II Directive (Council Directive 96/82/EC). The objective of Seveso II was to prevent serious chemical accidents and to minimize their human and environmental consequences by including new requirements for safety systems and emergency planning, and communicating risk information to the

---

[*] Ortwin Renn, "Risk Communication at the Community Level: European Lessons from the Seveso Directive," *JAPCA* 39:10 (1989), 1302.

[†] Bruna De Marchi, "Public Information about Major Accident Hazards: Legal Requirements and Practical Implementation," *Organization & Environment* 5: (1991), 241.

[‡] James Cummings-Saxton, Samuel J. Ratick, Frederick W. Talcott, Charlotte P. Dougherty, Amy Vander Vliet, Amy J. Barad, and Anne E. Crook, "Accidental Chemical Releases and Local Emergency Response: Analysis Using the Acute Hazardous Events Data Base," *Organization & Environment* 2:2 (1988), 140.

public.* The Seveso II Directive was later expanded upon by Directive 2003/105/EC. Recently, the Seveso III Directive (Directive 2012/18/EU) was created to amend and eventually repeal the Seveso II Directive. The objectives of the Seveso III Directive, among other aims, are to reinforce public access to information and strengthen inspection standards.[†]

Love Canal Disaster

In the 1920s, the Love Canal in Niagara Falls, New York, was turned into a chemical dumpsite. In 1953, the Hooker Chemical Company covered the canal and sold it to the Department of Education, which built a school.[‡] Homes were later built in that area. Eventually, the toxic chemicals buried beneath the homes in the area were exposed. The residents in this area suffered medical conditions ranging from asthma and mental disorders to cancer due to exposure to the toxic chemicals. For the first time in U.S. history, in 1978, the government declared the Love Canal incident, a human-made disaster, as a federal disaster.[§]

Bhopal Disaster

In 1984, Union Carbide India Limited (UCIL) released 30 metric tons of methyl isocyanate (or MIC) from its plant in Bhopal, India, exposing close to 200,000 individuals to the poisonous gas, killing approximately 20,000, and causing an estimated 60,000 to become ill—many of which required long-term treatment.[¶] In the area of Bhopal, reproductive and developmental impacts were observed in the form of stillbirths, spontaneous abortions, and increased infant mortality.[**] Several factors played a role in the Bhopal disaster: the location of the facility; the malfunction of the safety devices; inadequate staffing, qualifications, and training of employees; and the communication of the event to the public.

---

* Misse Wester-Herber and Lars-Erik Warg, "Did They Get It? Examining the Goals of Risk Communication within the Seveso II Directive in a Swedish Context," *Journal of Risk Research* 7:5 (2004), 496.

† "Introduction to the Seveso III Directive," *Health and Safety Executive* 2012, http://www.hse.gov.uk/seveso/introduction.htm.

‡ Robert E. Hess and Abraham Wandersman, "What Can We Learn From Love Canal?: A Conversation With Lois Gibbs and Richard Valinsky," *Prevention in Human Services* 4:1–2 (1985), 111.

§ Filemon A. Uriarte Jr., "Waste Management in ASEAN Countries," *Toxicology and Industrial Health* 7:5–6 (1991), 230.

¶ V. K. Vijayan, "Methyl Isocyanate (MIC) Exposure and Its Consequences on Human Health at Bhopal," *International Journal of Environmental Studies* 67:5 (2010), 637; Roli Varma and Daya R. Varma, "The Bhopal Disaster of 1984," *Bulletin of Science: Technology & Society* 25:1 (2005), 37–38.

** "Methyl Isocyanate," EPA, 2000, http://www.epa.gov/ttn/atw/hlthef/methylis.html cited in T. Mac Sheoin, "Waiting for Another Bhopal: Global Policies to Control Toxic Chemical Incidents," *Global Social Policy* 9:3 (2009), 413.

With respect to the location of the plant, at the time existing industry regulations (i.e., industry plan of August 25, 1975) required plants handling toxic chemicals to be located at least 24 km from the city.[*] Despite this, UCIL was granted a license to build a plant "on the outskirts of the city barely one km from the railway station and 3 km from two major hospitals."[†] Apart from the location of the facility, another contributing factor to the incident was the malfunctioning of the safety equipment. Specifically, two of the safety devices, the scrubber and the flare tower, were nonfunctional; the third safety device, the water spraying system, was ineffective as well.[‡]

The staff also contributed to the disaster. Particularly, overall, the staff at the plant had inadequate qualifications and training. Originally, those hired to work as operators at the facility had to have higher education degrees and take part in a six-month training program.[§] This policy was subsequently abandoned; the new policy allowed high school graduates to be hired and allowed workers from other plants to be hired and to work at the plant without taking part in the training.[¶] Moreover, the staff at the facility was significantly reduced. Originally, the staff consisted of "12 operators, 3 supervisors, 2 maintenance supervisors, and 1 superintendent per shift"; this was reduced to "6 operators, 1 supervisor, and no obligatory superintendent."[**]

The final factor contributing to the disaster was the manner in which the incident was communicated to the public. Following the incident, there was a significant delay in warning the nearby community of the poisonous gas leak. The warnings given in the aftermath were also disastrous. The alarm that was used to warn the public of the poisonous gas leak was the same alarm used for other emergencies.[††] Additionally, the instructions that were given following the alarm contributed to the harm and damage caused. Police instructed the population to run because

---

[*] "The Bhopal Tragedy: Night of December 2 to 3, 1984," French Ministry for Sustainable Development, No. 7022, June 2010, 6, http://www.aria.developpement-durable.gouv.fr/wp-content/files_mf/FD_7022Bhopalinde_1984_ang.pdf.

[†] Roli Varma and Daya R. Varma, "The Bhopal Disaster of 1984," *Bulletin of Science: Technology & Society* 25:1 (2005), 40.

[‡] Roli Varma and Daya R. Varma, "The Bhopal Disaster of 1984," *Bulletin of Science: Technology & Society* 25:1 (2005), 41.

[§] Ibid.

[¶] Ibid.

[**] Daya R. Varma, "Anatomy of the Methyl Isocyanate Leak in Bhopal," In Jitendra Saxena (Ed.), *Hazard Assessment of Chemicals* (Washington, DC: Hemisphere, 1986) cited in Roli Varma and Daya R. Varma, "The Bhopal Disaster of 1984," *Bulletin of Science: Technology & Society* 25:1 (2005), 41; "The Bhopal Gas Tragedy," ICFAI Center for Management Research, 702-006-1, 2012, 2, http://www.econ.upf.edu/~lemenestrel/IMG/pdf/bhopal_gas_tragedy_dutta.pdf.

[††] "The Bhopal Gas Tragedy," ICFAI Center for Management Research, 702-006-1, 2012, 2, http://www.econ.upf.edu/~lemenestrel/IMG/pdf/bhopal_gas_tragedy_dut ta.pdf.

poisonous gas was spreading; consequently, when the alarm sounded and the instructions were given, individuals "ran and inhaled more of the poison than they would have had they not run."* The warning that should have been given "was to ask people not to run but rather lie down on the ground and cover their faces with wet clothes."†

After the Bhopal incident, India created a legal framework to prevent major chemical disasters by passing: the Environment (Protection) Act of 1986; the Factories Act in 1987; the Hazardous Waste (Management and Handling) Rules of 1989; the Manufacture, Storage and Import of Hazardous Chemicals Rules of 1989; and the Public Liability Insurance Act of 1991.‡ Following the disaster, process safety, which refers to the "comprehensive, systematic approach encompassing the proactive identification, evaluation and mitigation or prevention of chemical releases that could occur as a result of failures in process, procedures, or equipment," was also promoted worldwide.§ Moreover, in the United States, in response to the Bhopal incident, the Emergency Planning and Community Right to Know Act of 1986 (42 U.S.C. 11001-11050) required industries to inform any neighboring communities of hazards and create on-site and off-site emergency response procedures. This act assists communities in preparing for emergencies that involve hazardous and toxic chemicals.¶ Furthermore, the 1992 Convention on the Transboundary Effects of Industrial Accidents was implemented after the Bhopal disaster. This Convention promotes international cooperation in industrial accidents.

Fires

Historically, many human-made fires have occurred, including the 1903 Iroquois Theater Fire in Chicago and the 1942 Cocoanut Grove fire in Boston. In the aftermath of each of these fires, a reevaluation of fire prevention and fire suppression strategies occurred. Irrespective of this process, however, many other fires followed, some of which had resulted from similar errors in fire protection and suppression strategies found

---

* Roli Varma and Daya R. Varma, "The Bhopal Disaster of 1984," *Bulletin of Science: Technology & Society* 25:1 (2005), 42.

† Ibid.

‡ T. Mac Sheoin, "Waiting for Another Bhopal: Global Policies to Control Toxic Chemical Incidents," *Global Social Policy* 9:3 (2009), 419.

§ Ernie Hood, "Lessons Learned? Chemical Plant Safety Since Bhopal," *Environmental Health Perspectives* 112:6 (2004), A354, cited in T. Mac Sheoin, "Waiting for Another Bhopal: Global Policies to Control Toxic Chemical Incidents," *Global Social Policy* 9:3 (2009), 415.

¶ "EPCRA Tier I and Tier II Reporting," EPA, November 1, 2013, http://www2.epa.gov/epcra-tier-i-and-tier-ii-reporting.

in the Iroquois Theater and in Cocoanut Grove (see analysis in the next sections).

Iroquois Theater Fire

In 1903, the Iroquois theater, which was promoted as absolutely fire-proof, experienced one of the worst fires in history. On December 30, 1903, the theater was filled overcapacity (2,000 patrons for the 1,600 seats). The fire started during the second act of a matinee performance of *Mr. Bluebeard*. After the fire started, the asbestos curtain was lowered to protect the audience from the fire; however, the curtain snagged midway and could not be lowered further. It was later found that the asbestos curtain was actually made from combustible materials and thus would not have done anything to protect patrons from the fire.

In the theater, many of the exit doors were covered by curtains and were not clearly labeled, making it extremely difficult for patrons to find them and escape the fire. Also, the doors were designed to open inward. As a result, when the crowd rushed to an exit, the crush of individuals prevented the doors from being opened. In addition, some doors were locked. Moreover, individuals in the gallery and the upper balconies were locked in their respective places; as such, the majority of the deaths were of individuals in these areas who could not escape. Furthermore, vents on the roof which were supposed to filter out smoke in case of a fire were unfinished and nailed shut; this caused the smoke to remain in the theater, resulting in numerous cases of suffocation from smoke inhalation. In the end, 602 individuals died, 212 of them were children.[*] In the aftermath of this fire, regulations were implemented in an attempt to prevent a similar disaster. Despite this regulation, more fires occurred under similar circumstances thereafter, one of which was the Cocoanut Grove club fire.

Cocoanut Grove Club Fire

On November 28, 1942, a fire started in the Cocoanut Grove, a restaurant/supper club in Boston, Massachusetts. In the fire, 492 individuals died.[†] It is believed that the fire started from a match lit by a bus-boy while he was attempting to locate a socket of a light bulb. The match

---

[*] Alberto Alvarez, Brian J. Meacham, Nicholas A. Dembsey, and Russell Thomas, "Twenty Years of Performance-Based Fire Protection Design: Challenges Faced and a Look Ahead," *Journal of Fire Protection Engineering* 23:4 (2013), 259; David Cowan, "A Tragic Reminder," *Chicago Tribune*, March 2, 2003, http://articles.chicagotribune.com/2003-03-02/entertainment/0303010007_1_iroquois-theatre-fire-chicago-fire-tragic-reminder/3.

[†] Travis Andersen, "Witness Transcripts from Cocoanut Grove Fire Released," October 31, 2012, http://www.bostonglobe.com/metro/2012/10/30/witness-transcripts-from-cocoanut-grove-fire-are-released-tell-dramatic-story-historic-boston-blaze/ErDncLdE682FvDmaBUrNqM/story.html.

was placed close to highly flammable ceiling decorations that caught fire in consequence. Once the fire started, patrons made their way toward the exits. However, only some were able to escape. The main entrance, a revolving door, soon became jammed from the crush of individuals trying to exit. Many individuals died by the doors, unable to escape the fire. Like the Iroquois Theater, exits in the Cocoanut Grove club were not easily identifiable, were largely inaccessible, and were locked. Also, similarly to the Iroquois theater, the doors of the Cocoanut Grove club opened inward. Consequently, only a few were able to escape before the crush of individuals prevented the doors from being opened.

Following this incident, regulations were implemented and building codes were amended. For instance, exits had to be clearly marked, exit doors were to remain unlocked and unblocked, revolving doors were only allowed if they were between two outward opening doors (to serve as emergency exits),* and the use of noncombustible building materials and decorations, an emergency lighting system, sprinklers, and smoke detection systems were required in establishments. Unfortunately, despite these requirements and regulations, more fires occurred because of blocked or locked exits, overcrowding, the use of combustible building materials, and a lack of sprinklers and smoke detection systems. One such fire that occurred on February 20, 2003, in West Warwick, Rhode Island, because of a lack of these requirements and regulations was the Station Nightclub Fire; in this fire, 100 people died.[†] Numerous other fires occurred under similar circumstances, such as: the September 11, 2012, fire that occurred at a textile factory in Karachi, Pakistan, killing 300 workers;[‡] the November 24, 2012, Bangladesh clothes factory fire where 112 deaths occurred;[§] and the June 3, 2013, poultry plant fire in China which killed 119 individuals.[¶] In these countries, the deaths were

---

[*] It is important to note that in the immediate aftermath of the fire, revolving doors were outlawed; they were reinstated afterward but only if they were placed between two outward pushing doors.

[†] William Grosshandler, Nelson Bryner, Daniel Madrzykowski, and Kenneth Kuntz, "Report of the Technical Investigation of the Station Nightclub Fire," National Institute of Standards and Technology (NIST) NCSTAR 2: Vol. I, June 2005, http://fire.nist.gov/bfrlpubs/fire05/PDF/f05032.pdf.

[‡] Zia Ur-Rehman, Declan Walsh, and Salman Masood, "More Than 300 Killed in Pakistani Factory Fires," New York Times, September 12, 2012, http://www.nytimes.com/2012/09/13/world/asia/hundreds-die-in-factory-fires-in-pakistan.html.

[§] Gardiner Harris, "Bangladeshi Factory Owners Charged in Fire That Killed 112," New York Times, December 22, 2013, http://www.nytimes.com/2013/12/23/world/asiabangladeshi-factory-owners-charged-in-fatal-fire.html?_r=0; Emily Thomas, "Bangladesh Clothing Factory Hit by Deadly Fire," BBC News, October 8, 2013, http://www.bbc.co.uk/news/world-asia-24453165.

[¶] Christopher Bodeen, "China Poultry Plant's Locked Doors Highlight Work-Safety Concern," Huffington Post, June 4, 2013, http://www.huffingtonpost.com/2013/06/04/china-work-safety-poultry-plant-fire_n_3382702.html.

attributed to poor safety cultures, systems, and regulations, and locked doors which prevented workers from escaping the fires. What was also lacking in these and the above-mentioned fires was the effective enforcement of existing fire code regulations.

Oil Spills

There have been several major oil spills, each with significant human, environmental, and economic consequences. Some of these consequences include (but are not limited to): illnesses, deaths, wildlife rehabilitation, cost of spilled substances, damage to natural resources, value of equipment damaged, public relations expenses, cleanup fees, containment costs, damage claims (e.g., legal fees, property damage, and loss of revenue), waste recovery, waste disposal, and fines and penalties.[*] The next sections examine three major oil spills and their respective costs: the Exxon Valdez oil spill; the Shetlands oil spill; and the Deepwater Horizon incident.

Exxon Valdez Oil Spill

On March 24, 1989, an oil tanker, Exxon Valdez, spilled over 11 million gallons of crude oil into the water in Prince William Sound, Alaska.[†] This oil spill caused significant environmental damage. Indigenous and migratory wildlife (e.g., seabirds, shorebirds, waterfowl, sea otters, harbor porpoises, sea lions, salmon, herring, and whales) sustained significant losses from the oil spill.[‡] In addition, those that suffered the greatest economic damage included fishing industries and seafood processing plants around the area.

The oil spill was the result of a combination of human and technical factors. An investigation following the incident revealed that the management of the vessel and the mishandling of the situation by the staff played a major role in the incident. Specifically, Exxon had failed to provide a rested and sufficient crew (with respect to the number of personnel) for the vessel.[§] The master of the vessel who was supposed to

---

[*] Franklin E. Giles, "Factors in Estimating Potential Response Costs of Spills and Releases," *Environmental Claims Journal* 22:1 (2010), 33.

[†] Thomas A. Birkland, "In the Wake of the Exxon Valdez: How Environmental Disasters Influence Policy," *Environment: Science and Policy for Sustainable Development* 40:7 (1998), 5.

[‡] S. D. Rice, R. B. Spies, D. A. Wolfe, and B. A. Wright, "The Effects of the Exxon Valdez Oil Spill on the Alaskan Coastal Environment," *American Fisheries Society Symposium* 18 (1996), 1–16; Duane A. Gill, J. Steven Picou, and Liesel A. Ritchie, "The Exxon Valdez and BP Oil Spills: A Comparison of Initial Social and Psychological Impacts," *American Behavioral Scientist* 56:1 (2012), 5.

[§] Susan L. Smith, "*Exxon Valdez*," Dustin R. Mulvaney (Ed.), *Green Energy: An A-to-Z Guide* (Thousand Oaks, CA: Sage, 2011).

be on duty at the time of the incident was in his stateroom and the third mate of the ship failed to effectively maneuver the vessel to avert disaster, potentially due to fatigue.* The investigation also revealed a technical issue; the vessel's radar system was inoperable.† To mitigate such disasters in the future, the human and technical factors likely to precipitate oil spills should be targeted. In addition, systems should be operational, vessels adequately staffed, and crew members well trained.

According to Richard Sylves, "how damaging an oil spill is depends in part on the degree of emergency preparedness in place before the event, the speed of response, and the effectiveness of recovery operations once a spill has occurred."‡ There were significant public and private failures in all three of these areas of emergency management. First, there were many issues that arose that prolonged the cleanup of the spill, including the remote location of the spill and its magnitude. The cleanup of the spill was also delayed because the oil booms and skimmers that were used were limited by the weather conditions (e.g., the weather was too cold; as such, the oil did not evaporate easily) and the location of the spill.

Second, the response organizations did not coordinate their actions. To be effective, a response organization should be able to coordinate the actions of all of those involved, direct response operations, and coordinate information sharing with government agencies and the media. In addition, this organization should be able to efficiently and effectively establish a command and control center and conduct and coordinate responses. What happened with the Exxon Valdez incident?

The United States government placed Exxon in charge of the oil spill cleanup. Accordingly, Exxon assumed responsibility for the salvage of the oil tanker Exxon Valdez and for the response operations. Existing emergency management plans had a state or federal agency taking the lead role in responding to a disaster. None of the existing emergency management plans had anticipated that a private company instead of a state or federal agency would manage the human-made disaster. In fact, the emergency management plan of the Coast Guard included the establishment of a regional response team where state and federal activities would be coordinated. In this plan, the state was represented by the Department of Environmental Conservation. However, the Alaskan

---

* "Oil Spill Facts: Questions and Answer," Exxon Valdez Oil Spill Trustee Council, http://www.evostc.state.ak.us/index.cfm?FA=facts.QA.

† Gregory Palast, "Ten Years after But Who Was to Blame?" *The Guardian* March 20, 1999, http://www.theguardian.com/business/1999/mar/21/observerbusiness.bp.

‡ Richard T. Sylves, "How the *Exxon Valdez* Disaster Changed America's Oil Spill Management," *International Journal of Mass Emergencies and Disasters* 16:1 (1998), 13; Richard T. Sylves and Louise K. Comfort, "The Exxon Valdez and BP Deepwater Horizon Oil Spills: Reducing Risk in Socio-Technical Systems," *American Behavioral Scientist* 56:1 (2012), 81.

Governor responded to the human-made disaster by creating his own independent response organization. Having three separate response organizations, the federal, state, and private response organizations, significantly hampered decision making in response to the oil spill. As a result of the separate organizational structures and their involvement in the handling of the oil spill, it took several weeks for a single, stable, and functioning decision-making organization to be created. This delay had significant adverse consequences.

In the aftermath of the disaster, the Marine Spill Response Organization (MSRO) was created. The MRSO is a not-for-profit oil spill removal organization, which offers its services to mitigate the potential damage caused to the environment by an oil spill.* In addition to the formation of the MRSO, the Oil Pollution Act (OPA) of 1990 was passed. This act required the public and private sectors to have more effective and efficient emergency management plans in place that can mitigate spills that have already occurred, by including detailed response and cleanup procedures within their plans. Also, these plans need to include the personnel and resources needed to respond to oil spills. In addition, these plans need to be able to handle worst-case oil spill scenarios.† Moreover, the National Contingency Plan (NCP) was revised as a result of OPA after the Exxon Valdez oil spill to include these changes.

Furthermore, OPA included liability and compensation provisions for those affected by the oil spill. OPA additionally included punitive damages in the event of an oil spill. OPA further consisted of sections dealing with recovery from oil spills. Here, an integral part of recovery is the determination of liability and compensation for cleanup costs and the repair of environmental damage caused by the disaster. In this incident, Exxon was held liable for the damage caused. Indeed, it is common practice in the United States to hold polluters responsible for the cleanup and repair of environmental damage. The same cannot be said about Europe; this became evident in the Shetland Islands oil spill.

Shetland Islands Oil Spill

On January 5, 1993, amid a hurricane, the oil tanker Braer spilled approximately 85,000 tons of oil near the Shetland Islands.‡ The hurricane brought the oil to land coating inhabitants, livestock, land, homes, and other property. Wildlife in the area was also affected by

---

* "About MSRC," Marine Spill Response Organization (MSRO), 2013, http://www. msrc.org/about/.
† "Facility Response Planning: Compliance Assistance Guide," U.S. Environmental Protection Agency, August 2002, 4, http://www.epa.gov/oem/docs/oil/frp/frpguide.pdf.
‡ Stephen C. Young, "The Shetland Oil Disaster," *Environmental Politics* 2:2 (1993), 33.

the oil spill. Additionally, the fishing industry and fish processing plants sustained significant economic losses.* Having anticipated that an oil spill could occur, emergency management plans had been developed in anticipation of such an incident.† The response of officials to the disaster and the oil on land, while swift, had significant adverse consequences. Specifically, authorities sprayed 120 tons of chemical dispersants, contaminating inhabitants, livestock, and agricultural land.‡ Consequently, agricultural lands and salmon farms were condemned because of the oil and the chemical dispersants.§

No warning was provided to residents concerning the spraying. As such, they were not warned to stay indoors nor evacuated from the area. According to Gregory Button, "[t]he official word from the Scottish Home Office from the first day of the spill was that there would be no long-term health effects from the spill or the use of dispersants. This claim was largely unsubstantiated."¶ Button further noted that

> almost immediately after the dispersants were sprayed, hundreds of Dunross Parish residents complained of eye and skin irritation, headaches, and diarrhea. Over 40 people experienced severe asthmatic responses. Later more than 250 people would demonstrate abnormal lung functioning. A smaller number would have test results that demonstrated renal and liver malfunction. Many of the local residents became alarmed.**

In Europe, the Seveso Directives I, II, and III delineate the responsibilities of public and private sectors in communicating information about hazardous substances and materials to the public. Likewise, the United States has similar policies in place. Nonetheless, by contrast to the United States and its "right to know" policy, Europe provides and gives access to information about hazardous substances and materials

---

* Mans Jacobsson, "Braer: Legal Aspects of a Major Oil Spill. International Oil Pollution Compensation Fund," 1995 Oil Spill Conference, 722, http://ioscproceedings. org/doi/pdf/10.7901/2169-3358-1995-1-721.

† Gerald L. Forbes, "The Braer Oil Spill Incident—Shetland, January 1993," *International Journal of Environmental Health Research* 4:1 (1994), 50.

‡ Gregory V. Button, "What You Don't Know Can't Hurt You: The Right to Know and the Shetland Island Oil Spill," *Human Ecology* 23:2 (1995), 245.

§ Gerald L. Forbes, "The Braer Oil Spill Incident—Shetland, January 1993," *International Journal of Environmental Health Research* 4:1 (1994), 53–54; Stephen C. Young, "The Shetland Oil Disaster," *Environmental Politics* 2(2) (1993), 338; Gregory V. Button, "What You Don't Know Can't Hurt You: The Right to Know and the Shetland Island Oil Spill," *Human Ecology* 23:2 (1995), 247.

¶ Gregory V. Button, "What You Don't Know Can't Hurt You: The Right to Know and the Shetland Island Oil Spill," *Human Ecology* 23:2 (1995), 250.

** Ibid., 248.

on a "need to know" basis.* UK policies have a strict "need to know" standard, where the public's "need to know" is determined by scientific advisors that provide a recommendation on behalf of and in the interest of the public based on the information they were given about the risks.† Information about the chemical dispersants and their safety for use for this oil spill was not immediately released. The Marine Pollution Control Unit, which at the time coordinated the United Kingdom's response to the oil spill,‡ later found that one of the dispersants used had not passed a toxicity test.§

The United Kingdom assumed much of the responsibility for the cleanup of the oil spill. Existing UK law (which is in accordance with the 1969 International Convention on Civil Liability for Oil Pollution Damage) restricted the liability of the owners of the vessel (this and other laws specifically addressing oil pollution are included in Table 8.2).¶ Because of the limited liability of the owners of the vessel, additional funds to cover costs, damages, and losses were provided to the victims by the International Oil Pollution Compensation Fund.** This is unlike the practice of the United States in comparable events, such as the Exxon Valdez oil spill (discussed in the previous section) and the Deepwater Horizon oil spill (discussed in the next section).

Deepwater Horizon Oil Spill

On April 20, 2010, the Macondo well erupted underneath the *Deepwater Horizon* oil rig in the Gulf of Mexico causing an explosion, killing 11 workers.†† The Deepwater Horizon oil rig sank two days later. Similar to the Shetland Islands oil spill, dispersants were also heavily used. Unlike oil that spilled in Alaska due to the Exxon Valdez spill, the oil from the Deepwater Horizon evaporated more easily because of the warmer

---

* J. van Eijndhoven, "Disaster Prevention in Europe," In S. Jasanoff (Ed.), *Learning from Disaster* (Philadelphia: University of Pennsylvania Press, 1994); Gregory V. Button, "What You Don't Know Can't Hurt You: The Right to Know and the Shetland Island Oil Spill," *Human Ecology* 23:2 (1995), 253.

† Gregory V. Button, "What You Don't Know Can't Hurt You: The Right to Know and the Shetland Island Oil Spill," *Human Ecology* 23:2 (1995), 253.

‡ Nowadays, the Maritime and Coastguard Agency's (MCA) Counter Pollution and Response Branch (CPR) is responsible for coordinating the UK's response to oil spills.

§ Gerald L. Forbes, "The Braer Oil Spill Incident—Shetland, January 1993," *International Journal of Environmental Health Research* 4:1 (1994), 52–53.

¶ By contrast, such limits on liability do not exist in U.S. law (i.e., in OPA).

** Mans Jacobsson, "Braer: Legal Aspects of a Major Oil Spill. International Oil Pollution Compensation Fund," 1995 Oil Spill Conference, 721, http://ioscproceedings.org/doi/pdf/10.7901/2169-3358-1995-1-721.

†† David Barstow, David Rohde, and Stephanie Saul, "Deepwater Horizon's Final Hours," *New York Times*, December 25, 2010, http://www.nytimes.com/2010/12/26/us/26spill.html?pagewanted=all.

TABLE 8.2   Survey of Laws and Regulations Dealing with Oil Pollution

1954	International Convention for the Prevention of Pollution of the Sea by Oil
1968	U.S. National Oil and Hazardous Substances Pollution Contingency Plan (42 USC §9601-9657)
1969	International Convention on Civil Liability for Oil Pollution Damage
1969	International Convention Relating to Intervention on the High Seas in Cases of Oil Pollution Casualties
1971	International Convention for the Establishment of an International Fund for Compensation for Oil Pollution
1972	The Convention on the Prevention of Marine Pollution by Dumping of Wastes and Other Matters
1971	UK Prevention of Oil Pollution Act (amended by the 1974 Health and Safety at Work Act)
1972	U.S. Clean Water Act (33 USC § 1251)
1973	International Convention for the Prevention of Pollution from Ships
1973	U.S. Trans-Alaska Oil Pipeline Act (43 USC § 1651)
1974	U.S. Disaster Relief Act of 1974 (42 USC § 3231)
1990	International Convention on Oil Pollution Preparedness, Response and Co-operation
1990	U.S. Oil Pollution Control Act (33 USC § 2701)
1996	UK Merchant Shipping (Prevention of Oil Pollution) Regulations
1998	UK Merchant Shipping (Oil Pollution Preparedness, Response and Co-operation Convention) Regulations

climate. Irrespective of this, a vast amount of oil was spilled; as such, the cleanup effort took several months. The spill itself was difficult to stop. Approximately 5 million barrels of oil was spilled until the well was finally capped on July 15, 2010[*] (Figure 8.3).

The Deepwater Horizon oil spill caused catastrophic human, environmental, and economic harm. The explosion at the Deepwater Horizon oil rig killed 11 workers. The Gulf's marine and coastal ecosystem was also adversely affected. The two industries that suffered the greatest economic damage were the tourism and fishing industries; these industries are "highly sensitive to both direct ecosystem harm and, indirectly, [to] public perceptions and fears of tainted seafood and soiled beaches."[†] In

---

[*] Campbell Robertson, "U.S. Puts Oil Spill Total at Nearly 5 Million Barrels," *New York Times*, August 2, 2010, http://www.nytimes.com/2010/08/03/us/03flow.html?fta=y.

[†] "Deep Water: The Gulf Oil Disaster and the Future of Offshore Drilling," National Commission on the BP Deepwater Horizon Oil Spill and Offshore Drilling, January 2011, 185, https://s3.amazonaws.com/pdf_final/DEEPWATER_ReporttothePresident_FINAL.pdf.

FIGURE 8.3   Rigs drilling a relief well and preparing the static kill are shown in the Gulf of Mexico July 31, 2010, over the Deepwater Horizon well 40 miles from the southern coast of Louisiana. (From the U.S. Coast Guard, DoD photo by Petty Officer 1st Class Sara Francis, U.S. Coast Guard, Released.)

addition, there was a temporary fishing ban and certain state fisheries started to close after the oil spill. Ultimately, the National Oceanic and Atmospheric Administration (NOAA) "prohibited all fishing in nearly 37 percent of the Gulf zone."* The Deepwater Horizon oil spill is considered one of the worst environmental disasters in U.S. history.

Given that it was one of the greatest environmental disasters, why did the United States not declare a state of emergency? The Robert T. Stafford Disaster Relief and Emergency Assistance Act (PL 100-707) was implemented to enable the federal government to declare a state of emergency, depending on its severity, in the aftermath of a disaster. If a state of emergency is declared, the federal government provides assistance, among other resources, to those requesting it. The U.S. presidents in both the Exxon Valdez (George H. W. Bush) and Deepwater Horizon

---

* Nancy G. Leveson, *Engineering a Safer World: Systems Thinking Applied to Safety* (Cambridge, MA: MIT Press, 2011), 376; "Deep Water: The Gulf Oil Disaster and the Future of Offshore Drilling," National Commission on the BP Deepwater Horizon Oil Spill and Offshore Drilling, January 2011, 140, https://s3.amazonaws.com/pdf_final/DEEPWATER_ReporttothePresident_FINAL.pdf.

(Barack Obama) disasters refused to declare a state of emergency, despite significant state and public pressure. If the presidents in both of these events had declared a state of emergency, monies from taxpayers would have been used for the cleanup of the oil spills. In both instances, and in similar situations, U.S. presidents have opted to hold the companies responsible for the oil spills. In the case of the Deepwater Horizon oil spill, those held responsible were British Petroleum (BP) and Transocean.

In the aftermath of the spill, certain factors were identified by the National Commission on the BP Deepwater Horizon Oil Spill and Offshore Drilling as leading to the eventual oil spill. Specifically, these factors included "well design, construction, monitoring and testing."* Another factor that contributed to the disaster was human error. This included not only the poor decision making in upper-level management on how to deal with the oil spill, but also their failure to train and prepare employees for the worst-case scenarios—such as a major blowout that causes explosions, fires, and a loss of power.

Other factors that contributed to the disaster were the lack of inspections by administrative agencies and lack of enforcement of existing regulations and policies. The latter contributed to the lack of accountability by companies running the oil rigs and drilling operations.† The absence of a "strong centralized oversight governmental authority and policies... encouraged [the] largely unregulated growth of domestic production [and] provided the necessary conditions for" the Deepwater Horizon oil spill.‡

Following the oil spill, new deepwater drilling, safety protocols, and regulations were drafted. However, the rules and regulations are only one part of the equation. Companies need to be held accountable for policy violations. This requires active enforcement and oversight over the implementation of existing rules and regulations. To achieve this, what is also required is more effective company oversight and more inspections of facilities. There is a way to prevent oil spills like the Deepwater Horizon incident from occurring; countries can stop deepwater drilling for oil. However, this can have a detrimental effect on U.S. energy independence.§

---

* National Commission on the BP Deepwater Horizon Oil Spill and Offshore Drilling, "Deep Water: The Gulf Oil Disaster and the Future of Offshore Drilling," January 2011, 87, https://s3.amazonaws.com/pdf_final/DEEPWATER_ReporttothePresident_FINAL.pdf.

† Ibid., 28.

‡ John Barnshaw, Kathryn Dolan, Fulya Apaydin, Tara Deubel, Karen Greiner, and Thuy Nguyen, "Crisis in the Gulf of Mexico: Discourse, Policy, and Governance in Postcatastrophe Environments," *Journal of Applied Social Science* 6:2 (2012), 135.

§ Energy security will be explored in Chapter 12 of this volume.

CONCLUDING THOUGHTS

Human-made disasters such as nuclear accidents, chemical accidents, fires, and oil spills, can have devastating short-term and long-term human, environmental, and economic impacts. The long-term impacts of some of the human-made disasters reviewed have yet to be fully assessed and are currently being explored (e.g., the Fukushima nuclear accident and Deepwater Horizon oil spill). A survey of disasters in this chapter revealed that key contributing factors to most human-made disasters are human errors, the lack of corporate accountability, and the lack of enforcement of existing policies, laws, and regulations. Strong safety cultures were also found to be absent.

Strong emergency management plans and procedures can mitigate the impact of human-made disasters. Apart from the creation of the emergency management plan, its practice by key personnel, and its communication to the public at large, public and private sectors should prepare for worst-case scenarios. Response organizations also need to coordinate their responses to a human-made disaster. Finally, recovery operations should be coordinated between public and private sectors as well. To lessen (to the extent possible) the likelihood that such incidents will come to fruition, those responsible for the human-made disaster should be held culpable and financially responsible for response and recovery operations. This responsibility should be extended to providing significant compensation and paying punitive damages in order to deter such conduct in the future.

CHAPTER 9

Infectious Diseases

Europe experienced infectious diseases throughout the centuries. In the 14th and 15th centuries, the bubonic pneumonic plague (known as the Black Death) devastated Medieval Europe. The plague is transmitted "from one rodent to another by flea ectoparasites and to humans either by the bite of infected fleas or when handling infected hosts."[*] If left untreated, mortality rates[†] from plague are extremely high.[‡] In the 19th century, turberculosis (TB) spread in Europe killing many until vaccines[§] were developed. Both of these diseases resurfaced in the 20th and 21st centuries with devastating consequences. For instance, drug resistant strains of TB have been found: extensively drug-resistant tuberculosis (XDR-TB) and multidrug-resistant tuberculosis (MDR-TB).[¶] In 2012, the bubonic plague resurfaced in Madagascar killing 60 individuals.[**] The following year, in 2013, 32 individuals died from a total of 84 suspected plague cases.[††] Of those suspected of infection, 60 individuals

---

[*] "Global Alert and Response (GAR): Plague," World Health Organization, http://www. who.int/csr/disease/plague/en/.

[†] The number of diseased individuals who lost their lives in a specific population.

[‡] "Global Alert and Response (GAR): Plague," World Health Organization, http://www. who.int/csr/disease/plague/en/.

[§] A vaccine is defined as "a biological preparation that improves immunity to a particular disease…[It] typically contains an agent that resembles a disease-causing microorganism, and is often made from weakened or killed forms of the microbe, its toxins or one of its surface proteins. The agent stimulates the body's immune system to recognize the agent as foreign, destroy it, and 'remember' it, so that the immune system can more easily recognize and destroy any of these microorganisms that it later encounters." "Vaccines," World Health Organization (WHO), http://www.who.int/ topics/vaccines/en/.

[¶] "Tuberculosis (TB): Frequently Asked Questions—XDR-TB," World Health Organization, http://www.who.int/tb/challenges/xdr/faqs/en/; "Tuberculosis (TB): Multidrug-Resistant Tuberculosis (MDR-TB)," World Health Organization, http://www.who.int/tb/challenges/ mdr/en/.

[**] *BBC News*, "Madagascar Village 'Hit by Bubonic Plague,'" December 10, 2013, http:// www.bbc.co.uk/news/world-africa-25324011.

[††]"Bubonic Plague Outbreak Kills 32 in Madagascar," *The Guardian*, December 20, 2013, http://www.theguardian.com/world/2013/dec/20/bubonic-plague-outbreak-deaths-madagascar.

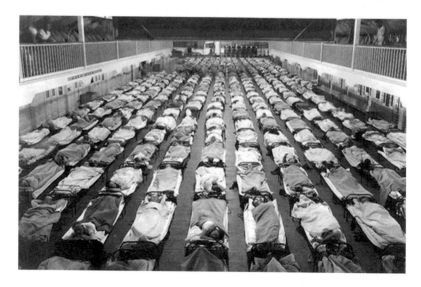

FIGURE 9.1 The Spanish influenza pandemic of 1918 killed millions around the globe. Naval Training Station, San Francisco, California. Crowded sleeping area extemporized on the Drill Hall floor of the Main Barracks, during World War I. Note bunks arranged in columns, with alternating headings. Signs on the wall at left forbid spitting on the floor to prevent the spread of disease. (Photograph from the U.S. Naval Historical Center.)

were believed to be infected with a more virulent strain of the disease (pneumonic or pulmonary plague).* This strain of the disease is transmitted to humans without bites or fleas or direct contact with infected animals. Instead, it is transmitted through inhalation. This strain has an extremely high fatality rate; if left untreated, an individual can die within 24 hours of infection.[†]

In the 20th century, the influenza pandemic of 1918 (i.e., the Spanish flu) killed millions throughout the world, irrespective of their age or health (Figure 9.1). Following the Spanish flu virus, two other influenza A viruses spread in 1957 and 1968 (the Asian and Hong Kong influenza, respectively) "caus[ing] significant morbidity[‡] and mortality globally."[§] Shortly thereafter, new diseases, such as human immunodeficiency virus/acquired immunodeficiency syndrome (HIV/AIDS), also surfaced.

---

* Ibid.

† "*Yersinia pestis* (Plague)," UPMC Center for Health Security, December 1, 2013, http://www.upmchealthsecurity.org/our-work/publications/plague-fact-sheet.

‡ Morbidity refers to the state of being unhealthy due to a specific cause.

§ "Influenza: Fact Sheet No. 211," World Health Organization, March 2003, http://www.who.int/mediacentre/factsheets/2003/fs211/en/.

What is particularly troubling about this and many other new infectious diseases is that to date there are no known cures available. The indiscriminate nature of infectious diseases illustrates the vulnerabilities of societies to this security threat. What's more, infectious diseases are not limited by territorial boundaries; thereby posing a significant threat to transnational security. A case in point is the West Nile virus. This virus is native to Africa, Asia, and the Middle East.[*] In 1999, the West Nile virus appeared in New York City, eventually spreading throughout the United States.[†]

This chapter critically evaluates major public health crises involving infectious diseases and measures taken to mitigate, respond to, prepare for, and recover from them. To do so, this chapter first examines how infectious diseases are spread. It then considers the economic, social, and political consequences of infectious diseases both nationally and internationally. Moreover, it covers the weaponization of infectious diseases. Furthermore, it explores how such crises are addressed at the national and international level. To what extent can technology be relied upon as a tool to address the issues that arise from infectious diseases? How prepared are agencies and organizations to deal with these crises? Special attention is paid to HIV/AIDS, Severe Acute Respiratory Syndrome (SARS), and H1N1.

THE SPREAD OF INFECTIOUS DISEASES

The spread of infectious diseases is described in terms of epidemics, outbreaks, and pandemics. The term given depends on the nature and extent of the infectious disease. Particularly, an epidemic is defined as "a widespread occurrence of an infectious disease in a community at a particular time."[‡] An outbreak refers to "the occurrence of cases of disease in excess of what would normally be expected in a defined community, geographical area or season."[§] Outbreaks and epidemics are often used interchangeably; however, the term outbreak usually refers to epidemics in small localized areas.[¶]

---

[*] Darrick T. Evensen and Christopher E. Clarke, "Efficacy Information in Media Coverage of Infectious Disease Risks: An Ill Predicament?" *Science Communication* 34:3 (2012), 395.

[†] Ibid.

[‡] Oxford Dictionary, s.v. "Epidemic" (Oxford, United Kingdom: Oxford University Press), http://www.oxforddictionaries.com/us/definition/american_english/epidemic.

[§] "Disease Outbreaks," WHO, http://www.who.int/topics/disease_outbreaks/en/.

[¶] Máire A. Connolly (Ed.), "Communicable Disease Control in Emergencies: A Field Manual," World Health Organization, 2005, 107, http://whqlibdoc.who.int/publications/2005/9241546166_eng.pdf?ua=1.

TABLE 9.1   Pandemic Influenza Phases

	Description
Phase 1	No viruses circulating among animals have been reported to cause infections in humans
Phase 2	An animal influenza virus circulating among domesticated or wild animals is known to have caused infection in humans, and is therefore considered a potential pandemic threat
Phase 3	An animal or human-animal influenza reassortant virus has caused sporadic cases or small clusters of disease in people, but has not resulted in human-to-human transmission sufficient to sustain community-level outbreaks
Phase 4	Verified human-to-human transmission of an animal or human-animal influenza reassortant virus able to cause "community-level outbreaks"
Phase 5	Human-to-human spread of the identified virus in at least two countries in one WHO region
Phase 6	In addition to the criteria defined in Phase 5, community level outbreaks exist in at least one other country in a different WHO region. This phase is known as the pandemic phase.

Source: Information for table retrieved from: WHO, http://www.who.int/influenza/resources/documents/pandemic_phase_descriptions_and_actions.pdf.

By contrast, a pandemic is "an epidemic occurring worldwide, or over a very wide area, crossing international boundaries and usually affecting a large number of people."[*] The World Health Organization created six pandemic influenza phases that are designed to communicate the risk of influenza viruses to the global community (see Table 9.1). The World Health Organization also developed actions that should be taken during each phase by both countries that are affected by the infectious diseases and those that have not yet been affected (see Table 9.2).

The 2013 World Economic Forum Global Risks report included infectious disease pandemics and chronic diseases as one of the top five global risks (according to impact and likelihood) between 2007 and 2010.[†] Even though infectious diseases were not among the top five global

---

[*] John Murray Last (Ed.), *A Dictionary of Epidemiology* (Fourth Edition) (New York: Oxford University Press, 2001); Heath Kelly, "The Classical Definition of a Pandemic Is Not Elusive," *Bulletin of the World Health Organization* 89:7 (2011), 540, http://www.who.int/bulletin/volumes/89/7/11-088815.pdf.

[†] Specifically, the global risk by impact was as follows: In 2007, pandemics ranked number 4; in 2008, pandemics ranked number 5; in 2009, chronic disease ranked number 4; and in 2010, chronic disease ranked number 4. With respect to the global risk by likelihood: In 2007, chronic disease in developed countries ranked number 2; in 2008, chronic disease in the developed world ranked number 5; in 2009, chronic disease ranked number 3; and in 2010, chronic disease ranked number 3. "Global Risks Report 2013," World Economic Forum, 2013, 13, http://www3.weforum.org/docs/WEF_GlobalRisks_Report_2013.pdf.

TABLE 9.2   Actions That Should Be Taken during Pandemic Influenza Phases

	Actions by Affected Countries	Actions by Unaffected Countries
Phase 1	Creating, implementing, practicing, and harmonizing national pandemic influenza preparedness and response plans with national emergency preparedness and response plans	Creating, implementing, practicing, and harmonizing national pandemic influenza preparedness and response plans with national emergency preparedness and response plans
Phase 2	Creating, implementing, practicing, and harmonizing national pandemic influenza preparedness and response plans with national emergency preparedness and response plans	Creating, implementing, practicing, and harmonizing national pandemic influenza preparedness and response plans with national emergency preparedness and response plans
Phase 3	Creating, implementing, practicing, and harmonizing national pandemic influenza preparedness and response plans with national emergency preparedness and response plans	Creating, implementing, practicing, and harmonizing national pandemic influenza preparedness and response plans with national emergency preparedness and response plans
Phase 4	Rapid containment	Readiness for pandemic response
Phase 5	Pandemic response where actions are taken according to national emergency response plans	Readiness for imminent response
Phase 6	Pandemic response where actions are taken according to national emergency response plans	Readiness for imminent response

Source: Information for table retrieved from: WHO, http://www.who.int/influenza/ resources/documents/pandemic_phase_descriptions_and_actions.pdf; "Strengthening Response to Pandemics and Other Public Emergencies, Report of the Review Committee on the Functioning of the International Health Regulations (2005) and on Pandemic Influenza (H1N1) 2009," World Health Organization, 2011, 18, http://apps.who.int/iris/bitstream/ 10665/75235/1/9789241564335_eng.pdf.

risks between 2011 and 2013, the Global Risks report focused extensively on the dangers of infectious diseases to human health as one of the three risk cases it analyzed.[*] This report also covered infectious diseases that were found to be resistant to antibiotics. In fact, one main health concern of 2013 was that new antibiotic resistant bacteria have rendered existing antibiotics ineffective. Nonetheless, the report noted that one antibiotic

---

[*] "Global Risks Report 2013," World Economic Forum, 11, http://www3.weforum.org/ docs/WEF_GlobalRisks_Report_2013.pdf.

resistant bacteria, methicillin-resistant staphylococcus aureus (MRSA), was stabilizing and decreasing;[*] whereas others, such as cases of K pneumonia, were increasing.[†] The 2013 Global Risks report revealed that the spread of the antibiotic resistant infectious diseases was attributed to poor hygiene, poor living conditions, polluted water supplies, and the overuse of antibiotics.[‡] The latter factor, the overuse of antibiotics, is considered a force multiplier of infectious diseases.[§] The first three factors have also been cited as causing the spread of other infectious diseases. A case in point is cholera, which is a bacterial infectious disease that is "caused by ingestion of food or water contaminated with the bacterium *Vibrio cholerae*."[¶] Nevertheless, even countries where citizens do not suffer from poor living conditions and hygiene have suffered from infectious diseases.

Pathogens are also spread through international travel, immigration, and/or the globalization of food supplies.[**] Consider Lassa fever. Lassa fever is endemic to the rodent population in West Africa.[††] It spreads to humans from contact "with food or household items contaminated with rodent excreta."[‡‡] It subsequently can spread from human to human through direct contact.[§§] Cases of Lassa fever have been observed in countries outside of West Africa due to travel to and from the region. Undeniably, the spread of infectious diseases depends on transnational patterns of travel, trade, and migration.

The existence of zoonotic diseases also plays a significant role in the spread of infectious diseases (Figure 9.2). Zoonotic diseases refer to diseases that are naturally transmissible from animals to humans. Indeed, viruses that infect animals have subsequently infected humans, such as the Nipah, Ebola, and Marburg viruses. The Nipah virus (NiV) is a

---

[*] Ibid., 29.

[†] Ibid.

[‡] Ramanan Laxminarayan and David L. Heymann, "Challenges of Drug Resistance in the Developing World," *British Medical Journal* 344:9 (2012); Ibid., 30.

[§] Mely Caballero-Anthony, "Combating Infectious Diseases in East Asia: Securitization and Global Public Goods for Health and Human Security," *Journal of International Affairs* 59:2 (2006), 110.

[¶] "Cholera, Fact Sheet No. 107," World Health Organization, July 2012, http://www.who.int/mediacentre/factsheets/fs107/en/.

[**] John C. Gannon, "The Global Infectious Disease Threat and Its Implications for the United States," *NIE 99-17D*, January 2000, http://www.fas.org/irp/threat/nie99-17d.htm.

[††] "Special Pathogens Branch: Lassa Fever," CDC, June 19, 2013, http://www.cdc.gov/ncidod/dvrd/spb/mnpages/dispages/lassaf.htm; "Global Alert and Response (GAR): Lassa Fever," World Health Organization, http://www.who.int/csr/disease/lassafever/en/index.html.

[‡‡] "Global Alert and Response (GAR): Lassa Fever," World Health Organization, http://www.who.int/csr/disease/lassafever/en/index.html.

[§§] D. I. H. Simpson, "Marburg/Ebola/Haemorrhagic Fevers," *The Journal of the Royal Society for the Promotion of Health* 100:2 (1980), 54.

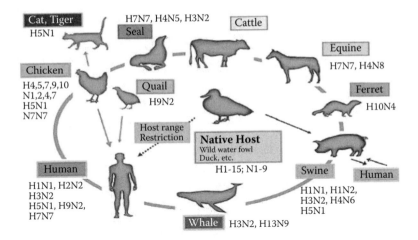

FIGURE 9.2 The existence of zoonotic diseases plays a significant role in the spread of infectious diseases as evidenced by this figure from the Centers for Disease Control. This is a schematic showing the host range of Type A influenza virus. (From the Centers for Disease Control and Prevention Influenza Branch.)

zoonotic infectious disease that is transmissible in animals and humans. The first case of an infected human was observed in 1998.[*] Humans become infected by coming in contact with infected animals or humans.[†] Another zoonotic disease, the Ebola virus, is particularly deadly with a fatality rate of 90% of those infected.[‡] Ebola is transmissible to humans "through close contact with the blood, secretions, organs or other bodily fluids of infected animals."[§] It can also be transmitted between humans "from close contact with the blood, secretions, organs or other bodily fluids of infected people."[¶] Similar to the Ebola virus, the Marburg virus is one of the "most virulent pathogens known to infect humans."[**] Like the Ebola virus, the Marburg virus is spread through direct contact with

---

[*] Stephen P. Luby, Emily S. Gurley, and M. Jahangir Hossain, "Transmission of Human Infection with Nipah Virus," *Clinical Infectious Diseases* 49:11 (2009), 1743.

[†] "Global Alert and Response (GAR): Nipah Virus (NiV) Infection," World Health Organization, http://www.who.int/csr/disease/nipah/en/; Stephen P. Luby, Emily S. Gurley, and M. Jahangir Hossain, "Transmission of Human Infection with Nipah Virus," *Clinical Infectious Diseases* 49:11 (2009), 1743–1746.

[‡] "Ebola Haemorrhagic Fever, Fact Sheet No. 103," World Health Organization, August 2012, http://www.who.int/mediacentre/factsheets/fs103/en/.

[§] Ibid.

[¶] Ibid.

[**] "Global Alert and Response (GAR): Marburg Haemorrhagic Fever," World Health Organization, http://www.who.int/csr/disease/marburg/en/.

infected individuals and animals.* More specifically, it is "transmitted by direct contact with the blood, body fluids and tissues of infected persons [and through the handling of ill or dead infected animals]."† No vaccine or specific treatment exists for animals and individuals infected with either the Nipah, Ebola, or Marburg virus.‡

IMPACT OF INFECTIOUS DISEASES

The mobility of infectious diseases makes dealing with them particularly challenging. For obvious reasons, infectious diseases directly impact health due to the resulting illnesses and/or deaths. However, infectious diseases also have social, political, and economic consequences. The social costs associated with outbreaks include the "significant social disruption through fear and anxiety about a disease (based on accurate or inaccurate information), the loss of people in key social positions due to illness or death, discrimination against groups affected by disease, and the loss of the majority of (or entire) specific demographic groups."§ With respect to political consequences, "the most obvious effect of disease that may result in the instability of the nation or region is the toll of some diseases that have high mortality rates."¶ Finally, the economic impact of infectious diseases includes the costs associated with treating infected individuals, the cost of vaccines, the impact on the tourism industry, and the impact on consumer confidence in regions where pandemics have occurred. Infectious diseases can also disrupt the distribution of goods and services in and between countries. For these reasons, the economic consequences of infectious diseases are significant; due, in large part, to the adverse impact that they have on "productivity, profitability, and foreign investment."**

---

* D. I. H. Simpson, "Marburg/Ebola/Haemorrhagic Fevers," *The Journal of the Royal Society for the Promotion of Health* 100:2 (1980), 54–55; "Marburg Haemorrhagic Fever," World Health Organization, November 2012, http://www.who.int/mediacentre/factsheets/fs_marburg/en/.

† "Global Alert and Response (GAR): Marburg Haemorrhagic Fever," World Health Organization, http://www.who.int/csr/disease/marburg/en/.

‡ "Global Alert and Response (GAR): Nipah Virus (NiV) Infection," World Health Organization, http://www.who.int/csr/disease/nipah/en/; "Ebola Haemorrhagic Fever," Fact Sheet No. 103, World Health Organization, August 2012, http://www.who.int/mediacentre/factsheets/fs103/en/; "Global Alert and Response (GAR): Marburg Haemorrhagic Fever," World Health Organization, http://www.who.int/csr/disease/marburg/en/.

§ Gary Cecchine and Melinda Moore, "Infectious Disease and National Security: Strategic Information Needs," RAND, 2006, 17, http://www.rand.org/pubs/technical_reports/TR405.html.

¶ Ibid.

** "National Intelligence Estimate: The Global Infectious Disease Threat and Its Implications for the United States," National Intelligence Council, January 2000, 36, http://www.wilsoncenter.org/sites/default/files/Report6-3.pdf.

Infectious diseases thus pose significant risks to domestic and international economies' trade and commerce. When infectious diseases, such as foot-and-mouth disease (FMD), avian influenza ("bird flu"), and bovine spongiform encephalopathy (BSE, "mad cow disease"), spread among animals, the countries with the infected animals suffered trade restrictions, reduced livestock production, increases in consumer costs, and an overall adverse impact on their economies.* FMD is described as "a severe, highly contagious viral disease" that "causes illness in cows, pigs, sheep, goats, deer, and other animals with divided hooves."† When an FMD outbreak occurred in Taiwan, it crippled the pork industry, shutting it down for a year.‡ A similar occurrence was observed with the avian flu outbreak in Hong Kong in 1997. This outbreak resulted in a decrease in air travel to the country, a decline in tourism, loss of poultry production, and a loss of commerce.

Furthermore, the spread of BSE also had adverse effects on economies. Particularly, concerns about the spread of mad cow disease through the international meat trade arose.§ These concerns led to the mass slaughter of cattle, a significant decrease in beef consumption, and embargoes on beef from countries where cases of the disease had been reported. For instance, when mad cow disease was found in Britain, the European Union banned British beef. Consequently, the "losses to the British economy were estimated by the WHO at $5.75 billion, including $2 billion in lost beef exports."¶

Government responses to infectious diseases are considered acceptable if they can effectively deal with them and do not result in considerable and unnecessary economic consequences. When dealing with infectious diseases, governments are faced with the dilemma of taking action; specifically, eliciting a response which constitutes neither an overreaction nor underreaction. An overreaction can cause widespread fear and have significant adverse short-term and long-term impacts on the economy. This was observed in India. Specifically, in 1994, domestic officials declared a plague outbreak in Surat, India. In response to this declaration, a mass exodus ensued, where half a million individuals fled

---

* John C. Gannon, "The Global Infectious Disease Threat and Its Implications for the United States," *NIE 99-17D*, January 2000, http://www.fas.org/irp/threat/nie99-17d.htm.

† "Foot-and-Mouth Disease," The Animal and Plant Health Inspection Service (APHIS), July 2013, http://www.aphis.usda.gov/publications/animal_health/2013/fs_fmd_general.pdf.

‡ John C. Gannon, "The Global Infectious Disease Threat and Its Implications for the United States," *NIE 99-17D*, January 2000, http://www.fas.org/irp/threat/nie99-17d.htm.

§ Sandra J. Maclean, "Microbes, Mad Cows and Militaries: Exploring the Links Between Health and Security," *Security Dialogue* 39:5 (2008), 481.

¶ John C. Gannon, "The Global Infectious Disease Threat and Its Implications for the United States," *NIE 99-17D*, January 2000, http://www.fas.org/irp/threat/nie99-17d.htm.

from Surat and the surrounding areas.[*] The government overreacted by placing any person with symptoms, such as "the sudden onset of fever, headache, chills, and weakness,"[†] into quarantine.[‡] The international community overreacted as well. Specifically, travel to and from India was banned by certain countries and trade restrictions were imposed (e.g., the United Arab Emirates, Oman, Qatar, and Bangladesh).[§] Other countries issued travel warnings (e.g., the United States, the United Kingdom, Canada, France, Germany, and Italy).[¶]

Underreactions have also been observed by countries with outbreaks of infectious diseases. Consider the BSE outbreak in Britain. In 1986, "the first cases of BSE were recorded in Britain. In spite of the rapid escalation of the BSE epidemic in 1987, UK policy makers did not take any regulatory actions because the risks of cross-species transmissibility were deemed unproven."[**] It was only after 1995, that the UK government responded to the spread of this infectious disease but only after a human contracted a new variant of Creutzfeldt–Jakob disease (CJD).[††] CJD is "one of the five human proteinaceous infectious particle (prion) diseases. It is also classified as a transmissible spongiform encephalopathy, a rapidly progressive, neurodegenerative disorder causing dramatic neuromuscular symptoms, profound dementia, and death."[‡‡] Of the two forms of this rare and fatal brain disorder, classic and variant CJD, the variant form is linked to BSE.[§§] Britain's delay in response to the cases of

---

[*] Gary Cecchine and Melinda Moore, "Infectious Disease and National Security: Strategic Information Needs," RAND, 2006, 20, http://www.rand.org/pubs/technical_reports/TR405.html.

[†] The symptoms of the plague vary occurring to the type of plague. For instance, in addition to the "sudden onset of fever, headache, chills, and weakness," individuals with pneumonic plague can experience (if left untreated) "a rapidly developing pneumonia with shortness of breath, chest pain, cough, and sometimes bloody or watery mucous." Likewise, in addition to the "sudden onset of fever, headache, chills, and weakness," individuals with bubonic plague also have "one or more swollen, tender and painful lymph nodes (called *buboes*)." "Plague: Symptoms," Centers for Disease Control (CDC), June 13, 2012, http://www.cdc.gov/plague/symptoms/.

[‡] Gary Cecchine and Melinda Moore, "Infectious Disease and National Security: Strategic Information Needs," RAND, 2006, 20, http://www.rand.org/pubs/technical_reports/TR405.html.

[§] Ibid., 21.

[¶] Ibid.

[**] Alessandra Arcuri, "Reconstructing Precaution, Deconstructing Misconceptions," *Ethics & International Affairs* 21:3 (2007), 359–360.

[††] Ibid., 360.

[‡‡] Clarissa Rentz, "Creutzfeldt–Jakob Disease: Two Case Studies." *American Journal of Alzheimer's Disease and Other Dementias* 18:3 (2003), 171.

[§§] Harash K. Narang, "Lingering Doubts about Spongiform Encephalopathy and Creutzfeldt–Jakob Disease," *Experimental Biology and Medicine* 226:7 (2001), 640.

BSE resulted not only in high human and agro-industry costs, but also resulted in a decrease in public confidence in government institutions.[*]

The reports of the spread of infectious diseases initiate national and international responses that could effectively control its spread and mitigate social (e.g., social disruption), political (e.g., government destabilization), and economic (e.g., loss of productivity) consequences. By contrast, the reporting of the spread of an infectious disease can result in devastating consequences for the reporting country. For instance, that country may experience significant disruptions in trade and travel and suffer other economic costs associated with international intervention measures. Consider the cholera outbreak in Peru in 1991. The temporary ban placed on Peruvian seafood exports in response to this outbreak devastated the fishing industry and trade.[†] Tourism to the country was also affected.[‡] Given this prospect, countries with outbreaks may be hesitant to report them to the international community.

Paradoxically, the country affected by an infectious disease suffers greater losses when it reports an outbreak to the international community.[§] In 1994, India suffered a $2 billion loss due to the plague scare.[¶] As noted above, the plague sparked a mass exodus from Surat (500,000 fled), various countries banned travel to and from India, and trade with India was stopped by certain countries.[**] Richard Cash and Vasant Narasimhan rightly pointed out that "if the interests of reporting countries are not protected," it is likely that countries will continue to

[*] Alessandra Arcuri, "Reconstructing Precaution, Deconstructing Misconceptions," *Ethics & International Affairs* 21:3 (2007), 360.

[†] John C. Gannon, "The Global Infectious Disease Threat and Its Implications for the United States," *NIE 99-17D*, January 2000, http://www.fas.org/irp/threat/nie99-17d.htm.

[‡] Ibid.

[§] Richard A. Cash and Vasant Narasimhan, "Impediments to Global Surveillance of Infectious Diseases: Consequences of Open Reporting in a Global Economy," *Bulletin of the World Health Organization* 78:11 (2000), 1364, http://whqlibdoc.who.int/bulletin/2000/Number%2011/78(11)1358-1367.pdf; Gary Cecchine and Melinda Moore, "Infectious Disease and National Security: Strategic Information Needs," RAND, 2006, 21, http://www.rand.org/pubs/technical_reports/TR405.html.

[¶] C. E. Levy and Kenneth L. Gage, "Plague in the United States, 1995–1997," *Infections in Medicine* 16:1 (1999), 54–64; Gary Cecchine and Melinda Moore, "Infectious Disease and National Security: Strategic Information Needs," RAND, 2006, 21, http://www.rand.org/pubs/technical_reports/TR405.html.

[**] John C. Gannon, "The Global Infectious Disease Threat and Its Implications for the United States," *NIE 99-17D*, January 2000, http://www.fas.org/irp/threat/nie99-17d.htm.

"conceal epidemics, and the goals of global surveillance [and information sharing] are unlikely to be fully achieved."[*]

WEAPONIZATION OF INFECTIOUS DISEASES

Concerns exist at national and international levels that infectious diseases may be weaponized by enemies. Historically, during the French and Indian War as well as the Revolutionary War, the British weaponized smallpox and used it against their enemies.[†] Likewise, during World War II, one of Japan's imperial army units (Unit 731) weaponized cholera and plague, among other infectious diseases, and tested these biological weapons on Chinese civilians.[‡] The potential weaponization of infectious diseases remains a significant threat to transnational security.

Information on the science and technology required to build biological weapons is readily available. Particularly, there has been information published in scientific journals that could be used for nefarious purposes. One recent example involves research that uses the genetic code sequence of the H1N1 virus to generate a virus identical to the Spanish flu virus of 1918, which caused the worst pandemic in the 20th century and resulted in millions of deaths. The findings were published in the journal *Science*. However, review by the National Science Advisory Board for Biosecurity (NSABB) concluded that the benefits of the future use of such information (e.g., the development of new vaccines and therapies to protect against a pandemic of this nature) in the academic community outweighs the risks involved in its publication.[§] Criminals, rogue states, or terrorists could use this research to reconstruct extinct virulent pathogens for

---

[*] Richard A. Cash and Vasant Narasimhan, "Impediments to Global Surveillance of Infectious Diseases: Consequences of Open Reporting in a Global Economy," *Bulletin of the World Health Organization* 78:11 (2000), 1365, http://whqlibdoc.who.int/bulletin/2000/Number%2011/78(11)1358-1367.pdf; Gary Cecchine and Melinda Moore, "Infectious Disease and National Security: Strategic Information Needs," *RAND*, 2006, 21, http://www.rand.org/pubs/technical_reports/TR405.html.

[†] John Duffy, "Smallpox and the Indians in the American Colonies," *Bulletin of the History of Medicine* 25:4 (1951), 340; Susan Peterson, "Epidemic Disease and National Security," *Security Studies* 12:2/3 (2002), 72.

[‡] Nicholas D. Kristof, "Unmasking Horror—A Special Report; Japan Confronting Gruesome War Atrocity," *New York Times*, March 17, 1995, http://www.nytimes.com/1995/03/17/world/unmasking-horror-a-special-report-japan-confronting-gruesome-war-atrocity.html; Peter Williams and David Wallace, *Unit 731: Japanese Army's Secret of Secrets* (London: Hodder and Stoughton, 1989); Susan Peterson, "Epidemic Disease and National Security," *Security Studies* 12:2/3 (2002), 72.

[§] Jocelyn Kaiser, "Resurrected Influenza Virus Yields Secrets of Deadly 1918 Pandemic," *Science* 310:5745 (2005), 28–29; Christian Enemark and Ian Ramshaw, "Gene Technology, Biological Weapons, and the Security of Science," *Security Studies* 18:3 (2009), 637.

use in biological weapons. Such published research can also aid in the development of novel, virulent pathogens (for which no vaccine exists) and the engineering of pathogens to avoid detection and delay diagnosis; this could cause significantly more deaths in consequence.

Consider the recent H5N1 research by virologist Ron Fouchier from Erasmus Medical Center in Rotterdam, the Netherlands. H5N1, which emerged in Hong Kong, is a highly pathogenic virus found in wild and domestic birds.[*] It is transmissible to humans primarily through direct avian contact. The impact of this virus can have significant adverse health consequences such as severe disease and death. Vaccines to prevent H5N1 infections have been created but are not yet ready for widespread use.[†] Currently, H5N1 is difficult to transmit from individual to individual.[‡] However, Fouchier's H5N1 research focuses on genetic mutations in H5N1 that made it more transmissible to humans. Prior to his research, "experts believed that the strain was transmissible from person-to-person only through very close contact"; however, "Fouchier mutated the strain, creating an airborne virus that could be easily transmitted through coughs and sneezes."[§] This research has sparked significant debate and concern over "gain-of-function" research.[¶] Initially, the NSABB declared that it would not publish the virologist's findings for fear of it being used by criminals, terrorists, or rogue states. The NSABB subsequently reversed its decision in March 2012. The danger of misuse of the H5N1 mutation by criminal elements still remains; so too does the fear that this virus could be accidentally leaked from the laboratory in which it is being developed.[**] This fear is all the more pronounced given

---

[*] Darrick T. Evensen and Christopher E. Clarke, "Efficacy Information in Media Coverage of Infectious Disease Risks: An Ill Predicament?" *Science Communication* 34:3 (2012), 395.

[†] "FAQs: H5N1 Influenza," World Health Organization, http://www.who.int/influenza/ human_animal_interface/avian_influenza/h5n1_research/faqs/en/.

[‡] Ibid.

[§] Mikaela Conley, "Dutch Scientist Agrees to Omit Published Details of Highly Contagious Bird Flu Findings," *ABC News*, December 21, 2011, http://abcnews. go.com/Health/dutch-scientist-agrees-omit-details-killer-bird-flu/story?id=15204649.

[¶] "Gain of function" research "introduces or amplifies a gene product. This type of research is intended to increase the transmissibility, host range, or virulence of pathogens." Malerie Briseno and Christina England, "Science and Security: The Moratorium on H5N1 'Gain-of-Function' Experiments," *Public Interest Report* 66:1 (Winter 2013), 1, http://blogs-cdn.fas.org/pir/wp-content/uploads/sites/8/2013/03/H5N1-Winter-2013.pdf; Bob Grant, "European Researchers Urge H5N1 Caution," *The Scientist*, January 2, 2014, http://www.the-scientist.com/?articles.view/articleNo/38776/title/ European-Researchers-Urge-H5N1-Caution/.

[**] Steve Connor, "Leading Scientists Condemn Decision to Continue Controversial Research into Deadly H5N1 Bird-Flu Virus," *The Independent*, January 23, 2013, http://www.independent.co.uk/news/science/leading-scientists-condemn-decision-to-continue-controversial-research-into-deadly-h5n1-birdflu-virus-8463863.html.

TABLE 9.3   H5N1 Human Cases and Deaths (since 2003)

Affected Countries	Human Cases	Human Deaths
Nigeria	1	1
Egypt	173	63
Turkey	12	4
Azerbaijan	8	5
Pakistan	3	1
Iraq	3	2
Djibouti	1	0
Bangladesh	7	1
Myanmar	1	0
China	45	30
Laos	2	2
Thailand	25	17
Cambodia	47	33
Vietnam	125	62
Indonesia	195	163
Canada	1	1
Totals	649	385

Note: Figures last updated on January 8, 2014.

Source: Information for table retrieved from CDC, "Highly Pathogenic Avian Influenza (H5N1), Human Cases and Deaths Since 2003," http://www.cdc.gov/flu/pdf/avianflu/avian-flu-human-world-summary.pdf.

that, to date, H5N1 has killed approximately 60% of the individuals infected by it (385 out of the total 649 infected; see Table 9.3).

In addition to publishing research on the mutations of infectious diseases, the Internet has enabled the rapid dissemination of scientific research on virulent pathogens, making this information not only easier to acquire but also more readily available to the general public. Moreover, other security issues exist beyond the publication and availability of this type of research. For example, national and international laboratory experiments working with such pathogens pose great safety risks, especially because research has shown that facilities that conduct these experiments are not adequately secured.[*] Concerns also exist that zoonotic and human pathogens can be introduced into the food supply. When such an

---

[*] Christian Enemark and Ian Ramshaw, "Gene Technology, Biological Weapons, and the Security of Science," *Security Studies* 18:3 (2009), 626.

action is deliberate, this is known as *agroterrorism*.[*] Agroterrorism is defined as "the deliberate introduction of an animal or plant disease with the goal of generating fear, causing economic losses, and/or undermining stability and disruption of consumer demand."[†] This action is not a new phenomenon; zoonotic and human pathogens have been used by both state and nonstate actors. For example, in 1979, Palestinian terrorists poisoned Jaffa oranges, which Israel exports to Europe[‡]; nobody died as a result of this incident, but several people were made ill and this incident adversely affected Israel's export of this product. To deter and prevent the introduction of such pathogens into the food supply, quarantine, port inspections, and the tracking of imported plants, animals, and their products have been implemented to great effect.[§] In what follows, three major pandemics are examined (i.e., HIV/AIDS, SARS, and H1N1), along with the resultant national and international responses to these threats.

HIV/AIDS

HIV/AIDS (Figure 9.3) was first diagnosed in the early 1980s.[¶] Of the novel emerging diseases, all but HIV/AIDS have had low mortality and morbidity rates. In fact, by 2012, 36 million people had died from HIV/AIDS worldwide.[**] That year, approximately 35,000,000 individuals around the globe were HIV-positive.[††] An estimated 69% of this figure were living in sub-Saharan Africa.[‡‡] Given this figure, it is no

---

[*] Roger Breeze, "Agroterrorism: Betting Far More Than the Farm," *Biosecurity and Bioterrorism* 2:4 (2004), 251–264; O. Shawn Cupp, David E. Walker II, John Hillison, "Agroterrorism in the U.S.: Key Security Challenge for the 21st Century," *Biosecurity and Bioterrorism* 2:2 (2004), 97–105; Calum G. Turvey, Benjamin Onyango, and William H. Hallman, "Political Communications and Terrorism," *Studies in Conflict & Terrorism* 31:10 (2008), 947.

[†] C. Ford Runge, "National Security and Bioterrorism: A U.S. Perspective," Prepared for the 8th Joint Conference on Food, Agriculture and the Environment (Red Cedar Lake, WI, August 25–28, 2002), as cited in Calum G. Turvey, Benjamin Onyango, and William H. Hallman, "Political Communications and Terrorism," *Studies in Conflict & Terrorism* 31:10 (2008), 948.

[‡] Ehud Sprinzak and Ely Karmon, "Why So Little? The Palestinian Terrorist Organizations and Unconventional Terrorism," International Institute for Counter-Terrorism, June 17, 2007, http://www.ict.org.il/Articles/tabid/66/Articlsid/246/currentpage/5/Default.aspx.

[§] Jim Monke, "Agroterrorism: Threat and Preparedness," *CRS Report for Congress*, August 13, 2004, 29, http://www.fas.org/irp/crs/RL32521.pdf.

[¶] J. M. Mann, "AIDS: A Worldwide Pandemic," In M. S. Gottlieb, et al. (Eds.), *Current Topics in AIDS* (Volume 2) (New York: John Wiley & Sons, 1989), 1–10.

[**] "HIV/AIDS, Fact Sheet No. 360," World Health Organization, October 2013, http://www.who.int/mediacentre/factsheets/fs360/en/.

[††] Ibid.

[‡‡] Ibid.

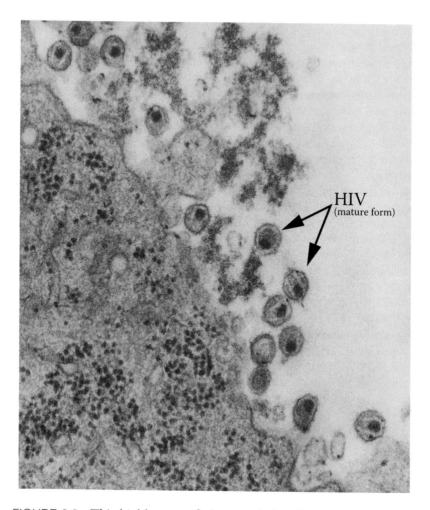

FIGURE 9.3 This highly magnified transmission electron micrographic (TEM) image revealed the presence of mature forms of the human immunodeficiency virus (HIV) in a tissue sample under investigation. The Human Immunodeficiency Virus (HIV), a retrovirus, was identified in 1983 as the etiologic agent for the Acquired Immunodeficiency Syndrome (AIDS). (From the U.S. Department of Health and Human Services, CDC.)

surprise that HIV/AIDS is one of the leading causes of death in developing countries. There is currently no universally recognized cure for HIV. Nevertheless, there is effective treatment that helps control the virus: highly active antiretroviral therapy (HAART). However, the benefits of HAART are limited if this therapy is taken by HIV/AIDS patients only at advanced stages of infection.

Initially, HIV/AIDS was treated solely as a health issue. Accordingly, during this time, it received little attention outside of health-based and development organizations. It was not until 2000 that it was declared a national and international security issue. In particular, it was UN Resolution 1308 that framed HIV/AIDS as a security concern. This resolution noted "that the HIV/AIDS pandemic, if unchecked, may pose a risk to stability and security."[*] UN Resolution 1308 also declared that HIV/AIDS was a threat to international security and peace. The same year of the resolution, the United States declared that the HIV/AIDS pandemic was a threat to national security.[†] Describing HIV/AIDS as a security threat helped raise international awareness and assisted in the obtainment of resources to help fight this infectious disease.[‡]

The best way to prevent HIV/AIDS is through awareness campaigns. Indeed, the absence or limiting of these campaigns contributes to the rise in high-risk behavior among populations. According to the WHO, high-risk behavior includes engaging in sex without a condom, sharing contaminated needles and syringes, and "receiving unsafe injections, blood transfusions, [and] medical procedures that involve unsterile cutting or piercing."[§] The Joint United Nations Programme on HIV/AIDS (UNAIDS) seeks to promote HIV/AIDS awareness and provide "universal access to HIV prevention, treatment, care and support."[¶] Funding to prevent HIV/AIDS and HIV/AIDS awareness campaigns is critical in raising awareness in the population and drawing attention to the fact that HIV/AIDS is still very prevalent today.

SARS

Severe Acute Respiratory Syndrome (SARS) is a highly contagious disease that "spread[s] to humans through the slaughter of infected animals

---

[*] UN Resolution 1308 (2000).

[†] Hakan Seckinelgin, Joseph Bigirumwami, and Jill Morris, "Securitization of HIV/AIDS in Content: Gendered Vulnerability in Burundi," *Security Dialogue* 41:5 (2010), 516.

[‡] Sandra J. Maclean, "Microbes, Mad Cows and Militaries: Exploring the Links between Health and Security," *Security Dialogue* 39:5 (2008), 478; Peter W. Singer, "AIDS and International Security," *Survival* 44:1 (2002), 145–158.

[§] "HIV/AIDS, Fact Sheet No. 360," World Health Organization, October 2013, http://www.who.int/mediacentre/factsheets/fs360/en/.

[¶] "Joint United Nations Programme on HIV/AIDS (UNAIDS): Mission/Vision of the UN Agency in Egypt," UN Egypt Coordination Office, http://www.un.org.eg/UNInner2.aspx?pageid=59.

in unsanitary and crowded markets."[*] The transmission of SARS is primarily airborne, which results in rapid spreading of the disease. In February 2003, a physician that had treated patients, who were later found to have SARS, subsequently traveled to Hong Kong. While there, 11 hotel guests came in contact with him and were consequently infected by the disease (unbeknownst to them).[†] They later traveled to their respective countries; in so doing, spreading the disease.[‡]

Those most at risk for exposure and contamination are healthcare workers that come in contact with individuals infected with the disease. For example, in Toronto, the contact of healthcare workers with the bedding of SARS infected patients increased the number of infections.[§] Additionally, many healthcare workers did not have the necessary training and expertise in infectious disease control.[¶] The resulting infections of healthcare workers occurred because of the little to no precautions taken to control the virus and prevent its spread. For instance, healthcare workers who were infected with SARS were not wearing gloves and surgical masks when coming in contact with patients. The same inadequate measures to control the spread of infectious disease in healthcare facilities were observed with the Ebola virus and Lassa fever.[**] Moreover, during the SARS outbreak in Toronto, existing infectious disease tracking and outbreak management computer software at Canadian hospitals were described as being "outdated and ineffective."[††] Furthermore, a new system, the integrated public-health information system (iPHS), had been acquired in 2000, but staff were not very familiar with its use.[‡‡] This hampered health workers' ability to treat, control, and contain SARS.

---

[*] Michael T. Osterholm, "Preparing for the Next Pandemic," *Foreign Affairs* 84:4 (July/August 2005), http://www.foreignaffairs.com/articles/60818/michael-t-osterholm/preparing-for-the-next-pandemic, cited in Gary Cecchine and Melinda Moore, "Infectious Disease and National Security: Strategic Information Needs," RAND, 2006, 21, http://www.rand.org/pubs/technical_reports/TR405.html.

[†] Roxana Salehi and S. Harris Ali, "The Social and Political Context of Disease Outbreaks: The Case of SARS in Toronto," *Canadian Public Policy/Analyse de Politiques* 32:4 (2006), 375.

[‡] Ibid.

[§] Ibid., 376.

[¶] Ibid., 377.

[**] "Ebola Haemorrhagic Fever, Fact Sheet No. 103." World Health Organization, August 2012, http://www.who.int/mediacentre/factsheets/fs103/en/; "Global Alert and Response (GAR): Lassa Fever," World Health Organization (n.d.), http://www.who.int/csr/disease/lassafever/en/index.html.

[††] Salehi, R. and S. H. Ali, "The Social and Political Context of Disease Outbreaks: The Case of SARS in Toronto," *Canadian Public Policy/Analyse de Politiques* 32:4 (2006), 377.

[‡‡] Ibid.

Several countries adopted stringent measures to screen and control visitors coming from SARS-affected countries. Thermal imaging technology was installed at airports and other entry/exit points to scan passengers for fevers. If fevers were detected, travelers were subjected to medical screening to determine if they were infected with SARS. Those with SARS were quarantined. Friends and families of SARS patients (those that come in contact with them) were also placed under home quarantine.[*] As a result, existing legislation on infectious disease in Hong Kong, Shanghai, and Toronto was amended to provide public health officials with far-reaching powers to investigate infectious diseases and issue isolation and quarantine orders.[†] Along with quarantine and traveler screening, travel restrictions were placed to SARS-affected countries. Passengers were strongly encouraged to avoid traveling to areas with high levels of SARS wherever possible. Specifically, travel alerts were issued by the World Health Organization warning passengers against traveling to SARS-affected countries.[‡] Other countries temporarily banned the entry of travelers from SARS-affected countries into their own territories.[§]

Media reports on SARS highlighted that it was a highly contagious fatal pathogen with no known cure.[¶] The means of transmission of SARS were also unclear.[**] This uncertainty was communicated to the public, along with images of infected areas and the number of those infected by the disease and those who died from it.[††] As a result, "juxtaposing the massive publicity about SARS against the medical unknowns boosted feelings of uncertainty and contributed to what could have been an overreaction, in some cases."[‡‡]

---

[*] Mely Caballero-Anthony, "SARS in Asia: Crisis, Vulnerabilities, and Regional Responses," *Asian Survey* 45:3 (2005), 484.

[†] Lesley A. Jacobs, "Rights and Quarantine during the SARS Global Health Crisis: Differentiated Legal Consciousness in Hong Kong, Shanghai, and Toronto," *Law & Society Review* 41:3 (2007), 520.

[‡] Mely Caballero-Anthony, "SARS in Asia: Crisis, Vulnerabilities, and Regional Responses," *Asian Survey* 45:3 (2005), 482.

[§] Ibid., 485.

[¶] Ibid., 483.

[**] Ibid.

[††] Ibid.

[‡‡] Bobbie Person, Francisco Sy, Kelly Holton, Barbara Govert, and Arthur Liang, "Fear and Stigma: The Epidemic within the SARS Outbreak," *Emerging Infectious Diseases* 10:2 (2004), Centers for Disease Control and Prevention, http://wwwnc.cdc.gov/eid/article/10/2/03-0750_article.htm; Asian Development Bank, "SARS: Economic Impacts and Implications. Economic and Research Department," *Policy Brief Series*, Number 15 (May 2003), http://www.adb.org/publications/sars-economic-impacts-and-implications; Mely Caballero-Anthony, "SARS in Asia: Crisis, Vulnerabilities, and Regional Responses," *Asian Survey* 45:3 (2005), 483.

What contributed to the consequences of SARS was China's delay in reporting the outbreak. The first outbreak of SARS was traced back to the Chinese province of Guangdong in November 2002. Nonetheless, it was not until March 12, 2003, that the World Health Organization issued a global health warning concerning SARS. When the health warning was finally provided, SARS had already spread to many areas in China, Hong Kong, Taiwan, Singapore, and Vietnam.* This handling of SARS provides an excellent example of what not to do during an outbreak or pandemic. By the time SARS was contained, 8,300 individuals were infected and close to 800 individuals had died in 28 countries.† It also disrupted the free movement of goods and individuals.

In the aftermath of SARS, the International Health Regulations (IHR) were amended and updated. The IHR consists of international legally binding rules for member states of the World Health Organization for controlling the potential spread of infectious diseases internationally.‡ The IHR are designed to prevent the spread of infectious diseases internationally by requiring countries to notify the international community of outbreaks. The IHR also requires countries to maintain public health facilities that can contain the affected and minimize the spread of infectious diseases. According to the IHR, countries are required to report infectious diseases to the World Health Organization.§ However, at the time of SARS, the IHR only listed three infectious diseases for which reporting was mandated—cholera, plague, and yellow fever.¶ Novel diseases, such as SARS (and H1N1 discussed in the next section), illustrate the inadequacy of this sole focus. In the aftermath of SARS, the 2005 International Health Regulations were implemented. The 2005 IHR sought to enhance national capacity building and collaboration between countries, surveillance and response capabilities, and develop the means to identify infectious diseases and notify the World Health Organization should an infectious disease be detected within the territory of the country. The 2005 IHR additionally require countries to provide information

---

* Mely Caballero-Anthony, "SARS in Asia: Crisis, Vulnerabilities, and Regional Responses," *Asian Survey* 45:3 (2005), 479.

† Sue Chan, "WHO: SARS Outbreak Nearing End," *CBS News*, June 13, 2003, http://www.cbsnews.com/news/who-sars-outbreak-nearing-end/.

‡ David L. Heymann, "The International Response to the Outbreak of SARS in 2003," *Philosophical Transactions: Biological Sciences* 35 (2004), 1127.

§ Mely Caballero-Anthony, "SARS in Asia: Crisis, Vulnerabilities, and Regional Responses," *Asian Survey* 45:3 (2005), 480–481.

¶ Roxana Salehi and S. Harris Ali, "The Social and Political Context of Disease Outbreaks: The Case of SARS in Toronto," *Canadian Public Policy/Analyse de Politiques* 32:4 (2006), 380; Mely Caballero-Anthony, "SARS in Asia: Crisis, Vulnerabilities, and Regional Responses," *Asian Survey* 45:3 (2005), 481.

on potential public health emergencies that concern the international community within 24 hours of their detection.[*]

H1N1

In 2009, the Centers for Disease Control and Prevention (CDC) described H1N1 as a contagious virus that spread from human to human through contact by way of coughing, sneezing, or talking by individuals with this form of influenza; individuals could also become infected by touching items or surfaces with the virus and touching their nose or mouth afterward.[†] H1N1 had significant adverse consequences for numerous people infected by it, including serious illnesses and death. The CDC estimated that anywhere "between about 195,000 and 403,000 H1N1-related hospitalizations" and approximately "8,870 and 18,300 2009 H1N1-related deaths occurred between April 2009 and April 10, 2010."[‡] In addition to humans, domestic animals were also infected with the 2009 H1N1 virus.[§]

The first cases of the pandemic occurred in Mexico in February and March 2009; the first cases in the United States were observed at the end of March 2009.[¶] In June 2009, the WHO declared that the 2009 H1N1 was a pandemic.[**] In the beginning of the pandemic, Mexico "suffered severe economic sanctions" from bans on pork importation (e.g., live swine, pork, and pork-containing products) from this country.[††] The pandemic was mistakenly labeled as swine flu; however, pork was not the source of the pandemic.[‡‡] Despite assurances from researchers, scientists, and international organizations that pork was not the source of the

---

[*] Sungwon Yoon, "Ideas, Institutions, and Interest in the Global Governance of Epidemics in Asia," *Asia–Pacific Journal of Public Health* 22:3 (2010), 128S.

[†] "Updated CDC Estimates of 2009 H1N1 Influenza Cases, Hospitalizations and Deaths in the United States, April 2009–April 10, 2010," CDC, May 14, 2010, http://www.cdc.gov/h1n1flu/estimates_2009_h1n1.htm#Table% 20Cumulative.

[‡] Ibid.

[§] "H1N1 Flu Virus: For Pet Owners (FAQ)," February 14, 2011, American Veterinary Medical Association, https://www.avma.org/KB/Resources/FAQs/Pages/2009-H1N1-FAQs-pets.aspx.

[¶] "Strengthening Response to Pandemics and Other Public Emergencies, Report of the Review Committee on the Functioning of the International Health Regulations (2005) and on Pandemic Influenza (H1N1) 2009," World Health Organization, 2011, 29, http://apps.who.int/iris/bitstream/10665/75235/1/9789241564335_eng.pdf.

[**] "The 2009 H1N1 Pandemic: Summary Highlights, April 2009–April 2010," CDC, June 16, 2010, http://www.cdc.gov/h1n1flu/cdcresponse.htm.

[††] "Strengthening Response to Pandemics and Other Public Emergencies. Report of the Review Committee on the Functioning of the International Health Regulations (2005) and on Pandemic Influenza (H1N1) 2009," World Health Organization, 2011, 37, http://apps.who.int/iris/bitstream/10665/75235/1/9789241564335_eng.pdf.

[‡‡] Ibid.

pandemic, bans were implemented nevertheless.* H1N1 subsequently spread through travel to the United States, Canada, Europe, Asia, South America, and parts of Africa, and contact with infected individuals.† The WHO officially declared that the pandemic ended in August 2010.‡

DEALING WITH INFECTIOUS DISEASES

Many measures have been taken nationally and internationally to combat the spread of infectious diseases. These measures have focused on preventing, mitigating, preparing for, and responding to outbreaks and pandemics. Strategies at the national and international level focus on prevention (wherever possible), mitigation, and control of infectious diseases.

Prevention and Mitigation

The prevention of infectious diseases may or may not be possible. This depends on the infectious disease and whether or not a vaccine is available. For instance, there is a vaccination for yellow fever (a disease that is transmitted to humans by infected mosquitos) to prevent infection of an individual.§ If infected, however, no specific treatment exists. Mass immunization campaigns have been created, promoted, and implemented in South America and Africa to prevent the spread of this disease.¶ Additionally, vaccines are recommended for travelers to these countries and many countries require that individuals traveling from countries that are at risk for yellow fever virus transmission be vaccinated before entering their territories.**

The World Health Organization (WHO) requires that countries have domestic measures that can control the spread of infectious diseases internationally. To accomplish this, countries need to first have nation-

---

* Ibid.
† "2009 H1N1 Flu: International Situation Update," CDC, May 14, 2010, http://www.cdc.gov/h1n1flu/updates/international/051410.htm.
‡ "WHO Declares End to 2009 H1N1 Influenza Pandemic," U.S. Department of Health and Human Services, August 10, 2010, http://www.hhs.gov/news/press/2010pres/08/20100810b.html.
§ "Yellow Fever," CDC, December 13, 2011, http://www.cdc.gov/yellowfever/; "Yellow Fever," World Health Organization, May 2013, http://www.who.int/mediacentre/factsheets/fs100/en/.
¶ "Global Alert and Response (GAR): Yellow Fever," World Health Organization, http://www.who.int/csr/disease/yellowfev/en/index.html.
** "Travel Vaccines & Malaria Information, by Country: Yellow Fever," CDC, August 1, 2013, http://wwwnc.cdc.gov/travel/yellowbook/2014/chapter-3-infectious-diseases-related-to-travel/travel-vaccines-and-malaria-information-by-country.

wide disease surveillance systems in place to detect infectious diseases within the confines of their borders. These systems also enable the early detection of unusual events that might indicate a pattern associated with existing influenza viruses or the emergence of a novel virus.[*] According to the WHO, this "surveillance...is [further] intended to give early warning in case of [the] emergence of significantly changed versions of existing circulating influenza viruses, changes that might result from an increase in virulence, for example, or the emergence of a novel influenza virus with different epidemiological characteristics."[†] Ultimately, such surveillance helps identify risk factors in individuals and vulnerabilities to infectious diseases. These systems also monitor health trends over time and evaluate the effectiveness of health interventions and services provided. Two examples of such surveillance systems include the Global Outbreak Alert and Response Network (GOARN), which links established individual surveillance and response networks around the world,[‡] and the WHO's Global Influenza Surveillance and Response System (GISRS)[§] that detects, monitors, and analyzes influenza viruses. These surveillance networks enable the real-time monitoring and analysis of reported data in existing surveillance networks. In addition, they facilitate worldwide tracking and monitoring of infectious diseases and their impact through data sharing. Data should be shared nationally and internationally to identify important features of the pandemic virus, and enable the prevention, mitigation, and control of the virus.[¶]

Preparedness

To prepare for the spread of infectious diseases, the United States has implemented several programs, the most notable of which is the Department of Health and Human Services' Biomedical Advanced Research and Development Authority (BARDA). BARDA "leads an integrated, systematic approach to the development and purchase of

---

[*] "Surveillance Recommendations for Member States in the Post-Pandemic Period," World Health Organization, August 12, 2010, 1, http://www.who.int/csr/resources/publications/swineflu/surveillance_post_pandemic.pdf.

[†] Ibid.

[‡] David L. Heymann, "The International Response to the Outbreak of SARS in 2003," *Philosophical Transactions: Biological Sciences* 359 (2004), 1127.

[§] The GISRS was previously known as the Global Influenza Surveillance Network (GISN). "Global Influenza Surveillance and Response System (GISRS)," WHO, http://www.who.int/influenza/gisrs_laboratory/en/.

[¶] "Strengthening Response to Pandemics and Other Public Emergencies. Report of the Review Committee on the Functioning of the International Health Regulations (2005) and on Pandemic Influenza (H1N1) 2009," World Health Organization, March 7, 2009, http://www.who.int/ihr/preview_report_review_committee_mar2011_en.pdf.

the necessary vaccines, drugs, therapies, and diagnostic tools for public health medical emergencies."[*] The United States and other countries have also prepared for outbreaks or pandemics by stockpiling (when and if sufficient resources are available) "antiviral drugs for domestic use, particularly at the start of a pandemic when mass vaccination is not an option and priority groups, such as front-line workers, need to be protected."[†]

An additional part of the preparedness (and mitigation) plan of countries is the research toward the creation of vaccines and antibiotics. Considering the infectious diseases that are resistant to existing antibiotics, incentives should be created to encourage pharmaceutical companies to develop new antibiotics (e.g., advanced purchase commitments).[‡] Currently, disincentives exist in such production—high investments and low sales and returns. Despite these disincentives measures have been taken toward the creation of antibiotics. Specifically, recent public–private partnerships have shown progress in new antibiotic discovery and development.[§] For instance, public–private partnerships in these areas are a part of the Innovative Medicines Initiative (IMI), an initiative of the EU Commission and the European Federation of Pharmaceutical Industries and Associations.[¶]

Response

The primary goal of the response phase is to contain infectious diseases. One way this occurs is through confinement. Confinement measures exist both in the response and preparedness phases of emergency management. International law allows for the implementation of confinement measures, such as quarantine and isolation of individuals, for

---

[*] "The Clock Is Ticking—A Progress Report on America's Preparedness to Prevent Weapons of Mass Destruction Proliferation and Terrorism," Commission on the Prevention of Weapons of Mass Destruction Proliferation and Terrorism, October 21, 2009, 12, http://www.teachingterror.net/resources/MDR-Final.pdf.

[†] "Responding to the Avian Influenza Pandemic Threats: Recommended Strategic Actions (WHO/CDS/CSR/GIP/2005.8)," World Health Organization, 2005, 14, http://www.who.int/csr/resources/publications/influenza/WHO_CDS_CSR_GIP_05_8-EN.pdf.

[‡] Chantal M. Morel and Elias Mossialos, "Stocking the Antibiotic Pipeline," *British Medical Journal* (2010), 340; "Global Risks Report 2013," World Economic Forum (2013), 32, http://www3.weforum.org/docs/WEF_GlobalRisks_Report_2013.pdf.

[§] Ibid.

[¶] Ibid; Margaret Chan, "Antimicrobial Resistance in the European Union and the World," World Health Organization, 2012, http://www.who.int/dg/speeches/2012/amr_20120314/en/index.html.

public health reasons.* However, such practices should only be used when a significant risk is posed to society and the intervention sought is the least invasive one available.

To contain infectious diseases, eradication measures are also used both in the response and preparedness phases of emergency management. For instance, in England, glanders† was eradicated by exterminating infected horses.‡ Additionally, in response to the foot and mouth disease§ outbreak in 2001, the United Kingdom burned the carcasses of infected animals that had died from the disease.¶

Another contagious and fatal infectious disease that affects all bird species is exotic Newcastle disease (END). END is transmitted through bird secretions from the nose, mouth, and eyes, and bird's excrements, and has been known to kill unvaccinated and vaccinated birds.** To eradicate this disease, infected birds are often destroyed. For example, the response to the 2002–2003 END outbreak in California "led to the depopulation of 3.16 million birds."†† In 2004, the H7N3 virus was found among chickens at poultry farms in the Fraser Valley community in British Columbia, Canada. In response to this contagious virus, the Canadian government decided to kill millions of poultry in the farms.‡‡ The avian influenza also resulted in the eradication of millions of poultry worldwide to contain the disease. Such instances of mass slaughter and

---

* According to Jacobs, "isolation is the separation of a patient known to have an infectious disease from otherwise healthy people"; whereas, "quarantine is the confinement of an individual who has been exposed to infectious disease but is asymptomatic. It involves an order by a public health official for a person to be separated from other people, restricted in his or her movement, and in a restricted area because there is a risk of the person becoming infectious. In essence, quarantine orders are only applicable to someone exposed to infectious disease but whose doctors do not know if he or she is infected." See Lesley A. Jacobs, "Rights and Quarantine during the SARS Global Health Crisis: Differentiated Legal Consciousness in Hong Kong, Shanghai, and Toronto," *Law & Society Review* 41:3 (2007), 513.

† "Glanders is an infectious disease that is caused by the bacterium *Burkholderia mallei*. While people can get the disease, glanders is primarily a disease affecting horses. It also affects donkeys and mules and can be naturally contracted by other mammals such as goats, dogs, and cats." See "Glanders," CDC, January 13, 2012, http://www.cdc.gov/glanders/.

‡ Aidan T. Cockburn, "Eradication of Infectious Diseases," *Science* 133:3458 (1961), 1056.

§ FMD is a fatal viral disease that affected cloven-hoofed animals.

¶ Jim Monke, "Agroterrorism: Threat and Preparedness," *CRS Report for Congress*, August 13, 2004, 32. http://www.fas.org/irp/crs/RL32521.pdf.

** "Exotic Newcastle Disease," The Animal and Plant Health Inspection Service (APHIS), http://www.aphis.usda.gov/animal_health/birdbiosecurity/end/.

†† "Exotic Newcastle Disease—California Historical Reflection," California Department of Food and Agriculture, http://www.cdfa.ca.gov/ahfss/Animal_Health/newcastle_disease_info.html.

‡‡ Ibid.

carcass disposal have led to the demand for the scientific community to seek alternatives to these practices. Attempts to eradicate infectious diseases without mass slaughter of infected animals have been successful. For example, in England, rabies was successfully eradicated by enforcing a six-month quarantine for all dogs and cats and requiring all dogs to wear muzzles for a year.[*]

An essential step in the containment of infectious diseases is the sharing of information. The media plays a critical role in the communication of information about infectious diseases. Indeed, much of the public's information about infectious diseases comes from the media.[†] The media's communication of a risk may heighten or allay public fears. Therefore, the information should be communicated to the public in such a way as to create a better informed populous that understands risks clearly and can take action in a way that can positively affect the health of individuals and communities.[‡] The mass media should not create hysteria and panic from their reporting of infectious diseases. This may occur if the media focuses exclusively on the symptoms of infectious diseases and the deaths and illnesses caused by infectious diseases. This may also occur if the media focuses on the lack of vaccines or lack of known causes of the virus. As Colin McInnes argued, "there is a difficult balance to be struck over the amount of information to release, particularly early on in an emergency, when saying too much may lead to an overreaction and appear panicky, while too little can appear complacent or conspiratorial."[§] Regardless of which approach is taken to contain and control infectious diseases, an international multistakeholder collaboration is required. This cooperation and coordination between public and private sectors is required on both the domestic and international level.

---

[*] Aidan T. Cockburn, "Eradication of Infectious Diseases," *Science* 133:3458 (1961), 1051.

[†] John P. Roche and Marc A. T. Muskavitch, "Limited Precision in Print Media Communication of West Nile Virus Risks," *Science Communication* 24 (2003), 353–365; Darrick T. Evensen and Christopher E. Clarke, "Efficacy Information in Media Coverage of Infectious Disease Risks: An Ill Predicament?" *Science Communication* 34:3 (2012), 395.

[‡] Charles Salmon and Charles Atkin, "Using Media Campaigns for Health Promotion," In Teresa L. Thompson (Ed.), *Handbook of Health Communication* (Mahwah, NJ: Lawrence Erlbaum Associates, 2003); Darrick T. Evensen and Christopher E. Clarke, "Efficacy Information in Media Coverage of Infectious Disease Risks: An Ill Predicament?" *Science Communication* 34:3 (2012), 395.

[§] Colin McInnes, *Health, Security and the Risk Society* (London: The Nuffield Trust and the UK Global Health Programme, 2005), 11.

CONCLUDING THOUGHTS

Infectious diseases remain a significant transnational security threat. New infectious diseases are emerging and older infectious diseases are evolving, becoming more virulent. Infectious diseases can cause a high rate of morbidity and mortality in a relatively short amount of time. The mobility of infectious diseases makes dealing with them particularly challenging. Infectious diseases have health, psychological, social, economic, and political consequences. Infectious diseases are spread through lifestyles, land use, poor immune systems, lack of adequate hygiene, mutations in pathogens, and trade, commerce, and travel.

Timely and accurate information about infectious diseases that threaten transnational security should be provided. This information and best practices in dealing with infectious diseases should be shared nationally and internationally. Strategies at the national and international level focus on prevention, mitigation, and control of infectious diseases. To prevent the spread of infectious disease and control its impact, wherever possible, vaccines should be used. Additionally, the mitigation strategies for infectious diseases should include building capacities to lessen the impact of an infectious disease in the event it materializes. Mitigation should also include having mechanisms in place to detect infectious diseases. Here, surveillance measures can detect infectious diseases at early stages. To accomplish this, risk factors in individuals and vulnerabilities to infectious diseases should be identified and communicated.

Finally, to control infectious diseases, containment measures should be implemented. The primary ways to contain infectious diseases is through eradication, if possible, and quarantine and isolation practices. Effective infectious disease surveillance measures and reporting mechanisms are required to contain the spread of infectious diseases. Although it should, the reporting of infectious diseases does not always occur in a timely manner. This was the case with China and the SARS outbreak. The SARS outbreak started in China. However, the Chinese government delayed in responding to SARS and notifying the international community of the outbreak. When the WHO was notified, the disease had already spread across borders. Early warning and communication of the threat is thus critical for containment. The lessons learned from SARS were that a failure to quickly respond to and adequately contain an infectious disease can have devastating economic, social, and political effects not only on the country that fails to report it but also other countries around the globe.

CHAPTER 10

Security Issues in Conflict and Post-Conflict Societies

The 20th century and the beginning of the 21st century have been marred by violence, conflict, and war committed in response to colonialism, instability, territorial disputes, ethnic polarization, and terrorism. This chapter covers the worldwide implications of societies experiencing civil strife and localized wars. Crimes against humanity, war crimes, genocide, ethnic cleansing, and refugee crises are also examined. The legal mechanisms in place to deal with these issues are additionally explored. Special attention is paid to the challenges posed by conflict and post-conflict societies to the international community.

MASS ATROCITIES

Mass atrocities are defined as "widespread and often systematic acts of violence against civilians or other noncombatants including killing; causing serious bodily or mental harm; or deliberately inflicting conditions of life that cause serious bodily or mental harm."[*] For a mass atrocity to be committed, an organization of some sort must exist, which seeks to strengthen a particular group in society while weakening another. Additionally, the actors seeking to commit mass atrocities must promote reasons for doing so that will resonate with the population. Common reasons promoted include the need to counter what they believe (whether real or perceived) is a serious existential threat and/or to change the ethnic or religious composition of a territory. Factors that serve as triggers to mass violence include "the loss of well-being, the threat to and frustration of basic needs, and a sense of injustice or relative deprivation in comparison

---

[*] Stephen Matthew Wisniew, "Early Warning Signs and Indicators to Genocide and Mass Atrocity," School of Advanced Military Studies, United States Army Command and General Staff College, Fort Leavenworth, KS (AY 2012-2) (2012), http://www.hsdl.org/?view&did=732038.

to others."* These feelings among the populace are used and directed by those in power toward a target group. These feelings are also used by those in power to gain supporters for their cause and to gain tolerance among the populace for what would otherwise be unjustified behavior (e.g., the use of violence and engagement in other crimes against the target group). The atrocities are advocated for and implemented as a means to an end. To execute such atrocities, the perpetrators also require a willing group or population to commit mass atrocities and the opportunity to do so.

Mass atrocities include crimes against humanity, war crimes, genocide, and ethnic cleansing. The first crime in this category, crimes against humanity, refers to the illicit and inhumane acts, which are part of a widespread systematic attack, that are intentionally designed to cause serious bodily harm or mental injury, and significant suffering in a target population. International law has specified which crimes are considered inhumane. Specifically, Article 6(c) of 1945 Charter of the International Military Tribunal (otherwise known as the Nuremberg Charter) holds that crimes against humanity are "murder, extermination, enslavement, deportation, and other inhumane acts committed against any civilian population, before or during the war,... or persecutions on political, racial, or religious grounds in execution of or in connection with any crime within the jurisdiction of the Tribunal, whether or not in violation of domestic law of the country where perpetrated." The International Criminal Tribunal for the former Yugoslavia (ICTY)[†] and International Criminal Tribunal for Rwanda (ICTR)[‡] added two more crimes to the list of crimes against humanity: rape and torture. The International Criminal Court[§] further expanded the list to include enforced disappearance of persons and apartheid.[¶]

The second crime in this category, war crimes, refers to crimes that are committed during conflict that are in violation of existing laws of war or international law. Article 6(b) of the Nuremberg Charter holds that

---

[*] Staub, Ervin, "Genocide and Mass Killing: Origins, Prevention, Healing and Reconciliation," *Political Psychology* 21(2) (2000), 372.

[†] An ad hoc criminal tribunal established by the United Nations to hold those responsible for committing mass atrocities "committed in the territory of the former Yugoslavia since 1991." See Article 1 of the Statute of the International Criminal Tribunal for the former Yugoslavia.

[‡] An ad hoc criminal tribunal established by the United Nations to hold those responsible for mass atrocities "committed in the territory of Rwanda and Rwandan citizens responsible for such violations committed in the territory of neighbouring States between 1 January 1994 and 31 December 1994." See Article 1 of the Statute of the International Criminal Tribunal for Rwanda.

[§] The International Criminal Court was established by the Rome Statute to initiate proceedings against those accused of serious crimes affecting the international community such as: war crimes, crimes against humanity, and genocides.

[¶] See Article 7(1)(i) and Article 7(i)(j) of the Rome Statute of the International Criminal Court.

such crimes "include, but [are] not be limited to, murder, ill-treatment or deportation to slave labor or for any other purpose of civilian population of or in occupied territory, murder or ill-treatment of prisoners of war or persons on the seas, killing of hostages, plunder of public or private property, wanton destruction of cities, towns, or villages, or devastation not justified by military necessity." The enlisting and use of child soldiers in war is also considered a war crime. Particularly, in *Prosecutor v. Thomas Lubanga Dyilo*, the International Criminal Court found Thomas Lubanga Dyilo guilty of perpetrating war crimes, which involved his conscripting and enlisting of children under the age of 15 into the Union of Congolese Patriots (Union des Patriotes Congolais)/ Patriotic Force for the Liberation of Congo (Force Patriotique pour la Libération du Congo) and using them as active participants in the hostilities.* His actions were in direct violation of Article 8 of the 1998 Rome Statute of the International Criminal Court (hereafter Rome Statute).†

The third crime in this category, genocide, refers to the systematic destruction of a particular group of individuals on the basis of their culture, disability, ethnicity, nationality, political affiliation, race, religion, or sex. The United Nations Convention on the Prevention and Punishment of the Crime of Genocide (hereafter Genocide Convention) was the first legally binding instrument that defined and outlawed genocide.‡ In particular, Article 2 of the Genocide Convention, defined it as acts, which are committed with the "intent[ion]...of destroy[ing], in whole or in part, a national, ethnical, racial or religious group," such as: killing members of a group; inflicting serious bodily or mental harm on members of a group; purposely imposing on a "group conditions of life calculated to bring about its physical destruction in whole or in part"; implementing "measures [that are] intended to prevent births within... [a] group"; and "forcibly transferring children of... [a] group to another group." Genocide should not be confused with ethnic cleansing (the final crime in this category). Ethnic cleansing refers to "the attempt to create ethnically homogeneous geographic areas through the deportation or forcible displacement of persons belonging to particular ethnic groups. Ethnic cleansing sometimes involves the removal of all physical vestiges of the targeted group through the destruction of monuments, cemeteries, and houses of worship."§ While those engaging in ethnic cleansing

---

* *Prosecutor v. Thomas Lubanga Dyilo* (Judgment pursuant to Article 74 of the Statute) ICC-01/04-01/06 (14 March 2012).

† Article 8(2)(e)(vii) of the Rome Statute criminalizes: "conscripting or enlisting children under the age of fifteen years into armed forces or groups or using them to participate actively in hostilities."

‡ The Genocide Convention was adopted in 1948 and entered into force in 1951.

§ George. J. Andreopoulos, *Encyclopedia Britannica* s.v. "Ethnic Cleansing," http://www. britannica.com/EBchecked/topic/194242/ethnic-cleansing.

may use genocide to do so, they can also achieve their goal of creating ethnically homogenous lands through other means that do not involve genocide.*

Genocide often involves conflict of the government with the groups in its citizenry or government and supporting coalitions against what the government believes to be rebel groups. Usually, countries justify using violence against groups or individuals in the population as a legitimate act of war or reprisal for harm done, which is considered necessary to protect and defend its citizens and territory. However, in the past, such violence has been found to be unjustified. Historically, leaders of governments have killed millions of innocent victims and not opponents of their regimes. A case in point is Adolf Hitler. Adolf Hitler sought to systematically eliminate the non-Aryan race from Germany by killing Jews en masse (the Holocaust). Specifically, the Holocaust involved the state-sponsored killing of European Jews between the 1930s and 1940s by the Nationalist Socialist German Workers Party (NSDAP or Nazi) regime and its supporters. During the Holocaust, 6 million Jews were killed (Figure 10.1).

Violence is usually incited or orchestrated by state officials, local leaders, military personnel, or local or national political figures. This was observed in the Bosnian genocide. Following the death of the President of Yugoslavia, Josip Broz Tito, grievances of the Serbs directed a wave of nationalism under Slobodan Milosevic. Milosevic subsequently created an ethnic national movement within the Serbs, which resulted in the ethnic conflict in Bosnia.† Under Milosevic's command, the Yugoslavian National Army (JNA) massacred and raped thousands of individuals. Additionally, the JNA engaged in the ethnic cleansing of an area which they proclaimed to be the Republic Srpska, by killing and otherwise forcibly removing Bosniaks from that area.‡ To forcibly displace individuals in the region, the JNA engaged in extreme measures. This was illustrated in *Prosecutor v. Momcilo Krajisnik*: "Serb municipal authorities and Serb forces created severe living conditions for Muslims and Croats which aimed, and succeeded, in making it practically impossible for

* Ibid.
† The common Yugoslav identity dissolved following Josip Broz Tito's death and the war in Bosnia ultimately signaled the end of the Federal Republic of Yugoslavia. V. P. Gagnon Jr., "Ethnic Nationalism and International Conflict: The Case of Serbia," *International Security* 19(3) (1994/1995), 130–166; Center for European Studies, "What Happened to Yugoslavia? The War, The Peace and the Future," University of North Carolina–Chapel Hill (2004), http://www.unc.edu/depts/europe/teachingresources/balkan-crisis.pdf.
‡ *The Prosecutor of the Tribunal against Ratko Mladic* (Amended Indictment) Case No. IT-95-5/18-I (October 2002), http://www.icty.org/x/cases/mladic/ind/en/mla-ai021010e.pdf.

FIGURE 10.1   Barbed wire in Auschwitz Camp I, a former Nazi extermination camp on October 22, 2012 in Oswiecim, Poland. It was the biggest Nazi concentration camp in Europe. (Image courtesy of Shutterstock.com.)

most of them to remain. The measures undertaken increased in severity by time, starting with dismissals from employment, house searches, and the cutting off of water, electricity, and telephone services."[*] By the end of the Bosnian mass atrocities, 100,000 people were killed and 2 million people were forcibly displaced; the civil war that led to these atrocities ended in 1995 with the signing of the Dayton Peace Accords.[†]

Countries have utilized military, paramilitary, and militia to commit mass killings against subgroups within their territory. For example, Rwanda utilized its military and militia forces to commit mass murder with the intention of exterminating Tutsis and moderate Hutus within their territory. These two groups had a history of conflict. Particularly, the Hutu were the majority group in Rwanda and the Tutsi were the minority group. The Tutsi minority group had dominated and held most of the power positions during the precolonial and postcolonial periods in Rwanda. Traditionally, the Tutsi owned land and cattle; whereas the Hutu worked in the agriculture, cattle keeping, construction, and fishing

---

[*] United Nations International Tribunal for the Former Yugoslavia, *Prosecutor v. Momcilo Krajisnik* (Judgment) Case No. IT-00-39-T (September 27, 2006), 347, http://www.icty.org/x/cases/krajisnik/tjug/en/kra-jud060927e.pdf.
[†] "The Conflicts," ICTY, http://www.icty.org/sid/322.

industries, among other areas.[*] Because the Tutsi held a monopoly over the power in Rwanda, the Hutu resented and hated Tutsis because of their domination over them. The discord between the two ethnic groups was mainly attributed to the existing power struggle and not economic domination.

The tipping point that led to the political violence between these two groups in Rwanda can be traced back to when Belgian political reforms[†] provided limited political space to the Hutu; this action challenged the privileged position of the Tutsi. The violence that ensued following these reforms led to numerous deaths and forced hundreds of thousands of Tutsi to seek refuge in neighboring countries (e.g., Uganda, Burundi, and Zaire).[‡] A rebel group known as the Rwanda Patriotic Front (RPF), which was predominantly made up of Tutsis, was subsequently formed from those exiled. The genocide began on April 6, 1994, when a plane carrying the Hutu presidents of Rwanda and Burundi (Juvenal Habyarimana and Cyprien Ntayamira, respectively,) was shot down.[§] Although it was believed at the time that the RPF was responsible for shooting down the plane, a report from a judicial investigation sanctioned by France revealed that the RPF could not have been responsible because the region during that period was under the control of Hutu extremists.[¶] The Minister of Foreign Affairs and government spokesperson in Rwanda, Louise Mushikiwabo, confirmed that this shooting down of the plane "was a coup d'état carried out by extremist Hutu elements and their advisers who controlled [the] Kanombe Barracks."[**] In the following 100 days after the plane was shot down, an estimated

---

[*] Audrey I. Richards (Ed.), *Economic Development and Tribal Change: A Study of Immigrant Labour in Buganda* (Cambridge: Heffer and Sons, 1952), 17, 118; Mahmood Mamdani, *Politics and Class Formation in Uganda* (London: Heinemann, 1977), 149, 154–155, cited in Ogenga Otunnu, "Rwandese Refugees and Immigrants in Uganda," In Howard Adelman and Astri Suhrke (Eds.), *The Path of a Genocide: The Rwanda Crisis from Uganda to Zaire* (New Brunswick, NJ: Transaction Publishers, 1999), 5.

[†] Belgium had colonial control of Rwanda after World War I.

[‡] Zaire is now known as the Democratic Republic of Congo.

[§] *BBC News*, "Rwanda President's Plane 'Shot Down,'" 1994, http://news.bbc.co.uk/onthisday/hi/dates/stories/april/6/newsid_2472000/2472195.stm.

[¶] This investigation was conducted by France because crew members onboard the aircraft that was shot down were French. "Report: Rebels Cleared in Plane Crash That Sparked Rwandan Genocide," *CNN*, January 11, 2012, http://www.cnn.com/2012/01/11/world/africa/rwanda-president-plane/.

[**] James Karuhanga and Edmund Kagire, "Habyarimana's Killing a Coup D'état–Report," *The New Times (Rwanda)*, January 11, 2012, http://www.newtimes.co.rw/news/index.php?i=14867&a=48966.

800,000 to 1,000,000 Tutsis and moderate Hutus were slaughtered.* During the genocide, "an estimated 150,000 to 250,000 women were also raped."†

While there are similarities in the illicit acts taken to commit mass atrocities, such as crimes against humanity, war crimes, and genocide, there are important differences between them. A main difference between crimes against humanity and genocide is that unlike genocide, the former does not require the intent to destroy in whole or in part a target group. Instead, to be considered a crime against humanity the action only needs to target a specific group and the perpetrator needs to carry out widespread or systematic violations. Furthermore, crimes against humanity and war crimes differ in an important way. Specifically, war crimes can only occur during times of war. Crimes against humanity, however, can occur both during periods of war and peace. Given the magnitude of devastation that could be caused in the event that any mass atrocity occurs, measures should be in place which seek to prevent them or at the very least mitigate the destruction that could be caused should they materialize. The next sections examine existing measures that deal with mass atrocities.

Dealing with Mass Atrocities

The key to dealing with mass atrocities is finding the appropriate balance between the protection of civilians, humanitarian action, and the prevention of mass atrocities. To accomplish this, the following plan of action is required, which focuses on: the prevention of conflict; the development and better use of early warning systems; protecting civilians in conflict societies; ending impunity of perpetrators of mass atrocities; repairing the harm done to victims; and addressing the refugee crises post-conflict.

Preventing Conflict

Establishing a framework for mass atrocity prevention is critical. This framework would include risk identification, choosing the most appropriate action based on the risk factors, prioritizing actions, and implementing

---

* See, for example, Bert Ingelaere, "The Gacaca Courts in Rwanda," In Luc Huyse and Mark Salter (Eds.), *Traditional Justice and Reconciliation after Violent Conflict: Learning from African Experiences* (Stockholm, Sweden: International Institute for Democracy and Electoral Assistance, 2008), 25; Paul Kagame, Preface, Phil Clark and Zachary D. Kaufman (Eds.), *After Genocide: Transitional Justice, Post-Conflict Reconstruction and Reconciliation in Rwanda and Beyond* (New York: Columbia University Press, 2008), xxi.

† "Outreach Program on the Rwanda Genocide and the United Nations, Rwanda: A Brief History of the Country," United Nations, http://www.un.org/en/preventgenocide/rwanda/education/rwandagenocide.shtml.

the most appropriate measures to prevent mass atrocities. The first step in prevention is the identification of risk factors in societies. The preconditions (or risk factors) of mass atrocities include the structural conditions that serve as triggers to violence. Certain structural conditions that give rise to mass atrocities include the presence of economic, social, and political grievances, the absence of legitimate means for nonviolent conflict resolution, and intergroup competition and conflict. An examination of previous mass atrocities reveals that structural conditions of poverty, unemployment, and inequality are often attributed to a target group in society. These structural conditions cause intergroup tensions that often precede mass atrocities. These structural conditions played a prominent role in the genocide in Rwanda. They were also present in the Holocaust. Indeed, the crippling economy led many Germans to subscribe to Nazi ideology. The Depression, which resulted in chronic unemployment and a loss of savings for many Germans, paved the way for Nazis to spread their message of hate to Germany, blaming Jews for the economic situation of German citizens. Other structural factors that create conditions in society that make conflict inevitable are bad governance, endemic corruption, and the denial of basic human rights. These factors, along with the existing conditions of extreme poverty and the desire to control the country's most valuable commodity, diamonds, led to Sierra Leone's brutal civil war between 1991 and 2002.

Other prominent risk factors associated with mass atrocities are: the organization of hate groups that are dedicated to vilifying a target group in society and the publication of hate propaganda toward that target group (see Table 10.1). The publication of hate propaganda[*] exists in all genocides. This hate propaganda is particularly designed to polarize society and classify the target group as the "others" in order to divide the population into those supporting those in power or those responsible for vilifying the "others" (us), and those in the target group, tolerant of the group, and those supporting the group (them). This propaganda commonly seeks to dehumanize them. With such propaganda, the "others" are often "equated with animals, vermin, insects or diseases."[†] Such dehumanization has been well documented in the Bosnian and Rwanda genocides, and the Holocaust.[‡] During the Bosnian genocide,

---

[*] Susan Benesch developed an analytical framework for monitoring and evaluating the dangerousness of speech, Susan Benesch, "Dangerous Speech: A Proposal to Prevent Group Violence," http://www.worldpolicy.org/sites/default/files/Dangerous%20 Speech%20Guidelines%20Benesch%20January%202012.pdf.

[†] Gregory H. Stanton, "The 8 Stages of Genocide," Genocide Watch, http://www. genocidewatch.org/aboutgenocide/8stagesofgenocide.html.

[‡] Arlen C. Moller and Edward L. Deci, "Interpersonal Control, Dehumanization, and Violence: A Self-Determination Theory Perspective," *Group Processes & Intergroup Relations* 13:1 (2010), 44.

TABLE 10.1   Examples of Warning Signs in Three Genocides

Genocide	Warning Signs
Holocaust	Dictatorship
	German nationalism
	Anti-Semitism
	Segregation
	Ghettos
	Death camps
	Unpunished violence
Bosnia	Serbian nationalism
	Anti-Bosniak propaganda
	Policy of ethnic cleansing
	Ghettos
	Unpunished violence
Rwanda	Ethic divisions
	Anti-Tutsi propaganda
	Killing of Rwanda and Burundi presidents
	Unpunished violence

propaganda was spread through the media to further Milosevic's cause.[*] Dehumanizing hate propaganda was also broadcasted on the radio in Rwanda. Indeed, the label of cockroaches (*inyenzi*) was given to Tutsis, and their collaborators or supporters were viewed as accomplices of the enemy (*ibyitso*).[†] The Radio Télévision Libre des Mille Collines (RTLM) broadcasted incitements to violence by calling for the extermination of the "Tutsi cockroach."[‡] Moreover, illicit actions against Tutsis and moderate Hutus were equated to the following: "killings were *umuganda*, collective work, chopping up men was 'bush clearing' and slaughtering women and children was 'pulling out the roots of the bad weeds.'"[§] Similar dehumanization of Jews was observed in the Holocaust. Jews were portrayed "as a plague infesting German stock whose eradication

---

[*] Mark A. Winton and Ali Unlu, "Micro–Macro Dimensions of the Bosnian Genocides: The Circumplex Model and Violentization Theory," *Aggression and Violent Behavior* 13 (2008), 47.

[†] Philip Gourevitch, *We Want to Inform You That Tomorrow We Will Be Killed with Our Families: Stories from Rwanda* (New York: Farrar, Straus and Giroux, 1998), 83; Ravi Bhavnani, "Ethnic Norms and Interethnic Violence: Accounting for Mass Participation in the Rwandan Genocide," *Journal of Peace Research* 43:6 (2006), 656.

[‡] "Outreach Program on the Rwanda Genocide and the United Nations, Rwanda: A Brief History of the Country," United Nations, http://www.un.org/en/preventgenocide/rwanda/education/rwandagenocide.shtml.

[§] Gérard Prunier, *The Rwanda Crisis: History of a Genocide* (New York: Columbia University Press, 1995), 142.

was supposed to play an essential, cleansing role in the German destiny."[*]
Moreover, "Nazi propaganda portrayed Jews as subhuman and unscrupulous beings,...undeserving of civil rights."[†]

Another key factor is the purging of the target group from governmental and military positions, while simultaneously expanding the recruitment of members in the dominant group to these positions. Commonly, the target group is marginalized through laws, policies, procedures, and measures seeking their exclusion from governments, schools, and more generally, employment. In certain genocides, these laws additionally extend to purging the target group from society. A case in point is the Cambodian genocide. The Khmer Rouge regime, led by Pol Pot, was responsible for the mass slaughter of an estimated 1.7 million in Cambodia between 1975 and 1979.[‡] Anyone who did not hold similar beliefs to the regime was killed. Specifically, the Khmer Rouge regime sought to purge society from the elite, intellectuals, businessmen, Buddhists, minorities, and foreigners.[§] The regime even passed a decree that banned all minorities: "In Kampuchea[¶] there is one nation, and one language, the Khmer language. From now on the various nationalities...do not exist any longer in Kampuchea."[**] This decree served as a justification for the extermination and forced assimilation of all non-Khmer ethnic minority groups (e.g., Chinese, Vietnamese, Cham, among other minorities) that followed.[††]

Another risk factor (or warning sign) observed before mass atrocities is the displacement and segregation of the target group from the dominant group. With respect to the latter, ghettos or camps for the target groups are established. This was evident in the Bosnian genocide and the Holocaust (see Table 10.1). In the Bosnian genocide, ghettos were created with poor quality of life conditions, which were designed to extinguish

---

[*] Jacob Schiff, "The Trouble with 'Never Again!' Rereading Levinas for Genocide Prevention and Critical International Theory," *Millennium—Journal of International Studies* 36:2 (2008), 224.

[†] Eric Sterling, "Indifferent Accomplices," Harry James Cargas (Ed.), *Problems Unique to the Holocaust* (Kentucky: The University Press of Kentucky, 2003), 113.

[‡] "Cambodian Genocide Program, The CGP, 1994–2013," Yale University, http://www.yale.edu/cgp/.

[§] Dan Fletcher, "A Brief History of the Khmer Rouge," *Time*, 2009, http://content.time.com/time/world/article/0,8599,1879785,00.html#ixzz2rRWsOzNT.

[¶] Kampuchea is Cambodia, in the Khmer language.

[**] Elizabeth Becker, *When the War Was Over: The Voices of Cambodia's Revolution and Its People* (New York: Simon & Schuster, 1986), 243 (quoting Khmer Rouge propaganda).

[††] Elizabeth Becker, *When the War Was Over: The Voices of Cambodia's Revolution and Its People* (New York: Simon & Schuster, 1986), 243; Beth Van Schaack, "The Crime of Political Genocide: Repairing the Genocide Convention's Blind Spot," *Yale Law Journal* 106:7 (1997), 2270; Robert Gellately and Ben Kiernan, *The Specter of Genocide: Mass Murder in Historical Perspective* (Cambridge: Cambridge University Press, 2003), 313–314.

TABLE 10.2   Eight Stages of Genocide

Stage 1	*Classification* (categorization of target population)
Stage 2	*Symbolization* (assigning symbols to target population; for example, yellow stars to the Jewish population during the Holocaust)
Stage 3	*Dehumanization* (labeling the target group as unhuman or subhuman)
Stage 4	*Organization* (creating control structures to strengthen and arm a group in society)
Stage 5	*Polarization* (distancing the target group from the rest of the population)
Stage 6	*Preparation* (taking steps to isolate the target group or otherwise make the next step, extermination, possible)
Stage 7	*Extermination* (engaging in mass atrocities against the target group)
Stage 8	*Denial* (refuting allegations of wrongdoing, covering up illicit actions and seeking to evade prosecution for acts)

Source: Gregory Stanton, "The 8 Stages of Genocide Briefing Paper," Genocide Watch (1998), http://www.genocidewatch.org/images/8StagesBriefingpaper.pdf.

the group within them.[*] During the Holocaust, a disproportionate number of Jews were sent to concentration camps where they were systematically murdered by the Nazis. In these concentration camps, Jews were beaten, shocked, shot, gassed, suffocated, hanged, or worked/starved to death. In addition to concentration camps, ghettos were set up. Similar to the concentration camps, the majority of the Jewish people in the ghettos died from disease (from the poor living conditions), starvation, and inhumane treatment. These camps and ghettos mark what is known as the preparation stage of the genocide (see Table 10.2). This is an important stage to detect because it immediately precedes the extermination stage, when mass atrocities such as genocide begin.

A final risk factor is the outbreak of violence against civilians, which, if it remains unchecked, will escalate to mass atrocities. Here, a conflict situation frequently leads to mass atrocities when impunity exists for perpetrators who commit acts of violence against a target population (see Table 10.1). By failing to adequately deal with such acts of violence, perpetrators are emboldened and escalate their violence. This cycle of impunity facilitates the escalation of violence. The only way to prevent mass atrocities at this stage is either for the existing regime to end the crisis or effective international intervention to be taken.

---

[*] Application of the Convention on the Prevention and Punishment of the Crime of Genocide (*Bosnia and Herzegovina v. Yugoslavia* (Serbia and Montenegro)) (Application of the Republic of *Bosnia and Herzegovina v. Yugoslavia*) International Court of Justice, General List No. 91 (20 March 1993), para. 75.

The analysis of the preconditions of mass atrocities can assist the international community in: determining which regions are especially vulnerable to conflict; identifying which areas in conflict might experience mass atrocities; and pinpointing the vulnerabilities in these societies that should be addressed to prevent mass atrocities from occurring. By understanding the factors that make mass atrocities likely in a particular territory, identifying key actors that may commit mass atrocities, and monitoring progress in the territory, decisive preventive measures can be taken. There are two forms of prevention that can be pursued: namely, structural and direct prevention.

Structural prevention focuses on identifying early warning signals and dealing with them accordingly. It encompasses economic development, security reforms, humanitarian relief, the establishment of the rule of law, and assistance with human rights issues.[*] Some strategies pursued include curtailing deprivation, reducing poverty, eradicating inequalities, and supporting local ownership, structural reform, and community development.[†] The key to a structural prevention strategy is to identify existing national capacity and the areas that require modification and assistance. Direct prevention includes the specific action or specific actions that seek to alter the behavior of the offenders. An example of a direct prevention measure is diplomacy. Direct prevention measures, such as diplomacy, work best when they involve the relevant parties and specifically focus on the issues at stake. Here, consensual agreements among conflicting parties should be pursued. Both forms of prevention, structural and direct prevention, seek to reduce the likelihood that mass atrocities will occur.

If an imminent threat of mass atrocity is detected, preventative measures that are designed to deter and/or persuade the individuals seeking to take such action should be taken. It is important to note that there is no one size fits all prevention strategy for mass atrocities. The strategy chosen will depend on the country, the conflict it is experiencing, and the international community's willingness and capacity to rapidly detect and respond to risk factors.

Early Warning Systems

An essential element in mass atrocity detection is early warning. However, early warning is only possible if appropriate and complete information is available. Civil society plays an essential role in the early

---

[*] "Preventing Conflict and Building Peace, A Manual of Issues and Entry Points, Development Assistance Committee," Organisation for Economic Co-operation and Development (OECD), 2005, http://www.oecd.org/development/incaf/35785584.pdf.

[†] Alex J. Bellamy, "Mass Atrocities and Armed Conflict: Links, Distinctions, and Implications for the Responsibility to Prevent, Policy Analysis Brief," The Stanley Foundation, 2011, http://www.stanleyfoundation.org/publications/pab/BellamyPAB22011.pdf.

warning process by comprehensively documenting mass atrocities and their impact on victims. In addition, they are often the ones that bring attention to mass atrocities around the globe; in so doing, galvanizing support for the victims and responses to the conflict. With respect to the former, civil society has been (and continues to be) instrumental in organizing and distributing humanitarian aid to conflict-affected areas. With respect to the latter, civil society has been instrumental in naming and shaming perpetrators and public and private enablers of mass atrocities.[*]

Social media and mobile technologies can also serve as potential tools for gathering information in threatened communities. Consider the postelection violence in Kenya in 2008.[†] Real-time information about the violence was communicated via blogs, Twitter, uploading images on websites, and posting videos on YouTube.[‡] The benefits of such tools can only be experienced by communities that have access to the Internet, computers, and related technologies. In many areas, "the lack of broadband access or limited mobile phone coverage beyond state capitals presents important hurdles for real-time and sustained communication from the... [rest of the world] to the areas in crisis as well as blocks or severely limits information flow from the affected region out to the... [rest of the world]."[§] Nevertheless, a competition known as the Tech Challenge for Atrocity Prevention, which was created by the United States Agency for International Development (USAID) and Humanity United, revealed technologies that could be used to enable communications in these areas. Specifically, one of the subchallenges for users was to "develop simple, affordable technologies that can be used to gather or verify atrocity-related data from hard-to-access areas, which can then be used to inform the international community."[¶] A winning proposal submitted in this subcategory involved the Portable Anonymous

---

[*] The responses to such enablers and perpetrators is explored in the "Ending Impunity" section of this chapter.

[†] Joshua Goldstein and Juliana Rotich, "Digitally Networked Technology in Kenya's 2007–2008 Post-Election Crisis," The Berkman Center for Internet and Society, *Harvard University*, Berkman Center Research Publication No. 2008-09, September 2008, http://cyber.law.harvard.edu/sites/cyber.law.harvard.edu/files/Goldstein&Rotich_Digitally_Networked_Technology_Kenyas_Crisis.pdf.

[‡] Patrick Meier and Jennifer Leaning, "Applying Technology to Crisis Mapping and Early Warning in Humanitarian Settings, Working Paper Series," *Harvard Humanitarian Initiative*, 2009, 4, http://hhi.harvard.edu/sites/default/files/In%20Line%20Images/working%20paper%20-%20applying%20tech.pdf.

[§] Patrick Meier and Jennifer Leaning, "Applying Technology to Crisis Mapping and Early Warning in Humanitarian Settings, Working Paper Series," *Harvard Humanitarian Initiative*, 2009, 5, http://hhi.harvard.edu/sites/default/files/In%20Line%20Images/working%20paper%20-%20applying%20tech.pdf.

[¶] "Tech Challenge for Atrocity Prevention," United States Agency for International Development (USAID), 2013, http://www.usaid.gov/atrocities.

Communication Technology (PACT), which "provides access to communications networks in remote areas with poor infrastructure."*

Technology has also been used in other ways to promote early detection of mass atrocities. A case in point is crisis mapping. Crisis mapping is a tool that has been effective in identifying the threats posed by conflict societies. Particularly, crisis mapping collates information that is collected using technologies, such as satellites, with reports provided by citizens in order to gather, analyze, and evaluate real-time mass atrocity preconditions (or risk factors) in conflict societies. Crisis mapping has helped establish conflict patterns and assisted in the understanding of how conflicts emerge.† An example of a crisis-mapping tool is the Satellite Sentinel Project. The Satellite Sentinel Project "fuse[s] together satellite imagery, on the ground field reporting, and crisis mapping applications into a unified monitoring platform to deter, detect and document threats to Sudanese civilians."‡ This project has located mass graves, tracked the intentional destruction of civilian homes, and monitored military airstrikes in Sudan.§ Crisis mapping technologies have the potential to proactively address risks before mass atrocities occur.

The Sentinel Project for Genocide Prevention has also sought to develop an early warning system for mass atrocities.¶ The early warning system (EWS) they developed consists of four stages: risk assessment, operational process monitoring, vulnerability assessment, and forecasting. The latter two, vulnerability assessment and forecasting, are still only in the conceptual stage. The former stage, the vulnerability assessment, "examine[s] the characteristics of the country and all [of] the actors within …[the country] to determine just how vulnerable to attack that the threatened community is. This phase begins the transition from prevention into the field of mitigation and will aid in building target

---

* Ibid.

† For more information on crisis mapping, see Shashi Kara (moderator), Jennifer Leaning, Colette Mazzucelli, and Zach Romanow, "Deconstructing Prevention: Crisis Mapping, Technology, and Genocide Prevention," February 26, 2013, Panel Discussion in NYC Conference co-organized by the Benjamin N. Cardozo School of Law Program in Holocaust, Genocide, and Human Rights Studies and the Auschwitz Institute for Peace and Reconciliation, Conference partners: Carnegie Council for Ethics in International Affairs, Institute for the Study of Genocide, and Heinrich Böll Stiftung North America, A video of the presentation can be seen at: http://www.youtube.com/watch?v=k_E_QCA8g64&index=5&list=PLuzaPqT98VixVzDPhbwyuXyTG7JrBpH6F.

‡ "Documenting the Crisis," Satellite Sentinel Project, http://www.satsentinel.org/documenting-the-crisis; "Program on Crisis Dynamics and Crisis Mapping," Harvard Humanitarian Initiative, http://hhi.harvard.edu/sites/default/files/publications/program%20on%20crisis%20dynamics%20and%20crisis%20mapping1.54.pdf.

§ "Documenting the Crisis," Satellite Sentinel Project, http://www.satsentinel.org/documenting-the-crisis.

¶ "Early Warning System Overview," The Sentinel Project for Genocide Prevention, http://thesentinelproject.org/our-work/early-warning-system-overview/.

group resilience in the event of the worst-case scenario."* The latter, the forecasting stage, seeks to "to predict when genocidal violence may... [occur], how severe it is likely to be (building upon information from the vulnerability assessment), and what the most likely perpetrator courses-of-action are. This will inform intervention, response, and evacuation efforts."† Both of these phases, when fully available for implementation, will enable authorities to intervene before the threat of mass atrocities materializes.

Measures have been (and should be) sought to strengthen national and international capacity to detect early warning signs of mass atrocities. Nationally, in 2012, U.S. President Barack Obama established the Atrocities Prevention Board (APB), an agency tasked with developing atrocities prevention and response strategies for the United States.‡ The APB additionally seeks to draw attention to at risk countries and ensure that they receive appropriate attention from policy makers in order to prevent mass atrocities. Moreover, the African Union established a Peace and Security Council (PSC) in 2004, which was responsible for anticipating and preventing conflicts.§ Internationally, the United Nations' capacity to detect early warning signals of mass atrocities should be strengthened. Particularly, to deal with mass atrocities more effectively, it is imperative that United Nations staff are trained in detecting early warning signs of atrocities. This is an essential element in early warning as the United Nations is best placed to assess the risk of mass atrocities because of their access to conflict regions. Accordingly, they are better positioned to obtain up-to-date information and monitor conflict situations.

Protecting Civilians

The protection of civilians is the primary responsibility of the state. State sovereignty refers to the principle of noninterference in the affairs of the state by others. Countries are, thus, restricted by the historical respect for state sovereignty and noninterference into the domestic affairs of other nations. In response to mass atrocities, however, countries have become willing to initiate humanitarian interventions, diplomatic sanctions, and the deployment of peacekeeping forces to the auspices of the United Nations. State sovereignty no longer serves as an appropriate

---

* Ibid.
† Ibid.
‡ The White House, President Barack Obama, "Remarks by the President at the United States Holocaust Memorial Museum," State of the Union, Office of the Press Secretary, April 23, 2012, http://www.whitehouse.gov/the-press-office/2012/04/23/remarks-president-united-states-holocaust-memorial-museum.
§ "Peace and Security Council (PSC)," Africa Union, July 23, 2013, http://www.peaceau.org/en/page/39-secretariat-psc.

excuse for other states' inaction against mass atrocities. State sovereignty also does not shield countries from international intervention. The international community has a responsibility to act when a state is in breach of its duties and allows mass atrocities to be perpetrated within its borders. The international community intervenes when a country is unwilling or unable to protect its own citizens. When such a situation arises, the responsibility to protect falls upon the international community.

Under the UN General Assembly Resolution 60/1 of October 24, 2005 (2005 World Summit Outcome), the responsibility to protect doctrine applies to the following mass atrocities: genocide, crimes against humanity, war crimes, and ethnic cleansing. According to this resolution,

> Each individual [s]tate has the responsibility to protect its populations from genocide, war crimes, ethnic cleansing and crimes against humanity. This responsibility entails the prevention of such crimes, including their incitement, through appropriate and necessary means...The international community should, as appropriate, encourage and help States to exercise this responsibility and support the United Nations in establishing an early warning capability.[*]

This resolution further delineated the responsibility of the international community to protect civilians from mass atrocities. Particularly, "[t]he international community, through the United Nations, also has the responsibility to use appropriate diplomatic, humanitarian and other peaceful means, in accordance with Chapters VI and VIII of the Charter, to help to protect populations from genocide, war crimes, ethnic cleansing and crimes against humanity."[†] States have a duty to act irrespective of any action taken by other entities, such as the United Nations. Indeed, the actions of other entities does not relieve countries from their obligation to take action to prevent mass atrocities from occurring within their borders and respond to them once they begin. The responsibility to protect principle, therefore, not only establishes the legal legitimacy to intervene but also creates a moral obligation to intervene.

There are many different ways in which the international community can intervene when mass atrocities are about to occur, are in progress, or have occurred. These measures have included governance measures such as:[‡] "building institutional capacity;" "ensuring the delivery of social services;" "supporting the diffusion or sharing of power;" "strengthening

---

[*] UN General Assembly Resolution 60/1 of October 24, 2005 (2005 World Summit Outcome), para. 138.
[†] UN General Assembly Resolution 60/1 of October 24, 2005 (2005 World Summit Outcome), para. 139.
[‡] Alex J. Bellamy, "Mass Atrocities and Armed Conflict: Links, Distinctions, and Implications for the Responsibility to Prevent," Policy Analysis Brief, The Stanley Foundation, 2011, 5, http://www.stanleyfoundation.org/publications/pab/BellamyPAB22011.pdf.

and supporting democracy;" "strengthening the independence of [the] judiciar[y];" "strengthening the rule of law;" "ending/preventing impunity;" "eradicating corruption;" and "strengthening local conflict resolution capacity." Social measures have also been created that are aimed at: strengthening and assisting civil society; criminalizing, preventing, and punishing incitement to violence and hate speech; educating the population on tolerance and diversity; enabling intergroup competence building; and promoting interfaith dialogue. Also, sanctions have been imposed on countries, embargoes have been enforced in the trading of arms, assets of perpetrators have been frozen, and diplomatic sanctions have been imposed.*

Additionally, military intervention has taken place in response to mass atrocities. In 1999, without UN authorization, "the North Atlantic Treaty Organization (NATO) conducted a three-month bombing campaign in an effort to prevent the...Serbian led ethnic cleansing in Kosovo," where approximately 600 individuals were killed and an estimated 750,000 Albanians were deported from that region.† Moreover, military intervention by the international community in 1945 defeated the Nazis and prevented the Germans from totally annihilating the European Jewish population.‡

Furthermore, diplomatic measures have been pursued, such as arbitration, conflict resolution, and peace agreements. Nevertheless, not all peace agreements have successfully ended mass atrocities. A case in point is the peace agreement that ended the Bosnian genocide; namely, the Dayton Peace Accords signed in November 1995. These accords separated the country into two federations, the Federation of Bosnia and Herzegovina (the Muslim and Croat federation), and the Republika Srpska.§ Despite these accords, Bosnian society remained fragmented and ethnically divided, and violence continued for several years afterward until NATO intervened in Kosovo in 1999.¶

It is imperative that the international community intervenes when a disproportionate number of a country's population is suffering due to mass atrocities. This, however, does not always occur. In fact, in the past, the international community has failed to protect civilians when

---

* Ibid.
† "Confronting Crimes Against Humanity," United States Institute of Peace, 12, http://www.usip.org/sites/default/files/file/09sg.pdf; *BBC News*, "Flashback to Kosovo's War," July 10, 2006, http://news.bbc.co.uk/2/hi/europe/5165042.stm.
‡ "Overview of the Holocaust: 1933–1945," Anti-Defamation League, 7, http://www.adl.org/assets/pdf/education-outreach/Overview-of-the-Holocaust-NYLM-Guide.pdf.
§ Evers, Frank, "Mission Information Package Bosnia and Herzegovina," Centre for OSCE Research, Institute for Peace Research and Security Policy at the University of Hamburg (IFSH), (December 2003), http://www.core-hamburg.de/documents/MIP_BiH.pdf.
¶ Ibid.

mass atrocities were taking place. In the case of the Bosnian and Rwanda genocide, states' unwillingness to act had devastating consequences for both countries. For example, the UN's failure to protect the safe area of Srebrenica in Bosnia resulted in the disappearance of 8,000 individuals in the area.* The international community also failed to protect the citizens in Rwanda. Indeed, once violence began in Rwanda, Belgium withdrew many of its troops by reducing its force from over 2,000 to less than 300, after 10 of its peacekeepers were slaughtered in a massacre at the residence of the Prime Minister, Agathe Uwilingiyimana.† Clearly, despite its responsibility to protect, the international community has, at times, failed to do so.

The G-Word   The need for swift and decisive action needs to be taken when, despite all national and international efforts, mass atrocities are occurring or are about to occur. Consider genocide. Despite the existence of the Genocide Convention, the international community has been hesitant to use the word genocide (i.e., the "g-word") when a genocide is suspected. Salih Booker and Ann-Louise Colgan had argued that the Rwanda genocide brought home the lesson that in order to stop genocide, the word must first be used.‡ During the Rwanda crisis, politicians and government officials were instructed not to utter the "g-word," which would require U.S. intervention in the region. This "ban on saying 'genocide' by the Clinton administration arose out of a briefing compiled by the Office of the Secretary of Defense. Inside the May 1994 briefing (later declassified by the National Security Archives), State Department lawyers said they were worried that a finding of genocide might obligate the administration 'to actually "do something"' [about the genocide]."§

---

* It is believed that these individuals were killed or executed, "The Fall of Srebrenica and the Failure of UN Peacekeeping: Bosnia and Herzegovina," Human Rights Watch, October 1995, 7(13), 69; Helge Brunborg and Henrik Urdal, "Report on the Number of Missing and Dead from Srebrenica," ICTY, February 12, 2000, http://www.icty.org/x/file/About/OTP/War_Demographics/en/krstic_srebrenica_000212.pdf.

† "Rwanda: A Brief History of the Country," Outreach Program on the Rwanda Genocide and the United Nations, http://www.un.org/en/preventgenocide/rwanda/education/rwandagenocide.shtml.

‡ Salih Booker and Ann-Louise Colgan, "Genocide in Darfur," *The Nation*, July 12, 2004, http://www.thenation.com/article/genocide-darfur; Scott Straus, "Darfur and the Genocide Debate," *Foreign Affairs* (January/February 2005), 129, http://users.polisci.wisc.edu/straus/Straus.pdf.

§ For a declassified discussion paper on Rwanda, see http://www2.gwu.edu/~nsarchiv/NSAEBB/NSAEBB53/rw050194.pdf; Rebecca Hamilton, "Inside Colin Powell's Decision to Declare Genocide in Darfur," *The Atlantic* (August 17, 2011), http://www.theatlantic.com/international/archive/2011/08/inside-colin-powells-decision-to-declare-genocide-in-darfur/243560/.

This belief is linked to the provisions of the Genocide Convention, which require contracting states to prevent and punish genocide.[*]

Nonetheless, the use of the "g-word" does not necessarily mean that international intervention will occur. This became evident in the Darfur genocide, where the Sudanese government mobilized and armed a militia, known as Janjaweed, to kill more than 70,000 non-Arab Darfuris and displace an estimated 1.8 million.[†] Particularly, in 2004, the United States Congress passed a resolution that labeled Darfur as a genocide.[‡] That same year, the Secretary of State, Colin Powell, stated before the Senate Foreign Relations Committee "that genocide has been committed in Darfur and that the government of Sudan and the Janjaweed bear responsibility."[§] Despite the use of the "g-word," no military action was taken by the United States. In fact, it was determined by the United States and others, such as the United Nations, that sanctions were a sufficient response to the mass atrocities committed in Sudan.[¶]

Sanctions, however, are insufficient to deal with perpetrators of mass atrocities who often deny their involvement in them. Denial allows the perpetrator moral justification for the atrocities he or she committed. In addition, perpetrators often block the international community's investigations of mass atrocities.[**] These perpetrators create mass graves, burn entire sites where atrocities have been committed, and take other actions to cover up evidence of their crimes.[††] Perpetrators are often not held accountable for their crimes. However, this lack of accountability increases the likelihood that events will repeat themselves. Indeed, existing weak justice institutions in countries have given rise to a culture of impunity. Accordingly, mechanisms are required that can end the culture of impunity in countries by holding perpetrators responsible for their crimes.

---

[*] See Article 8 of the Genocide Convention. Scott Straus, "Darfur and the Genocide Debate," *Foreign Affairs* (January/February 2005), 129, http://users.polisci.wisc.edu/straus/Straus.pdf.

[†] Scott Straus, "Darfur and the Genocide Debate," *Foreign Affairs* (January/February 2005), 123, 126–127, http://users.polisci.wisc.edu/straus/Straus.pdf.

[‡] U.S. Congress Resolution 467 (108th Congress, 2003–2004), "Declaring Genocide in Darfur, Sudan" 108th Congress (June 24, 2004), http://www.gpo.gov/fdsys/pkg/BILLS-108hconres467rfs/pdf/BILLS-108hconres467rfs.pdf.

[§] Glenn Kessler and Colum Lynch, "U.S. Calls Killings in Sudan Genocide," *Washington Post*, September 10, 2004, http://www.washingtonpost.com/wp-dyn/articles/A8364-2004Sep9.html.

[¶] Dianne E. Rennack, "Sudan: Economic Sanctions," *CRS Report for Congress*, RL32606, October 11, 2005, http://www.au.af.mil/au/awc/awcgate/crs/rl32606.pdf.

[**] Gregory Stanton, "The Eight Stages of Genocide Briefing Paper," Genocide Watch (1998), http://www.genocide watch.org/images/8StagesBriefingpaper.pdf.

[††] Ibid.

Ending Impunity

> You were fully aware of the power of words, and you used the radio—the medium of communication with the widest public reach—to disseminate hatred and violence....Without a firearm, machete or any physical weapon, you caused the deaths of thousands of innocent civilians (ICTR comments during sentencing of radio journalist, Ferdinand Nahimana, for his role in the Rwanda genocide).[*]

Measures have been implemented by national and international governments and institutions to deal with the threats posed by conflict societies. The most promising measures implemented by the international community to deal with mass atrocities are the creation of justice mechanisms for the criminal prosecution of perpetrators of these crimes. To sustain peace in the aftermath of conflict, the establishment and promotion of the rule of law in the region is required. This sends the message to citizens and the government alike that all are accountable to existing laws and will be prosecuted for violations of the law.

In 1945, the Agreement for the Prosecution and punishment of the major war criminals of the European Axis, and Charter of the International Military Tribunal, established the International Military Tribunal (IMT) to prosecute World War II war criminals. The trials held in the IMT are widely known as the Nuremberg trials. In these trials, Nazis were prosecuted for war crimes. The International Military Tribunal for the Far East was established in Tokyo in order to prosecute Japanese defendants who were accused of war crimes. Other justice mechanisms that have been established to prosecute perpetrators of mass atrocities include the International Criminal Court (ICC) established by the Rome Statute and the ad hoc tribunals that were established by the United Nations; namely, the International Criminal Tribunal for the former Yugoslavia (ICTY) and International Criminal Tribunal for Rwanda (ICTR). These institutions strengthen the rule of law in post-conflict societies and abated victims' feelings and needs of vengeance by promoting ideals that no one is above or outside the law and that crimes of mass atrocities will be punished.[†]

While these measures have been effective in appropriating accountability and largely ending impunity for mass atrocities, they are limited in effect. Specifically, these measures are taken only after mass atrocities have taken place. A case in point is the ICC. The ICC is considered a court of last resort; that is, countries should only turn to this court if

---

[*] *The Prosecutor v. Ferdinand Nahimana, Jean-Bosco Barayagwiza, Hassan Ngeze* (Judgment and Sentence), ICTR-99-52-T (3 December 2003).

[†] Martha Minow, *Between Vengeance and Forgiveness: Facing History after Genocide and Mass Violence* (Boston: Beacon Press, 1998), 26.

they are unable or unwilling to prosecute these crimes. The ICC prosecutes perpetrators of genocide, crimes against humanity, war crimes, and ethnic cleansing, after these serious crimes have taken place. The ICC, therefore, lacks any preventative capacity against these crimes. The ICC also lacks the capacity to prosecute all of the persons involved in mass atrocities; at times, the sheer number of the perpetrators alone renders the prosecution of all of them in this court prohibitive (e.g., this had been observed in Rwanda). The ICC limits those that it prosecutes to those perpetrators that are deemed to be the most responsible for the crimes. Other perpetrators are prosecuted in international courts, truth commissions, and indigenous reconciliation proceedings.

The courts, commissions, and proceedings seek to punish perpetrators for the crimes that they have committed. States can be held responsible for mass atrocities committed in their territories. Consider the dispute brought before the International Court of Justice (ICJ)* by the government of the Republic of Bosnia and Herzegovina against the Federal Republic of Yugoslavia (Serbia) concerning alleged violations of the Genocide Convention (hereafter *Bosnia and Herzegovina v. Serbia and Montenegro*).† In this case, the ICJ held that both individuals and governments can conduct genocide and can be responsible for violations under the Genocide Convention. In fact, Article 4 of the Genocide Convention clearly states that "responsible rulers, public officials, and private individuals" can be punished pursuant to the Convention. Under the Genocide Convention, governments are obligated from both refraining from and not being complicit in the commission of genocide. Governments are also required to take action to prevent genocide in both their own territories and other countries when warranted. In *Bosnia and Herzegovina v. Serbia and Montenegro*, the ICJ clarified the obligation of a country to prevent genocide. The court held that states had more than just a responsibility to punish the perpetrators of the crime, they were also obligated to prevent genocide.‡ In 2007, the ICJ pointed out that a country's duty to prevent genocide is activated as soon as the country is aware or should have been aware that genocide

---

* The International Court of Justice "is the principal judicial organ of the United Nations (UN). It was established in June 1945 by the Charter of the United Nations and began work in April 1946....The Court's role is to settle, in accordance with international law, legal disputes submitted to it by States and to give advisory opinions on legal questions referred to it by authorized United Nations organs and specialized agencies." For more information, see International Court of Justice, "The Court," http://www.icj-cij.org/court/index.php?p1=1.

† *Application of the Convention on the Prevention and the Punishment of the Crime of Genocide (Bosnia and Herzegovina v. Serbia and Montenegro)*, Judgment, ICJ 2007, http://www.icj-cij.org/docket/files/91/13685.pdf.

‡ Ibid., para. 428–438 (prevent) and 439–450 (punish).

was occurring; certainty of the event is not required.[*] In its judgment, the court delineated the manner in which states can be held accountable for breaching their legal duty to prevent genocide within their territories. This duty to prevent requires governments to "employ all means reasonably available to them, so as to prevent the genocide so far as possible."[†] Governments can violate the Genocide Convention by failing to take all of the measures that they have within their power to prevent the genocide.[‡]

Many regimes have tried behind their arguments of state sovereignty to dissolve them of responsibility in dealing with mass atrocities perpetrated in their own territories. State sovereignty, however, does not shield them from international concern and action. Heads of state have been charged with mass atrocities. Nonetheless, not all perpetrators have been held accountable. A case in point is Sudanese President Omar al-Bashir. In particular, two arrest warrants have been issued for al-Bashir in 2009 and 2010 for committing crimes against humanity and war crimes in Darfur. Specifically, the indictment that led to the first warrant charged al-Bashir as an indirect perpetrator or as an indirect coperpetrator under Article 25(3)(a) of the Rome Statute for five counts of crimes against humanity, murder, extermination, forcible transfer, torture, and rape, in violation of Articles 7(1)(a), 7(1)(b), 7(1)(d), 7(1)(f), and 7(1)(g) of the Rome Statute, and two counts of war crimes, direct attacks on civilians and pillaging, in violation of Articles 8(2)(e)(i) and 8(2)(e)(v) of the Rome Statute.[§] This arrest warrant marks the first indictment and warrant issued against a sitting head of state by the ICC. The indictment that led to the second warrant (which does not substitute or repeal the first one) charged al-Bashir as an indirect perpetrator or as an indirect coperpetrator under Article 25(3)(a) of the Rome Statute for three counts of genocide against the Fur, Masalit, and Zaghawa ethnic groups, which include: "genocide by killing," in violation of Article 6(a) of the Rome Statute; "genocide by causing serious bodily or mental harm," in violation of Article 6(b) of the Rome Statute; and "genocide by deliberately inflicting conditions of life calculated to bring about physical destruction," in violation of Article 6(c) of the Rome Statute.[¶] In addition to these arrest warrants, UN Security Resolutions were passed that emphasized Sudan's responsibility in protecting its population. For instance, UN Security Council Resolution 1556 of 30 July 2004 stated that "the Government of Sudan bears the primary responsibility to respect human

---

[*] Ibid., para. 431–432.

[†] Ibid., para. 430.

[‡] Ibid., para. 160 and 430.

[§] *The Prosecutor v. Omar Hassan Ahmad Al Bashir* ("Omar Al Bashir") (Warrant of Arrest for Omar Hassan Ahmad Al Bashir) ICC-02/05-01/09 (4 March 2009).

[¶] Ibid.

rights while maintaining law and order and protecting its population within its territory." This obligation was reiterated in UN Security Council Resolution 1564 of 18 September 2004.* This resolution also called on "the Government of Sudan to end the climate of impunity in Darfur by identifying and bringing to justice all those responsible, including members of popular defense forces and Janjaweed militias, for the widespread human rights abuses and violations of international humanitarian law, …insist[ing] that the Government of Sudan take all appropriate steps to stop all violence and atrocities."†

To date, the Sudanese government has refused to cooperate with the ICC. What's more, mass atrocities continue to be perpetrated in Sudan. This shows that punishment for mass atrocities has not been consistently certain; accordingly, the deterrent effects of these courts are doubtful. As Daniel Donovan rightly pointed out, "[t]he ICC depends on the cooperation of the states that have ratified it to turn over suspects, and help in the information gathering process to speed up and actually complete fair and efficient trials."‡ For the ICC to be more effective, international cooperation is critical. In addition, it is important to note that not all countries have signed or ratified the Rome Statute, even three of the permanent members of the UN Security Council; namely Russia, China, and the United States.§ Accordingly, without international cooperation and states' taking action against mass atrocities committed in their territories, the success of the ICC will be limited.¶

Apart from heads of state, journalists are also not immune from prosecution for their role in mass atrocities. Consider Rwanda. The

---

* This resolution stated "that the Sudanese Government bears the primary responsibility to protect its population within its territory, to respect human rights, and to maintain law and order, and that all parties are obliged to respect international humanitarian law."

† Recital 7, UN Security Council Resolution 1564 (2004).

‡ Daniel Donovan, "International Criminal Court: Successes and Failures of the Past and Goals for the Future," *International Policy Digest*, March 23, 2012, http://www.internationalpolicydigest.org/2012/03/23/international-criminal-court-successes-and-failures-of-the-past-and-goals-for-the-future/.

§ Russia is a signatory of the Statute but has not ratified it. China is not a signatory to the Statute and while originally the United States was a signatory in 2000, the Bush Administration in 2002, withdrew from it. Jess Bravin, "U.S. Accepts International Criminal Court," *Wall Street Journal*, April 26, 2008, http://online.wsj.com/news/articles/SB120917156494046579; Kofi A. Annan, "Justice vs. Impunity," *New York Times*, May 30, 2010, http://www.nytimes.com/2010/05/31/opinion/31iht-edannan.html?_r=0.

¶ Daniel Donovan, "International Criminal Court: Successes and Failures of the Past and Goals for the Future," *International Policy Digest*, March 23, 2012, http://www.internationalpolicydigest.org/2012/03/23/international-criminal-court-successes-and-failures-of-the-past-and-goals-for-the-future/; Kofi A. Annan, "Justice vs. Impunity," *New York Times*, May 30, 2010, http://www.nytimes.com/2010/05/31/opinion/31iht-edannan.html?_r=0.

radios and in print media were used to spread hate speech and incite violence among the population. Because of this, the journalists Hassan Ngeze, the founder and editor of an in print local newspaper (Kanguara), and Jean-Bosco Barayagwiza and Ferdinand Nahimana, founders of the Radio-Télévision Libre des Molles Collines (RTLM), were prosecuted for their roles in the genocide and crimes against humanity.* Specifically, Hassan Ngeze, Jean-Bosco Barayagwiza, and Ferdinand Nahimana were each found guilty of genocide, conspiracy to commit genocide, direct and public incitement to commit genocide, and crimes against humanity (persecution and extermination).†

The ICC and ad hoc tribunals have also held perpetrators responsible for being complicit in genocide. In fact, complicity in genocide is a violation of the Genocide Convention.‡ According to the ICJ, complicity in genocide refers to providing "the means to enable or facilitate the commission of the crime."§ Consequently, the enablers of the mass atrocities can be (and should be) held accountable for their crimes. Those who commit or enable mass atrocities can include individuals, businesses, and countries. An individual, business, or country enables mass atrocities when it provides resources, goods, services, and support in the commission of the atrocities.¶ Agencies have been created that seek to hold enablers responsible. Specifically, the U.S. Atrocities Prevention Board (APB) seeks to hold enablers of mass atrocities accountable for their acts.** Governments have also imposed sanctions against enablers. For example, an Executive Order was passed in the United States, which sanctioned individuals or businesses that provided goods, services, or technologies to Syria and Iran to facilitate human rights abuses through the use of goods, services, or technologies to monitor, track, and target specific civilians for attacks.†† Another example involved the Democratic Republic of Congo, where businesses that extracted and traded minerals

---

* *The Prosecutor v. Ferdinand Nahimana, Jean-Bosco Barayagwiza, Hassan Ngeze* (Judgment and Sentence), ICTR-99-52-T (3 December 2003); Elizabeth Baisley, "Genocide and Constructions of Hutu and Tutsi in Radio Propaganda," *Race & Class* 55:3 (2014), 39.

† *The Prosecutor v. Ferdinand Nahimana, Jean-Bosco Barayagwiza, Hassan Ngeze* (Judgment and Sentence), ICTR-99-52-T (3 December 2003).

‡ See Article 3(e) of the Genocide Convention.

§ *Application of the Convention on the Prevention and the Punishment of the Crime of Genocide (Bosnia and Herzegovina v. Serbia and Montenegro)*, ICJ Judgment of 26 February 2007, para. 419, http://www.icj-cij.org/docket/files/91/13685.pdf.

¶ "Disrupting the Supply Chain for Mass Atrocities: How to Stop Third-Party Enablers of Genocide and Other Crimes against Humanity," Human Rights First, July 2011, 1. https://www.humanrightsfirst.org/wp-content/uploads/pdf/Disrupting_the_Supply_Chain-July_2011.pdf.

** "Atrocities Prevention Board," Human Rights First, May 2012, http://www.humanrightsfirst.org/wp-content/uploads/pdf/Fact_Sheet-APB.pdf.

†† Executive Order 13608.

in the Democratic Republic of Congo aided armed groups that controlled the mines by assisting them in generating revenue that was then used to facilitate the perpetration of mass atrocities against civilians.*

The decisions of the above-mentioned courts demonstrate that senior officials and any other individuals involved in mass atrocities are not immune from prosecution (with few exceptions, such as al-Bashir). These courts thus lay essential groundwork for efficient and transparent international justice, which aids the post-conflict development of the region.

Repairing Harm Done

Post-conflict societies face a very high risk of relapsing to conflict. To prevent conflicts from re-emerging, the risk factors that led to the original conflict need to be removed or at the very least reduced. Additionally, the conflict that has most likely generated grievances among the population also needs to be addressed. Such grievances cannot solely be dealt with through retributive justice, which focuses explicitly on punishing the wrongs committed. Survivors of mass atrocities and victims' families also seek reparation and restorative justice.

Reparations are viewed as compensation given to the victim to redress any harm or wrong done. A victim's right to reparation is enshrined in international human rights instruments, such as the Universal Declaration on Human Rights.† Moreover, the Inter-American Court of Human Rights has held that reparation consists of "full restitution..., which includes the restoration of the prior situation, the reparation of the consequences of the violation, and indemnification for patrimonial and non-patrimonial damages, including emotional harm."‡ This court further stated that "every violation of an international obligation which results in harm creates a duty to make adequate reparation."§ In addition to human rights instruments, international law has also addressed reparation. For instance, Article 75 of the Rome Statute provided the legal basis for victim reparation. This provision outlined the responsibilities of the ICC in affording justice to victims for violations under the Rome Statute.

---

* Department of State, "Report Submitted to the Committee on Foreign Relations," U.S. Senate and the Committee on Foreign Affairs U.S. House of Representatives, Country Reports on Human Rights: Practices for 2010 (Volume 1), 112th Congress 1st Session (112–30), U.S. Government Printing Office, 2010, http://www.gpo.gov/fdsys/pkg/CPRT-112SPRT66165/html/CPRT-112SPRT66165-VolumeI.htm.
† "Everyone has the right to an effective remedy by the competent national tribunals for acts violating the fundamental rights granted him by the constitution or by law." Article 8 of the Universal Declaration on Human Rights.
‡ *Valasquez Rodriguez v. Honduras* (Judgment on Reparations), 21 July 1989, para. 26.
§ Ibid., para. 25.

Reparation has been provided by governments to those affected by the conflict. Consider Chile. Victims who suffered from mass atrocities under the Pinochet regime were provided with pensions and special healthcare programs.[*] Similar reparation programs have been developed by other countries for survivors of mass atrocities and the families of those who died from mass atrocities. A case in point is the reparation program between the German government and Jewish victims for Nazi crimes, which included compensation for material losses and pension support.[†]

In addition to reparation, reconciliation has been sought post-conflict. This can be achieved through restorative justice. Restorative justice is a "process whereby all the parties with a stake in a particular offense come together to resolve collectively how to deal with the aftermath of the offense and its implications for the future."[‡] This process seeks to restore, to the extent possible, the victim, offender, and community to their pre-mass atrocity status. Using this process, victims (or families of deceased victims) can reconcile with the offender, if they choose to, and negotiate reparation. The community has a primary role in this process, in respect of mediating the reconciliation.[§] Research findings reveal that victims choose to engage in the restorative justice process in order to obtain information from the perpetrator (e.g., motive for crime, confession of the crime, or information concerning the killing of a relative), the victim's need to tell their story, and the need to gain some sense of closure.[¶] Through this process, offenders are encouraged to express remorse, to accept responsibility, and to apologize.

---

[*] "Reparations," International Center for Transitional Justice, http://www.ictj.org/our-work/transitional-justice-issues/reparations.

[†] See 1952 Luxembourg Agreement signed by Moshe Sharett, Israeli Prime Minister, and Konrad Adenauer, West German Chancellor. The reparation program has been updated and amended throughout the years and is still in effect today. Menachem Z. Rosensaft and Joana D. Rosensaft, "The Early History of German-Jewish Reparations," *Fordham International Law Journal* 25:6 (2001), S-45.

[‡] Tony F. Marshall, "The Evolution of Restorative Justice in Britain," *European Journal on Criminal Policy and Research* 4:4 (1996), 37; Lucia Zedner, *Criminal Justice* (Oxford, UK: Oxford University Press, 2004), 101.

[§] Linda Keller, "Seeking Justice at the International Criminal Court: Victims' Reparations," *Thomas Jefferson Law Review* 29:2 (2007), 190.

[¶] Howard Zehr, *Changing Lenses* (Waterloo, Ontario: Herald Press, 1990), 26; Howard Zehr, *The Little Book of Restorative Justice* (Intercourse, PA: Good Books, 2002) 14; Elmer G. M. Weitekamp, Stephan Parmentier, Kris Vanspauwen, Marta Valiñas, and Roel Gerits, "How to Deal with Mass Victimization and Gross Human Rights Violations. A Restorative Justice Approach," In Uwe Ewald and Ksenija Turkovic (Eds.), *Large-Scale Victimization as a Potential Source of Terrorist Activities* (Amsterdam: IOS, 2006), 230; Ines Staiger, "Restorative Justice and Victims of Terrorism," In Rianne Letschert, Antony Pemberton, and Ines Staiger (Eds.), *Assisting Victims of Terrorism: Towards a European Standard of Justice* (Dordrecht, The Netherlands: Springer, 2010), 270.

Restorative justice, however, is not a substitute for retributive justice. The perpetrators of mass atrocities are still punished for their crimes. A hybrid model of justice that includes both retributive and restorative elements is the Gacaca courts in Rwanda. Gacaca courts "promote reconciliation by providing a means for victims to learn the truth about the death of their family members and relatives. They also gave perpetrators the opportunity to confess their crimes, show remorse and ask for forgiveness in front of their community."* This citizen-based justice system involves the community at every level: Rwandans are the judges, witnesses, suspects, and victims. Following the genocide, Rwanda had suffered from a complicated reintegration process. To assist in the reintegration and reconciliation process, Gacaca courts heard genocide cases. These courts were additionally developed to deal with the overwhelming number of perpetrators in the Rwanda genocide. The objectives of the Gacaca courts go beyond providing restitution to victims, to seeking to repair the harm or the injuries caused by a crime to the person(s) victimized and the broader community. Specifically, the Gacaca courts sought to "establish the truth about what happened; accelerate the legal proceedings for those accused of genocide crimes; eradicate the culture of impunity; reconcile Rwandans and reinforce their unity; and use the capacities of Rwandan society to deal with its problems through a justice based on Rwandan custom."† Although these measures seek to repair the harm done to victims, they are not widely available nor widely used. What's more, they cannot deal with a direct outcome of many mass atrocities today; namely, refugees.

Refugee Crises

The United Nations High Commission on Refugees (UNHCR) was set up to assist approximately 1 million individuals that were displaced following World War II.‡ The UNHCR is the primary agency responsible for providing international protection and assistance to individuals in

---

* UN Department of Public Information, "Background Note: The Justice and Reconciliation Process in Rwanda. Published," The Outreach Programme on the Rwanda Genocide and the United Nations, April 2013, http://www.un.org/en/preventgenocide/rwanda/pdf/Backgrounder%20Justice%202013.pdf.

† Bert Ingelaere, "The Gacaca Courts in Rwanda," In Luc Huyse and Mark Salter (Eds.), "Traditional Justice and Reconciliation after Violent Conflict: Learning from African Experiences," International Institute for Democracy and Electoral Assistance (IDEA), 2008, 38, cited in Megan M. Westberg, "Rwanda's Use of Transitional Justice after Genocide: The Gacaca Courts and the ICTR," *University of Kansas Law Review* 59:2 (2011), 337.

‡ "Refugee Numbers," United Nations High Commission on Refugees, http://www.unhcr.org/pages/49c3646c1d.html.

need, especially during conflicts.[*] The types of individuals the UNHCR protects are refugees and internally displaced persons. Pursuant to Article 1(2) of the 1951 UN Convention Relating to the Status of Refugees, a refugee refers to any person

> owing to well-founded fear of being persecuted for reason of race, religion, nationality membership of a particular social group or political opinion, is outside the country of his nationality and is unable or, owing to such fear, is unwilling to avail himself of the protection of that country; or who not having a nationality and being outside the country of his former habitual residence as a result of such events, is unable or, owing to such fear, is unwilling to return to it.

Under the 1998 Guiding Principles on Internal Displacement, internally displaced persons are defined as "persons or groups of persons who have been forced or obliged to flee or to leave their homes or places of habitual residence, in particular as a result of or in order to avoid the effects of armed conflict, situations of generalized violence, violations of human rights or natural or human-made disasters, and who have not crossed an internationally recognized State border."

Both the UNHCR and the International Organization for Migration (IOM) have set up campuses and facilities for those that have been forced to leave their countries. In addition to these responsibilities, the IOM provides national and international migration services to displaced persons, refugees, and anyone else in need of their services.[†] Similarly, the International Federation of Red Cross and Red Crescent Societies, among other responsibilities, coordinates and provides international assistance to refugees and victims of conflict.[‡]

In addition to internally displaced persons, the large number of refugees seeking to leave the country during or after the conflict poses a significant transnational security threat. Countries are often unwilling to accept refugees seeking safety abroad. Indeed, "[t]he citizenry and governments in many developed and developing states have increasingly viewed mass refugee flows as a liability rather than an asset."[§] Consider the Holocaust. According to Monica Duffy Toft, "[m]any times during the war, groups of Jewish refugees—most small, some larger—escaped the fate of their fellows, only to be turned back at European borders or to

---

[*] "Humanitarian Assistance and Assistance to Refugees," United Nations, May 21, 1999, http://www.un.org/ha/general.htm.

[†] "About IOM," International Organization for Migration (IOM), http://www.iom.int/cms/about-iom.

[‡] "Who We Are," International Federation of Red Cross and Red Crescent Societies, http://www.ifrc.org/en/who-we-are/.

[§] Robert Mandel, "Perceived Security Threat and the Global Refugee Crisis," *Armed Forces & Society* 24:1 (1997), 77.

be prevented from docking at European and U.S. ports."[*] The Evian Conference convened in 1938 in France to discuss the Jewish refugee crisis.[†] The goals of the conference were to persuade countries to admit more Jewish refugees into their respective territories and to find a solution to Hitler's oppressive rule against the Jews. However, of the attendees at the conference, almost all of them refused to accept more Jewish refugees by relaxing their immigration restrictions because of concern that these refugees would pose further economic hardships on their countries.

The influx of displaced persons and refugees is taxing on the host countries because the additional arrival of individuals puts a strain on available resources and social services for an indeterminate amount of time. This was observed in the aftermath of Darfur. In fact, UN Security Resolution 1556 of 30 July 2004, noted "with grave concern that up to 200,000 refugees have fled to the neighboring State of Chad, which constitutes a serious burden upon that country." As of 2012, "more than 1.4 million displaced people still rely on food handouts in camps throughout Darfur, and many others have fled the country."[‡] Indeed, a large number of refugees can adversely impact the economy, society, and public order.[§]

In 2013, the UNHCR reported that an estimated 15 million refugees are in need of repatriation, local integration, or resettlement.[¶] Among these options, repatriation, which involves returning refugees to their country of origin, is the policy of choice.[**] However, repatriation may not always be possible; especially when a refugee, when returned, may be subjected to persecution, reprisal, or unsafe conditions that puts them at risk of emotional or physical harm.[††] When repatriation is not possible, refugees either pursue "local integration in the initial country of asylum, or resettlement to a third country."[‡‡] To aid in the appropriate place-

---

[*] Monica Duffy Toft, "The Myth of the Borderless World: Refugees and Repatriation Policy," *Conflict Management and Peace Science* 24:2 (2007), 145.

[†] Eric Estorick, "The Evian Conference and the Intergovernmental Committee," *The ANNALS of the American Academy of Political and Social Science* 203:1 (1939), 136.

[‡] James Copnall, "Darfur Conflict: Sudan's Bloody Stalemate," *BBC News*, April 29, 2013, http://www.bbc.co.uk/news/world-africa-22336600.

[§] Eric Estorick, "The Evian Conference and the Intergovernmental Committee," *The ANNALS of the American Academy of Political and Social Science* 203:1 (1939), 138.

[¶] "Refugee Numbers," United Nations High Commission on Refugees, http://www.unhcr.org/pages/49c3646c1d.html.

[**] Monica Duffy Toft, "The Myth of the Borderless World: Refugees and Repatriation Policy," *Conflict Management and Peace Science* 24:2 (2007), 147.

[††] Megan Bradley, *Refugee Repatriation: Justice, Responsibility and Redress* (Cambridge: Cambridge University Press, 2013), 20; Monica Duffy Toft, "The Myth of the Borderless World: Refugees and Repatriation Policy," *Conflict Management and Peace Science* 24:2 (2007), 147.

[‡‡] "Durable Solutions," UNHCR, http://www.unhcr.org/pages/49c3646cf8.html; See also Recommendation 28 in "Handbook on Voluntary Repatriation: International Protection," UNHCR, 1996, http://www.unhcr.org/3bfe68d32.html.

ment of refugees, international cooperation is required. International support is also needed for those countries that do not have the resources and funding to absorb refugees. The Syrian refugee crisis illustrates the costs and consequences of absorbing refugees without sufficient international assistance.[*] In 2014, the Assistant Secretary of the U.S. Bureau of Population, Refugees, and Migration stated the following during her testimony to the Senate Committee on the Judiciary, Subcommittee on the Constitution, Civil Rights and Human Rights:

> The impact on many communities across the region is overwhelming. Schools have moved to double-shifts to accommodate Syrian children. Hospital beds are filled by Syrian patients. Rents have risen and wages have fallen as a result of the competition for housing and jobs. There are water shortages in Jordan and Lebanon. The drain on water resources is especially severe in Jordan due to its relative lack of water; the Government of Jordan is already struggling to cover subsidies for water for Jordanian citizens. The governments of these countries—as well as the Governments of Iraq and Turkey—are concerned that they must stretch the services they provide to their own citizens to reach the overwhelming numbers of vulnerable refugees living in their countries.[†]

While funds have been provided by the U.S. State Department and USAID to humanitarian organizations, "the wider international community...[should also] support...neighboring countries as they respond to the [crisis in] Syria."[‡] These practices should be enforced for future conflict and post-conflict situations around the globe.

CONCLUDING THOUGHTS

A significant challenge for the international community is dealing with violent conflict within states, which is manifested in civil wars and mass atrocities. A conflict in society escalates to become an eventual mass atrocity through: the emergence of some crisis situation that produces social conflict; the mobilization of an armed group (or groups); and the outbreak of violence against civilians, which, if it remains unchecked,

---

[*] Rochelle Davis and Abbie Taylor, "Syrian Refugees in Jordan and Lebanon: A Snapshot from Summer 2013," The Center for Contemporary Arab Studies, The Institute for the Study of International Migration, Georgetown University, 2013, http://ccas.georgetown.edu/document/1242799693627/Syrian+Refugee+Report+Sept+2013.pdf.

[†] Anne C. Richard, Syrian Refugee Crisis, Assistant Secretary, "Bureau of Population, Refugees, and Migration Statement Submitted for the Record to the Senate Committee on the Judiciary," Subcommittee on the Constitution, Civil Rights and Human Rights Washington, DC, January 7, 2014, http://iipdigital.usembassy.gov/st/english/texttrans/2014/01/20140107290103.html#axzz2s1P9ooRE.

[‡] Ibid.

will escalate to mass atrocities. Countries have committed mass atrocities to counter purported political threats to ensure their political survival. These mass atrocities are committed by a national leader and/or political party against its people or a dominant group against a minority group.

The most prominent risk factors associated with mass atrocities are: the organization of hate groups that are dedicated to vilifying a target group in society; publication of hate propaganda toward that target group; purging the target group from governmental and military positions; expanding recruitment of members in the dominant group; creating, arming, and training militias; targeted violence against specific civilians; and the impunity of perpetrators for committing such illicit acts.

Along with the identification of these risk factors, what is also needed is the real-time analysis of information from conflict societies. Early warning analysis is critical as it demonstrates the risk factors that give rise to conflict in countries during peacetime. Accordingly, national and international capacity should be strengthened to detect early warning signs of mass atrocities. To effectively counter mass atrocities, the monitoring of emerging conflicts is required. Early intervention is also required to counter mass atrocities. Humanitarian intervention can include nonmilitary and military interventions. International intervention, however, is not a substitute for prevention.

The responsibility to protect asserts that states have a legal and ethical responsibility to protect their citizens; however, if the state is unable or unwilling to do so the responsibility to protect falls on the international community. The responsibility to protect principle not only establishes the legal legitimacy to intervene but also the moral obligation to intervene. There have been historical incidents, however, when countries and the international community have fallen short of this responsibility. Countries have been held accountable for failing to take all of the measures that they have within their power to prevent mass atrocities. Apart from the courts, other measures have been implemented which seek to hold accountable those responsible for the crimes. Consider enablers. One of the key elements in preventing and responding to mass atrocities is the targeting of enablers; in so doing, restricting perpetrators' access to resources that they need to commit their illicit activities. With respect to enablers, sanctions have been provided not only to governments but also to the individuals and companies that enable them to commit mass atrocities.

Besides requiring countries to fulfill their own internal responsibility to protect, it is imperative that the United Nations has the support and resources it needs to deal with mass atrocities. Some of the measures that can be used to respond to mass atrocities include short-term measures, such as diplomatic isolation, travel restrictions, the curtailment and withdrawal of investment, and media campaigns that involve the naming and shaming of the perpetrators.* Long-term measures, such as power-sharing agreements, democratic institution building, and funds for development, can also be implemented.†

Mass atrocities have an adverse social and political impact on both the country in conflict and the international community. In addition, apart from their significant adverse effects on humans and their quality of life, mass atrocities can damage the economic well-being of the region by, for example, disrupting trade and transport routes for both exports and imports. Furthermore, mass atrocities have resulted in a large number of refugees. Many countries, however, have been unable or unwilling to accept these refugees. Accordingly, the refugee crisis is unlikely to diminish anytime soon. It is likely to remain among the top five global challenges until 2050.‡

---

* "Confronting Crimes against Humanity," United States Institute of Peace, 15, http://www.usip.org/sites/default/files/file/09sg.pdf.

† Ibid.

‡ Kirsten Gelsdorf, "Global Challenges and their Impact on International Humanitarian Action," *OCHA Occasional Policy Briefing Series* Brief No. 1: Global Challenges and Their Impact on International Humanitarian Action, 20, January 2010, https://docs.unocha.org/sites/dms/Documents/Global_Challenges_Policy_Brief_Jan10.pdf.

CHAPTER 11

The Fight for
Natural Resources
Seeking Food and Water Security

Natural resources, such as food and water, are not inexhaustible. These resources should meet the needs of the current and future generations. The 2013 World Economic Forum Global Risks report included food shortage crises as one of the top five global risks in 2012.[*] Additionally, this report included water supply crises as one of the top five global risks between 2012 and 2013.[†] This chapter examines the threat of food and water insecurity in various areas of the world and what it means for transnational security. The fight over natural resources by certain countries is also examined. Finally, this chapter considers access to and the availability of nutritious food and clean water as a fundamental human right.

FOOD SECURITY

According to the 1996 World Food Summit, "[f]ood security exists when all people, at all times, have physical and economic access to sufficient, safe and nutritious food to meet their dietary needs and food preferences

---

[*] Specifically, food shortage crises ranked number 3 in 2012; "Global Risks Report 2013," World Economic Forum, 2013, 13, http://www3.weforum.org/docs/WEF_GlobalRisks_Report_2013.pdf.

[†] Particularly, in 2012, concerning global risk by impact, water supply crises ranked number 2, and in 2013, water supply crises ranked number 2. Additionally, in 2012, concerning global risk by likelihood, water supply crises ranked number 5 and in 2013, water supply crises ranked number 4. "Global Risks Report 2013," World Economic Forum, 2013, 13, http://www3.weforum.org/docs/WEF_GlobalRisks_Report_2013.pdf.

for an active and healthy life."* Despite popular belief, food security does not only encompass issues of availability. Availability of food is only one part of the multidimensional problem. The United Nations Food and Agriculture Organization (FAO) identified four major dimensions of food security: food availability, access, use, and stability.†

The first element, food availability, refers to the consistent availability of an adequate amount of food. This dimension focuses exclusively on ensuring that food exists and can be measured by food production, supply, stocks, and trade. The second dimension of food security is access, which requires that individuals have the necessary resources to obtain the foods they need for a nutritional diet. This encompasses the economic and physical accessibility to food, which is primarily concerned with individuals' and nations' ability to purchase food. To enable access to food, it needs to be affordable and within one's reach—either on one's farm, neighboring farms, or at the market. Yet, when individuals have access to food, it may not be safe to eat; quality food may not be available.

The third dimension concerns the proper utilization of food, which ensures that it is prepared in a nutritional manner. Specifically, this dimension of food security encompasses the nutritional value of the meal and how it is prepared and distributed in a household. According to the FAO, "[u]tilization refers to the proper use of food and includes the existence of appropriate food processing and storage practices, adequate knowledge and application of nutrition and child care and adequate health sanitation services."‡ Nutritional foods provide individuals with the nutrients they need to sustain a healthy lifestyle. The lack of a nutritional diet can result in increases in illnesses and even death. The fourth and final dimension concerns the stability of the three aforementioned dimensions over time (food availability, access, and use). Food security is achieved when all four of these dimensions are fulfilled concurrently.§

---

* Recital 1 of 1996 World Food Summit Plan of Action, http://www.fao.org/docrep/003/w3613e/w3613e00.htm.

† EC—FAO Food Security Programme, "An Introduction to the Basic Concepts of Food Security," *Food Security Information for Action: Practical Guides*, 2008, 1, http://www.fao.org/docrep/013/al936e/al936e00.pdf.

‡ Marc J. Cohen, Cristina Tirado, Noora-Lisa Aberman, and Brian Thompson, "World Food Insecurity and Malnutrition: Scope, Trends, Causes and Consequences," In *Impact of Climate Change and Bioenergy on Nutrition*, FAO, 2008, ftp://ftp.fao.org/docrep/fao/010/ai799e/ai799e02.pdf, cited in Emmy Simmons, "Harvesting Peace: Food Security, Conflict, and Cooperation," *Environmental Change and Security Program*, 2013, 16, http://wilsoncenter.org/sites/default/files/HarvestingPeace.pdf.

§ EC—FAO Food Security Programme, "An Introduction to the Basic Concepts of Food Security," *Food Security Information for Action: Practical Guides*, 2008, 1, http://www.fao.org/docrep/013/al936e/al936e00.pdf.

Food Insecurity

Food insecurity refers to "the state of being without reliable access to a sufficient quantity of affordable, nutritious food."[*] This is a real threat that is often invisible except to those who feel its effects over time. It has an adverse impact on individuals' health, economic well-being, and their productivity.[†] These households that suffer the most from food insecurity are those with special populations (e.g., the disabled, the elderly, the chronically sick, and orphans).[‡]

Two types of food insecurities have been identified by the European Commission (EC)—Food and Agriculture Organization (FAO) Food Security Programme: short-term (transient) food insecurity and longer-term (chronic) food insecurity.[§] Transient (acute) food insecurity occurs when "there is a sudden drop in the ability to produce or access enough food to maintain a good nutritional status," due to "short-term shocks and fluctuations in food availability and food access, including year-to-year variations in domestic food production, food prices and household incomes."[¶] Chronic food shortages occur when individuals' need for food exceeds existing food supply and production capabilities. By contrast, chronic food insecurity occurs when "people are unable to meet their minimum food requirements over a sustained period of time," as a result of "extended periods of poverty, lack of assets and inadequate access to productive or financial resources."[**]

Hunger

Hunger refers to "the want or scarcity of food in a country" or region.[††] The International Food Policy Research Institute (IFPRI) developed the Global Hunger Index (GHI), a worldwide measurement and tracking mechanism, in order to assess global hunger. Specifically, to measure

---

[*] Oxford Dictionary s.v. "Food Insecurity," http://www.oxforddictionaries.com/us/definition/american_english/food-insecurity.

[†] Monica Fisher and Paul A. Lewin, "Household, Community, and Policy Determinants of Food Insecurity in Rural Malawi," *Development Southern Africa* 30:4–5 (2013), 451–467.

[‡] Paul Bukuluki, Firminus Mugumya, Stella Neema, Agatha Kafuko, and Eric Ochen, "Gender, Food Security, and AIDS in Internally Displaced People's Camps in Uganda: Implications for HIV Responsive Policy and Programming," *International Food Policy Research Institute Brief* 17 (2008), http://programs.ifpri.org/renewal/pdf/RFbrief17.pdf.

[§] EC—FAO Food Security Programme, "An Introduction to the Basic Concepts of Food Security," *Food Security Information for Action: Practical Guides*, 2008, 1, http://www.fao.org/docrep/013/al936e/al936e00.pdf.

[¶] Ibid.

[**] Ibid.

[††] "2013 World Hunger and Poverty Facts and Statistics," World Hunger Education Service, http://www.worldhunger.org/articles/Learn/world%20hunger%20facts%202002.htm.

global hunger, the IFPRI examined three indicators: the proportion of the population that was undernourished; the prevalence of underweight children of the population; and the mortality rate of children in the population.[*] The GHI is calculated by country and region.[†]

The 2013 GHI reflects information about worldwide hunger between 2008 and 2012. The data on the three indicators of hunger from 120 developing countries and those in transition are calculated to determine the countries ranking in the GHI. According to the GHI, global hunger has improved. However, food security is still considered a significant transnational security issue because an estimated 842 million people live in hunger[‡] (Figure 11.1). To date, South Asia and South Africa have the

FIGURE 11.1   August 15, 2011: Unidentified children stretch out their hands at the Dadaab refugee camp, where thousands of Somalians wait for help because of hunger in Dadaab, Somalia. (Image courtesy of Shutterstock.com.)

---

[*] Rajendra Prasad, "Population Growth, Food Shortages and Ways to Alleviate Hunger," *Current Science* 105:1 (July 10, 2013), 34, http://www.currentscience.ac.in/Volumes/105/01/0032.pdf.

[†] International Food Policy Research Institute (IFPRI), "Global Hunger Index," http://www.ifpri.org/book-8018/ourwork/researcharea/global-hunger-index.

[‡] "Hunger Statistics," World Food Programme, http://www.wfp.org/hunger/stats; Food and Agriculture Organization of the United Nations, "Global Hunger Down, But Millions Still Chronically Hungry," FAO, http://www.fao.org/news/story/en/item/198105/icode/.

TABLE 11.1   Alarming Global Hunger Index (GHI) Scores

Timor-Leste	Haiti
Sudan	Sierra Leone
Chad	Burkina Faso
Yemen	Mozambique
Ethiopia	India
Madagascar	Tanzania
Zambia	Democratic Republic of Congo
Central African Republic	Niger

Source: "Global Hunger Index: The Challenge of Hunger: Building Resilience to Achieve Food and Nutrition Security," International Food Policy Research Institute (IFPRI), http://www.ifpri.org/sites/default/files/publications/ghi13. pdf.

greatest GHI scores. In total, 19 countries had alarming GHI scores, which reflected their levels of hunger. Of these countries, three of them had extremely alarming GHI scores; namely, Burundi, Comoros, and Eritrea. These three countries had the "highest proportion of undernourished people—more than 60 percent of the population."[*] The remaining 16 countries (see Table 11.1), had alarming GHI scores. From these countries, India and Timor-Leste had "the highest prevalence of underweight children under five—more than 40 percent in both countries," and Mali, Sierra Leone, and Somalia had "the highest under-five mortality rate, ranging from approximately 18 to about 19 percent."[†]

There are several drivers of global hunger, each one is explored in the next section.

Drivers of Hunger   There are nine main drivers of hunger. The first driver is poverty, which is directly related to the lack of available and appropriate employment opportunities. Individuals in poverty are unable to afford food—let alone nutritious food—for themselves and their families. In Burundi, many agricultural households are poor, thereby

---

[*] "Although the Democratic Republic of Congo and Somalia are likely to have high proportions of undernourished as well, they could not be included in this comparison because of lack of reliable data." International Food Policy Research Institute (IFPRI), "Global, Regional, and National Trends: 2013 Global Hunger Index," http://www. ifpri.org/ghi/2013/global-regional-national-trends?print.

[†] International Food Policy Research Institute (IFPRI), "Global Hunger Index: The Challenge of Hunger: Building Resilience to Achieve Food and Nutrition Security," *IFPRI*, 14, http://www.ifpri.org/sites/default/files/publications/ghi13.pdf.

contributing to the existing food insecurity.* This is especially problematic for children because undernourishment and malnourishment have an adverse impact on a child's development; sometimes this impact is irreversible. In fact, studies have shown that children "whose nutrition is compromised before ... [the age of two] suffer [irreversible] personal harm to their cognitive and physical capacities."†

The second driver is the lack of an effective agriculture industry. Here, land use, fertilizers, crop cultivation, irrigation, the purchase and affordability of seeds, transportation systems, roads, and storage facilities play critical roles in the efficacy of the agricultural infrastructure. Fluctuations in agriculture production may be observed due to soil degradation, weather changes, and damage by pests and pathogens. For example, in Malawi, food security in the region depends on maize development and access to it. Food insecurity in Malawi results from insufficient rainfall, nitrogen deficient soils, limited ability to purchase food (as a consequence of declining soil fertility), inadequate labor availability for agriculture, and poor transport infrastructure.‡ Fluctuations in agriculture production may be avoided in the short term by relying on existing food supplies and food trade across the borders. Food trade, however, can be affected by poor transportation infrastructure and conflict situations.

Consider the humanitarian relief provided after the drought in Southern Africa between 1990 and 1991. Particularly, in response to the drought, "[n]early, 8 million tons of food grains were imported...for

---

* Marijke D'Haese, Stijn Speelman, Ellen Vandamme, Tharcisse Nkunzimana, Jean Ndimubandi, and Luc D'Haese, "Recovering from Conflict: An Analysis of Food Production in Burundi," Paper submitted for the Joint 3rd African Association of Agricultural Economists and 48th Agricultural Economists Association of South Africa Conference, Cape Town, September 19–23, 2010, http://ageconsearch.umn.edu/bitstream/96829/2/145.%20Recovering%20from%20conflict_Burundi.pdf; Emmy Simmons, "Harvesting Peace: Food Security, Conflict, and Cooperation," Environmental Change and Security Program, 2013, 28, http://wilsoncenter.org/sites/default/files/HarvestingPeace.pdf.

† Emmy Simmons, "Harvesting Peace: Food Security, Conflict, and Cooperation," Environmental Change and Security Program, 2013, 4, http://wilsoncenter.org/sites/default/files/HarvestingPeace.pdf.

‡ Carol McSweeney, Mark New, and Gil Lizcano, "UNDP Climate Change Country Profiles: Malawi," 2008, http://ncsp.undp.org/sites/default/files/Malawi.oxford.report.pdf; Quentin Wodon and Kathleen Beegle, "Labor Shortages Despite Underemployment? Seasonality in Time Use in Malawi," In C. Mark Blackden and Quentin Wodon (Eds.), Gender, Time Use, and Poverty in Sub-Saharan Africa (Washington, DC: World Bank, 2006), 97–116; Monica Fisher and Paul A. Lewin, "Household, Community, and Policy Determinants of Food Insecurity in Rural Malawi," Development Southern Africa 30:4–5 (2013), 451–467; Rachel Bezner Kerr, "Food Security in Northern Malawi: Gender, Kinship Relations and Entitlements in Historical Context," Journal of Southern African Studies 31:1 (2005), 60.

the 10 countries affected…This substantial increase in imports resulted in pressure on the region's distribution systems, leading to a number of problems which would not have been significant in 'normal' years."[*] Here, aid distribution was complicated due to infrastructural and non-infrastructural constraints. Infrastructural constraints included physical obstacles to the transport of food, such as "steep gradients and tight curves at which points grain was stolen from the slow-moving wagons."[†] Noninfrastructural constraints included "general security problems along the corridor, regulatory constraints for cargo destined for Zambia, conflict between humanitarian requirements and commercial concerns, poor labor management systems in ports (where there were no incentives to work more than necessary), and transit toll fees in Mozambique."[‡] In this case, food insecurity was the result of the lack of effective distribution systems and not the lack of food.

The third driver is adverse climates and weather. Indeed, natural disasters, such as floods, hurricanes, typhoons, tsunamis, and droughts, all adversely affect food security. The latter, droughts, have affected numerous regions in Africa by causing crops to fail and livestock to die. For instance, droughts have had a detrimental effect on livestock, which, by consequence, have negatively impacted the income and availability and access to nutritional food in Kenya.[§] Oxfam has provided aid to Kenya by buying their weakest livestock in order to ensure that the owners obtain income before their animals die.[¶] The meat from the livestock is then distributed to the population for food.[**] Ethiopia is also vulnerable to land degradation, climate change, and extreme weather events.[††] In the 1980s, the droughts in Ethiopia devastated the crop harvest. Ultimately, the droughts led to food insecurity. At the time, the Ethiopian government's attention was directed toward the ongoing civil war, and the international community significantly delayed its

---

[*] Peter J. Gregory, John S. I. Ingram, and Michael Brklacich, "Climate Change and Food Security," *Philosophical Transactions of the Royal Society B: Biological Sciences*, 360:1463 (November 29, 2005), 2144.

[†] Ibid., 2144–2145.

[‡] Ibid., 2145.

[§] "East Africa Food Crisis," Oxfam International, http://www.oxfam.org/en/emergencies/east-africa-food-crisis; UK Met Office, "Climate Impacts on Food Security and Nutrition: A Review of Existing Knowledge," Met Office and United Nations World Food Programme's Office for Climate Change, Environment and Disaster Risk Reduction, 2012, http://www.metoffice.gov.uk/media/pdf/k/5/Climate_impacts_on_food_security_and_nutrition.pdf.

[¶] Oxfam International, "East Africa Food Crisis," http://www.oxfam.org/en/emergencies/east-africa-food-crisis.

[**] Ibid.

[††] European Union—Joint Cooperation Strategy for Ethiopia, January 27, 2013, http://www.entwicklung.at/uploads/media/EU_Joint_Cooperation_Strategy_01.pdf.

involvement. When the international community provided food aid and supplies, the Ethiopian government diverted them to its military and not to those in need. Millions of individuals in the region were at risk of starvation because the food production at the time fell short of meeting the demands of the population and food aid did not reach the starving population. In the end, the resulting food crisis claimed the lives of an estimated 1 million people.[*]

The fourth driver is conflict. Conflicts in society affect all dimensions of food security.[†] Conflicts, such as civil wars and mass atrocities, have had an adverse impact on food security by disrupting farming, food supplies, and food distribution. Civil wars and mass atrocities also lead many individuals to leave their homes and in so doing their livelihoods, employment, and access to food. For example, in Mali, thousands have fled their homes due to conflict in the region.[‡]

Grievances are especially pronounced in countries where the wealth and benefits of the export of rich domestic natural resources (such as diamonds and oil) do not translate into great benefits and even food security for all of the population. Often the wealth benefits of these resources are exclusive to an elite class; normally, as a result of widespread and endemic corruption in government positions that control these natural resources.[§] According to Henk-Jan Brinkman and Cullen Hendrix, "[s]ome of the countries most plagued by the conflict during the past 20 years are characterized by widespread hunger, such as Angola, DRC [Democratic Republic of Congo], Papua New Guinea, and Sierra Leone. The mixture of hunger—which creates grievances—and the availability of valuable commodities—which can provide opportunities for rebel funding—is a volatile combination."[¶] Moreover, according to Ban Ki-Moon, the Secretary General of the United Nations, "severe drought and food insecurity in many countries in the Sahel had created the conditions for instability and undermined stabilization efforts."[**] Furthermore, in

---

[*] *BBC News*, "Flashback 1984: Portrait of a Famine," April 6, 2000, http://news.bbc. co.uk/2/hi/africa/703958.stm.

[†] Emmy Simmons, "Harvesting Peace: Food Security, Conflict, and Cooperation," Environmental Change and Security Program, 2013, 37, http://wilsoncenter.org/sites/ default/files/HarvestingPeace.pdf.

[‡] Ibid., 37.

[§] Ibid., 21.

[¶] Henk-Jan Brinkman and Cullen S. Hendrix, "Food Insecurity and Violent Conflict: Causes, Consequences, and Addressing the Challenges," World Food Programme, Occasional Paper No. 24, July 2011, 5–5, http://ucanr.edu/blogs/food2025/blogfiles/ 14415.pdf.

[**] "Security Council Statement Stresses Conflict Prevention in Africa Must Address: Root Causes—Poverty, Poor Governance, Political Exclusion," UN Security Council, SC/10970, http://www.un.org/News/Press/docs/2013/sc10970.doc.htm.

some regions, inequality in the distribution of services and food aid has triggered civil wars. Cases in point are Liberia and Sierra Leone. In fact, in these countries one of the underlying causes of their civil wars was the disparity that existed in the distribution of services and food assistance between cities and rural areas.[*]

Conflict can arise in countries due to the scarcity of resources such as land for agriculture and water resources. Indeed, conflict arises between countries or between groups within society for the control of natural resources, such as food or water.[†] Those suffering from food insecurity may join insurgencies or other groups due to their beliefs that it will improve their situation. Actually, countries that suffer from food insecurity often become breeding grounds for terrorist organizations; for instance, al-Shabaab in Somalia and Tigrayan Peoples' Liberation Front and the Ethiopian Peoples' Revolutionary Democratic Front in Ethiopia. Conflicts in societies also interfere with food distribution by international organizations, such as the UN. For example, terrorist groups often interfere with the international community's effort to provide aid to conflict regions. This was observed in the aftermath of the 2011 drought that devastated East Africa including Ethiopia, Djibouti, Kenya, Somalia, and Uganda. Al-Shabaab prevented humanitarian aid from reaching those affected by the famine.

The fifth driver is food waste. Much of the food that is produced annually is not consumed.[‡] This is extremely problematic given the number of individuals in the world that are hungry and die of starvation. Some countries even have a food surplus. The issue, therefore, is not the lack of food, but its uneven distribution in the world population. The fact that not all food that is produced is consumed also illustrates the waste of another vital resource; namely, water, which is used to produce food. In fact, food security is directly affected by access to and use of natural resources such as water.

The sixth driver of hunger is the increase in food prices. In 2013, it was reported that the global grain reserves had hit critically low levels

---

[*] Woodrow Wilson International Center for Scholars, "Event—Harvesting Peace: Food Security, Conflict, and Cooperation (Report Launch)," Environmental Change and Security Program, September 12, 2013, http://www.wilsoncenter.org/event/harvesting-peace-food-security-conflict-and-cooperation-report-launch.

[†] Emmy Simmons, "Harvesting Peace: Food Security, Conflict, and Cooperation," Environmental Change and Security Program, 2013, 4, http://wilsoncenter.org/sites/default/files/HarvestingPeace.pdf.

[‡] Alexandra Silver, "UN: One-Third of Food Produced for Human Consumption Is Uneaten," Time, May 13, 2011, http://newsfeed.time.com/2011/05/13/un-one-third-of-food-produced-for-human-consumption-is-uneaten/.

TABLE 11.2   African Riots between 2007 and 2008

Guinea	Mozambique	Madagascar
Mauritania	Burkina Faso	Somalia
Morocco	Cote d'Ivoire	Tunisia
Senegal	Ethiopia	Zimbabwe
Cameroon	Egypt	

Source: Julia Berazneva and David R. Lee, "Explaining the African Food Riots of 2007–2008: An Empirical Analysis," CSAE 25th Anniversary Conference 2011: Economic Development in Africa, March 20–22, 2011, 30, St. Catherine's College, Oxford, http://www.csae.ox.ac.uk/conferences/2011-EDiA/papers/711-Berazneva.pdf.

and that rising food prices led to conflicts and unrest in different regions.[*] This, however, was not the first time that rising food prices threatened to create or created conflict. The food riots and demonstrations in several countries in Africa between 2007 and 2008 are a prime example (see Table 11.2). This conflict resulted from the global inflation of food prices, among other governmental and economic issues.[†]

The seventh driver of hunger is population growth. Food production often cannot keep up with the rate of population growth. Ethiopia's food security has been adversely affected by increases in its population.[‡] Food shortages may also be provoked by the influx of individuals who migrate from rural areas to urban centers.

The eighth driver of hunger is illness, which can also affect food security. For instance, HIV/AIDS adversely affects households due to the inevitable increase in healthcare spending, higher demands for care of these infected, and a decrease in work productivity.[§] Consider Swaziland, where "the HIV and AIDS epidemic, along with high income inequality, has severely undermined food security despite [the] growth [experienced] in [its] national income."[¶]

---

[*] John Vidal, "UN Warns of Looming Worldwide Food Crisis in 2013," *The Guardian*, October 13, 2012, http://www.theguardian.com/global-development/2012/oct/14/un-global-food-crisis-warning.

[†] Julia Berazneva and David R. Lee, "Explaining the African Food Riots of 2007–2008: An Empirical Analysis," March 2011, 30, http://www.csae.ox.ac.uk/conferences/2011-EDiA/papers/711-Berazneva.pdf.

[‡] European Union—Joint Cooperation Strategy for Ethiopia, January 27, 2013, http://www.entwicklung.at/uploads/media/EU_Joint_Cooperation_Strategy_01.pdf.

[§] FAO, "The Impact of HIV/AIDS on Food Security," Committee on World Food Security, 27th Session (28 May–1 June 2001), http://www.fao.org/docrep/meeting/003/y0310e.htm#P89_4486.

[¶] International Food Policy Research Institute (IFPRI), "Global, Regional, and National Trends: 2013 Global Hunger Index," http://www.ifpri.org/ghi/2013/global-regional-national-trends?print.

The ninth driver of hunger is inequality. Consider Malawi, where even though food security is a high priority,* existing gender inequality contributes to food insecurity. In fact, in Malawi, women were disadvantaged, having less access to food and water. As Rachel Bezner Kerr has argued, "gender relations affect who suffers more during periods of food shortages."† Unlike women, men have easier access to labor, income, capital and land during natural disasters, emergencies, and conflict situations. In addition, gender inequality exists in reference to the opportunities for women in the workforce; males are often afforded greater work opportunities than women. Also, Kerr's study has revealed that women in Malawi were responsible for caring for sick relatives within and beyond the household, which ultimately affected their income and household food security. This study also showed that women were less likely to receive support from kin in the form of seeds, cash, labor, or food. Additionally, husbands did not always provide their wives with the funds they obtained. Moreover, in Malawi, women commonly engage in informal labor in farms (*ganyu*) for which they are provided meager payment, either food or cash.‡ Unlike women, men can receive higher wages by migrating to other areas for work.§ Kerr's study further demonstrated that no major decision-making powers over major production issues were given to women. What's more, women had unequal access to land and power over its use.

Poor households do not have the funds needed to purchase fertilizer. Households that are poor often have to obtain credit to purchase fertilizer for their soil.¶ Gender inequalities also exist in the ability to obtain credit; men are more likely than women to obtain credit to

---

* Monica Fisher and Paul A. Lewin, "Household, Community, and Policy Determinants of Food Insecurity in Rural Malawi," *Development Southern Africa* 30:4–5 (2013), 451–467.

† Rachel Bezner Kerr, "Food Security in Northern Malawi: Gender, Kinship Relations and Entitlements in Historical Context," *Journal of Southern African Studies* 31:1 (2005), 61.

‡ John McCracken, "Planters, Peasants and the Colonial State: The Impact of the Native Tobacco Board in the Central Province of Malawi," *Journal of Southern African Studies* 9:2 (1982), 186; Martin Whiteside, "Ganyu Labour in Malawi and Its Implications for Livelihood Security Interventions: An Analysis of Recent Literature and Implications for Poverty Alleviation," *Agricultural Research and Extension Network Paper* 99 (2000), 1; Rachel Bezner Kerr, "Food Security in Northern Malawi: Gender, Kinship Relations and Entitlements in Historical Context," *Journal of Southern African Studies* 31:1 (2005), 58.

§ Rachel Bezner Kerr, "Food Security in Northern Malawi: Gender, Kinship Relations and Entitlements in Historical Context," *Journal of Southern African Studies* 31:1 (2005), 58.

¶ Ibid., 60.

purchase fertilizer.* Given the inability to obtain credit, women engage in *ganyu* at other farms in order to obtain funds to purchase fertilizer; however, this provides them with low wages or food as remuneration.† By engaging in *ganyu*, women limit their ability to work on their own farms. Food insecurity in Malawi is thus primarily attributed to a lack of entitlements (e.g., wages, soil fertility, labor, etc.) of women.‡ Despite these limitations, women have a greater role in providing for the household and are expected to feed their families during natural disasters, emergencies, and conflict situations; even though they had fewer means to do so.

Dealing with Food Insecurity

Food insecurity may result from the lack of an effective agriculture industry, the growth in population, extreme weather conditions or natural disasters, climate change, soil degradation, water scarcity, poverty, conflict, terrorism, war, trade imbalances, increases in food prices, food waste, illnesses, and inequality.§ To effectively deal with food insecurity, the drivers of global hunger need to be addressed. For example, since poverty can cause food insecurity, measures should be put in place that seek to eradicate poverty, as this can improve individuals' access to food. Therefore, to effectively deal with food insecurity, measures need to be taken that will provide immediate assistance to those most vulnerable to hunger, such as enabling short- and long-term sustainable food security, agricultural development, and nutritional programs to alleviate the root causes of hunger.

The vulnerabilities of food systems to climate change can be reduced by increasing food production, improving food distribution, and increasing economic access to food.¶ Funding is also needed to assist those in farming that do not have the necessary funds and resources. According to Rajendra Prasad, the primary way to alleviate hunger is improving

---

* Ibid., 61.

† Pauline E. Peters, "Failed Magic or Social Context? Market Liberalization and the Rural Poor in Malawi," *Development Discussion Paper 562* (Cambridge, MA: Harvard Institute for International Development, 1996), 17.

‡ Rachel Bezner Kerr, "Food Security in Northern Malawi: Gender, Kinship Relations and Entitlements in Historical Context," *Journal of Southern African Studies* 31:1 (2005), 61.

§ 1996 Rome Declaration on World Food Security, http://www.fao.org/docrep/003/w3613e/w3613e00.htm.

¶ Peter J. Gregory, John S. I. Ingram, and Michael Brklacich, "Climate Change and Food Security," *Philosophical Transactions: Biological Sciences* 360:1463 (November 29, 2005), 2139–2148.

agriculture in developing countries and those in transition.[*] For example, farmers have been able to use fertilizer nitrogen to grow crops on the lands that would have been left uncultivated due to the reduced soil fertility.[†] Pesticides have also been used to prevent crops from being lost to insects, other pests, diseases, and weeds.[‡] However, the overuse of fertilizer nitrogen results in the pollution of surface and groundwater making such water toxic to marine life and the overuse of pesticides has been found to be harmful to humans.[§] When used in proper amounts, these can help aid food security efforts. In fact, effective and efficient use of fertilizer and agrochemicals and the prevention of their overuse has been promoted as a way to ensure sufficient food production and alleviate hunger.[¶]

Food insecurity can also be minimized by improving the agricultural and transportation infrastructure. In addition, existing crops in regions have provided insight into sustainable farming. For example, many farmers in African countries have over-farmed soils and are unable to purchase fertilizer. Given these conditions, they often plant *Oryza glaberrima* (or *O. glaberrima*) on their weaker soils; this type of rice (also known as African Rice) is highly adaptable to adverse climates, poor soils, and weedy conditions.[**] Moreover, assistance needs to be provided to better enable farmers to deal with changing climate conditions. Furthermore, land needs to be managed more effectively and water needs to be used more efficiently. These agricultural developments aid in food production and help to alleviate hunger in different parts of the world. In line with this, the 2009 L'Aquila Food Security Initiative called for a comprehensive approach in investing in agriculture to ensure food security in

---

[*] Rajendra Prasad, "Population Growth, Food Shortages and Ways to Alleviate Hunger," *Current Science* 105:1 (July 10, 2013), 32, http://www.currentscience.ac.in/Volumes/105/01/0032.pdf.

[†] Ibid.

[‡] Ibid.; Ibrahim Y. Dugje, Friday Ekeleme, Alpha Y. Kamara, Lucky O. Omoigui, Amare Tegbaru, Issa A. Teli, and Johnson E. Onyibe, "Guide to Safe and Effective Use of Pesticides for Crop Production," Canadian International Development Agency, April 2008, http://old.iita.org/cms/articlefiles/92-Pesticide%20guide%20web%20final.pdf.

[§] Clifford S. Synder, "Nutrient and Hypoxia in the Gulf of Mexico—An Update on Progress," *Better Crops* 92 (2008), 16–22; S. B. Mittal, Raj Kumar Jhorar, Konrad Miegel, Guru Prem, and A. K. Kapoor, "Nitrate Contamination in Haryana—Is Nitrogen Fertilizer Responsible," *Indian Journal of Fertilisers* 5 (2009), 55–62; Rajendra Prasad, "Population Growth, Food Shortages and Ways to Alleviate Hunger," *Current Science* 105:1 (July 10, 2013), 33, http://www.currentscience.ac.in/Volumes/105/01/0032.pdf.

[¶] Rajendra Prasad, "Population Growth, Food Shortages and Ways to Alleviate Hunger," *Current Science* 105:1 (July 10, 2013), 35, http://www.currentscience.ac.in/Volumes/105/01/0032.pdf.

[**] Paul Richards, "The History and Future of African Rice: Food Security and Survival in a West African War Zone," *Africa Spectrum* 41:1 (2006), 79.

countries, maintaining food security commitments around the globe, and seeking to advance efforts in promoting worldwide food security.[*]

Another measure that is used to promote food security around the globe is aid. Nonprofit organizations, such as Oxfam, have supplied Somalia with therapeutic feeding centers, water systems, support for farmers, and public health communications.[†] The distribution of food in the event of an emergency is only a temporary solution. At times, those that have sought to distribute food supplies and aid to people in regions that need them the most have been unable to do so. A prime example of this is Somalia. Somalia is one of the most difficult places in the world to deliver aid.[‡] On occasion, food aid became a "source of competition, diversion, and manipulation" in certain regions. In such situations, "[t]o prevent losses, food aid transporters were required to pay a deposit equal to the value of the food in order to ensure its arrival at the intended destination... [Nonetheless,] [f]ears about the loss or diversion of food aid ma[d]e donors more wary and access by agencies more difficult."[§]

Some external intervention has also been found to be detrimental in the long run. For example, increased imports of food and free distribution of food are meant to be a temporary solution to an acute food shortage. The ultimate goal of food aid is to help the region rebound and be subsequently self-sufficient in respect to food supply and distribution, and the development of an agricultural infrastructure. Sometimes, the short-term solutions have competed with local food production and distribution, thus adversely impacting local livelihoods due to the loss of income sustained. To ensure the sustainability of food security, the emphasis of measures, investments, and aid should be on the self-reliance of local farmers.

Several international agencies and nongovernmental organizations (NGOs) deal with food security. Two main international agencies that seek to provide transnational food security are the World Food Programme (WFP) and the FAO. The WFP is the main agency that is responsible for providing food assistance during emergency situations

---

[*] "2012 L'Aquila Food Security Initiative Final Report 2012," Department of State, http://www.state.gov/s/global foodsecurity/rls/rpt/laquila/index.htm.

[†] "East Africa Food Crisis," Oxfam International, http://www.oxfam.org/en/emergencies/east-africa-food-crisis.

[‡] Ibid.

[§] International Federation of Red Cross and Red Crescent Societies (IFRC), *World Disasters Report 2011: Focus on Hunger and Malnutrition* (Geneva, Switzerland, 2011), 127–128, http://ifrc.org/PageFiles/89755/Photos/307000-WDR-2011-FINAL-email-1.pdf; Emmy Simmons, "Harvesting Peace: Food Security, Conflict, and Cooperation," Environmental Change and Security Program, 2013, 13, http://wilsoncenter.org/sites/default/files/HarvestingPeace.pdf.

and to countries in need.* This food assistance is organized by the Central Emergency Response Fund. The FAO is an international agency that collects, maintains, and disseminates comprehensive information on global food consumption.†

Other strategies that have been promoted by international agencies and NGOs that seek to maximize the availability of adequate and nutritional types of food include: reducing food waste; enabling income generation; providing education on nutrition; and introducing new crops into the regions.‡ For example, in the Horn of Africa, nongovernmental organizations, such as Oxfam, have provided clean and safe water, sought to improve sanitation and public health, attempted to rebuild livelihoods, increased access to food, markets, and services, and promoted long-term approaches to dealing with existing and future food crises.§

Since food insecurity contributes to conflict, influential agencies, such as the United States Agency for International Development (USAID), have sought to improve individuals' access to food and increase the availability of food to those in conflict and post-conflict societies. The goal of USAID is to ensure that individuals have consistent access to food in these regions. The United States has also created a program known as Feed the Future to ensure food security in particular countries (see Table 11.3). This program, which is led by USAID, targets 19 countries that experience food insecurity and conflict.¶ The agencies involved with

TABLE 11.3   Feed the Future Countries

Bangladesh	Haiti	Mali	Tajikistan
Cambodia	Honduras	Mozambique	Tanzania
Ethiopia	Kenya	Nepal	Uganda
Ghana	Liberia	Senegal	Zambia
Guatemala	Malawi		

Source: "Countries," Feed the Future, http://www.feedthefuture.gov/countries.

---

* "Mission Statement," World Food Programme, http://www.wfp.org/about/mission-statement.

† "About FAO," Food and Agriculture Organization of the United Nations, http://www.fao.org/about/en/.

‡ Food and Agriculture Organization of the United Nations, "Promotion of Food and Dietary Diversification Strategies to Enhance and Sustain Household Food Security," In Agriculture Food and Nutrition for Africa, 1997, http://www.fao.org/docrep/w0078e/w0078e06.htm.

§ "East Africa Food Crisis," Oxfam International, http://www.oxfam.org/en/emergencies/east-africa-food-crisis.

¶ Emmy Simmons, "Harvesting Peace: Food Security, Conflict, and Cooperation," Environmental Change and Security Program, 2013, 5, http://wilsoncenter.org/sites/default/files/HarvestingPeace.pdf.

Feed the Future* work with governments to develop their agricultural sector and break the cycle of poverty and hunger.†

Chronic food insecurity "can be overcome with…typical long term development measures also used to address poverty, such as education or access to productive resources…They may also need more direct access to food to enable them to raise their productive capacity."‡ By contrast, transient (acute) food insecurity "is relatively unpredictable and can emerge suddenly. This makes planning and programming more difficult and requires different capacities and types of intervention, including early warning capacity."§ With respect to the latter, measures have been (and should continue to be) sought to strengthen national and international capacity to detect early warning signs of food insecurity. However, early warning is only possible if appropriate and complete information is available. One type of early warning measure that provides up-to-date and accurate information about food security is the Global Information and Early Warning System on Food and Agriculture (GIEWS).¶ Specifically, the GIEWS

> warns of imminent food crises, so that timely interventions can be planned and suffering avoided…monitors food supply and demand in all countries of the world on a continuous basis,…..compiles and analyzes information on global production, stocks, trade and food aid; monitors export prices and developments on main grain exchanges; [and] reacts to man-made or natural disasters by sending rapid evaluation missions to the countries affected and issuing Special Alerts/ Reports that are quickly disseminated to the international community.**

Other early warning measures include: database and mapping systems; data analysis tools; and methodologies and initiatives for food

---

* These agencies include USAID, the Millennium Challenge Corporation, Overseas Private Investment Corporation, U.S. Department of Agriculture, U.S. Department of State, Peace Corps, U.S. Department of Treasury, U.S. Trade Representative, and the U.S. African Development Foundation.
† "About," Feed the Future, http://www.feedthefuture.gov/about.
‡ EC—FAO Food Security Programme. "An Introduction to the Basic Concepts of Food Security." Food Security Information for Action: Practical Guides, 2008, 1, http:// www.fao.org/docrep/013/al936e/al936e00.pdf.
§ Ibid.
¶ "Global Information and Early Warning System on Food and Agriculture (GIEWS)," Food and Agriculture Organization of the United Nations, 3, http://www.fao.org/ giews/english/giews_en.pdf.
** Ibid., 3.

security analysis.* The GIEWS is an example of a database and mapping system. Another example is CountryStat, which includes national and subnational information on food and agriculture.† The FAO developed two data analysis tools, the National Basic Food Price—Data and Analysis Tool and the FAO Agri-Market, to analyze and monitor market data. Another tool that has been created is the Crop Monitoring and Forecasting Tool. This tool analyzes information about the weather and assesses its impact on crop production.‡ Another tool, the Climate Change Impact Tool, assesses the impact of climate change on agriculture.§ Furthermore, an example of an initiative for food security analysis is the Food Insecurity and Vulnerability Information and Mapping Systems (FIVIMS). The FIVIMS involves a "collaborative effort of the major United Nations agencies charged with responsibility for organizing and monitoring international programs for children... food, and agriculture."¶ In addition to these measures, other international organizations and NGOs monitor food availability in the countries and regions where they operate.

The Right to Food and the Right to Be Free from Hunger

Governments are required to provide their populations with access to sufficient food. The right to food and the right to be free from hunger are enshrined in international law and human rights instruments. For example, this right to food is included in the 1948 Universal Declaration of Human Rights and the 1966 International Covenant on Economic, Social and Cultural Rights.** Specifically, Article 25(1) of the Universal

---

* Paolo Romano, "Data Management and Mapping Tools and Systems for Food Security," Support to the EC Programme on Linking Information and Decision-Making to Improve Food Security for Selected Greater Mekong Sub-Regional Countries, June 2010, http://www.foodsec.org/fileadmin/user_upload/eufao-fsi4dm/docs/Romano%20Lao%20PDR%20Food%20Security%20Data%20Management%20Requirement%20Analysis%20and%20Technical%20Capacity%20Assessment.pdf.

† CountryStat, https://countrystat.org/; Ibid., v.

‡ FAO, "Crop Monitoring and Forecasting," http://www.fao.org/nr/climpag/aw_3_en.asp; Paolo Romano, "Data Management and Mapping Tools and Systems for Food Security," Support to the EC Programme on Linking Information and Decision-Making to Improve Food Security for Selected Greater Mekong Sub-Regional Countries, June 2010, v, http://www.foodsec.org/fileadmin/user_upload/eufao-fsi4dm/docs/Romano%20Lao%20PDR%20Food%20Security%20Data%20Management%20Requirement%20Analysis%20and%20Technical%20Capacity%20Assessment.pdf.

§ Ibid., v.

¶ Ibid., vi; Ezzeddine Boutrif, "Establishing a Food Insecurity and Vulnerability Information and Mapping System," FAO, http://www.fao.org/docrep/w5849t/w5849t09.htm.

** Entry into force January 3, 1976.

Declaration of Human Rights (UDHR) states that "[e]veryone has the right to a standard of living adequate for the health and well-being of himself and of his family, including food, clothing, housing and medical care and necessary social services." Likewise, Article 11(1) of the International Covenant on Economic, Social and Cultural Rights (ICESCR) includes "the right of everyone to an adequate standard of living for himself and his family, including adequate food, clothing and housing, and to the continuous improvement of living conditions." Pursuant to Article 11(2), the ICESCR also established "the fundamental right of everyone to be free from hunger." Article 11(2) further included a country's responsibility in ensuring that this right is respected. Particularly, countries are, pursuant to Article 11(2)(a), required "[t]o improve methods of production, conservation and distribution of food by making full use of technical and scientific knowledge, by disseminating knowledge of the principles of nutrition and by developing or reforming agrarian systems in such a way as to achieve the most efficient development and utilization of natural resources." Additionally, Article 11(2)(b) holds that countries are required "to ensure [that] an equitable distribution of world food supplies [exists] in relation to need."

General Comment No. 12 of the UN Committee on Economic, Social and Cultural Rights (CESCR) explained the right to adequate food under Article 11 of the ICESCR.* In particular, paragraph 6 of General Comment No. 12 of the CESCR stated that "[t]he right to adequate food is realized when every man, woman and child, alone or in community with others, have physical and economic access at all times to adequate food or means for its procurement." In addition, paragraph 7 of General Comment No. 12 of the CESCR further stated that food availability and accessibility should be sustainable; here, "[t]he notion of sustainability is intrinsically linked to the notion of adequate food or food security, implying food being accessible for both present and future generations." Moreover, paragraph 8 of General Comment No. 12 of the CESCR clarified what "adequate food" refers to: "[t]he availability of food in a quantity and quality sufficient to satisfy the dietary needs of individuals, free from adverse substances, and acceptable within a given culture." Furthermore, paragraph 14 of General Comment No. 12 of the CESCR delineated the responsibilities of the state "ensur[ing] for everyone under its jurisdiction access to the minimum essential food which is

---

* UN Committee on Economic, Social and Cultural Rights (CESCR), General Comment No. 12: The Right to Adequate Food (Art. 11 of the Covenant), 12 May 1999, http://www.refworld.org/docid/4538838c11.html.

sufficient, nutritionally adequate and safe, to ensure their freedom from hunger." The ICESCR is thus violated if a country "fails to ensure the satisfaction of, at the very least, the minimum essential level required to be free from hunger."*

The rights of women and children with respect to food are enshrined in the 1979 Convention on the Elimination of All Forms of Discrimination Against Women (CEDAW)† and the 1989 Convention on the Rights of the Child (CRC),‡ respectively. The Preamble to the CEDAW states that women in situations of poverty should have access to food. Article 12(2) of CEDAW further states that women should have access to "adequate nutrition during pregnancy and lactation." With respect to children, Article 24(2)(c) of the CRC seeks to combat malnutrition. It also includes the responsibility of countries in implementing measures that provide children with nutritious foods. Another part of the Convention that relates to food security is Article 27(1) of the CRC. Specifically, this article "recognize[s] the right of every child to a standard of living adequate for the child's physical, mental, spiritual, moral and social development." This article relates to food security given the impact of food on a child's development.

The rights of those with disabilities with regard to food are included in the 2006 Convention on the Rights of Persons with Disabilities (CRPD).§ Particularly, under Article 28(1) of the CRPD, countries are required to "recognize the right of persons with disabilities to an adequate standard of living for themselves and their families, including adequate food, clothing and housing, and to the continuous improvement of living conditions, and shall take appropriate steps to safeguard and promote the realization of this right without discrimination on the basis of disability." Article 25(f) of the CRPD also includes a provision to prevent the discriminatory withholding of food on the basis of disability. In fact, on the whole, discriminatory withholding of food is considered unjustified. Indeed, paragraph 18 of General Comment No. 12 of the UN Committee on Economic, Social and Cultural Rights (CESCR) held that "any discrimination in access to food, as well as to means and entitlements for its procurement, on the grounds of race, color, sex, language, age, religion, political or other opinion, national or social origin, property, birth or other status...constitutes a violation of the Covenant."

---

* Paragraph 17 of General Comment No. 12 of the CESCR.
† Entry into force September 3, 1981.
‡ Entry into force September 2, 1990.
§ Entry into force May 3, 2008.

WATER SECURITY

Water is the most vital life-sustaining resource. The security of this life-sustaining resource is thus paramount. Water security refers to "the capacity of a population to safeguard sustainable access to adequate quantities of acceptable quality water for sustaining livelihoods, human well-being,* and socio-economic development, for ensuring protection against water-borne pollution and water-related disasters, and for preserving ecosystems in a climate of peace and political stability."†

Available literature on water security refers to water poverty, water stress, and water scarcity. Water poverty refers to "the condition of not having access to sufficient water, or water of an adequate quality, to meet one's basic needs."‡ According to the UN, water poverty exists when available water resources are below 1000 cubics per individual per annum.§ By way of extension, "water stress occurs when the demand for water exceeds the available amount during a certain period or when poor quality restricts its use."¶ Water stress encompasses both the quantitative and qualitative deterioration of water.** Quantitatively, existing water resources are being depleted (e.g., overexploitation of aquifers). Qualitatively, existing water sources are safe for use (e.g., unpolluted).

Water scarcity (or water shortage) is the condition that exists when available water resources cannot meet the demand for water in an area. More specifically, according to the United Nations, "[w]ater scarcity is defined as the point at which the aggregate impact of all users impinges on the supply or quality of water under prevailing institutional arrangements to the extent that the demand by all sectors, including

---

* "Human well-being has multiple constituents, including basic material for a good life, freedom of choice and action, health, good social relations, and security," Food and Agriculture Organization of the United Nations. "Key Definitions: Well-Being," Millennium Ecosystem Assessment, 2005, http://www.fao.org/nr/kagera/tools-and-methods/key-defintions/en/.

† UNESCO-IHP, "(Draft) Strategic Plan of the 8th Phase of IHP," International Hydrological Programme, 20th Session of the Intergovernmental Council (Paris, June 4–7, 2012), http://unesdoc.unesco.org/images/0021/002164/216434e.pdf; UN Water, "Water Security & the Global Water Agenda: A UN-Water Analytical Brief," United Nations University, 2013, vi, http://www.unwater.org/downloads/watersecurity_analyticalbrief.pdf.

‡ Oxford Dictionaries, "Water Poverty," http://www.oxforddictionaries.com/us/definition/american_english/water-poverty.

§ Stephen Nortcliff, Gemma Carr, Robert B. Potter, and Khadija Darmame, "Jordan's Water Resources: Challenges for the Future," Geographical Paper No. 185, 2008, 8, http://www.reading.ac.uk/web/FILES/geographyandenvironmentalscience/GP185.pdf

¶ "Water Stress," European Environment Agency, http://www.eea.europa.eu/themes/water/wise-help-centre/glossary-definitions/water-stress.

** Ibid.

TABLE 11.4   Most Water Stressed Countries in the World

Bahrain	United Arab Emirates
Qatar	Yemen
Kuwait	Saudi Arabia
Libya	Oman
Djibouti	Egypt

Source: "Water Stress Index 2012: New Products and Analysis," Maplecroft, http://maplecroft.com/about/news/water_stress_index_2012.html.

the environment, cannot be satisfied fully."[*] The United Nations further noted that "[w]ater scarcity is both a natural and a human-made phenomenon. There is enough freshwater on the planet for 7 billion people but it is distributed unevenly and too much of it is wasted, polluted and unsustainably managed."[†] Kuwait, Bahrain, Qatar, and the United Arab Emirates, among other countries, are faced with water shortages.[‡]

Attempts have been made to measure water scarcity. A case in point is the Water Stress Index (WSI) developed by Maplecroft.[§] The WSI is determined "by calculating the ratio of domestic, industrial and agricultural water consumption, against renewable supplies of water from precipitation, rivers and groundwater."[¶] In 2012, 10 countries in the Middle East and North Africa out of a total 186 countries evaluated, were ranked as the most water stressed countries in the world (see Table 11.4). Among the many countries that were evaluated, India was ranked as a "high risk" country.[**] Furthermore, the United States was classified as a "medium risk" country; however, certain states (i.e., Arizona, California, Kansas, Nebraska, New Mexico, and Texas) were classified as "high risk" and "extremely high risk" due to their depletion of groundwater resources.[††]

---

[*] "International Decade for Action 'Water for Life' 2005–2015," Water Scarcity, United Nations, http://www.un.org/waterforlifedecade/scarcity.shtml.

[†] Ibid.

[‡] Mohamed J. Abdulrazzak, Mey Jurdi, and Shiraz Basma, "The Role of Desalination in Meeting Water Supply Demands in Western Asia," *Water International* 27:3 (2002), 397.

[§] Other measures of water scarcity also exist.

[¶] "Water Stress Index: New Products and Analysis," Maplecroft, http://maplecroft.com/about/news/water_stress _index.html.

[**] "Water Stress Index 2012: New Products and Analysis," http://maplecroft.com/about/news/water_stress_index_2012.html.

[††]Ibid.

Drivers of Water Scarcity

There are four main drivers to water scarcity. The first is population growth.[*] Indeed, growing populations contribute to the declining availability of water, due to the inevitable increase in the demand for and consumption of water and decrease in the availability of water per person. Population growth also leads to an increase in food consumption and agricultural production. Agricultural production relies heavily on water; in fact, the majority of water is utilized in agricultural production.[†] Accordingly, water scarcity adversely impacts food availability.

The second driver of water scarcity is changes in consumer, industrial, government, and agricultural behaviors. This encompasses behavior that overexploits and overuses available water resources.[‡] For consumers, this type of behavior can include buying bottled mineral water.[§] For governments, this includes the country's mismanagement of groundwater resources by overexploitation of them. Most notable is the case of India, where the overuse of groundwater resources is currently unsustainable and has resulted in a critical depletion of existing water.[¶]

The third driver of water scarcity is the deterioration of the existing quality of water. Here, contaminated water reduces the availability of usable water.[**] Contaminated water has devastating human health and agricultural consequences. Countries in the Arabian Peninsula can draw water from groundwater aquifers. However, the groundwater reserves in the region are limited in capacity for storage and use, especially in regards to meeting the increased demands for water in the region.[††] In addition, the quality of the water in these aquifers has deteriorated.[‡‡] The

---

[*] Peter H. Gleick, "Water in Crisis: Paths to Sustainable Water Use," *Ecological Applications* 8:3 (August 1998), 574.

[†] "Briefing: Water Scarcity," UNEP, September 2011, http://www.unep.org/research4policy/Portals/24104/KNOSSOS%20POLICY%20PAPER%20MAIN%20BRIEFING-16sept_PHILLIP.pdf.

[‡] Mohamed J. Abdulrazzak, Mey Jurdi, and Shiraz Basma, "The Role of Desalination in Meeting Water Supply Demands in Western Asia," *Water International* 27:3 (2002), 403.

[§] European Environment Agency, "Water Resources across Europe—Confronting Water Scarcity and Drought," EEA Report No. 2/2009, European Environment Agency, 2009, 5.

[¶] Water Papers, "India Groundwater Governance: Case Study," 2011, http://www.groundwatergovernance.org/fileadmin/user_upload/groundwatergovernance/docs/Country_studies/GWGovernanceIndia.pdf; Paul Wyrwoll, "India's Groundwater Crisis," Global Water Forum, July 30, 2012, http://www.globalwaterforum.org/2012/07/30/indias-groundwater-crisis/comment-page-1/.

[**] Peter H. Gleick, "Water in Crisis: Paths to Sustainable Water Use," *Ecological Applications* 8:3 (August 1998), 574.

[††] Mohamed J. Abdulrazzak, Mey Jurdi, and Shiraz Basma, "The Role of Desalination in Meeting Water Supply Demands in Western Asia," *Water International* 27:3 (2002), 395.

[‡‡] Ibid.

lack of quality water exists in other regions as well. In fact, the majority of individuals without access to clean water are in Asia.[*] In certain countries, sewage, poisons, and harmful chemicals have been dumped into bodies of water, such as rivers and lakes.

The fourth and final driver of water scarcity is climate change and variability.[†] In Ethiopia, extreme weather events have had an adverse impact on the water supply. In addition, arid and semiarid environments have detrimental effects on water resources. These effects are particularly pronounced in countries that are located in the Arabian Peninsula that have harsh climates. The water supplies of other countries have also been negatively impacted by extreme weather conditions. For example, Israel has faced many droughts; each of which adversely impacted Israel's water reserves.

Water Conflicts

Water, as a vital and valuable resource, often leads to conflicts between societies. Water scarcity also played a role in the conflict in Darfur.[‡] Countries sharing transboundary water resources are particularly vulnerable to conflict because of the fear that countries sharing the resource might overuse it. Indeed, one country's use of the resource impacts the availability of the resource to other countries that use it. Conflicts in relation to water uses include: conflicts concerning the distribution of water resources (e.g., the amount consumed); conflicts concerning the relative distribution of water resources (e.g., the amount of water that is used for energy generation); and conflicts concerning pollution or degradation of water resources.[§] Conflicts are pronounced among societies that share water resources. A case in point is the prolonged conflict between Israelis and Palestinians concerning the allocation of land currently

---

[*] United Nations Development Report, "Beyond Scarcity: Power, Poverty and the Global Water Crisis," Summary: Human Development Report, 2006, http://www.cooperazioneallosviluppo.esteri.it/pdgcs/italiano/speciali/acqua/Pdf/Undp_Rapporto_2006.pdf.

[†] Peter H. Gleick, "Water in Crisis: Paths to Sustainable Water Use," *Ecological Applications* 8:3 (August 1998), 574.

[‡] Lydia Polgreen, "A Godsend for Darfur, or a Curse?" *New York Times*, July 22, 2007, http://www.nytimes.com/2007/07/22/weekinreview/22polgreen.html?pagewanted=all&_r=0.

[§] Stephan Libiszewski, "International Conflicts over Freshwater Resources," In Mohamed Suliman (Ed.), *Ecology, Politics & Violent Conflict* (London: ZedBooks, 1995), 55; Simon A. Mason, "From Conflict to Cooperation in the Nile Basin," Dissertation for Ph.D. in Sciences, Swiss Federal Institute of Technology Zurich, 2003, http://www.css.ethz.ch/publications/pdfs/From_Conflict_to_Cooperation.pdf.

belonging to Israel.[*] Each side believes that the land is theirs for religious and historical reasons. Water in the contested territories is also scarce. The conflict, therefore, also includes a fight for water resources.

In some countries, the right to use water is tied to the ownership of land.[†] For example, in Yemen, common water resources are being accessed and utilized by private persons who can access it from their own lands.[‡] Between countries, the rights and allocations of water from transboundary water systems are often disputed. Consider transboundary rivers—differing perspectives exist on the rights of use of transboundary rivers between those countries that are upstream and those that are downstream. More specifically,

> upstream users generally tend to favor the 'doctrine of absolute sovereignty', which maintains the absolute right of a sovereign to use the waters flowing through its territory, whereas downstream users, where water development schemes have the longest history, tend to favor allocation based on the "doctrine of absolute riverine integrity," which holds that all riparian territories have a right to use, undegraded, the waters naturally in their province.[§]

The Jordan River is an example of a transboundary river. Israel, Jordan, Lebanon, Syria, and the West Bank are located within or border the Jordan River basin. Thus, these countries compete for this limited water resource. Shared transboundary aquifers have also been a source of contention (e.g., the mountain and coastal aquifers shared by the Israelis and Palestinians).[¶]

Previous water sharing arrangements, such as the U.S. Johnston plan of the 1950s and the Yarmouk River Proposal in the 1970s, have failed. Despite this and other failures in water sharing agreement attempts, there have been some successful water sharing arrangements. Consider India and Pakistan—where conflict arose between the two countries over water resources. To resolve the conflict, a water sharing agreement, the Indus Waters Treaty of 1960, which was mediated by the World Bank,

---

[*] For more information about the conflict, see Marie-Helen Maras, *Counterterrorism* (Burlington, MA: Jones & Bartlett, 2012), 323–328.

[†] V. Ratna Reddy, "Water Security and Management: Lessons from South Africa," *Economic and Political Weekly* 37:28 (July 13–19, 2002), 2879.

[‡] Gerhard Lichtenthaeler "Water Conflict and Cooperation in Yemen," *Middle East Research and Information Project*, MER 254:40 (Spring 2010), http://www.merip.org/mer/mer254/water-conflict-cooperation-yemen.

[§] Mark F. Giordano, Meredith A. Giordano, and Aaron T. Wolf, "International Resource Conflict and Mitigation," *Journal of Peace Research* 42:1 (2005), 56.

[¶] David Brooks and Julie Trottier, "Confronting Water in an Israeli–Palestinian Peace Agreement," *Journal of Hydrology* 382 (2010) 103–114.

was subsequently created and agreed upon. This treaty is considered to be one of the most successful water sharing agreements to date.

International measures have also been implemented to improve the sharing of transboundary water resources; notably, the UN General Assembly Resolution on the Law of Transboundary Aquifers.[*] This resolution promotes the creation of bilateral and regional arrangements to appropriately manage transboundary aquifers and control the pollution of shared aquifers.[†] The need for proper management of transboundary aquifers was reiterated in UN General Assembly Resolution 66/104 (2011).[‡] Cooperation in the use of water resources provides a sound and solid basis for existing and future peace negotiations.[§]

Dealing with Water Insecurity

To overcome existing and future water insecurity, the drivers of water scarcity need to be addressed. This encompasses improving agricultural practice, reducing domestic and industrial demand, and expanding the existing water supply.[¶] It also includes mitigating the effects of natural disasters, climate change and variation, and reducing existing and further pollution and contamination of water. These objectives were included in the EU Water Framework Directive (Directive 2000/60/EC). Other short-term and long-term goals that can be implemented to ensure water security include "agricultural development [that takes the scarcity of water resources into account], capacity building, water pricing, reduction of subsidies, development and application of appropriate technology, and an enhanced institutional infrastructure, which is capable of formulating and managing complex water policies."[**] Oxfam has worked towards implementing some of these goals. Specifically, in the Horn of Africa, Oxfam has provided clean and safe water.[††] It has also assisted communities in Ethiopia by building more efficient and sustainable

---

[*] Resolution adopted by the General Assembly on 11 December 2008 [on the report of the 6th Committee (A/63/439)] UN General Assembly Resolution 63/124.

[†] Ibid.

[‡] Resolution adopted by the General Assembly on 9 December 2011 [on the report of the 6th Committee (A/66/477)] UN General Assembly Resolution 66/104.

[§] Wouter Meindertsma, Wilfried G. J. H. M. van Sark, and Clive Lipchin, "Renewable Energy Fueled Desalination in Israel," *Desalination and Water Treatment* 13:1–3 (2010), 462.

[¶] Rudolf Baten and Karen Stummeyer, "How Sustainable Can Desalination Be?" *Desalination and Water Treatment* 51:1–3 (2013), 44.

[**] Mohamed J. Abdulrazzak, Mey Jurdi, and Shiraz Basma, "The Role of Desalination in Meeting Water Supply Demands in Western Asia," *Water International* 27:3 (2002), 405.

[††] "East Africa Food Crisis," Oxfam International, http://www.oxfam.org/en/emergencies/east-africa-food-crisis.

sources of water.* Oxfam further provided water supplies to those who were far removed from water resources.†

Cooperation and coordination of policies within and between countries is an essential element for an efficient and effective water management system worldwide. For better water management, more rainwater should be harvested and seepage losses in canals should be reduced.‡ Water management can only improve the efficiency of water use. It cannot, however, increase the country's water supply. To increase water supplies, desalination has been used. Desalination is a long-established method used to make freshwater. Israel has been able to increase its water production and availability despite the country's limited natural water resources. Israel has not only continued to seek to increase its recycling of water (e.g., by recycling wastewater), but also to increase its desalination capacity. Desalination in Israel relies mainly on seawater. The desalination of seawater and brackish water§ occurs in other countries as well, such as Saudi Arabia, United Arab Emirates, Kuwait, and Jordan.

The introduction of desalinated water into existing water supplies helps improve the quality of the water. As Wouter Meindertsma, Wilfried van Sark, and Clive Lipchin have noted, "[b]y blending the high quality water from the desalination plants with the lower quality water from conventional water resources, the hardness and the nitrate levels of the water decrease."¶ One main disadvantage of desalinated water is that its production requires significant energy resources.** Indeed, "[e]nergy costs represent a major portion of the total cost of the desalination process."†† In fact, "desalinated seawater consumes much more energy than the extraction of water from conventional sources in Israel, such as the Lake of Galilee."‡‡ Attempts, however, have been made to make desalination plants more energy efficient. Another disadvantage is that desalination technology is

---

* Ibid.
† Ibid.
‡ Rajendra Prasad, "Population Growth, Food Shortages and Ways to Alleviate Hunger," *Current Science* 105:1 (July 10, 2013), 35, http://www.currentscience.ac.in/Volumes/105/01/0032.pdf.
§ Brackish water has more salinity than freshwater, but less salinity than seawater.
¶ Wouter Meindertsma, Wilfried G. J. H. M. van Sark, and Clive Lipchin, "Renewable Energy Fueled Desalination in Israel," *Desalination and Water Treatment* 13:1–3 (2010), 453.
** Energy security will be examined in the next chapter, Chapter 12.
†† Mohamed J. Abdulrazzak, Mey Jurdi, and Shiraz Basma, "The Role of Desalination in Meeting Water Supply Demands in Western Asia," *Water International* 27:3 (2002), 403.
‡‡ Wouter Meindertsma, Wilfried G. J. H. M. van Sark, and Clive Lipchin, "Renewable Energy Fueled Desalination in Israel," *Desalination and Water Treatment* 13:1–3 (2010), 455.

expensive; so too is its maintenance and use. At present, desalination costs cannot be easily sustained by countries.

Apart from desalination, other measures can be implemented to alleviate water insecurity in regions: the "further[ing of] surface water development from dams, mining of groundwater, tertiary wastewater treatment,... and short and long distance [water] conveyance systems" (e.g., through pipelines, aqueducts, and water tankers).* Additionally, to deal with water insecurity, storage in existing reservoirs should be expanded and effective and efficient water distribution system systems should be created.†

In addition to increasing existing water supplies, to avoid future conflicts over water resources, countries need to work together to find a resolution that is satisfactory to all parties. As the demand for water access increases, so too will the need and opportunities for all countries to engage in discussions to resolve transboundary water disputes. With cooperation of efforts, transnational security threats, such as water insecurity, can be prevented from escalating to resource-driven conflict in entire regions.

The Right to Water

Governments are required to provide their populations with access to sufficient water. In 2010, the UN General Assembly adopted a resolution (Resolution 64/292) that explicitly declared that water was a human right.‡ This right is also included in international conventions. For instance, Article 24(2)(c) of the Convention on the Rights of the Child includes the responsibility of countries to implement measures that provide children with clean drinking water. In addition, under Article 14(2)(h) of the Convention on the Elimination of All Forms of Discrimination Against Women, women have the right "to enjoy adequate living conditions, particularly in relation to housing, sanitation, electricity and water supply, transport and communications." Moreover, Article 25(f) of the Convention on the Rights of Persons with Disabilities includes a provision that prevents the discriminatory withholding of fluids.

---

* Mohamed J. Abdulrazzak, Mey Jurdi, and Shiraz Basma, "The Role of Desalination in Meeting Water Supply Demands in Western Asia," *Water International* 27:3 (2002), 403.

† Rajendra Prasad, "Population Growth, Food Shortages and Ways to Alleviate Hunger," *Current Science* 105:1 (July 10, 2013), 35, http://www.currentscience.ac.in/Volumes/105/01/0032.pdf.

‡ UN General Assembly Resolution 64/292 (July 28, 2010).

While not explicitly enshrined in the International Covenant on Economic, Social and Cultural Rights (ICESCR), the Committee on Economic, Social and Cultural Rights (CESCR) clarified in paragraph 3 of General Comment No. 15 (2002) that "the right to water clearly falls [under Article 11 of the ICESCR] within the category of guarantees essential for securing an adequate standard of living, particularly since it is one of the most fundamental conditions for survival." The CESCR in paragraph 10 of General Comment No. 15 (2002) further elucidated that the

> right to water contains both freedoms and entitlements. The freedoms include the right to maintain access to existing water supplies necessary for the right to water, and the right to be free from interference, such as the right to be free from arbitrary disconnections or contamination of water supplies. By contrast, the entitlements include the right to a system of water supply and management that provides equality of opportunity for people to enjoy the right to water.

Furthermore, the CESCR in paragraph 12 of General Comment No. 15 (2002) reveals three dimensions of the right to water: it must be available, of sufficient quality, and (economically and physically) accessible to all in the population.

CONCLUDING THOUGHTS

The right to food, the right to be free from hunger, and the right to water are fundamental human rights. Individuals need to fulfill their basic physiological needs to ensure their survival; these needs primarily include having nutritional food to eat and clean water to drink in order to maintain a healthy and active lifestyle. The availability of food and water is only one part of the equation. The quality of the food and water needs to also be of adequate quality to prevent sickness and disease. Often individuals have access to food and water; however, the food may be unsafe and the water may be contaminated.

Food and water security are adversely impacted by population growth, climate change, and extreme weather variations, and governmental, consumer, industrial, and agricultural behaviors. Food insecurity can also occur from poverty, trade imbalances, and increases in food prices. For certain members of the population food and water insecurity are more pronounced; especially for the elderly, the disabled, the infirm, children, and women. Food and water insecurity additionally arises when access to these resources is interrupted. Emergencies and conflicts in societies frequently lead to such interruptions as well.

CHAPTER 12

Energy Security
Current Issues

As a result of the uneven distribution of the world's natural resources, nations have become interdependent when it comes to sources of energy. As such, energy security is a global problem affecting developing and developed nations alike. A shortage of energy could threaten state sovereignty and power while causing security threats, such as riots, instability, physical harm, and even death. This chapter discusses the different sources of energy and current issues in energy security. Special attention will be paid to the energy geopolitics of Turkey and the energy resources in the Persian Gulf.

ENERGY SOURCES

Energy is obtained from five primary sources: oil, coal, natural gas, nuclear, and renewable sources. The first three sources, oil, coal, and natural gas, are fossil fuels (see Figure 12.1a and 12.1b). Oil is used primarily for transportation, while smaller amounts are used for heat and electricity.[*] Coal is primarily used for electricity; and less commonly used for heat.[†] Natural gas is used for electricity, hot water, heating, and cooking. Natural gas is cleaner than other fossil fuels and emits much less carbon dioxide, nitrogen oxides, and sulfur oxides.[‡]

---

[*] "Clean Energy: Oil," Environmental Protection Agency, September 25, 2013, http://www.epa.gov/cleanenergy/energy-and-you/affect/oil.html.

[†] "Clean Energy: Coal," Environmental Protection Agency, September 25, 2013, http://www.epa.gov/cleanenergy/energy-and-you/affect/coal.html.

[‡] "Air Emissions," Environmental Protection Agency, September 25, 2013, http://www.epa.gov/cleanenergy/energy-and-you/affect/air-emissions.html; "Clean Energy: Natural Gas," Environmental Protection Agency, September 25, 2013, http://www.epa.gov/cleanenergy/energy-and-you/affect/natural-gas.html.

(a)

(b)

FIGURE 12.1   A coal yard (a) and a petrochemical industrial plant (b).

Fossil fuels are nonrenewable energy sources; so too are the fuels used to power nuclear power plants; namely, uranium.[*] Nuclear energy is the primary source of power for certain countries.[†] A case in point is France, which "derives over 75% of its electricity from nuclear energy."[‡] There are grave concerns regarding the use of nuclear energy; for example, countries engaging in nuclear proliferation and nuclear power plants malfunctioning.[§] Other countries, such as Ireland and Australia, do not use nuclear energy. Instead, these countries rely on other energy sources, both nonrenewable and renewable.

Given that fossil fuels are limiting and depleting resources, it is critical for alternative energy sources to be developed and used. Renewable energy sources consist of energy obtained from solar, wind, water, geothermal sources (i.e., heat from the earth), and biomass sources (e.g., crops, crop residues, wood, and manure).[¶] These sources can be used for electricity, transportation, heating, and cooling. Specifically, solar energy can be used to create electricity, heat, and cooling; wind energy can be used to generate electricity; water energy can be used to create electricity (or hydropower); geothermal energy can be used to generate heat and electricity; and biomass energy sources can be used to produce heat (e.g., wood for fireplace), electricity (i.e., wood is burned to produce steam that drives the turbines and produces electricity), and fuel for vehicles (e.g., ethanol and biodiesel).[**]

Today, renewable energy sources are considered the most sustainable forms of energy. Notably, "[t]hey are free from constraints on fuel supply, produce no or few greenhouse gas emissions and are geographically widely available; [in addition] technological advances are expected to bring down [its] costs."[††] Despite this, their widespread use has been met with opposition; especially with respect to industries. Specifically, the infrastructures of existing industries are primarily designed to work with traditional forms of energy (e.g., fossil fuels). Accordingly, any shift

---

[*] "Clean Energy: Nuclear Energy," Environmental Protection Agency, October 22, 2013, http://www.epa.gov/clean energy/energy-and-you/affect/nuclear.html.

[†] Nuclear energy will not be discussed in detail.

[‡] "Nuclear Power in France," World Nuclear Association, January 2014, http://www.world-nuclear.org/info/Country-Profiles/Countries-A-F/France/.

[§] In this volume, see Chapter 3 for information on nuclear proliferation and Chapter 8 for nuclear power plant accidents.

[¶] "Non-Hydroelectric Renewable Energy," Environmental Protection Agency, September 25, 2013, http://www.epa.gov/cleanenergy/energy-and-you/affect/non-hydro.html.

[**] "Sustainable Energy," World Nuclear Association, June 2013, http://www.world-nuclear.org/info/Energy-and-Environment/Sustainable-Energy/; "Renewable Energy and Electricity," World Nuclear Association, October 24, 2013, http://www.world-nuclear.org/info/Energy-and-Environment/Renewable-Energy-and-Electricity/.

[††] Anthony Froggatt and Michael A. Levi, "Climate and Energy Security Policies and Measures: Synergies and Conflicts," *International Affairs* 85:6 (2009), 1134.

to renewable energy sources, even if it were a partial shift, would require a significant investment on the part of the industries; therefore, without significant government subsidies such a shift may not be possible (especially for small- and medium-size companies). Moreover, it may not be economically sound as certain countries with government subsidies, such as Germany and Denmark, have some of the highest energy prices in the world.* In sum, the extremely high capital costs of renewable energy, despite incentives of government subsidies, serve as a deterrent to its widespread use.

THE PURSUIT OF ENERGY SECURITY

Energy security is equated with the availability of and continual access to affordable energy resources. The perception of energy security and what it entails differs by country. Particularly, energy security means "different things to different countries based on their geographical location, their geological endowment, their international relations, their political system and their economic disposition."[†]

Many countries are energy dependent and/or interdependent on other countries to fulfill their energy needs. Consider, for example, that the Ukraine is highly dependent on Russia for its energy resources of oil, natural gas, and nuclear fuel. However, developed countries, like Japan, may also be highly dependent on other countries for energy because they have limited domestic resources.[‡] In fact, Japan was ranked one of the largest net fossil fuel importers in the world; second only to China.[§] Despite having vast coal reserves, China has had to seek energy resources outside of its own country to meet increasing energy demands. The same holds true for India (see Tables 12.1 and 12.2).[¶]

The United States also depends on other countries for energy resources. Specifically, the United States currently imports its energy resources primarily from Latin America (e.g., Mexico and Venezuela), Canada, the Persian Gulf (e.g., Saudi Arabia), and Africa (e.g., Nigeria). Importing

---

* "Why Is Renewable Energy So Expensive?" *The Economist*, http://www.economist.com/blogs/economist-explains/2014/01/economist-explains-0.

† Gal Luft and Anne Korin, "Energy Security: In the Eyes of the Beholder," In Gal Luft and Anne Korin (Eds.), *Energy Security Challenges for the 21st Century* (Santa Barbara, CA: ABC-CLIO, 2009), 5–6.

‡ "Japan: Overview," U.S. Energy Information Administration, October 29, 2013, http://www.eia.gov/countries/cab.cfm?fips=ja.

§ "Japan Is the Second Largest Net Importer of Fossil Fuels in the World," U.S. Energy Information Administration, November 7, 2013, http://www.eia.gov/todayinenergy/detail.cfm?id=13711.

¶ Tanvi Madan, "India's International Quest for Oil and Natural Gas: Fueling Foreign Policy?" *India Review* 9:1 (2010), 2–37.

TABLE 12.1   Top 10 Coal Producing Countries (2012)

People's Republic of China	Russia
United States	South Africa
India	Germany
Indonesia	Poland
Australia	Kazakhstan

Source: "Coal Facts 2013" (based on 2012 IEA and BP data published in 2013), World Coal Association, http://www.worldcoal.org/resources/coal-statistics/.

TABLE 12.2   Top Coal Importers (2012)

People's Republic of China	Chinese Taipei
Japan	Germany
India	United Kingdom
South Korea	

Source: "2013 Edition of IEA Cola Information" and "2013 Edition on the BP Statistical Review of World Energy" cited in "Coal Facts 2013" (based on 2012 IEA and BP data published in 2013), World Coal Association, http://www.worldcoal.org/resources/coal-statistics/.

energy from other countries is neither politically desirable nor an economically sustainable practice. Energy security is obtained by the ability of a country to be energy independent, or at the very least to reduce its energy dependence on other countries. This requires a country to increase its own production and supply of energy resources to its population. For example, the United States has invested in deepwater drilling technology in the Gulf of Mexico to bolster U.S. energy security. Indeed, the resources extracted from the Gulf of Mexico are helping the United States minimize its dependency on other countries for energy.[*]

Increases in the energy needs of nations are an inevitable consequence of the exponential population growth and the population's energy consumption. In addition to increases in population growth, other drivers of energy insecurity are societal conflicts, political instability, and human-made and natural disasters. Serious crimes, such as terrorism and organized crime, can also lead to disruptions in the supply of energy resources, thereby resulting in energy insecurity. For instance, the Kurdistan Worker's Party has conducted terrorist attacks against oil and natural gas pipelines in Turkey causing significant economic damage

---

[*] "U.S. Gulf of Mexico Fact Sheet," U.S. Energy Information Administration, http://www.eia.gov/special/gulf_of_mexico/.

to the country.* Likewise, Colombia's pipelines have been targeted on numerous occasions by terrorist groups, such as the National Liberation Army (Ejército de Liberación Nacional or ELN) and the Revolutionary Armed Forces of Colombia (Fuerzas Armadas Revolucionarios de Colombia); these attacks resulted in significant economic and environmental damage.† Similarly, in India, a terrorist group known as the United Liberation Front of Assam (ULFA) conducted several attacks against the Assam pipeline causing major economic and property damage.‡ Terrorist attacks on oil and/or natural gas pipelines can undermine efforts to maintain energy security and stability. This was observed in Yemen in 2012, where the terrorist attacks on pipelines temporarily halted oil production and cost the government over $1 billion in lost oil production and revenue.§

National and transnational criminals engage in cross-border trafficking of goods, such as nonrenewable energy resources (i.e., energy trafficking). For example, on January 24, 2014, in Operation Alisuyo, Interpol dismantled the fuel trafficking rings of two organized crime networks.¶ Fuel was trafficked by these networks across Peru and Ecuador. Energy trafficking occurs in one of three ways. First, inexpensive fossil fuels that are obtained in one country can be sold in another for great profit. For instance, oil illicitly obtained in Nigeria is then distributed to other countries in West Africa; especially in Cameroon, Benin, Chad, and Niger, where oil prices are much higher than those in Nigeria.** Second, bunkering can also occur. Bunkering involves the direct theft of fossil fuels from pipelines. According to a UNODC report, "classic oil bunkering involves stealth; attaching an unauthorized secondary pipeline to a company mainline by the techniques known as hot and cold tapping."††

---

* Andrew S. Weiss, F. Stephen Larrabee, James T. Bartis, and Camille A. Sawak, "Promoting International Energy Security," Volume 2, Turkey and the Caspian, RAND, 2012, xii, http://www.rand.org/content/dam/rand/pubs/technical_reports/2012/RAND_TR1144z2.sum.pdf.

† Ali M. Koknar, "The Epidemic of Energy Terrorism," In Gal Luft and Anne Korin (Eds.), *Energy Security Challenges for the 21st Century* (Santa Barbara, CA: ABC-CLIO, 2009), 22.

‡ Gal Luft, "Pipeline Sabotage Is Terrorist's Weapon of Choice," *Pipeline & Gas Journal*, March 28, 2005, http://www.iags.org/n0328051.htm.

§ Hakim Almasmari, "Militants Blow Up Major Oil Pipeline in Yemen," *CNN*, December 28, 2013, http://www.cnn.com/2013/12/28/world/meast/yemen-pipeline-damaged/.

¶ "Fuel Smuggling Rings Dismantled in INTERPOL Coordinated Operation," Interpol, January 24, 2014, http://www.interpol.int/News-and-media/News/2014/N2014-007.

** "Transnational Trafficking and the Rule of Law in West Africa: A Threat Assessment," United Nations Office on Drugs and Crimes (UNODC), July 2009, 22, http://www.unodc.org/documents/data-and-analysis/Studies/West_Africa_Report_2009.pdf.

†† "Transnational Trafficking and the Rule of Law in West Africa: A Threat Assessment," United Nations Office on Drugs and Crimes (UNODC), July 2009, 20, http://www.unodc.org/documents/data-and-analysis/Studies/West_Africa_Report_2009.pdf.

Here, hot tapping involves "creating a [concealed] branch connection to a pipeline in which the oil is flowing under pressure;" whereas cold tapping refers to the attempts made by those seeking to steal fossil fuels to put a pipeline temporarily out of use in order to siphon the fossil fuel (e.g., by bombing the pipeline).[*] On occasion, stolen fossil fuels are distributed in the country of origin within which they were taken. This was observed in Nigeria.[†] Commonly, fossil fuels are trafficked short distances. Accordingly, they are usually trafficked between neighboring countries. For example, petrol was siphoned from Algeria and then trafficked to Morocco.[‡] Third, fossil fuels trafficking may also involve governments and private industries. Specifically, fossil fuels may be produced in excess of the licensed amounts. In order to do this, corrupt energy officials and fossil fuel companies falsify production documents to show that only the licensed amount was produced; the excess fossil fuel is then sold for great profit to third parties. Countries that are believed to engage in this type of illicit activity are Angola, Iraq, Nigeria, Russia, and Saudi Arabia.[§]

Energy security may also be disrupted from cyberattacks. A case in point is the Iranian energy industry, which has experienced numerous instances of malware being introduced into the industrial control systems and the government and company computers of their energy industry with the intention of damaging and obtaining information from these systems. A well-known form of malware that infected the industrial control system of an Iranian nuclear facility is the Stuxnet computer worm. This malware was designed to maintain a façade of normal operations, while the centrifuges were malfunctioning.[¶] Stuxnet "is believed to be the first known malware that targets the controls at industrial facilities, such as power plants. At the time of its discovery, the assumption was that espionage lay behind the effort, but subsequent analysis by Symantec uncovered the ability of the malware to control plant operations outright."[**] It was particularly designed to attack a specific type of

---

[*] Ibid., 20–21.

[†] "Transnational Trafficking and the Rule of Law in West Africa: A Threat Assessment," United Nations Office on Drugs and Crimes (UNODC), July 2009, 22, http://www. unodc.org/documents/data-and-analysis/Studies/West_Africa_Report_2009.pdf.

[‡] Isabelle Mandraud, "Algeria Turns off Tap on Morocco's Smuggled Petrol Trade," *The Guardian*, October 15, 2013, http://www.theguardian.com/world/2013/oct/15/algeria-morocco-petrol-trafficking.

[§] Raymond Baker, *Capitalism's Achilles Heel: Dirty Money and How to Renew the Free-Market System* (Hoboken, NJ: Wiley, 2005), 167.

[¶] David Kushner, "The Real Story of Stuxnet," *IEEE Spectrum*, February 26, 2013, http://spectrum.ieee.org/telecom/security/the-real-story-of-stuxnet.

[**] Elinor Mills, "Stuxnet: Fact vs. Theory," *CNET*, October 5, 2010, http://news.cnet.com/8301-27080_3-20018530-245.html.

Siemens industrial control system,* such as those used in Iranian nuclear facilities. That following year, in 2011, a form of malware named Stars also targeted the Iranian energy industry. A third form of malware known as Duqu subsequently targeted the Iranian energy industry. Both Stars and Duqu were designed to surreptitiously obtain data from industrial control systems of critical infrastructure (e.g., energy, water, and nuclear facilities). Unlike Stuxnet, Stars and Duqu were designed to spy on systems and gather data (a form of cyberespionage). Stars is believed to be part of Duqu.† In 2012, another form of malware targeted Iran's oil industry; namely, Flame. This malware enabled the stealing of information and the spying on systems. It was designed to map and monitor oil industry computer systems. In addition to Stuxnet, Stars, Duqu, and Flame, the Iranian Oil Ministry and the National Iranian Oil Company were targeted by a malware known as Wiper. Wiper was an aggressive piece of malware that was designed to both steal and destroy data within systems.‡ To prevent the spread of this malware, "[t]he [M]inistry disconnected all oil facilities, operations and even oil rigs from the Internet to prevent this virus from spreading."§ Iranian officials reported that the malware did not affect oil production or distribution because of existing backups of both essential and nonessential data.¶

Iran is not the only country that has been subjected to cyberattacks against its energy industry. On August 15, 2012, an individual with privileged access to Aramco's computer system unleashed the Shamoon virus, which subsequently erased the majority of the information stored

---

* Existing literature on Stuxnet has mislabeled it as a virus. Stuxnet is actually a computer worm as it was particularly programmed to spread and target centrifuges without any user activity. See, for example, Bruce Schneier, "The Story behind the Stuxnet Virus," *Forbes*, October 7, 2010, http://www.forbes.com/2010/10/06/iran-nuclear-computer-technology-security-stuxnet-worm.html; Yaakov Katz, "Stuxnet Virus Set Back Iran's Nuclear Program by 2 Years," *The Jerusalem Post*, December 15, 2010, http://www.jpost.com/Iranian-Threat/News/Stuxnet-virus-set-back-Irans-nuclear-program-by-2-years; Jim Finkle, "Stuxnet Weapon Has at Least Four Cousins," *Reuters*, December 28, 2011, http://www.reuters.com/article/2011/12/28/us-cybersecurity-stuxnet-idUSTRE7BR1EV20111228.

† Robert McMillan, "Update: Iran Says It Was Targeted with Second Worm, 'Stars,'" *Computerworld*, April 25, 2011, http://www.computerworld.com/s/article/9216140/Update_Iran_says_it_was_targeted_with_second_worm_Stars_.

‡ Kim Zetter, "Wiper Malware That Hit Iran Left Possible Clues of Its Origins," *Wired Magazine*, August 29, 2012, http://www.wired.com/threatlevel/2012/08/wiper-possible-origins/.

§ Thomas Erdbrink, "Facing Cyberattack, Iranian Officials Disconnect Some Oil Terminals from Internet," *New York Times*, April 23, 2012, http://www.nytimes.com/2012/04/24/world/middleeast/iranian-oil-sites-go-offline-amid-cyberattack.html?_r=0.

¶ Kim Zetter, "Wiper Malware That Hit Iran Left Possible Clues of Its Origins," *Wired Magazine*, August 29, 2012, http://www.wired.com/threatlevel/2012/08/wiper-possible-origins/.

on its corporate computers, "[and] replac[ed]...[the deleted data] with an image of a burning American flag."* Iranian-based hackers were believed to be responsible for these cyberattacks in the Persian Gulf,† even though the words Arabian Gulf were in the code (Iran is vehemently opposed to the use of Arabian Gulf to refer to the Persian Gulf).‡ Later that month, another malware attack occurred that similarly targeted the energy industry in the Persian Gulf. Specifically, a computer virus was used to attack the systems of RasGas, a Qatari natural gas producer. RasGas shut down its website and e-mail servers in response to the attack.§ The company reported that the malware had not infected the "computers that control the production and delivery of gas."¶

The energy industry of the United States has been targeted as well. In 2012, the computer systems of U.S. natural gas pipeline companies were targeted by a spear phishing scheme.** Spear phishing schemes occur as follows: A user that is part of a particular organization receives an e-mail from what appears to be a trusted source (usually an authority figure within the same company as the user). This e-mail is designed to trick the user into revealing confidential and/or personal data. U.S. authorities are concerned that employees of natural gas and oil pipeline companies are susceptible to these and other attacks that may include malicious software designed to steal information or gain control of the systems and its data.†† U.S. authorities have expressed concern over the vulnerability of energy companies to these and other attacks, such as malware being surreptitiously introduced into their industrial control

---

* Nicole Perlroth, "In Cyberattack on Saudi Firm, U.S. Sees Iran Firing Back," *New York Times*, October 23, 2012, http://www.nytimes.com/2012/10/24/business/global/cyberattack-on-saudi-oil-firm-disquiets-us.html?pagewanted=all.

† Lolita C. Baldor, "U.S.: Hackers in Iran Responsible for Cyberattacks," *The Washington Times*, October 12, 2012, http://www.washingtontimes.com/news/2012/oct/12/us-hackers-iran-responsible-cyberattacks/?page=all.

‡ Nicole Perlroth, "In Cyberattack on Saudi Firm, U.S. Sees Iran Firing Back," *New York Times*, October 23, 2012, http://www.nytimes.com/2012/10/24/business/global/cyberattack-on-saudi-oil-firm-disquiets-us.html?pagewanted=all.

§ Siobhan Gorman and Julian E. Barnes, "Iran Blamed for Cyberattacks," *Wall Street Journal*, October 12, 2012, http://online.wsj.com/news/articles/SB10000872396390444465780457805293155576700.

¶ Kim Zetter, "Qatari Gas Company Hit with Virus in Wave of Attacks on Energy Companies," August 30, 2012, *Wired Magazine*, http://www.wired.com/threatlevel/2012/08/hack-attack-strikes-rasgas/.

** Elinor Mills, "U.S. Warns of Cyberattacks on Gas Pipeline Companies," *CNET*, May 7, 2012, http://news.cnet.com/8301-1009_3-57429617-83/u.s-warns-of-cyberattacks-on-gas-pipeline-companies/.

†† Elinor Mills, "U.S. Warns of Cyberattacks on Gas Pipeline Companies," *CNET*, May 7, 2012, http://news.cnet.com/8301-1009_3-57429617-83/u.s-warns-of-cyberattacks-on-gas-pipeline-companies/.

systems to control operations and steal information.[*] In 2013, U.S. authorities claimed that Iranian backed hackers obtained access to the industrial control systems software, which would enable them to launch attacks against oil and gas pipelines in the United States.[†]

A critical component of energy security is the avoidance of major disruptions in the supply of energy resources. These disruptions are not always the result of political instability, serious crime, and human-made and natural disasters. They may also occur due to pricing disputes between supplier and transit countries. In fact, this was observed between Russia and the Ukraine during their natural gas pricing disputes in 2006 and 2009, which disrupted the supply of natural gas not only to the Ukraine, but also to the European Union (EU).[‡] During both disputes, natural gas supplies were turned off, leaving the EU without natural gas. This is particularly problematic due to the EU's dependency on Russia for natural gas. This overreliance on Russia for natural gas has made the EU energy insecure.

The natural gas supply disruptions that resulted from the pricing disputes have led some EU Member States to seek natural gas imports from other areas, such as Norway.[§] Countries in the EU have also been exploring alternative energy resources and have even sought to build pipelines to obtain natural gas from other sources. One such pipeline project is the "Trans-Anatolian natural gas pipeline (TANAP), which would connect to the Trans Adriatic Pipeline (TAP), which goes from the Turkish border through Greece and Albania, and ends in Italy."[¶] This, and other alternatives (e.g., importing natural gas from different areas and pursuing greater usage of renewable energy resources), can help minimize EU dependency on Russian imports.

These events illustrated that countries' energy wealth could be used as instruments of foreign policy. Therefore, natural gas and oil pipelines

---

[*] Mark Clayton, "Alert: Major Cyber Attack Aimed at Natural Gas Pipeline Companies," *Christian Science Monitor*, May 5, 2012, http://www.csmonitor.com/USA/2012/0505/Alert-Major-cyber-attack-aimed-at-natural-gas-pipeline-companies.

[†] Siobhan Gorman and Danny Yadron, "Iran Hacks Energy Firms, U.S. Says," *Wall Street Journal*, May 23, 2013, http://online.wsj.com/news/articles/SB10001424127887323336104578501601108021968.

[‡] Michael Ratner, Paul Belkin, Jim Nichol, and Steven Woehrel, "Europe's Energy Security: Options and Challenges to Natural Gas Supply Diversification," *Congressional Research Service*, R42405, August 20, 2013, 1, http://www.fas.org/sgp/crs/row/R42405.pdf.

[§] Lionel Beehner, "Russia's Energy Disputes," Council on Foreign Relations, February 3, 2010, http://www.cfr.org/oil/russias-energy-disputes/p12327.

[¶] Michael Ratner, Paul Belkin, Jim Nichol, and Steven Woehrel, "Europe's Energy Security: Options and Challenges to Natural Gas Supply Diversification," *Congressional Research Service*, R42405, August 20, 2013, 1–2, http://www.fas.org/sgp/crs/row/R42405.pdf.

that travel through particular countries can provide these transit countries with significant political leverage against the suppliers and (to a lesser extent) the consumer countries. When considering the developments of pipelines, countries need to make strategic choices and, wherever and to the extent possible, bypass countries that might seek to exploit the pipelines running through their territories.

Energy Geopolitics of Turkey

Even though Turkey does not have large oil, natural gas, and coal reserves, it "play[s] a crucial role in the energy supply–demand dynamics of the region because of its geostrategic location as a transit country for energy resources."[*] Indeed, Turkey is one of the few countries that have a strategic geopolitical energy position;[†] in fact, its geographic location makes it a key energy player. Echoing this sentiment, Taner Yildiz, the Minister of Energy in Turkey, asserted that "Turkey is indispensable when it comes to addressing some of the key global energy problems. Turkey is also at the center of energy geopolitics."[‡]

Turkey is predominantly a transit country for energy resources, serving as a bridge between the East and the West. Indeed, it is strategically located between countries with major oil and natural gas reserves.[§] It is also strategically located between major world suppliers and consumers of energy.[¶] Indeed, "pipelines from Russia and Azerbaijan bring significant quantities of oil and natural gas into Turkey...Turkey also provides an important outlet for Iraqi crude via the Kirkuk–Ceyhan oil pipeline."[**] Also, the Baku–Tbilisi–Ceyhan oil pipeline connected the Caspian oil basin with the Mediterranean, thereby providing a more

---

[*] Ksenia Krauer-Pacheco, "Turkey as a Transit Country and Energy Hub: The Link to Its Foreign Policy Aims," *Forschungsstelle Osteuropa* No. 118 (December 2011), 28, http://www.forschungsstelle.uni-bremen.de/UserFiles/file/fsoAP118.pdf.

[†] Geopolitics refers to "[t]he study of the impact of geographical distributions and divisions on the conduct of world politics." John Agnew, *Geopolitics: Re-Visioning World Politics* (New York: Routledge, 1998), 128.

[‡] Taner Yıldız, "Turkey's Energy Economy and Future Energy Vision," *Turkish Policy Quarterly* 9:2 (October 2010), 13–18.

[§] Hasan Alsancak, "The Role of Turkey in Global Energy: Bolstering Energy Infrastructure Security," *Journal of Energy Security*, May 18, 2010, http://www.ensec.org/index.php?option=com_content&id=247:the-role-of-turkey-in-the-global-energy-bolstering-energy-infrastructure-security&catid=106:energysecuritycontent05 10&Itemid=361.

[¶] Ibid.

[**] Ksenia Krauer-Pacheco, "Turkey as a Transit Country and Energy Hub: The Link to Its Foreign Policy Aims," *Forschungsstelle Osteuropa* No. 118 (December 2011), 16, http://www.forschungsstelle.uni-bremen.de/UserFiles/file/fsoAP118.pdf.

direct route of oil to Western markets.[*] In addition to natural gas and oil pipelines, Turkey is an important "transit point for seaborne-traded oil," where "volumes of Russian and Caspian oil are being sent by tanker via the Turkish Straits to Western markets, while a terminal on Turkey's Mediterranean coast at Ceyhan serves as an outlet for oil exports from northern Iraq and Azerbaijan."[†]

Turkey's reliance on energy resources imports has increased over the last few years. The local demand for energy has far exceeded that which can be obtained from available domestic energy resources. As a result, Turkey has had to rely primarily on other countries for energy resources, such as oil, natural gas, and coal.[‡] Specifically, much of Turkey's oil imports originate from Iran, Iraq, and Russia.[§] Moreover, most of the natural gas that Turkey imports is from Russia, Iran, and Azerbaijan.[¶] Furthermore, even though it produces some coal, Turkey imports approximately 90% of the coal it consumes, primarily from the United States, Russia, and Australia.[**] Like other countries, Turkey is seeking to reinforce its energy security by decreasing reliance on imported energy resources and increasing its use of domestic nonrenewable and renewable resources.[††]

Persian Gulf Energy Resources

The Persian Gulf plays a pivotal role in the energy security of other nations. Bahrain, Iran, Iraq, Kuwait, Oman, Qatar, Saudi Arabia, and the United Arab Emirates border the Persian Gulf. Out of the top 10 countries with the greatest proven oil reserves (see Table 12.3), five of them are located in the Persian Gulf: Saudi Arabia, Iran, Iraq, Kuwait, and the United Arab Emirates. The country from the Persian Gulf with

---

[*] Ibid., 31–32.

[†] "Turkey," U.S. Energy Information Administration, February 1, 2013, http://www.eia. gov/countries/cab.cfm? fips=TU.

[‡] Ibid.

[§] Ibid.

[¶] International Energy Agency, "Turkey," Oil & Gas Security: Emergency Response of IEA Countries, 2013, https://www.iea.org/publications/freepublications/publication/ 2013_Turkey_Country_Chapterfinal_with_last_page.pdf.

[**] "Turkey," U.S. Energy Information Administration, February 1, 2013, http://www.eia. gov/countries/cab.cfm? fips=TU.

[††] Tuncay Babali, "The Role of Energy in Turkey's Relations with Russia and Iran," Center for Strategic and International Studies, March 29, 2012, http://csis.org/files/ attachments/120529_Babali_Turkey_Energy.pdf.

TABLE 12.3   Countries with the Largest Proven Oil Reserves (2013)

Venezuela	Kuwait
Saudi Arabia	United Arab Emirates
Canada	Russia
Iran	Libya
Iraq	Nigeria

Source: U.S. Energy Information Administration, December 5, 2013, http://www.eia.gov/countries/cab.cfm?fips=tc.

the second greatest oil reserves in the world is Saudi Arabia. Saudi Arabia is also one of the largest oil producers and exporters in the world.[*]

The next greatest oil reserves are located in Iran, which is ranked as having the fourth largest oil reserves in the world. Even though it has these great oil reserves, Iran has actually decreased its oil production. This decrease has been the result of international sanctions.[†] Consider U.S. sanctions. These energy sanctions are designed to put pressure on Iran by targeting its economy and denying Iran the resources it needs to further develop its nuclear program and support for terrorism.[‡] The sanctions are also designed to "force foreign firms to choose between participating in the U.S. market and continuing to conduct various energy-related transactions with Iran."[§] In addition to sanctions, in 2012, the European Union declared an embargo on Iranian oil.[¶] At the time, the European Union accounted for an estimated 20% of Iran's total oil revenue.[**] In addition to the EU oil embargo, Iranian oil production dropped due to the "decisions by other Iranian oil customers to obtain exemptions from U.S. sanctions by reducing purchases of Iranian oil."[††] This has had a significant

---

[*] Aarti Nagraj, "Top 10 Countries with the World's Biggest Oil Reserves," *Gulf Business*, April 14, 2013, http://gulfbusiness.com/2013/04/top-10-countries-with-the-worlds-biggest-oil-reserves/#.Uv-04rTu3-F.

[†] Ibid; Alex Lawler and Jonathan Saul, "Exclusive: Iran's Oil Sales Rise as Sanctions Pressure Eases—Sources," *Reuters*, January 22, 2014, http://www.reuters.com/article/2014/01/22/us-iran-oil-exports-idUSBREA0L12520140122; Kenneth Katzman, "Iran Sanctions," *Congressional Research Service*, RS20871, January 31, 2014, https://www.fas.org/sgp/crs/mideast/RS20871.pdf.

[‡] The U.S. has labeled Iran as a state sponsor of terrorism.

[§] Kenneth Katzman, "Iran Sanctions," *Congressional Research Service*, RS20871, January 31, 2014, 9, https://www.fas.org/sgp/crs/mideast/RS20871.pdf.

[¶] Kenneth Katzman, "Iran Sanctions," *Congressional Research Service*, RS20871, January 31, 2014, https://www.fas.org/sgp/crs/mideast/RS20871.pdf.

[**] Farnaz Fassihi and John M. Biers, "EU Bans Imports of Iran's Oil, Raising Pressure on Tehran," *Wall Street Journal*, January 24, 2012, http://online.wsj.com/news/articles/SB10001424052970203718504577178231285985826.

[††] Kenneth Katzman, "Iran Sanctions," *Congressional Research Service*, RS20871, January 31, 2014, https://www.fas.org/sgp/crs/mideast/RS20871.pdf.

adverse impact on Iran's economy, which heavily depends on oil and natural gas revenues. In fact, according to the World Bank, "[r]evenues from oil and gas exports accounted for about 60 percent of government revenues in 2011/12 and are Iran's chief source of foreign exchange."[*] Indications of the significant adverse impact that the sanctions and embargoes have had on Iran's economy include the drop in gross domestic product (GDP), the decline of its currency, and inflation.[†] On November 24, 2013, Iran accepted an interim agreement, the Joint Plan of Action, where it agreed to "halt…[the] further expansion of …[its] nuclear program in exchange for temporary and modest sanctions relief."[‡] The effects of this relaxation of the sanctions on Iran's economy remain to be seen.

Iraq and Kuwait also have some of the greatest oil reserves in the world; they are ranked fifth and sixth, respectively. Iraq and Kuwait are additionally two of the top producers and exporters of oil in the world.[§] The final country in the Persian Gulf with some of the greatest oil reserves in the world is the United Arab Emirates; it is ranked seventh in the world. Furthermore, the United Arab Emirates is one of the largest oil producers in the world.[¶] The other countries in the Persian Gulf, Bahrain, Oman, and Qatar, lack the oil wealth of their neighbors.[**]

Many of the countries with the greatest oil reserves in the world are part of the Organization of the Petroleum Exporting Countries (OPEC). There are currently 12 members of the OPEC (see Table 12.4);[††] half of the members of OPEC are located in the Persian Gulf. This organization was created to "coordinate and unify the petroleum policies of its Member Countries and ensure the stabilization of oil markets in order to secure an efficient, economic and regular supply of petroleum

---

[*] "Iran Overview," World Bank, September 2013, http://www.worldbank.org/en/country/iran/overview.

[†] Kenneth Katzman, "Iran Sanctions," *Congressional Research Service*, RS20871, January 31, 2014, 52–53, https://www.fas.org/sgp/crs/mideast/RS20871.pdf.

[‡] Kenneth Katzman, "Iran Sanctions," *Congressional Research Service*, RS20871, January 31, 2014, https://www.fas.org/sgp/crs/mideast/RS20871.pdf.

[§] "Iraq," U.S. Energy Information Administration, April 2013, http://www.eia.gov/countries/country-data.cfm?fips=iz; "Kuwait," U.S. Energy Information Administration, July 8, 2013, http://www.eia.gov/countries/country-data.cfm?fips=KU.

[¶] "United Arab Emirates," U.S. Energy Information Administration, December 5, 2013, http://www.eia.gov/countries/cab.cfm?fips=tc.

[**] "Oman," U.S. Department of State, http://www.state.gov/outofdate/bgn/oman/40666.htm; Bureau of Near Eastern Affairs, "U.S. Relations with Bahrain," U.S. Department of State, September 13, 2013, http://www.state.gov/r/pa/ei/bgn/26414.htm; Christopher M. Blanchard, "Qatar: Background and U.S. Relations," *Congressional Research Service*, RL31718, https://www.fas.org/sgp/crs/mideast/RL31718.pdf.

[††] Gabon and Indonesia were also part of OPEC, but suspended their membership in 1995 and 2009, respectively. "Member Countries," Organization of the Petroleum Exporting Countries (OPEC), http://www.opec.org/opec_web/en/about_us/25.htm.

TABLE 12.4   Members of the Organization of the Petroleum Exporting Countries (OPEC)

Iran	Venezuela	Algeria
Iraq	Qatar	Nigeria
Kuwait	Libya	Ecuador
Saudi Arabia	United Arab Emirates	Angola

Source: "Member Countries," Organization of the Petroleum Exporting Countries (OPEC), http://www.opec.org/opec_web/en/about_us/25.htm.

TABLE 12.5   Countries with the Largest Proven Natural Gas Reserves (2013)

Russia	Turkmenistan
Iran	United Arab Emirates
Qatar	Venezuela
United States	Nigeria
Saudi Arabia	Algeria

Source: U.S. Energy Information Administration, December 5, 2013, U.S. Energy Information Administration, http://www.eia.gov/countries/cab.cfm?fips=tc.

to consumers, a steady income to producers and a fair return on capital for those investing in the petroleum industry."*

Out of the top 10 countries with the greatest natural gas reserves (see Table 12.5), four of them are located in the Persian Gulf: Iran, Qatar, Saudi Arabia, and the United Arab Emirates. The country from the Persian Gulf with the second greatest natural gas reserves in the world is Iran. The next largest natural gas reserves are located in Qatar, which is ranked as having the third largest natural gas reserves in the world. Saudi Arabia was ranked fifth in the world and the United Arab Emirates was ranked as having the seventh greatest natural gas reserves in the world. It is because of these vast natural gas and oil reserves that the Persian Gulf has a critical role in world energy security.

Some of the countries that are invested in the Persian Gulf and operate within it are the United States, Russia, China, the United Kingdom, and France. The United States has expressed a particular stake in the energy resources in the Persian Gulf. This stake was identified by U.S. President Jimmy Carter. Specifically, on January 23, 1980, President Carter asserted that the United States, if need be, would use military force to defend its interests in the Persian Gulf (the Carter Doctrine). Particularly, he declared: "Let our position be absolutely clear: An

---

* "Our Mission," Organization of the Petroleum Exporting Countries (OPEC), http://www.opec.org/opec_web/en/about_us/23.htm.

attempt by any outside force to gain control of the Persian Gulf region will be regarded as an assault on the vital interests of the United States of America, and such an assault will be repelled by any means necessary, including military force."* This proclamation was made in the aftermath of the 1979 Soviet invasion of Afghanistan in order to deter the U.S.S.R. from seeking hegemony in the Persian Gulf. Essentially, the Carter doctrine asserted the legitimacy of the use of military force to protect U.S. oil interests in the Persian Gulf. This national interest was reasserted by the 1990 Bush Doctrine.† Specifically, U.S. President George Bush stated that U.S. "interest...[and] involvement in the Gulf is not transitory... there will be a lasting role for the United States in assisting the nations of the Persian Gulf."‡ Despite the threat of military action, the supply of energy resources from the Persian Gulf are still vulnerable to threats posed by serious criminals (e.g., terrorists and pirates); nowhere is this more pronounced than in the transportation of energy supplies.

TRANSPORTING ENERGY RESOURCES: DISRUPTIONS AND VULNERABILITIES

Approximately half of the world's oil supply is moved through maritime transportation.§ Consequently, energy security depends on the unobstructed delivery of energy resources through this transport medium. Certain maritime routes that are used for energy resources transport include the Turkish Straits, which divide Asia and Europe, and are the most difficult to navigate; and the Danish Straits, which serve as a primary route for Russian oil supplies to Europe.¶ Specific maritime routes that are used for transport are considered chokepoints, because they consist of narrow straits which restrict movement and the size of vessels that can navigate through them.** The use of these chokepoints are dangerous because the oil tankers traveling through them are vulnerable to accidents, theft from pirates, acts of terrorism, and conflict in surrounding regions (e.g., wars)††; however, in some cases, there are

---

* Jimmy Carter, "State of the Union Address 1980," Jimmy Carter Library, January 23, 1980, http://www.jimmycarterlibrary.gov/documents/speeches/su80jec.phtml.

† George Bush, "Address before a Joint Session of the Congress on the Persian Gulf Crisis and the Federal Budget Deficit," George Bush Presidential Library and Museum, September 11, 1990, http://bushlibrary.tamu.edu/research/public_papers. php?id=2217&year=1990&mon th=9.

‡ Ibid.

§ "World Transit Chokepoints," U.S. Energy Information Administration, August 22, 2012, http://www.eia.gov/countries/regions-topics.cfm?fips=wotc&trk=p3.

¶ Ibid.

**Ibid.

††Ibid.

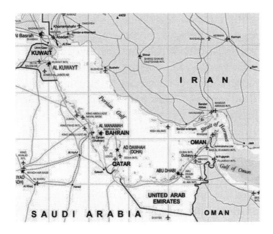

FIGURE 12.2   Map of the Persian Gulf and the Strait of Hormuz.

FIGURE 12.3   Map of the Strait of Malacca. (From the Annual Report to Congress, Military Power of the Peoples' Republic of China 2006, U.S. Department of Defense, 2006. Washington, DC.)

no viable alternatives to using these chokepoints to transport energy resources. In what follows, four major chokepoints are discussed: the Strait of Hormuz (Figure 12.2), Strait of Malacca (Figure 12.3), Suez Canal, and Bab-el-Mandeb.*

A major chokepoint is the Strait of Hormuz, which links the Gulf of Oman and the Arabian Sea with the Persian Gulf. Given the vast amount of oil transported through the Strait of Hormuz, it is considered the most important oil transit chokepoint in the world.† The Strait

---

* There are actually seven chokepoints. The Bosporus Straits (discussed earlier), the Panama Canal, and the Danish Straits will not be discussed in this chapter.
† "The Strait of Hormuz Is the World's Most Important Oil Transit," U.S. Energy Information Administration, January 4, 2012, http://www.eia.gov/todayinenergy/detail.cfm?id=4430.

of Hormuz is vulnerable to the threats posed by serious criminals. In August 2010, an oil tanker traveling through the Strait of Hormuz was subjected to a terrorist attack; no injuries or deaths occurred, and the damage was quickly repaired.* There is no viable and equivalent maritime transport alternative to the Strait of Hormuz. If this strait closes, alternative methods to transport fossil fuels need to be chosen. There are certain pipelines that bypass the Strait of Hormuz, such as the: Iraqi-owned Kirkuk–Ceyhan pipeline (which transfers oil from Iraq to Turkey); the Saudi Arabian-owned Petroline pipeline (i.e., the East–West pipeline, which runs from Saudi Arabia to the Red Sea); and the Abu Dhabi Crude Oil pipeline owned by the United Arab Emirates (i.e., the Habshan–Fujairah pipeline that transfers oil from the United Arab Emirates to the Gulf of Oman).† However, these alternatives are not able to sustain, in the long term, the delivery of the same amount of oil that is currently transported through the Strait of Hormuz.

In the past, Iranian officials warned that they would retaliate against attacks on their nuclear program, oil embargoes, and sanctions imposed on them by blocking the Strait of Hormuz.‡ This demonstrates how Iran has used the Strait of Hormuz in its foreign policy. To date, Iran has not closed the Strait of Hormuz. The closure of the Strait of Hormuz would have devastating consequences around the world. Nonetheless, there are some who argue that the closing of the Strait of Hormuz is unlikely.§ Specifically, should such a closure occur, it would have an overwhelming adverse impact on the oil revenue in Iran. This action would also most likely result in multilateral and military intervention; especially given countries' assertion of national interests in the Persian Gulf (for example, the United States). Despite the adverse consequences on Iran, others argue that Iran is likely to (temporarily) block the Strait of Hormuz.¶ Irrespective of which side of the argument one subscribes to,

---

* "UAE: Terrorists Attacked Oil Tanker," *CNN*, August 6, 2010, http://www.cnn.com/2010/WORLD/meast/08/06/uae.tanker.explosion/.
† "World Transit Chokepoints," U.S. Energy Information Administration, August 22, 2012, http://www.eia.gov/countries/regions-topics.cfm?fips=wotc&trk=p3.
‡ Farnaz Fassihi and John M. Biers, "EU Bans Imports of Iran's Oil, Raising Pressure on Tehran," *Wall Street Journal*, January 24, 2012, http://online.wsj.com/news/articles/SB10001424052970203718504577178231285985826.
§ Caitlin Talmadge, "Closing Time: Assessing the Iranian Threat to the Strait of Hormuz," *International Security* 33:1 (2008), 82–117; Eric Watkins, "Watching the World: Showdown in Hormuz?" *Oil and Gas Journal* 107:45 (December 7, 2009), http://www.ogj.com/articles/print/volume-107/issue-45/general-interest/watching-the-world.html.
¶ Caitlin Talmadge, "Closing Time: Assessing the Iranian Threat to the Strait of Hormuz," *International Security* 33:1 (2008), 82–117; Sabahat Khan, "Iranian Mining of the Strait of Hormuz—Plausibility and Key Considerations," Institute of Near East and Gulf Military Analysis (INEGMA), INEGMA Special Report No. 4 (January 2010), http://www.inegma.com/Admin/Content/File-29122013113155.pdf.

it is clear that Iran's control of the Strait of Hormuz presents a constant transnational security threat.

Maritime transportation of oil in other regions is able to rebound in certain situations without major disruptions if obstacles are encountered. A second chokepoint is the Strait of Malacca. Eugene Gholz and Daryl Press argue that if an oil tanker encountered obstacles in this strait (e.g., accident or pirate activity), the tanker could be diverted through the Straits of Lombok and Makassar.[*] The Strait of Malacca is another important transport chokepoint, connecting the Persian Gulf suppliers with the consumers in the Pacific Rim. This strait is under constant threat of maritime piracy, theft, and hijackings. While the threat of maritime piracy still exists today, it is not as significant of a threat as it was in the past. For instance, in 2004, 38 pirating incidents were reported in the Strait of Malacca alone; this was the second highest total of hijackings around the world that year (it was superseded only by the number of hijackings Indonesia experienced that year).[†] At the time when the pirating incidents peaked, Indonesia, Malaysia, and Singapore, located in the Strait of Malacca, were not patrolling the water and security of the strait effectively. The exponential increase in pirating incidents added impetus for these three countries to work together to secure the strait. The measures these countries took to decrease (but not eradicate) pirating incidents included: the conducting of sea patrols; the sharing of information about potential, attempted, and realized pirate activity; and the use of planes to monitor the waters for pirate activity.[‡] Despite these measures, in October 2013, an oil tanker was hijacked by pirates, who subsequently transferred oil from the tanker to another boat.[§] A similar incident occurred in the strait the following month in November 2013.[¶] To minimize disruptions in the supply of energy resources through the region, a pipeline has been created to bypass the Strait of Malacca; namely, the Myanmar–China Oil and Gas Pipeline.[**]

---

[*] Eugene Gholz and Daryl G. Press, "Protecting 'The Prize': Oil and the U.S. National Interest," *Security Studies* 19:3 (2010), 462.

[†] Michael Schuman, "How to Defeat Pirates: Success in the Strait," *Time Magazine*, April 22, 2009, http://content.time.com/time/world/article/0,8599,1893032,00.html.

[‡] Michael Schuman, "How to Defeat Pirates: Success in the Strait," *Time Magazine*, April 22, 2009, http://content.time.com/time/world/article/0,8599,1893032,00.html.

[§] Keith Wallace, "Tanker Hijackings Raise Piracy Concerns in Seas around Singapore," *Reuters*, November 12, 2013, http://www.reuters.com/article/2013/11/12/us-shipping-singapore-piracy-idUSBRE9AB06420131112.

[¶] Amrutha Gayathri, "Pirates Attack Tanker in the Malacca Strait, One of the World's Busiest Shipping Channels and Asia's Most Strategic Oil Chokepoint," November 11, 2013, http://www.ibtimes.com/pirates-attack-tanker-malacca-strait-one-worlds-busiest-shipping-channels-asias-most-strategic-oil.

[**] "World Transit Chokepoints," U.S. Energy Information Administration, August 22, 2012, http://www.eia.gov/countries/regions-topics.cfm?fips=wotc&trk=p3.

The Suez Canal is a third maritime chokepoint (Figure 12.4a and 12.4b). It "is located between Egypt and connects the Red Sea and Gulf of Suez with the Mediterranean Sea."[*] The inability to transport energy resources through the Suez Canal could result in significant adverse economic consequences. In fact, during the 1967 Arab–Israeli War, the Suez Canal closed, causing significant economic damage, especially to Great Britain.[†] Alternate routes exist if this canal would close; however, these routes would take significantly longer than travel through the Suez Canal thereby disrupting oil supply and distribution. Specifically, the alternate shipping route from the Middle East to Europe would be to transport energy resources all the way around the southern tip of Africa; in so doing, incurring significant additional costs and increasing the time that it takes to transport the energy resources.[‡] In addition to alternate travel routes, the Suez–Mediterranean Pipeline (SUMED) could be used to bypass the canal and to transport energy sources; this been used when cargo or vessels are too large to pass through the canal.[§]

The Bab-el-Mandeb is a fourth maritime chokepoint. It is located between Djibouti, Eritrea, and Yemen. The closure of this strait would directly impact oil tankers by preventing them from transporting their shipment from the Persian Gulf to the Suez Canal.[¶] These oil tankers would have to find alternate routes that would increase the time and cost for transport of the shipment. Oil tankers traveling in the strait have experienced acts of terrorism and maritime piracy. In addition to disruptions in maritime and pipeline energy transportation, energy security is also adversely impacted by energy price spikes and reduced fossil fuel production, which are direct consequences of oil embargoes.

Oil Embargoes and World Energy Security

Oil embargoes have affected energy security around the globe. Some believe that U.S. energy vulnerability to conflict and disruption in the Persian Gulf is exaggerated due to the flexibility of the energy market.[**]

---

[*] "World Transit Chokepoints," U.S. Energy Information Administration, August 22, 2012, http://www.eia.gov/countries/regions-topics.cfm?fips=wotc&trk=p3.

[†] Moshe Gat, "Britain and the Occupied Territories after the 1967 War," *Middle East Review of International Affairs* 10:4 (December 2006), 70, http://www.gloria-center.org/meria/2006/12/Gat.pdf.

[‡] Eugene Gholz and Daryl G. Press, "Protecting 'The Prize': Oil and the U.S. National Interest," *Security Studies* 19:3 (2010), 463.

[§] "World Transit Chokepoints," U.S. Energy Information Administration, August 22, 2012, http://www.eia.gov/countries/regions-topics.cfm?fips=wotc&trk=p3.

[¶] Ibid.

[**] Eugene Gholz and Daryl G. Press, "Protecting 'The Prize:' Oil and the U.S. National Interest," *Security Studies* 19:3 (2010), 477.

FIGURE 12.4   A map of Egypt and the Suez Canal (a) and a photograph
(b) of ships passing through the Suez Canal.

TABLE 12.6   Members of the Organization of Arab Petroleum Exporting Countries (OAPEC)

Algeria	Libya
Bahrain	Qatar
Egypt	Saudi Arabia
Iraq	Syria
Kuwait	United Arab Emirates

Source: Encyclopedia Britannica, s.v. "Organization of Arab Petroleum Exporting Countries (OAPEC)," 2013 http://www.britannica.com/EBchecked/topic/31502/Organization-of-Arab-Petroleum-Exporting-Countries-OAPEC.
Note: Tunisia was originally part of OAPEC but ceased being a member in 1987.

However, this is not the case.[*] The cost of energy would be directly impacted by such situations. This became evident in the 1973 energy crisis. The energy crisis resulted from an oil embargo placed on several countries and a reduction of oil production by the Organization of Arab Petroleum Exporting Countries (OAPEC). This oil embargo was the direct result of them losing the Yom Kippur War, which was fought on October 6, 1973. Egypt and Syria engaged in a simultaneous surprise military attack in the Sinai Peninsula and Golan Heights on the holiest day for the Jewish people, the Day of Atonement. During the oil embargo, members of OAPEC (see Table 12.6) banned the provision of oil to countries that were allies of Israel and those that assisted Israel during the war, such as the United States and the Netherlands. The United States provided military support, whereas, the Netherlands supported Israel, condemned the war, and called for a return to the Israeli–Palestinian boundaries and settlements agreed upon by UN Security Council Resolution 242 (1967).[†] This embargo ultimately led the 1973 energy crisis, because of the drastic increase in oil prices and the decrease in the availability of oil.

---

[*] Patrick Clawson and Simon Henderson, "Reducing Vulnerability to Middle East Energy Shocks: A Key Element in Strengthening U.S. Energy Security," The Washington Institute for Near East Policy, Policy Focus #49, November 2005, http://www.washingtoninstitute.org/html/pdf/PolicyFocus49.pdf.

[†] Joris J. C. Voorhoeve, *Peace, Profits and Principles: A Study of Dutch Foreign Policy* (The Hague: Martinus, Nijhoff, 1979), 238 cited in Roy Licklider, "The Power of Oil: The Arab Oil Weapon and the Netherlands, the United Kingdom, Canada, Japan, and the United States," *International Studies Quarterly* 32:2 (June 1988), 209.

DEALING WITH ENERGY INSECURITY

Many nations have prepared for disruptions in the supply of energy. One way this preparation occurs is by increasing the output of oil in the non-OPEC countries; for example, countries such as Russia, the United States, and Canada. This provides them with oil for temporary shortages. The 1973–1974 OAPEC oil embargo also prompted countries targeted by the embargoes to implement comprehensive measures that promoted energy conservation, the greater use of nuclear energy, and the development and use of renewable energy resources. With respect to the latter, countries should pursue greater investments in renewable energy sources to lessen their nonrenewable energy dependence on other nations. Countries should additionally minimize their energy dependence with volatile countries and conflict regions; instead relying on domestic production and, wherever needed, nonrenewable energy resources from allies.

Given the energy interdependence of nations of the world, international laws were needed to harmonize measures that should be taken in an effort to ensure energy security. To achieve this, the 1994 Energy Charter Treaty (ECT) was implemented. The ECT is a legally binding multilateral agreement that promotes international cooperation in energy security, including cooperation in the exploration of energy resources, their production, distribution, and use.[*] The ECT also seeks to achieve energy security through competitive markets, which respect state sovereignty over energy resources and their use.[†] The ECT further encourages signatories (see Tables 12.7 and 12.8) to work towards energy efficiency and the lessening of the harmful environmental effects of energy production and use.[‡]

Moreover, national measures have been implemented to lead countries toward energy independence. A case in point is the U.S. Energy Independence and Security Act (the Clean Energy Act) of 2007. This act seeks to move the United States away from energy dependence on other countries. Indeed, it seeks to promote U.S. energy independence by calling for the increase in domestic production of energy, in general, and the production and use of clean and renewable energy, in particular.[§]

---

[*] Energy Charter, "1994 Treaty," http://www.encharter.org/index.php?id=28.
[†] Ibid.
[‡] Ibid.
[§] "Summary of the Energy Independence and Security Act: Public Law 110-140 (2007)," U.S. Environmental Protection Agency, http://www2.epa.gov/laws-regulations/summary-energy-independence-and-security-act.

TABLE 12.7   Signatories That Have Ratified the Energy Charter Treaty
(as of June 2013)

Afghanistan	Kyrgyzstan
Albania	Latvia
Armenia	Liechtenstein
Austria	Lithuania
Azerbaijan	Luxembourg
Belgium	Malta
Bosnia and Herzegovina	Moldova
Bulgaria	Mongolia
Croatia	The Netherlands
Cyprus	Poland
Czech Republic	Portugal
Denmark	Romania
Estonia	Slovakia
Finland	Slovenia
Former Yugoslav Republic of Macedonia	Spain
France	Sweden
Georgia	Switzerland
Germany	Tajikistan
Greece	Turkey
Hungary	Turkmenistan
Ireland	Ukraine
Italy	United Kingdom
Japan	Uzbekistan
Kazakhstan	

Source: "Status of Ratification of the Energy Charter Treaty as of June 2013,"
Energy Charter Secretariat, http://www.encharter.org/fileadmin/user_
upload/document/ECT_ratification_status.pdf.

This act reinforces Executive Order 13423, which called for energy conservation and the use of renewable energy sources by federal agencies.[*]
Investing in renewable energy alliances with critical energy resource rich
regions, diplomacy, and uniform energy security policies can also help
minimize the risk of energy insecurity.

---

[*] "Executive Order 13423 of January 24, 2007, Strengthening Federal Environmental,
Energy, and Transportation Management," *Federal Register* 72:17 (January 26, 2007),
http://www.gpo.gov/fdsys/pkg/FR-2007-01-26/pdf/07-374.pdf.

TABLE 12.8   Signatories That Have Not Ratified the Energy
Charter Treaty (as of June 2013)

Australia	Iceland	Russia[b]
Belarus[a]	Norway	

Source: "Status of Ratification of the Energy Charter Treaty as of June
2013," Energy Charter Secretariat, http://www.encharter.org/
fileadmin/user_upload/document/ECT_ratification_status.pdf.

[a] Belarus applies the treaty only provisionally.
[b] Russia applied the treaty provisionally until October 18, 2009.

CONCLUDING THOUGHTS

Energy security involves the availability of and access to affordable
energy sources. Energy security is critical as it directly impacts individuals' quality of life. The energy security of a nation differs according to
the nation's energy resource needs. Energy sources vary; they include oil,
natural gas, coal, nuclear fuel, and renewable energy (solar, wind, water,
geothermal, and biomass).

Energy security requires access to affordable energy resources without significant disruptions in supply. However, there are many factors
that adversely impact the stability of energy security. For example, conflict and political instability in a region can adversely impact the supply of energy resources; so too can human-made and natural disasters.
Terrorist attacks on pipelines and ships transporting energy resources
have also undermined efforts to maintain such stability. In addition,
serious crimes such as organized crime or cyberattacks against energy
infrastructure can disrupt the provision of energy. To mitigate or prevent
damage to oil and natural gas pipelines and energy infrastructure, more
generally, the following measures should be implemented: surveillance
equipment should be installed and used to monitor pipelines and facilities; aerial and ground patrols of infrastructure should be conducted;
industrial control systems should be protected against cybersecurity
incidents; and corporate and government computer system redundancy
(i.e., backups) of the energy industry should be augmented.[*]

Oil embargoes can additionally disrupt the provision of energy
resources. When fewer fossil fuels are produced and prices of oil increase,
stockpiles are usually distributed in the market to offset these conditions and the costs, and absorb the shocks to the market. However, this

---

[*] Gal Luft, "Pipeline Sabotage Is Terrorist's Weapon of Choice," *Pipeline & Gas Journal*,
March 28, 2005, http://www.iags.org/n0328051.htm.

serves only as a temporary solution to the shortage of energy resources; it is unsustainable in the long term. Furthermore, disruptions in maritime transportation of energy resources, such as accidents, theft, piracy, and terrorism, have adversely impacted energy security. In some situations, maritime energy transportation is able to rebound from obstacles without any major disruptions (e.g., transportation through the Strait of Malacca). Other routes, as indicated in the previous section, however, are less immune to interruptions (e.g., Suez Canal). Using alternative routes in such situations would significantly increase the costs and time it would take to transport energy resources. For some transport routes, there is no viable and equivalent alternative (e.g., the Strait of Hormuz). Here, alternative routes are either underdeveloped or too costly.

Certain countries and regions play critical roles in energy security, albeit outside their own jurisdiction. For example, Turkey has a strategic geopolitical energy position because it serves as an energy bridge between the East and the West. Certain countries have attempted to exploit their energy position and use their position in foreign policy; for example, Iran. Such exploitation is possible because many countries are energy interdependent. A case in point are Member States of the European Union and Russia. The European Union heavily relies on Russia for natural gas. Due to the shut off of one of the European gas pipelines during pricing disputes between Russia and the Ukraine, many European consumers were left without natural gas. Subsequent to the incident, the European Union placed greater emphasis on implementing measures and technologies to secure its energy independence. To achieve energy security, countries make strategic decisions in order to minimize their energy interdependence and maximize their energy security. In pursuit of this energy independence, countries have invested in (and should continue to invest in) domestic energy production, energy diversification, renewable energy, and the creation of more energy efficient technologies.

CHAPTER 13

The Future of Transnational Security
Concluding Remarks

This chapter provides concluding remarks on the lessons learned in security practices and the future of transnational security. It does this by first examining the structural issues that trigger many transnational security threats. It then considers environmental issues; notably, climate change. Finally, it explores "new" transnational security threats. Special attention is paid to the role of interconnectivity in transnational security.

STRUCTURAL ISSUES IN TRANSNATIONAL SECURITY

The previous chapters focused on a variety of transnational security issues, analyzing their causes and the factors that influenced them. These chapters further examined the policy responses and the measures implemented to deal with these threats. This chapter examines the underlying causes of many transnational security threats. More specifically, in addition to the threats examined in the previous chapters, this last chapter is dedicated to examining the structural issues that underlie most of the existing transnational security threats; namely poverty, inequality, corruption, and climate change.

Poverty

Certain structural conditions trigger transnational security threats; many of these structural issues are also interrelated. Consider poverty. Poverty is an underlying cause of food insecurity. It is also a trigger that serves as a catalyst for some within the population to turn to organized crime, terrorism, or cybercrime to support themselves and their families.

Creating opportunities for employment would help reduce transnational security threats which involve criminal behavior. Indeed, the lack of available and legitimate job opportunities in Eastern Europe and Russia have led some individuals with cybersecurity skills to work for organized crime groups.[*]

Poverty has also been linked with hunger, the spread of infectious diseases, and individuals' sense of helplessness in dealing with these factors, all of which serve as triggers to violent behavior; especially if states fail to adequately intervene to assist and protect their populations from these threats. Conflict societies lack the ability to protect their populations. This inability is often exploited by terrorists who use these territories as a safe haven and launching ground to prepare, plot, and execute terrorist attacks. A case in point is Al-Shabaab in Somalia.

There are some transnational security threats that can aggravate present structural conditions in societies, such as poverty. An example of a threat that can exacerbate existing poverty conditions is a natural disaster. Specifically, natural disasters have been found to aggravate poverty in developing countries.[†] Natural disasters also disproportionately impact the poor; especially individuals that are unemployed and do not have access to insurance, credit, and/or loans.[‡]

Poverty truly is a transnational security threat; however, developed and developing countries experience poverty in different ways. In 2012, the United States reported that there were 46.5 million individuals living in poverty.[§] Generally, individuals within the United States that are living in poverty are eligible to receive governmental assistance. This assistance enables individuals to meet their most basic human needs of

---

[*] John Blau, "Russia—A Happy Haven for Hackers," *Computer Weekly*, May 26, 2004, http://www.computerweekly.com/feature/Russia-a-happy-haven-for-hackers; Peter Warren, "Hunt for Russia's Web Criminals," *The Guardian*, November 14, 2007, http://www.theguardian.com/technology/2007/nov/15/news.crime; Joseph D. Serio and Alexander Gorkin, "Changing Lenses: Striving for Sharper Focus on the Nature of the 'Russian Mafia' and Its Impact on the Computer Realm," *International Review of Law, Computers and Technology* 17:2 (July 2003), 191–202.

[†] Paul K. Freeman, Michael Keen, and Muthukumara Mani, "Being Prepared: Natural Disasters Are Becoming More Frequent, More Destructive, and Deadlier, and Poor Countries Are Being Hit the Hardest," *Finance and Development* 40:3 (2003), 42–45; Kristian Thor Jakobsen, "In the Eye of the Storm: The Welfare Impacts of a Hurricane," *World Development* 40 (2012), 2578–2589.

[‡] Michael R. Carter, Peter D. Little, Tewodaj Mogues, and Workneh Negatu, "Poverty Traps and Natural Disasters in Ethiopia and Honduras," *World Development* 35:5 (2007), 835–856; Stefan Dercon, "Growth and Shocks: Evidence from Rural Ethiopia," *Journal of Development Economics* 74 (2004), 309–329.

[§] United States Census Bureau, "Income, Poverty and Health Insurance in the United States: 2012—Highlights," http://www.census.gov/hhes/www/poverty/data/incpovhlth/2012/highlights.html.

food, shelter, and healthcare. Such forms of assistance, however, are not available in all countries, especially developing countries.

Poverty is measured in monetary terms; "captured by levels of income or consumption per capita or per household."[*] The extreme poverty rate is calculated at those living at or below $1.25 a day. An estimated "1.2 billion people live in extreme poverty—about 21 percent of the population in the developing world."[†] Certain international organizations such as the World Bank have taken measures to reduce extreme poverty. For instance, in Nepal, the World Bank helped reduce those living in poverty by 50% (from 2003 to 2011).[‡]

Specific measures that need to be taken to eradicate extreme poverty are combating the spread of infectious diseases (such as HIV/AIDS) and bolstering the economy.[§] In regards to infectious diseases, one of the United Nations Millennium Development Goals is to combat HIV/ AIDS, malaria, and other diseases, through prevention, treatment, and education campaigns.[¶] To bolster the economy, measures should be taken to strengthen trade and create job opportunities for the population. Several programs have been implemented to create a stronger workforce in particular countries around the globe. A case in point is Bosnia and Herzegovina. Specifically, United Nations agencies (such as the UN Development Programme or UNDP) "partnered with the Government of Spain to establish 16 centers in Bosnia and Herzegovina to provide career counseling to unemployed youth. In the first 14 months of operation, the centers provided skills training to more than 6,800 young people, of whom almost 1,800 gained their first work experience."[**]

Providing access to modern energy sources is another step toward alleviating poverty. Currently, many countries are experiencing energy poverty; that is, individuals do not have access to modern and clean energy sources. Modern and clean energy sources refer to "household access to electricity and clean cooking facilities (e.g., fuels and stoves that do not cause air pollution in houses)."[††] In addition, to eradicate

---

[*] "Poverty: The Official Numbers," United Nations, 13, http://www.un.org/esa/socdev/rwss/docs/2010/chapter2.pdf.

[†] "Annual Report 2013," World Bank, 22, https://openknowledge.worldbank.org/bitstream/handle/10986/16091/9780821399378.pdf?sequence=1.

[‡] "Goal 1: Eradicate Extreme Poverty and Hunger by 2015," World Bank, http://www.worldbank.org/mdgs/poverty_hunger.html.

[§] "Ending Extreme Poverty," USAID, February 13, 2014, http://www.usaid.gov/endextremepoverty; "Goal 1: Eradicate Extreme Poverty and Hunger by 2015," World Bank, http://www.worldbank.org/mdgs/poverty_hunger.html.

[¶] "The Millennium Development Goals Report 2013," United Nations, 34, http://www.un.org/millenniumgoals/pdf/report-2013/mdg-report-2013-english.pdf.

[**] "Fact Sheet: Goal 1: Eradicate Extreme Poverty and Hunger," "We Can End Poverty: Millennium Goals and Beyond 2015," United Nations, 1–2, http://www.un.org/millenniumgoals/pdf/Goal_1_fs.pdf.

[††] "Energy Poverty," International Energy Agency, http://www.iea.org/topics/energypoverty/.

poverty, food security should be increased (by investing in the agricultural industry).* For example, to help alleviate poverty, a program was implemented in Cambodia. In this program, which was spearheaded by the Food and Agriculture Organization of the United Nations (FAO), participants in 15 villages were able to "improve ... [their] food security and income generation by increasing off-farm production and improving quality, management, and marketing" of their products.† Moreover, measures that should be taken to eradicate poverty include the improving and promoting of education among the population, and the lessening of gender inequalities. These two factors are explored in the next section.

Inequality

Equality and nondiscrimination are fundamental human rights. These rights are enshrined in international human rights instruments. For instance, Article 2.1 of the International Covenant on Civil and Political Rights requires that "[e]ach State Party...undertakes to respect and to ensure to all individuals within its territory and subject to its jurisdiction the rights recognized in the present Covenant, without distinction of any kind, such as race, color, sex, language, religion, political or other opinion, national or social origin, property, birth or other status." Article 3 of the Covenant further notes that countries should "ensure the equal right of men and women to...[enjoy] all civil and political rights set forth in the present Covenant." This Covenant also holds that "[a]ll persons are equal before the law and are entitled without any discrimination to the equal protection of the law. In this respect, the law shall prohibit any discrimination and guarantee to all persons equal and effective protection against discrimination on any ground such as race, color, sex, language, religion, political or other opinion, national or social origin, property, birth or other status." These rights are additionally included in Article 2.2‡ and

---

* "Ending Extreme Poverty," USAID, February 13, 2014, http://www.usaid.gov/ endextremepoverty; "Goal 1: Eradicate Extreme Poverty and Hunger by 2015," World Bank, http://www.worldbank.org/mdgs/poverty_hunger.html.

† "Fact Sheet: Goal 1: Eradicate Extreme Poverty and Hunger," "We Can End Poverty: Millennium Goals and Beyond 2015," United Nations, 2, http://www. un.org/millenniumgoals/pdf/Goal_1_fs.pdf.

‡ Article 2.2 of the International Covenant on Economic, Social and Cultural Rights holds that: "The States Parties to the present Covenant undertake to guarantee that the rights enunciated in the present Covenant will be exercised without discrimination of any kind as to race, color, sex, language, religion, political or other opinion, national or social origin, property, birth or other status."

Article 3* of the International Covenant on Economic, Social and Cultural Rights. Equality and nondiscrimination rights are also included in other conventions, such as the International Convention on the Protection of the Rights of All Migrant Workers and Members of Their Families,† and the International Labour Organization (ILO) Convention No. 111 on Discrimination (Employment and Occupation).‡

Furthermore, gender inequality is specifically addressed in the Convention on the Elimination of All Forms of Discrimination against Women. In fact, Article 2 of the Convention calls on "States Parties [to] condemn discrimination against women in all its forms, [and] agree to pursue by all appropriate means and without delay a policy of eliminating discrimination against women." Gender inequality is inextricably linked to other transnational security threats such as poverty, food shortages, transnational organized crime (e.g., human trafficking), and infectious diseases. Research has shown that women are also disproportionately affected by human-made and natural disasters because of the general lack of availability of economic support and social services to women in certain regions following disasters (such support and services are primarily provided to men).§

Girls and women also lack equal access to education. The lack of education deprives women of productive employment. The promotion of gender equality and the empowerment of women is one of the UN's Millennium Development Goals. To achieve this goal, measures were implemented to narrow the gender gaps in access to education and the

---

* Article 3 of the International Covenant on Economic, Social and Cultural Rights holds that: "the States Parties to the present Covenant undertake to ensure the equal right of men and women to the enjoyment of all economic, social and cultural rights set forth in the present Covenant."

† Article 7 of the International Convention on the Protection of the Rights of All Migrant Workers and Members of Their Families holds that: "States Parties undertake, in accordance with the international instruments concerning human rights, to respect and to ensure to all migrant workers and members of their families within their territory or subject to their jurisdiction the rights provided for in the present Convention without distinction of any kind such as to sex, race, color, language, religion or conviction, political or other opinion, national, ethnic or social origin, nationality, age, economic position, property, marital status, birth or other status."

‡ Article 2 of the International Labour Organization (ILO) Convention No. 111 on Discrimination (Employment and Occupation) holds that: "Each Member for which this Convention is in force undertakes to declare and pursue a national policy designed to promote, by methods appropriate to national conditions and practice, equality of opportunity and treatment in respect of employment and occupation, with a view to eliminating any discrimination in respect thereof."

§ World Health Organization, "Gender and Women's Health: Gender and Disaster," WHO Regional Office for South-East Asia, January 19, 2005; "Gender and Women's Health: Gender and Disaster," The Global Fund for Women, December 2005, 1, http://www.globalfundforwomen.org/storage/images/stories/downloads/disaster-report.pdf.

workforce.* For example, in Somalia, scholarships were provided to girls to receive an education.† These programs that promote education also seek to fulfill another UN Millennium Development Goal, the attainment of universal primary education.‡

Other measures that have been implemented to combat gender inequality have focused on more than one structural transnational security threat; notably, the World Food Programme's (WFP) Food For Girls' Education Programme. This program sought to improve food security and increase the number of children obtaining an education, by providing incentives to families to send their children to school. In Yemen, for example, girls, overall, were not receiving an education. To promote the education of girls, the WFP provided families that sent their girls to obtain an education at school with "an annual ration of wheat and fortified vegetable oil."§

Corruption

Corruption involves dishonest or fraudulent activity by governments. Instruments have been developed to measure corruption. However, these instruments rely on subjective assessments of this security threat; namely, they measure perceived levels of public sector corruption. A case in point is the Corruption Perception Index. This index, which was developed by Transparency International (a nongovernmental organization), assesses the perceived level of corruption in 177 countries and territories.¶ In this index, countries with a score of 0 are very corrupt and those with a score of 100 are uncorrupt. In 2013, the top two countries (with the exact same scores) that were considered uncorrupt were Denmark and New Zealand. By contrast, the most corrupt countries were found to be Somalia, North Korea, and Afghanistan. These countries were closely followed by Sudan and South Sudan.

Structural conditions, such as corruption, poverty, unemployment, and the general lack of legitimate work opportunities, have served as catalysts to transnational organized crime, cybercrime, and terrorism.

---

* "Fact Sheet: Goal 3: Promote Gender Equality and Empower Women," "We Can End Poverty: Millennium Goals and Beyond 2015," United Nations, 1, http://www.un.org/millenniumgoals/pdf/Goal_3_fs.pdf.

† Ibid., 2.

‡ "The Millennium Development Goals Report 2013," United Nations, 14, http://www.un.org/millenniumgoals/pdf/report-2013/mdg-report-2013-english.pdf.

§ "Fact Sheet: Eradicate Extreme Poverty and Hunger," "We Can End Poverty: Millennium Goals and Beyond 2015," United Nations, 1–2, http://www.un.org/millenniumgoals/pdf/Goal_1_fs.pdf.

¶ "Corruption Perceptions Index 2013," Transparency International, http://cpi.transparency.org/cpi2013/.

These types of threats thrive under these conditions. Corruption exacerbates existing structural issues, such as inequality; in fact, it is usually the underlying reason for the uneven distribution of public resources. It is also commonly the reason for ineffective and dysfunctional criminal justice systems. Moreover, abject poverty is found in corrupt countries.[*] Corrupt countries are characterized by "bad governance wast[ing] public resources and discourag[ing] private investment."[†] With respect to the latter, "[e]conomic development is stunted because foreign direct investment is discouraged and small businesses within the country often find it impossible to overcome the 'start-up costs' required because of corruption."[‡] To eradicate poverty, therefore, good governance and accountable and transparent government institutions are required.[§]

The Way Forward

To ensure progress in the field of transnational security, academicians, policy makers, government officials, politicians, lawmakers, and practitioners should focus their efforts on the structural conditions that make transnational security threats possible, and at times, more severe (poverty, inequality, and corruption, to name a few). The structural transnational security threats mentioned earlier have often been viewed one-dimensionally; that is, security officials have sought to deal with them in an isolated manner. For example, with corruption, the solutions promoted are often those seeking to remove those that exhibit this behavior from the government. However, this method does not accurately deal with corruption. To be effective, the approach taken should be multidimensional. Consider poverty. Poverty is influenced by a lack of (or inadequate) income, unemployment, lack of education, inadequate living conditions, poor health, and inequality, among other factors. By viewing poverty in this manner, one realizes its complexity and the multidimensional approach required to effectively deal with this threat. Likewise, to deal with corruption, and other structural threats, multidimensional approaches are required. Ultimately, measures should be aimed at targeting the underlying causes of threats; without which, a security strategy could not be successful.

---

[*] The Millennium Development Goals Report 2013, United Nations, 7, http://www.un.org/millenniumgoals/pdf/report-2013/mdg-report-2013-english.pdf.

[†] Ibid.

[‡] "International Anti-Corruption Day," United Nations, https://www.un.org/en/events/anticorruptionday/.

[§] "Annual Report 2013," World Bank, 22, https://openknowledge.worldbank.org/bitstream/handle/10986/16091/9780821399378.pdf?sequence=1.

ENVIRONMENTAL ISSUES: CLIMATE CHANGE

A significant environmental transnational security threat is climate change. Climate change refers to "a change of climate which is attributed directly or indirectly to human activity that alters the composition of the global atmosphere and which is in addition to natural climate variability observed over comparable time periods."* The general scientific consensus about climate change is that it is real and affected directly or indirectly by human activity.† The sources of contention about climate change concern the magnitude of its impact on individuals' way of life and the speed with which these effects will be felt by societies worldwide.

The primary piece of international legislation covering climate change is the 1992 United Nations Framework Convention on Climate Change.‡ The ultimate objective of this Convention is the "stabilization of greenhouse gas§ concentrations in the atmosphere at a level that would prevent dangerous anthropogenic interference with the climate system."¶ To accomplish this, the Convention calls on states to "gather and share information on greenhouse gas emissions, [to implement]...strategies for addressing greenhouse gas emissions...[, and to] cooperate in preparing for adaptation to the impacts of climate change."** To assist nations in fulfilling these obligations, the 1997 Kyoto Protocol was implemented.†† This protocol set internationally binding emission reduction targets for developed countries. However, this protocol only mandates that developed countries cut greenhouse gas emissions; developing countries can volunteer to do this. This is extremely problematic given that two countries exempted from implementing this protocol, China and India, are significant greenhouse gas emitters. Since these countries are not covered by the Kyoto Protocol, the United States, which is also a significant emitter of greenhouse gases, opted out from implementing the protocol.

---

* See Article 1(2) of the 1992 United Nations Framework Convention on Climate Change.
† William R. L. Anderegg, James W. Prall, Jacob Harold, and Stephen H. Schneider, "Expert Credibility in Climate Change," *Proceedings of the National Academy of Sciences* 107:27 (2010), 12107–12109; Naomi Oreskes, "Beyond the Ivory Tower: The Scientific Consensus on Climate Change," *Science* 306:5702 (2004), 1686; Peter T. Doran and Maggie Kendall Zimmerman, "Examining the Scientific Consensus on Climate Change," *Eos Transactions American Geophysical Union* 90:3 (2009), 22–23; "Climate Change: Consensus," NASA, http://climate.nasa.gov/scientific-consensus.
‡ This Convention entered into force on March 21, 1994.
§ According to Article 1(5) of the UN Framework Convention on Climate Change, greenhouse gases refer to "those gaseous constituents of the atmosphere, both natural and anthropogenic, that absorb and re-emit infrared radiation."
¶ Article 2 of the UN Framework Convention on Climate Change.
** "The United Nations Framework Convention on Climate Change," United Nations, http://unfccc.int/essential_background/convention/items/2627.php.
†† Entry into force on February 16, 2005.

Accordingly, three countries that are well known as being significant greenhouse gas emitters are not implementing the emission reduction targets in the protocol. In light of this, Canada renounced the protocol, claiming that in its current state it was unworkable because the main greenhouse gas emitters in the world have not agreed to the protocol.[*] Notwithstanding, in the 2011 Durban, South Africa, Climate Change Conference, China, the United States and India pledged to join the new global emissions treaty that is being developed.[†] To effectively deal with climate change, all countries must cooperate in reducing greenhouse gas emissions.

Domestic efforts have also been made to reduce climate change. The U.S. Environmental Protection Agency (EPA) is primarily responsible for developing standards concerning greenhouse gas emissions.[‡] The EPA has found that "[g]reenhouse gas pollution, through its contribution to global climate change, presents a significant threat to Americans' health and to the environment upon which [the U.S.] economy and security depends."[§] The EPA's role in regulating greenhouse gas emissions was delineated in the case of *Massachusetts v. EPA*,[¶] and the court's interpretation of the Clean Air Act. Other national agencies are also concerned with climate change. For example, the National Aeronautics and Space Administration (NASA) published a report outlining the potential risks associated with climate change and its impact on national security.[**] This report observes that climate change could have significant adverse consequences on food, water, and energy security.[††] Nonetheless, these are not the only consequences of climate change.

Scientists have predicted that natural disasters will become more frequent as a consequence of climate change. Natural disasters have great adverse impacts on affected countries. Notably, the proximate effects of natural disasters include population displacement, hunger, and the

---

[*] "Kyoto Protocol Fast Facts," *CNN*, July 26, 2013, http://www.cnn.com/2013/07/26/world/kyoto-protocol-fast-facts/.

[†] Patrick McGroarty, "China, India, U.S. Take Steps toward Emissions Deal," *Wall Street Journal*, December 12, 2011, http://online.wsj.com/news/articles/SB10001424052970203518404577092571113144672.

[‡] "Regulatory Initiatives," EPA, http://www.epa.gov/climatechange/EPAactivities/regulatory-initiatives.html.

[§] Opening Statement of Regina McCarthy, Assistant Administrator for Air and Radiation, U.S. Environmental Protection Agency, "Hearing on EPA Regulation of Greenhouse Gases," Subcommittee on Energy and Power, Committee on Energy and Commerce, U.S. House of Representatives, June 29, 2012, http://www.epa.gov/ocir/hearings/pdf/2012_GHG_testimony_final.pdf.

[¶] 549 U.S. 497 (2007).

[**] Peter Schwartz and Doug Randall, "An Abrupt Climate Change Scenario and Its Implications for United States National Security" (Pasadena, CA: NASA Jet Propulsion Laboratory, 2003).

[††] Ibid., 14.

outbreak of infectious diseases.* Developing countries are most at risk
to the more severe consequences of natural disasters due to their lack of
resources and poor infrastructure. The population of developing countries are also at risk when countries do not prioritize their population's
safety over political demands. Consider Myanmar, which was devastated
by one of the deadliest cyclones in history, Cyclone Nargis. The death toll
for this cyclone was estimated at 140,000 individuals.† Cyclone Nargis
also adversely affected 2.4 million individuals and resulted in approximately $4.1 billion in losses and economic damage.‡ After the cyclone
hit Myanmar, the government refused international aid for political reasons. Specifically, Myanmar blocked visas for aid workers to prevent
them from entering the country and refused to accept relief aid, which
included basic necessities such as food and water; in so doing, causing
unnecessary hardships on its people. Natural disasters can additionally
"affect the structures of society by disrupting economic development,
increasing income and wealth inequality, marginalizing certain groups,
and by leading to large-scale migrations. Crucially, natural disasters can
also weaken state capacity and legitimacy, creating opportunities for the
disgruntled to engage in violent resistance."§

"NEW" TRANSNATIONAL SECURITY THREATS

Security officials are concerned with certain so-called "new" threats,
which have not yet fully materialized; namely, cyberwarfare and cyberterrorism. Consider one such new threat cyberwarfare, which is similar
to traditional forms of war, and can be commenced only by nation states
or organizations/groups connected to nation states. A person or group
of persons acting on their own, or for a criminal organization, cannot commit cyberwarfare. Instead, cyberwarfare can be thought of as a
state-sponsored cyberattack against another state's computers or information networks. Put simply, pursuant to the laws of war (or laws of
armed conflict), to be considered cyberwarfare, a cyberattack must: be
state-sponsored; be conducted in conjunction with a real-world, physical

---

* Philip Nel and Marjolein Righarts, "Natural Disasters and the Risk of Violent Civil
  Conflict," *International Studies Quarterly* 52:1 (2008), 165.
† "Myanmar Cyclone," Oxfam, http://www.oxfam.org/en/emergencies/myanmar-
  cyclone.
‡ Ibid.
§ Philip Nel and Marjolein Righarts, "Natural Disasters and the Risk of Violent Civil
  Conflict," *International Studies Quarterly* 52:1 (2008), 162.

attack; and amount to an "armed attack," which is an "action [that] is either intended to cause injury, death, damage or destruction."*

One cyberattack has been labeled by some as a cyberwarfare incident. Specifically, the 2008 cyberattacks on Georgia have been labeled as an act of cyberwarfare.† On August 8, 2008, Russia launched a military strike against Georgia that lasted for five days. Almost simultaneously, distributed denial of service (DDoS) attacks‡ were launched against Georgian government websites, as well as Georgian banks, news, and media websites. These cyberattacks disrupted the flow of information from Georgia to the outside world. Preceding these attacks, individuals were encouraged online to assist in launching cyberattacks against Georgia.§ In addition, a target list of Georgian government websites was published (which were alleged to have been tested for access) and the types of malware that could be used against these websites.¶ Russia was believed to be responsible for the cyberattacks; this, however, was not proven.

International law clearly delineates state responsibility. States have a legal obligation to prevent their territories from being used to plan, organize, direct, and implement attacks against other countries. If states refuse to prevent these incidents, they can be held responsible for them. Nevertheless, the assessment of a country's responsibility is inherently complex due to the attribution problem in cybercrime: especially with political cybercrimes. Usually, the evidence obtained during a cybercrime investigation cannot determine with certainty who was actually using the computer to commit the crime. For example, a trace can lead back to the computer used, but not, with certainty, to the perpetrator who was using the computer. As a result, it is extremely difficult to

---

* Michael N. Schmitt, "Wired Warfare: Computer Network Attack and *jus in bello*," *International Review of the Red Cross* 84:846 (2002), 372; Eneken Tikk, Kadri Kaska, Kristel Rünnimeri, Mari Kert, Anna-Maria Talihärm, and Lii Vihu, "Cyber Attacks against Georgia: Legal Lessons Identified," NATO Unclassified, November 2008, 20, http://www.carlisle.army.mil/DIME/documents/Georgia%201%200.pdf.

† John Markoff, "Before the Gunfire, Cyberattacks," *New York Times*, August 12, 2008, http://www.nytimes.com/2008/08/13/technology/13cyber.html; Jon Swaine, "Georgia: Russia 'Conducting Cyber War,'" *Telegraph*, August 11, 2008, http://www.telegraph.co.uk/news/worldnews/europe/georgia/2539157/Georgia-Russia-conducting-cyber-war.html.

‡ A DDoS involves an attempt to gain control over multiple computers and then use them to launch an attack against a specific target or targets. Marie-Helen Maras, Computer Forensics: *Cybercriminals, Laws and Evidence* (Second Edition) (Burlington, MA: Jones & Bartlett, 2014), 8.

§ Eneken Tikk, Kadri Kaska, Kristel Rünnimeri, Mari Kert, Anna-Maria Talihärm, and Lii Vihu, "Cyber Attacks against Georgia: Legal Lessons Identified," NATO Unclassified, November 2008, 13–14, http://www.carlisle.army.mil/DIME/documents/Georgia% 201%200.pdf.

¶ Ibid.

determine who the perpetrator is in cyberspace. To date, the Russian government has not accepted responsibility for the incident; as such, this incident cannot be described as cyberwarfare.

Similarly to cyberwarfare, an incident of cyberterrorism has not yet occurred.[*] Cyberterrorism can be defined as the politically, religiously, or ideologically motivated use of computers (or related technology) by an individual, group, or state targeting critical infrastructure with the intention of harming persons and/or damaging property in order to influence the population (or segment of the population) or cause a government to change its policies. One incident that has been erroneously labeled as an act of cyberterrorism involved Vitek Boden. Boden was a contractor for Hunter Watertech, an Australian firm that had installed the Supervisory Control and Data Acquisition (SCADA) controlled sewage equipment for the Maroochy Shire Council in Queensland, Australia.[†] He later applied for a position at Maroochy Shire Council but was not hired for the job. To exact revenge, he remotely hacked into the systems of the sewage treatment plant and leaked hundreds of thousands of gallons of raw sewage into the grounds, parks, and rivers neighboring the facility.[‡] Even though Boden targeted critical infrastructure and intended (and did) cause harm, his act cannot be classified as an act of cyberterrorism because he was merely trying to exact revenge on those who rejected him for a position he applied to. As a result, he was not motivated by a political, religious, or ideological goal nor was he trying to influence a government or population. Instead his actions can be classified as a cybercrime, which is often perpetrated for revenge purposes and economic gain.

The underlying cause of many "new" transnational security threats is the interconnectivity of systems; especially with respect to computer and information technology, and critical infrastructure. Interconnectivity makes it possible for a small yet determined adversary to cause widespread destruction; depending on the attack chosen, the perpetrator may

---

[*] For an in-depth analysis of the cases that have been erroneously labeled as incidents of cyberterrorism, see Chapter 7 of Marie-Helen Maras, *Computer Forensics: Cybercriminals, Laws and Evidence* (Second Edition) (Burlington, MA: Jones & Bartlett, 2014).

[†] Department of Justice, "Malicious Control System Cyber Security Attack Case Study— Maroochy Water Services, Australia," National Institute of Standards and Technology, Computer Security Resource Center, October 17, 2008, 1, http://csrc.nist.gov/groups/SMA/fisma/ics/documents/Maroochy-Water-Services-Case-Study_report.pdf; Marie-Helen Maras, *Computer Forensics: Cybercriminals, Laws and Evidence* (Second Edition) (Burlington, MA: Jones & Bartlett, 2014), 184.

[‡] Ben Wyld, "Cyberterrorism: Fear Factor," Computer Crime Research Center, July 20, 2004, http://www.crime-research.org/analytics/501/; Todd Datz, "Scada System Security: Out of Control," *CSO*, August 4, 2004, http://www.csoonline.com/article/219486/scada-system-security-out-of-control; Marie-Helen Maras, *Computer Forensics: Cybercriminals, Laws and Evidence* (Second Edition) (Burlington, MA: Jones & Bartlett, 2014), 184.

also be able to do this at a low cost (i.e., with few human and economic resources). Interconnectedness creates vulnerabilities in these systems, which would otherwise have been considered secure. Systems are connected for convenience purposes, economic benefits, and to increase processing powers' capabilities. However, these connections come at a cost—namely, security.

Without such connections, discussions about, for example, critical infrastructure protection would center on the physical security of facilities, the proper vetting of employees, restriction of employees' access to these systems, and the monitoring of such access. The current trend to connect critical infrastructure systems to administrative or corporate systems that are linked to the Internet exposes these critical infrastructure systems to unnecessary risks; risks that would not have been present had these systems been air gapped.* Consider the 2003 Slammer worm incident at a U.S. nuclear power plant. In this incident, "the Slammer worm penetrated a private computer network at Ohio's Davis–Besse nuclear power plant...disabl[ing] a safety monitoring system for nearly five hours, despite a belief by plant personnel that the network was protected by a firewall."† This incident illustrates a growing "trend of linking operations networks with corporate ...[local area networks]... because of the economic benefits of giving engineers easy access to plant data. An increase in plant efficien[cy] of a couple percentage points 'can translate to millions upon millions of dollars per year.'"‡ Unfortunately, despite incidents like the Slammer worm in the critical infrastructure industry, these connections are becoming increasingly commonplace due to their economic benefits and their permittance by domestic regulation.

There are certain critical infrastructure systems that an outsider—and more specifically, a hacker§—will never gain access to due to the setup of the systems. The systems themselves are standalone; that is, they are not connected to other systems. Only insiders can access these systems. Today, these systems are encountered less frequently. Irrespective of what type of system security officials are dealing with (standalone or networked), comprehending their vulnerabilities can enable a proper assessment of: existing measures and policies designed to protect critical infrastructure; the ability of these measures and policies to effectively deal with internal and external threats; and whether new measures and policies are required to counter potential threats to critical infrastructure.

---

* Air gapping seeks to secure computers and their networks by physically isolating them from unsecured networks, such as the Internet.
† Kevin Poulsen, "Slammer Worm Crashed Ohio Nuke Plant Network," *Security Focus*, August 19, 2003, http://www.securityfocus.com/news/6767.
‡ Ibid.
§ A hacker is someone who seeks to gain unauthorized access into computers.

The increasing use of and reliance on communications, information, and computer technologies has also altered the meaning of borders in the context of security. New and changing manifestations of vulnerability are present nowadays as a result of this increased dependency on communications, information, and computer technology, and its pervasiveness in society. And yet, interconnectivity can be considered as a great transnational security threat even beyond the cyberrealm. This becomes evident when examining other transnational security threats, such as the energy dependence and interdependence of nations.* In these and other transnational threats, the security decisions of one state affect the security of other states. Accordingly, today's interconnected world creates unprecedented vulnerabilities in nations around the globe. Consider the terrorist attacks on September 11, 2001. The impacts of these attacks were felt worldwide. In a less connected world, the impact of these attacks would have been limited to the national level. However, due to the interconnectivity of the world and its respective economies, this terrorist attack adversely impacted the global economic system. For these reasons, the interconnectedness of today's global society mandates a shared responsibility and necessity to collectively solve the transnational security issues that impact and threaten countries and their populations worldwide. To achieve this, national and international cooperation and coordination among public and private sectors around the globe is required.

---

* For information on energy security, see Chapter 12 of this volume.

Index